The Working Class in American History

Editorial Advisors

David
Alice
David
Sean

Women in

Series
Mari
Jacque
Anne

Lists of books in the series appear at the end of this volume.

Labor's Flaming Youth

Labor's Flaming Youth

Telephone Operators and Worker Militancy, 1878-1923

STEPHEN H. NORWOOD

UNIVERSITY OF ILLINOIS PRESS
Urbana and Chicago

Publication of this book was supported in part by a grant from the Andrew W. Mellon Foundation.

This book is printed on acid-free paper.

Library of Congress Cataloging-in-Publication Data

Norwood, Stephen H. (Stephen Harlan), 1951-
  Labor's flaming youth : telephone operators and worker militancy,
1878-1923 / Stephen H. Norwood.
    p.   cm. — (The Working class in American history) (Women in American history)
  Bibliography: p.
  Includes index.
  ISBN 0-252-01633-5 (alk. paper)
    1. Telephone operators—United States—History.   2. Trade-unions--
Telephone workers—United States—History.   3. Women in trade -
unions—United States—History.   I. Title.   II. Series.   III. Series: Women in Ameri-
can history.
  HD6073.T32U56   1990
  331.4'8138465'0973—dc20   89-31945
                                                                       CIP

To Eunice G. Pollack

Contents

Acknowledgments   xi

Introduction: The Flapper as Trade Unionist   1

1 The Work Experience, 1878–1923   25

2 Women Follow Men   73
Telephone Operators in the West, 1902–8

3 Protest and the Networks of Class and Gender   91
Boston, 1900–1913

4 Women in a Men's Union, 1913–18   128

5 The State against the Telephone Operator   156
The War and Its Aftermath, 1917–19

6 Women in Their Own Union   216
The Making of the Trade Union Woman

7 The Trade Union Woman   254
Isolation, Conflict, and Defeat, 1920–23

Epilogue   301

Bibliography   315

Index   333

Illustrations on pp. 53–60 and 171–79.

Acknowledgments

My interest in the subject of this book dates back at least to the summer of 1971, which I spent living with my grandmother, Rose Finkelstein Norwood, in Boston. A longtime labor organizer, my grandmother had over several decades led organizing drives among laundry and garment workers, telegraphers, retail clerks, building service workers, librarians, shipyard workers, and jewelry workers, and she had served as president of the Boston Women's Trade Union League. Now she was retired and completely forgotten by a very quiescent labor movement. But my grandmother didn't feel she was missing much, and she could make a rather strong case that she had lived in the "best times." Nearly every evening, she told me about some labor meeting, organizing campaign, or picket line in which she had been involved, and she brought the labor movement of the early twentieth century, and many of its long-dead activists, back to life.

Some of my grandmother's most exciting stories concerned the Boston Telephone Operators' Union and its dramatic strikes of 1919 and 1923. She had joined the union as a charter member in 1912, at the age of twenty, had served on its executive board, and had taken part in the 1919 strike. Sometimes other veterans of the Telephone Operators' Union dropped by and joined our conversations, including Julia O'Connor Parker, who had led the 1919 and 1923 strikes. These women provided me with important insights about their work experience, their contribution to the labor and women's movements, and the youth culture of the 1910s which had so strongly influenced them. It was shortly after Julia O'Connor Parker's death in 1972 that I decided to interview the few remaining women who had participated in the telephone operators' movement and to write its history.

In the earliest stages of my work, I received strong encouragement from the late Francis Moloney, then Assistant Director of the Boston Public Library and a source of limitless information about Boston, and from Don Mahoney, international representative of the

International Brotherhood of Electrical Workers (IBEW) and a great admirer of the old Telephone Operators' Union. I worked with Mahoney on the IBEW Telephone Organizing Committee during its New England campaign among commercial service representatives in 1973.

This book grew out of my doctoral dissertation at Columbia University. While the work was in its dissertation stage, I received helpful criticism from James Shenton, Eric Foner, David Rothman, Carolyn Heilbrun, and Eric Hirsch. I would like to take this opportunity to thank Professor Shenton for the encouragement and support he gave me all through graduate school. As I revised the manuscript for publication, I benefited greatly from the rigorous criticism and vast knowledge of women's labor history of Alice Kessler-Harris and Susan Porter Benson, who read the manuscript for the University of Illinois Press. I also very much appreciate the generous assistance I received from Milton Cantor, Bruce Laurie, and Kai Erikson, each of whom read an earlier draft of the manuscript in its entirety and contributed valuable suggestions. I would like to thank Jane Hunter for directing my attention to some of the recent studies of high school youth culture, and Sally Parker Swerbilov for all the information she provided me about her mother, Julia O'Connor Parker, in the many conversations we had over the years. And I very much appreciate the support I received from my parents, Bernard Norwood and Janet Lippe Norwood, who always endorsed my interest in history and who from the beginning took a deep interest in this study.

Financial support for this project was provided by a University of Oklahoma Junior Faculty Summer Research Fellowship, two grants from the University of Oklahoma Research Council, a Memphis State University Faculty Research Grant Award, and an NEH Travel Grant. I would like to thank Martha Penisten for typing the final draft of the book. Jane Mohraz was an excellent copy editor.

My deepest debt is to my wife, Eunice G. Pollack, who took endless hours from her own dissertation in social history to engage in discussions about the telephone operators, out of which came many of the insights in the book, and who provided a twenty-nine page, single-spaced critique of an earlier draft. I hope I have contributed as much to her work, and to her life, as she has to mine.

Introduction
The Flapper as Trade Unionist

In October, 1919, President Julia O'Connor opened the first convention of the Telephone Operators' Department of the International Brotherhood of Electrical Workers (IBEW) by praising union telephone operators across the country for displaying a "courage rare in the annals of labor." They had in the last year fought "more battles than falls to the lot of the average International organization in a decade." Strikes and lockouts had been "innumerable," as the telephone operators were put to the test by telephone company and federal government officials determined to "exterminate" their union movement.[1] Yet the movement had not only survived but grown stronger. It had scored some notable victories, particularly in New England, where eight thousand union telephone operators had won a highly favorable settlement after totally paralyzing telephone service for six days in the most massive strike across that region since the shoeworkers' strike of 1860.

The union movement among telephone operators had emerged only a few years before; its members were nearly all very young, with little experience in either the workplace or the labor movement. Yet Julia O'Connor expressed her confidence that the telephone operators would continue to strengthen their organization and establish themselves as a powerful presence in the labor movement throughout the country. "Our strength must come from the fearlessness, and enthusiasm, and undaunted spirit of youth," she declared.[2]

O'Connor extolled the rank-and-file telephone operator not only for her militancy and trade union commitment but for the competence and dependability she displayed in performing her daily duties at the switchboard. She provided an "indispensable public service"; telephone operating was a "high calling" requiring "intelligence, devotion, and esprit de corps."[3]

The delegates Julia O'Connor addressed in New Orleans represented a union movement that had attained its peak strength. Composed of young women, almost all in their teens and early twenties, telephone operators' locals spanned the continent and stood squarely in the center of the labor movement in New England, along the Pacific Coast, in Montana, and in parts of the Midwest. The operators had even developed an extensive organization in the Southeast, where women's unionism was almost unknown. There were locals in over thirty states and in several Canadian provinces.

The Telephone Operators' Department constituted in effect the first national trade union controlled and officered by women.[4] Established after years of agitation by telephone operators demanding equal rights for women in the labor movement, it allowed the operators full self-government within the IBEW and freedom from domination by male trade unionists. As the New Orleans *Times-Picayune* noted in reporting on the convention, the telephone operators had for the most part "fought their own battles in their own way without male help."[5]

The telephone operators' achievement is striking considering that women workers who attempted to organize in the early twentieth century confronted formidable obstacles which did not affect men, obstacles most male trade unionists believed to be insurmountable. Despite the upsurge in women's employment outside the home after 1900, it was generally assumed that women in the labor force were primarily oriented not to work but to family, which provided their major source of influence and identity. Unlike their male counterparts, women workers were for the most part very young and unmarried, earned low wages, and displayed little job persistence. Their meager earnings made it nearly impossible for them to live independent of their families. They remained supplementary wage earners, working only a few years while waiting to wed. In the cities especially, young working women were increasingly drawn to the new commercialized amusements; social life, rather than the job, seemed to be their main interest. Yet trade unionism demanded that workers view their jobs as their central concern in life. Unions could not survive if their members were too poorly paid to contribute dues or there was a high degree of turnover on the job.

Ruth Milkman has pointed out that "any successful struggle to organize women had first to challenge the ideology of 'women's place'—a problem that did not arise in organizing men."[6] In the early twentieth century, both employers and the labor movement could agree that women's primary role was in the home, not the workplace. Employers never defined women's work in terms of preparing women for upward job mobility. Desirable jobs were those that imparted such qualities as solicitousness, neatness, and cleanliness that would better prepare a woman to be a wife and mother.[7] The labor movement itself feared work would damage a woman's capacity to perform her future duties. Male trade unionists tended to accept the patriarchal definition of women as a "weaker sex" poorly equipped to withstand the strain of toil in the workplace. Many believed women would be better off entirely out of the work force. The labor movement was concerned about women primarily because they were low-wage competitors who threatened men's jobs. In any case, it devoted little attention to workers confined to unskilled and semiskilled occupations without craft traditions.

Until recently, most historians emphasized the docility of women workers and viewed them as peripheral to the labor movement. Even scholars writing from a feminist perspective have stressed women workers' indifference to organization. Nancy Woloch, for example, in one of the principal recent surveys of American women's history, describes women workers in the early twentieth century as "usually passive and tractable."[8] Leslie Woodcock Tentler has maintained that women were unlikely to develop an interest in unionization because they viewed their sojourn in the labor force as minor in the course of their life. Segregated in a low-paying and low-prestige secondary labor market, they could not achieve economic independence from their families. Since they lacked any long-term commitment to the job or any prospects for upward job mobility, they were unable to identify as workers and retained the traditional perception of themselves as dependents. Indeed, they viewed economic independence and a concern for job mobility as "not appropriate to their sex." Women's low wages "underscored the need for male economic protection, thus directing women . . . to devote their best energies to social life and eventual marriage." In the workplace, women's thoughts centered around fantasies of romance and marriage, not job conditions and protest. In short, since their work experience left them dependent and marginal, their families alone provided the locus of any search for self-esteem and influence.[9]

There is a growing body of scholarship, however, which suggests the record of women's labor militancy has been understated.[10] The decade following the "Uprising of the 20,000" in 1909—a strike by young, immigrant women garment workers that was one of the largest in the United States until that time—represented the high point of women's labor activism and influence in the labor movement. Female trade union membership increased fivefold during the 1910s.[11] While women garment workers in this period recently have received much attention, the telephone operators have been largely ignored, even though the Bell System, which dominated the telephone service, constituted the nation's largest employer of women in the early twentieth century.[12] In no other industry in the first half of the twentieth century were women workers able to build a national, woman-led labor organization. In the garment industry and in the other industries in which significant numbers of women were employed—such as textiles and boot and shoe—men administered unions above the local level, even when the membership was overwhelmingly female.

During the 1910s, the women garment workers and the telephone operators not only formed viable trade unions but were more militant than the men in their industries. In both cases, organization was made possible by a new and exogenous factor, a large and diversified women's movement that was expanding in influence after 1910 and increasingly was devoting attention to women workers and workplace reform. The women's group most important in preparing the operators to organize and administer a trade union was the National Women's Trade Union League (WTUL), a coalition of upper- and middle-class women reformers and working women. The WTUL had been established in 1903 to organize working women into trade unions, and it served as the principal link between the labor and women's movements. Influenced by the WTUL, the telephone operators, like the garment workers, gave particular attention to elaborating "woman-centered" social and educational programs to promote trade union commitment, and they formed autonomous women's institutions within the labor movement.[13]

This approach assumed the needs of women workers were significantly different from those of men because of their dissimilar experience in the labor force. Addressing the interests of men, who were in the labor force for a lifetime or close to it and for whom upward job mobility was usually a central concern, the trade unions focused almost exclusively on the issues of the workplace. They largely ignored the social concerns of the young, since the male workplace was numerically dominated by middle-aged men to whom adolescent boys necessarily deferred. But the operators' youth and expectation of short-term employment forced women organizing in the telephone service to address their social life as well as their workplace issues.

Organizers sought to identify "gay times" with labor activism and to provide an alternative "community of women" for those whose families and peers disapproved of trade unionism.[14]

Telephone operator unionists sponsored dances, parties, social hours, excursions, and bazaars to develop group spirit among the rank and file. They also stressed female-controlled workers' education programs, designed in part to transform traditional gender roles and attributes: to increase, for example, the assertiveness and self-esteem of young and inexperienced telephone operators. The Boston telephone operators' local, the largest in the country, even purchased a vacation house in an effort to encourage its members to spend a greater portion of their leisure time with their fellow workers rather than with their families. Operators' locals affiliated with Women's Trade Union League chapters where they existed, and as a result many members became active in such "women's causes" as suffrage and world peace and disarmament. Alice Kessler-Harris has noted that female organizers' efforts to address the needs and interests of young women workers through these social activities and workers' education programs "seem to have been as effective at galvanizing loyalty and discipline among women as appeals to bread-and-butter issues were among men."[15]

While operator unionists were sensitive to the concerns of the rank and file as women and as youth, they always maintained a central focus on issues of the workplace. Indeed, operator unionists saw themselves as committed workers as well as women and youth, and they displayed a pride in their craft approaching that of men in the skilled trades. The operator unionists were particularly committed to strengthening woman's identity as worker. Because of these concerns, the operators were readily able to participate actively with men in the mainstream labor movement. Operators' locals affiliated with and sent delegates to central labor unions in the cities and to state federations of labor, where some of them even served as officers.

The locals of the Telephone Operators' Department extended from coast to coast and from Edmonton, Alberta, to the Panama Canal Zone, but organization was sustained for a significant length of time in only one region, New England. Well over one-third of the international membership was concentrated in New England, primarily in the huge Boston local. This study traces the history of the union movement among the telephone operators from its emergence in Montana in the early years of the twentieth century until its collapse in the 1923 New England telephone strike, and it explains the reasons for its unparalleled success in New England. It also investigates the sections of the country where operators' organization was less permanent, where it exerted considerable strength—in some cases, even winning strikes—but was unable to sustain itself for more than a few years.

Telephone operating was always low-paying and became an increasingly regimented and alienating form of labor in the early twentieth century, but working conditions alone cannot account for operator militancy. I find insufficient the analysis advanced by Maurine Weiner Greenwald in the chapter on telephone operators in her *Women, War, and Work*. Greenwald views telephone operating in the 1880s and 1890s as "extremely desirable" employment for women, characterized by personal and often friendly contact with subscribers and a relaxed pace of work. Supervision was minimal and operating was interspersed with other duties, such as collecting bills from subscribers, which released operators from the switchboard and made their work less monotonous. But the application of scientific management techniques and the tightening of supervision during the first decade of the twentieth century intensified the pace of work and undermined operator initiative. Relations with subscribers became completely impersonal. Telephone operating was transformed into something unrelievedly dreary. According to Greenwald, "As new business methods reshaped the nature of telephone operating, militancy among women operators developed in direct response."[16]

There is no question that telephone operating was a highly disagreeable form of work in the early twentieth century. Julia O'Connor called the operator's job "the toughest in industry."[17] Yet the same changes in work processes occurred throughout the Bell System and were introduced in the larger cities almost simultaneously, while operator militancy was confined to a relatively small number of localities. Nor were working conditions in the period when operators organized always inferior to those in the late nineteenth century, a point that is developed in chapter 1. Some aspects of the job actually improved during the early twentieth century. Moreover, because of the high rate of turnover among telephone operators, the women exposed to the scientific management, strict discipline, and regimentation of the 1910s were not the same operators who had experienced the slower pace, greater autonomy, and wider responsibilities of the late nineteenth century. The degradation of work in itself is thus not sufficient to explain why operator militancy and organization developed in some localities and not in others.

A more complete understanding requires an analysis of the

sources of labor power in localities where telephone operators organized. The mediating factors explaining the success of operators' unionism in Boston were a strong women's movement that provided continuous support and leadership, the existence of workers' institutions of long standing, and a local tradition of labor struggle. These are explored in chapter 3.

The telephone operators' ethnicity also worked to their advantage in Boston. Overwhelmingly Irish-American, they were members of an ethnic group which comprised the vast majority of Boston's laboring population and dominated the trade union movement. These shared ethnic ties translated into public support during strikes, especially against a corporation controlled by men of "old stock" background. Telephone operators' strikes were ethnic as well as labor conflicts, pitting Irish against Yankee.

Because Irish-Americans dominated Boston's city government from the beginning of the twentieth century, the telephone operators also benefited from its support. First elected in the 1880s, Irish-American mayors held office for sixteen of the years between 1902 and 1923. Irish-Americans also constituted most of Boston's Democratic party delegation in the state legislature, which generally supported bills favorable to labor. The New England Telephone Company was several times a target of attack in the state legislature by such Boston Irish-American delegates as Martin Lomasney, the powerful ward leader of the North End.[18]

The women's movement, however, was the most critical source of support for the telephone operators. It encouraged them to organize in Boston in 1912, and it allowed them to resist domination by male unionists and to develop as a forceful and independent presence within the labor movement. Several small mining and railroad shop towns in Montana and the South also provided a highly favorable climate for telephone operators' unionism; these were closed-shop towns where trade unions enjoyed wide community support. In three such towns—Helena, Montana; Fort Smith, Arkansas; and Palestine, Texas—telephone operators' walkouts even sparked general strikes. Yet in these towns, the absence of a women's movement invariably caused the operators' unions, which had been organized by male unionists, to fall under the domination of a masculinist labor movement that viewed itself as the protector of the "weaker sex."

The rise of telephone operators' unionism was also greatly influenced by a new youth culture emerging in the early twentieth century, which emphasized peer networks and greater independence from adults. This new solidarity of youth had potentially important consequences for women workers, who were nearly all in their teens or twenties. Any labor-management conflict involving telephone operators was also a confrontation between the young and the old. Telephone operators' bargaining and strike committees were always composed of women in their twenties and teens; management was always represented by middle-aged men.

The telephone operators' youth helps explain the festive nature of many of their strikes, which featured spirited picketing, parades, singing and dancing, and frenzied mass meetings. Michelle Perrot's observation that the strike represents the workers' "great holiday" has particular pertinence for youth. The strike provided a "happy escape" from rigid hours and the tedium of unremitting work.[19] Young workers were more energetic than older workers but were less able to concentrate on the job. In New England, the spontaneous protest of Boston toll operators in 1912 which sparked unionization, the Boston telephone operators' vote to strike in 1913 which forced union recognition, and the 1919 strike all occurred in the spring, when young people found the workplace especially unbearable.[20]

For the telephone operators, the high school was the single most important institution for elaborating the new youth culture. The educational qualifications for telephone operators were considerably higher than for most other women workers and even male telephone workers. Operators in the Bell companies had to have at least a grammar school education, and in the larger cities most had attended high school. In Boston, a considerable number were high school graduates, even in the prewar period.[21] The head of the New England Telephone Company's employment bureau in Boston stated in 1910 that telephone operators hired by the company averaged two years of high school.[22] In 1913, the press secretary of the Boston Telephone Operators' Union claimed a majority of the members had graduated from high school.[23] Their high school background gave the operators a sense of group identity and a competence in administration, which grew out of participation in extracurricular activities and student government and proved invaluable in forming and sustaining a trade union.

High school training was not, of course, a necessary prerequisite for women's labor activism. Few women garment workers, for example, had more than a few years of schooling. Women militants in the garment industry were largely of East European Jewish origin; their labor activism was shaped by ethnocultural values that validated assertive behavior by women in the workplace. The women garment workers, however, never developed a national, woman-controlled labor organization in their industry; nor did they wage as effective a struggle for women's rights in the labor movement as the telephone operators did.

The high school became an increasingly important institution for working-class youth, and girls in particular, in the early twentieth century. Before the turn of the century, only a small, relatively affluent section of the population attended high school, which was largely devoted to preparing students for colleges and professional schools.[24] But the bureaucratization accompanying the enormous industrial expansion of the late nineteenth century greatly increased the demand for educated workers to fill a multitude of new white-collar positions. Public high schools became much more open to the working class, and enrollment increased about three times as fast as the population between 1890 and 1914. The costliness and monumental character of the new public high school buildings underlined their new importance to the society.[25] Because a boy's earning potential was greater than a girl's, working-class families more often forced their sons to leave school to seek employment. Many parents also hoped the high school would give their daughters a "cultural polish" that would help them attract a spouse of a higher social class.[26] Far more girls than boys attended high school during the early twentieth century. Nearly 50 percent more girls than boys graduated from high school between 1900 and 1920.[27]

In high school, students shifted their emotional commitment from the family to the peer group and developed considerably more social distance from adults. The lengthening of the school day, the establishment of cafeterias which allowed students to eat lunch at school, and the proliferation of extracurricular activities sharply diminished the amount of time spent at home. Using special study rooms and the library, students could even do their homework at school.[28] Extracurricular activities were particularly important for the emerging high school youth culture. A special period, the homeroom, largely centered around the coordination of these activities.[29] During the early twentieth century, student organizations, clubs, athletics, dances, and other social events assumed as much importance as the academic program.[30] The after-school clubs were nominally sponsored by teachers but were to a great extent shaped by the students themselves. Public schoolteachers, who were poorly paid, tended to resent having to spend additional time on these clubs and therefore devoted little energy to supervising them.[31]

The school officials' campaign against high school fraternities and sororities indicates the strength of peer networks and reveals adults' growing alarm over the independence of the young. The 1905 convention of the National Education Association condemned high school fraternities and sororities, and by the 1920s they had been outlawed in seventeen states, beginning with Massachusetts in 1909, and in innumerable school districts. School officials denounced these societies because they were exclusive and thus undermined school unity and "spirit." But perhaps even more important was the officials' fear that the societies' secrecy would not permit adequate supervision by adults. That school officials gave them so much attention indicates adults feared that the standards and behavior of the young differed too much from their own.[32]

Extracurricular activities involved students directly in organizing and administration, which undoubtedly helped the telephone operators in building trade unions. Student self-government was a central feature of high school extracurricular activities.[33] Although student councils were directed by teachers and administrators, they allowed young people to develop some sense of how to govern, familiarizing them with parliamentary procedure, accounting and record-keeping, and elections, all important to running a trade union. Girls were well represented as student council delegates in coeducational public schools.[34] School newspapers, magazines, and yearbooks helped instill a group consciousness among the students and became vehicles in which they sometimes expressed opposition to the views of teachers and administrators. Except for Waistmakers' Local 25 of the International Ladies' Garment Workers' Union in New York, the Telephone Operators' Department appears to have been the only women's trade union at any level, from local on up, to regularly publish its own magazine. High school provided the operators with the experience and literary skill to do it. Debating clubs trained students to express themselves and helped them acquire a familiarity with current political controversies, both invaluable for trade unionists. Girls were frequent participants in debates and often formed a separate debating club in the school.[35]

The telephone operators' movement must also be viewed within the context of a profound cultural reorientation that produced a new definition of femininity. The system of separate spheres, in which men and women were accorded vastly different roles and responsibilities and were seen as complete opposites, was weakening. This was occurring in part because increasing numbers of women were leaving the "female" sphere, the home, for the "male" sphere, the workplace. The distance between the sexes further narrowed as women claimed the right to sensual pleasure and individual expression previously reserved for men. Less emphasis was placed on female passivity and dependency. The "new woman" of the 1910s, who by 1920 had come to be known as the "flapper," was more physically active, energetic, independent, and self-indulgent than the woman of the late nineteenth century. She was a "determined pleasure-seeker," who "avidly cultivated beauty of face and form."[36] Her self-indulgence, even exhibitionism, is reflected in the enormous attention she gave to clothes and cosmetics. She rejected the corset for clothing that was much less constricting. Newspaper descriptions of striking telephone operators in the 1910s and early 1920s nearly always refer to their being dressed in the latest fashions, "putting on style" on the picket lines. The flapper was more assertive toward men, "pugilistically inclined when called the weaker sex," and capable of holding her own in fast repartee.[37] This "new woman"—the telephone operator of the 1910s and early 1920s—could readily assume a confrontational posture, whether with the all-male Bell Company management or with male trade unionists antagonistic to women's rights in the labor movement.

New commercialized forms of recreation—dance halls, amusement parks, and movie theaters—encouraged young women's participation and profited from their vitality and desire for excitement. These "cheap amusements," affordable for the working class, drew young women out of the home, away from family and adult supervision. The prewar dance craze, which revolutionized social dancing between 1912 and 1914, acquainted young people with dances unknown to adults. The dances emphasized spontaneous body movement, close physical contact with one's partner, and a less precise sequence of steps. Over a hundred new dances were introduced during these years, most of them strongly influenced by ragtime. The names of the new dances, taken from the barnyard—the bunny hug, the turkey trot, the grizzly bear, and the fox trot, to name a few of the most popular—suggested an exuberance and lack of inhibition far removed from the formalism and restraint of the preceding period. In sharp contrast to late-nineteenth-century dances that were usually sponsored by adult groups, these dances were performed by young people in unsupervised dance halls. Young people also went to amusement parks and movie theaters unaccompanied by adults.[38]

The consumer culture that emerged in the early twentieth century encouraged women to seek fulfillment by purchasing from among a dazzling array of new commodities made available by the country's massive industrial expansion. The huge urban department stores— the new "palaces of consumption"—appealed primarily to women and drew them in droves to the downtown streets, previously a male domain. By 1915, women were doing over 80 percent of the consumer purchasing in the United States.[39] The department stores' colorful and exotic displays associated consuming with sensuous pleasure. Floors were decorated to look like Egyptian temples or Japanese gardens. The festive atmosphere was enhanced by spectacular fountains illuminated by colorful lights, and mirrors multiplied the images of commodities to infinity. The appearance of city streets was dramatically altered by the introduction of plate-glass display windows, which became a major instrument of advertising for merchants. By 1915, great banks of store windows extended not only along the streets but under them as well, at subway stops in many cities. These displays, designed particularly for women, made "window-shopping" a new female pastime.[40]

There is no question that telephone operators in cities like Boston were drawn into this culture of consumption, given their penchant for walking the picket line in fur coats, high heels, and fashionable headgear. Many urban telephone exchanges were clustered in downtown districts near department stores, allowing the operator to shift into the role of window-shopper or customer during her lunch hour or after work. The pages of the *Union Telephone Operator*, the magazine of the Telephone Operators' Department, are replete with advertisements for jewelry, fur chokers, dresses, millinery, and beauty services. Rather than return home directly, Boston's delegation to the 1921 Telephone Operators' Department convention held in St. Louis preferred to stop off in New York for several days to see "the bright lights and advertised things."[41] While capable of distracting women from issues of serious concern, the consumer culture could also encourage unionization by heightening expectations about enjoying commodities, which could not be purchased with low wages.[42]

Telephone company management's lack of understanding of the changing high school youth culture and emerging "new woman" of the 1910s was a major source of tension in the telephone exchanges. As I will show in chapter 1, management in many ways treated the operators as schoolgirls of a previous generation; telephone operating was a sort of "thirteenth grade." Management imposed a harsh discipline over the operators at the switchboard, which it admitted was even stricter than in the high school.[43] Even during their brief rest breaks, the operators were under the careful scrutiny of older women called "matrons," charged with curbing boisterous conduct. Management explicitly referred to these matrons as "mothers" and to the operators as "their girls." The operators, however, were more likely to view the matrons as "police officers."[44] The companies also expected matrons to advise operators about personal hygiene and "proper dress," which many operators felt was an intrusion. Management sometimes compared the exchange building with the school. The Pacific Telephone Company, for example, declared that the "dainty rest room" it provided its operators in Los Angeles resembled "the reading or sewing room of Miss———'s private school for girls."[45] The telephone companies were seeking to reimpose a parental control that the operators, as independent high schoolers, had already evaded.

The Bell companies denounced the new fashions in dress and attempted to persuade—or in earlier years even compel—its operators to wear more conservative styles. The New York Telephone Company called on its operators to appear at work "well dressed," explaining that "well dressed does not imply expense, gaudiness, slippers so perilously high heeled . . . skirts so short or narrow."[46] The telephone operators' rejection of a company-imposed dress code was a major issue in the first big-city strike initiated by operators in San Francisco in 1907.

The telephone operators' formation of a militant international trade union with strong ties to the women's movement calls into question the stereotype of the flapper as frivolous and apolitical. This stereotype is based in part on the assumption that the flapper emerged in the 1920s, rather than the 1910s, a decade which represented the high point of both women's labor militancy and the women's suffrage movement. Scholars counterpose the self-indulgent, pleasure-oriented, heterosocial flapper to the altruistic women activists of the Progressive Era, still guided by the separate spheres, whose belief in female moral superiority motivated them to enter the public sphere to engage in social reform activities. Trained in women's seminaries and colleges, the reformers of the Progressive Era formed strong homosocial relationships and married less frequently than any generation before or since. Their sense of women's special reform mission was reflected in repeated attempts to establish women's congresses and parliaments, often at the international level.[47] It was these "social housekeepers" who led the settlement house and women's suffrage movements in the early twentieth century. Most scholars view the flapper as the complete antithesis of the "social housekeeper" and depict a vast and insurmountable gulf between the two generations of women. Mary Ryan, for example, in one of the major surveys of American women's history, states that the flapper "symbolized a gay abandonment of social housekeeping [and] women's organizations. . . ."[48]

The National Women's Trade Union League did much to bridge

the gulf between the two generations of women. The WTUL sought to establish an alliance between working women and middle-class "allies" to organize women into trade unions and promote protective legislation. Such a cross-class alliance was highly unusual, since virtually all American women's organizations until then, whether feminist or not, had been composed of middle- and upper-class women only.[49] While scholars have situated the WTUL fully within the social reform movement of the Progressive Era, young women who could be called "flappers" comprised a significant part of its membership. The Telephone Operators' Union represented the most important component of the Boston chapter, one of the three largest in the nation. The older generation of women reformers strongly influenced many of the telephone operators active in the union movement, especially in Boston. It was the "social housekeepers," as allies in the WTUL, who drew the telephone operators into the campaigns for women's suffrage and world peace and disarmament. Telephone operators accompanied prominent settlement house leaders as delegates to the International Congress of Women at The Hague in 1915 and the International Congress of Working Women at Washington in 1919.

Yet even as they forged close bonds with the older generation of women reformers, the big-city telephone operators of the 1910s and 1920s displayed the frenetic energy, need for fun and excitement, and exhibitionism of the flapper. As I show in chapters 4 and 6, from 1913 the operators' locals developed social programs centered around the entertainment of the heterosocial youth culture. The operators were always described as calling attention to themselves by dressing in the latest, flashiest styles. Boston's newspapers during the 1923 telephone operators' strike devoted much coverage to the aggressive picketing of young women they explicitly called "flappers," who jeered and sometimes fought strikebreakers, policemen, and other male "bimbos" supporting the company.[50] A columnist in the *Union Telephone Operator*, discussing her role during "Telephone Week," when the New England Telephone Company invited the public into its Boston exchanges to observe its operators at work, bragged that she had divided her time between "showing off my new dress" and "showing off my swell operating."[51] The conventions of the Telephone Operators' Department were marked by riotous midnight parties, and delegates interspersed dates with union business meetings.[52] Only the Telephone Operators' Union could select a beauty contest winner to lead its picket line at one of the major Boston exchanges in the 1923 strike: "Miss Telephone," an operator who had been chosen "the prettiest girl in the service."[53]

For the Irish-American Catholics who comprised the vast majority of the New England membership of the Telephone Operators' Union, as well as most of the national leadership, labor and feminist activism and the flapper life-style represented a sharp break from the standards for female behavior established by the Catholic church. The church adhered to a highly conservative interpretation of the separate spheres doctrine. It assigned men to the public sphere of work and politics and held women primarily responsible for the household and for perpetuating the race. Women were not to be in the labor force unless it was absolutely necessary for the family's support. The church viewed women as morally superior to men but, unlike the reformers of the Progressive Era, did not believe this justified their entry into the realm of politics. Women were passive and passionless, modest and delicate. The church called upon girls to emulate the humble, self-effacing nun, who served the needy while subordinating herself to male authority, the priests and the church hierarchy.

The cultural transformation of the 1910s which gave rise to the flapper horrified the Catholic church. The church issued continual denunciations of the "new woman," warning that she threatened civilization itself. Everything about the flapper profaned "true womanhood." Boston's leading Catholic magazine, the *Sacred Heart Review*, declared in 1916 that American women "had lost all sense of modesty." The flapper's "indecent exposure" made her little more than a prostitute: "The exhibitions at our bathing beaches and ocean resorts are disgusting. Young girls walk our streets with raiment which speaks of the brothel. The short skirt, the low cut neck and the display of hose are . . . bad enough in any one but it is intolerable in Catholic women."[54] The flapper's use of cosmetics was yet another "barbarous practice" that should be left to "the women of heathendom." Nor were cosmetics and "paganism in dress" the only dangers; equally frightening were the new dances with their "vulgar movements," like the trot, tango, toddle, and shimmy.[55] Pope Benedict in an encyclical letter in 1921 condemned "those barbarous and exotic dances," which "tear away the shreds of modesty."[56] The church also found the flapper's assertive behavior appalling, calling it more masculine than feminine; it made her a "swaggering . . . sheathed imitation of a boy."[57] To preserve the "dainty femininity" it cherished, the church warned the adolescent girl to avoid involvement in peer groups and sought to strengthen parental control.

In parochial schools, whose enrollments in grades ten through twelve were almost entirely female, the nuns tried to ensure that none of the students would become flappers.[58] They enforced strict discipline and refused to tolerate any display of youthful spontaneity. A student who attended parochial high school in Boston during the 1910s recalled that "the Eve in us was quietly subdued . . . instead Notre Dame, our model, was placed before us, with her virtues of Valor, Delicacy, and Modesty."[59] The nuns were so intimidating that a former student of the parochial high school in Woburn, just outside Boston, stated twenty-five years after her graduation, "I can even hear sister's voice, 'Will the girl chewing gum please deposit it in the waste basket?' and nine girls rose to obey." One of a group of students at the same school who had put on "an exhibition of dancing" when left briefly unsupervised in the school hall shuddered at the memory years later: "You can imagine what happened when Sister returned unexpectedly, and it is certain that we did no more dancing that term."[60]

The nuns' admonitions had little effect on the telephone operators, in part because the overwhelming majority attended public rather than parochial high schools. Archbishop John Williams, who headed the Boston church from 1866 until his death in 1907, had not been convinced that Boston's Catholics needed a separate school system and did little to encourage the establishment of parochial schools.[61] Constituting the majority of Boston's population, Catholics had considerable influence over the public school system. As early as 1888, half of the positions on the Boston school board were held by Catholics.[62] The largely working-class, Catholic population found supporting two school systems very burdensome. As a result, few Boston parochial schools went beyond the elementary grades; less than 2 percent of the students in parochial schools in 1900 were in grades ten through twelve.[63] Perhaps also because parochial schools were valued mainly for religious indoctrination and grammar schools were viewed as adequate for that purpose, most Catholic parents were satisfied in sending their children to public high schools.[64]

The church was a militant opponent of feminism and a major force against the women's suffrage movement. Believing all women could be best fulfilled in the role of "queen over the household," it consigned the public realm to men. Feminists, by contrast, called upon women to enter the public realm, to engage in politics and social reform. From the standpoint of the church, this meant abandoning family duties. It would also encourage aggressive, boisterous, and competitive behavior that could only make a woman more masculine while undermining her delicate constitution. The church continually denounced suffragists as "amazons" and "wild women."[65] Like the flapper, the suffragist was "conspicuous," whereas the ideal woman was quiet and modest. For the church, the family was adequately represented at the ballot box by its head, the husband. Granting women the vote would promote "individualism" at the expense of the family unit. The National American Woman Suffrage Association was able in 1900 to list only six Catholic clergymen in the entire country who supported women's suffrage.[66]

The union telephone operators not only ignored the church's standards for female conduct but also placed themselves under the tutelage of Protestant women who were active in the settlement house movement and were their allies in the Women's Trade Union League. The settlement house movement was heavily dominated by Protestants, and for this reason it was viewed with great distrust by the church. Few Catholics ever became settlement workers. But perhaps because it was run largely by women, the settlement house movement appealed strongly to the telephone operators. Boston's settlement houses were also generally friendly to the labor movement, which was not the case with Boston's church hierarchy, under William Cardinal O'Connell. O'Connell, who dominated the church in New England for most of the first half of the twentieth century, was very conservative on social and economic issues. His position was to "support the rich as benevolent and paternalistic while arguing for patience on the part of workers."[67] Boston's older priests openly preached that it was useless to organize strikes for higher wages, and the editors of the *Sacred Heart Review* generally urged workers to submit to unfair working conditions.[68]

The WTUL allies drew the telephone operators into the campaign for women's suffrage, in which very few Catholic women were involved. In 1902, when the Massachusetts Woman Suffrage Association attempted to set up a special committee to work among Catholics, it could not find any Catholic women to serve on it.[69] The telephone operators' suffrage activity, which will be discussed in chapter 4, brought them into sharp conflict with Boston's church hierarchy. The operators did receive some support on this issue from male Catholic trade unionists, another indication that the church was out of step with the labor movement. The Boston Central Labor Union and the Massachusetts State Federation of Labor, dominated by Irish Catholics, endorsed women's suffrage. Such prominent Catholic labor leaders as John Tobin, president of the Boot and Shoe Workers' Union, and Michael Murphy of the Stablemen's Union testified for women's suffrage before the Massachusetts legislature.[70] But Cardinal O'Connell was strongly hostile to feminism and women's suffrage, as was Boston's Catholic newspaper *The Pilot*.[71]

Scholars generally assume that Irish-American women were largely governed by traditional values and the needs of the family economy, while conceding that in some ways they did not conform to the separate spheres. Hasia Diner, in the most important study of Irish-American women in the nineteenth century, argues that women behaved assertively within the family and in the economic realm. Irish culture "defined the worth of women in highly economic terms," and Irish-Americans were tolerant of single women working outside the home. The Irish-American desire for economic security justified trade union activism for women, although Diner believes the vast majority of Irish-American women viewed this only as a device to improve their earning power and nothing more.[72] On women's issues they were highly conservative: "These women subscribed to religious imperatives and conformed to a set of behavioral patterns enunciated by the Catholic Church and by the traditional structures of Irish life which had no use for the feminist-women's rights model of the 'new woman.'" Women did leave the private sphere for wage work to assist the family, but they never questioned male dominance of the public sphere: "Politics . . . clubs, and organizations belonged to men. . . ."[73] There was almost no female participation in the Irish nationalist movement, which devoted little attention to the status of women in Ireland.[74] Diner, however, overlooks such Irish-American militants as Mary Kenney O'Sullivan, Leonora O'Reilly, Mary Donovan, and Elizabeth Gurley Flynn, who combined labor and political activism.[75]

Diner's portrayal of the late nineteenth-century Irish-American woman as apolitical and strongly influenced by traditional values certainly does not apply to the union telephone operators of the 1910s and early 1920s. These young women were drawing away from family control and disregarded church strictures on female conduct. They were also very much involved in the "male" world of politics. The Telephone Operators' Union actively supported the Irish nationalist movement and devoted coverage to it in its magazine, the *Union Telephone Operator*. The union's national president, Julia O'Connor, even travelled to Ireland to meet with nationalist leaders. The union also gave considerable attention to the peace movement. Even more important, the union operators consistently lobbied for labor legislation and social welfare bills like the Sheppard-Towner Maternity and Infancy Protection Act. Annie Molloy, the first president of the Boston operators' local, ran for the Boston city council in 1922, when no woman had ever held public elective office in the city, apart from school boards. As will be shown in chapter 4, the telephone operators also waged a long campaign against male trade unionists for self-determination within the labor movement.

The Telephone Operators' Union struggled not only to improve the material conditions of its members but to develop a confident and assertive "trade union woman" who strongly identified with the working class and the labor movement. That so many telephone operators could assume this role was due in large part to the women's movement, at peak strength in the 1910s, which provided models of forceful, politically committed women. The telephone operators were also greatly influenced by the workers' education movement, discussed in chapter 6. Led by progressive labor activists, intellectuals, and feminists, this movement devoted a great deal of attention to the woman worker. It provided education not for social mobility out of the working class but for the worker to better serve the labor movement.

Shaping the sinews of the trade union woman was the work itself. Despite the low wages and harsh discipline, telephone operators derived a greater sense of self-esteem from their work than did most other women. The operator exercised considerable responsibility in emergency situations, summoning physicians, police, and firemen to assist people threatened with serious injury or death. Emergency service during fires and floods sometimes exposed operators to great physical risk; the Bell System even offered a special award, the Vail medal, for "heroism." Telephone operating thus required characteristics identified by society as male: the ability to be level-headed in an emergency and to show initiative and courage. This made it easier for operators not only to disregard the constricting stereotypes of women as passive and dependent but to organize like men and to meet men on equal terms in the labor movement.

The company often reminded its operators that their services were essential to the nation's commercial life. In fact, the economic and social importance of the telephone in the early twentieth century allowed the operators to wield considerable power, far more than women workers in any other occupation. A telephone strike seriously inconvenienced subscribers and could prove devastating to business. The relatively high educational attainments of telephone operators, many of whom had completed high school, also allowed them to feel more efficacious than other women workers. These factors, all of which are more fully treated in the chapters that follow, help explain how the telephone operators managed to organize themselves into a powerful trade union whose impact extended far beyond its members.

NOTES

1. "Report of the Department President," in *Proceedings of the First Regular Convention of the Telephone Operators' Department, IBEW*, New Orleans, La., 1919, p. 12, Julia O'Connor Parker Papers, Schlesinger Library, Radcliffe College, Cambridge, Mass.

2. Ibid., p. 22.

3. Ibid.

4. The New Orleans *Times-Picayune* called the convention "the first trade union convention composed entirely of women that has ever been held in the United States. . . . " Ibid., October 2, 1919.

5. New Orleans *Times-Picayune*, October 5, 1919.

6. Quoted in Sharon Hartman Strom, "Challenging 'Woman's Place': Feminism, the Left, and Industrial Unionism in the 1930s," *Feminist Studies* 9 (Summer, 1983):360.

7. Alice Kessler-Harris, "Independence and Virtue in the Lives of Wage-Earning Women: The United States, 1870–1930," in Judith Friedlander et al., eds., *Women in Culture and Politics: A Century of Change* (Bloomington: Indiana University Press, 1986), p. 9.

8. Nancy Woloch, *Women and the American Experience* (New York: Alfred A. Knopf, 1984), p. 240.

9. Leslie Woodcock Tentler, *Wage-Earning Women* (New York: Oxford University Press, 1979), pp. 25, 60, 80.

10. Recent scholarship documenting women's labor militancy includes Ruth Milkman, ed., *Women, Work, and Protest* (Boston: Routledge and Kegan Paul, 1985); Jacquelyn Dowd Hall et al., *Like a Family* (Chapel Hill: University of North Carolina Press, 1987); Susan Levine, *Labor's True Woman* (Philadelphia: Temple University Press, 1984); Dolores Janiewski, *Sisterhood Denied* (Philadelphia: Temple University Press, 1985); Meredith Tax, *The Rising of the Women* (New York: Monthly Review Press, 1980); Alice Kessler-Harris, *Out to Work* (New York: Oxford University Press, 1982); Maurine Weiner Greenwald, *Women, War, and Work* (Westport, Conn.: Greenwood Press, 1980); and Thomas Dublin, *Women at Work* (New York: Columbia University Press, 1979).

11. Nancy McLean, "The Culture of Resistance: Female Institution Building in the International Ladies' Garment Workers' Union, 1905–1925," *Michigan Occasional Paper in Women's Studies*, no. 21 (Winter, 1982):4.

12. There is only one other scholarly study of telephone operators in the late nineteenth and early twentieth centuries: chapter 5 of Greenwald, *Women, War, and Work*.

13. Colette A. Hyman, "Labor Organizing and Female Institution-

Building: The Chicago Women's Trade Union League, 1904–1924," in Milkman, ed., *Women, Work, and Protest*, pp. 28–33; McLean, "The Culture of Resistance," passim.

14. Hyman, "Labor Organizing," p. 30.

15. Alice Kessler-Harris, "Problems in Coalition-Building: Women and Trade Unions in the 1920s," in Milkman, ed., *Women, Work, and Protest*, pp. 119–20.

16. Greenwald, *Women, War, and Work*, pp. 185, 194–96, 201.

17. Lawrence *Telegram*, July 9, 1923.

18. John Buenker, "The Mahatma and Progressive Reform: Martin Lomasney as Lawmaker, 1911–1917," *New England Quarterly* 44 (September, 1971):400, 407.

19. Michelle Perrot, *Workers on Strike* (New Haven, Conn.: Yale University Press, 1987), p. 146.

20. Michelle Perrot states in her study of strikes in France in the period 1871–90 that strikes occur disproportionately in the spring: "In May the factory seems unbearable. Even today a thrill runs through it at the first sight of sun." Ibid., p. 146.

21. This meant the telephone operators were an especially well-educated group within the working class, since as late as the early 1920s, less than 12 percent of urban children finished high school. David Montgomery, *The Fall of the House of Labor* (New York: Cambridge University Press, 1987), p. 131.

22. M. E. Harrington, "The Training of Operators in Boston," *New England Telephone Topics* [hereafter, *NETT*], June, 1910, p. 18.

23. Alice J. Donovan, "Description of Boston Telephone Operators' Troubles," *Journal of Electrical Workers and Operators* [hereafter, *JEWO*], May, 1913, p. 942; Letter from Alice J. Donovan, *JEWO*, August, 1913, p. 1094.

24. Paula Fass, *The Damned and the Beautiful* (New York: Oxford University Press, 1977), p. 210.

25. David Snedden, "High School Education as Social Enterprise," in Charles Hughes Johnston, ed., *The Modern High School* (New York: Charles Scribner's Sons, 1914), p. 21.

26. Reed Ueda, "Avenues to Adulthood: Urban Growth and the Rise of Secondary Schools in Somerville, Massachusetts, 1800–1930" (Ph.D. dissertation, Harvard University, 1980), p. 87.

27. Margery Davies, *Woman's Place Is at the Typewriter* (Philadelphia: Temple University Press, 1982), p. 180.

28. Warren Leon, "High School: A Study of Youth and Community in Quincy, Massachusetts" (Ph.D. dissertation, Harvard University, 1979), p. 76.

29. Joel Spring, *Education and the Rise of the Corporate State* (Boston: Beacon, 1972), p. 99.

30. Edward Krug, *The Shaping of the American High School*, vol. 2,

1920–41 (Madison: University of Wisconsin Press, 1972), p. 136; Spring, *Education,* p. 125.

31. Henry Sheldon, *Student Life and Customs* (New York: D. Appleton, 1901), p. 290.

32. Fass, *The Damned and the Beautiful,* pp. 214–15. For an example of the conflicting views of students and school officials on this matter in the Boston area, see "Editorial," *The Radiator* [student magazine of Somerville High School], December, 1906, p. 48, strongly defending high school fraternities and sororities; and "Student Organizations in High Schools," in City of Somerville, *Annual Report for 1905* (Somerville, Mass.: Somerville Journal Print, 1906), which attacks high school fraternities and sororities.

33. Joseph Kett, *Rites of Passage* (New York: Basic Books, 1977), p. 186.

34. Ueda, "Avenues," p. 216. Class offices were also usually evenly divided, although boys monopolized the presidency and usually the position of treasurer, with girls holding the positions of vice-president and secretary. Some public high schools in the cities remained all-female, and in these girls could hold all the student council positions and class offices. A good example is Girls' High School in Boston, which produced Mary E. June, one of the principal leaders of the Boston Telephone Operators' Union.

35. See, for example, *The Radiator,* November, 1914, p. 31; October, 1915, p. 12; and March, 1916, p. 16. The girls' debating teams of Somerville, Brookline, and Newton high schools comprised a Girls' Interscholastic Debating League. See also the *Cambridge Review* [student magazine of Cambridge High School], November, 1917, p. 7, and December, 1917, p. 13.

36. James McGovern, "The American Woman's Pre-World War I Freedom in Manners and Morals," *Journal of American History* 55 (September, 1968):325, 327.

37. Mary Ryan, *Womanhood in America* (New York: Franklin Watts, 1983), p. 228.

38. Lewis Erenberg, *Steppin' Out* (Westport, Conn.: Greenwood Press, 1981), pp. 146–57; Lois Banner, *American Beauty* (New York: Alfred A. Knopf, 1983), pp. 195–201; Kathy Peiss, *Cheap Amusements* (Philadelphia: Temple University Press, 1986), passim.

39. Gunther Barth, *City People* (New York: Oxford University Press, 1980), p. 129; William Leach, "Transformations in a Culture of Consumption: Women and Department Stores, 1890–1925," *Journal of American History* 71 (September, 1984):319, 339.

40. Leach, "Transformations," 325.

41. Letter from Para Chords [pseudonym], *Union Telephone Operator* [hereafter, *UTO*], January, 1922, p. 9.

42. Peiss, *Cheap Amusements,* p. 188.

43. E. H. Ansell, "The Human Element in a Telephone Operating Force," n.d., p. 17, Julia O'Connor Parker Papers.

44. "Life in Our Operators' Quarters," *NETT,* June, 1916, p. 35.

45. "The Development of the Telephone in Los Angeles," *Pacific Telephone Magazine,* January, 1913, p. 6.

46. "Style and the Girl!" *Telephone Review,* November, 1918, p. 307.

47. Ryan, *Womanhood in America,* pp. 206, 210.

48. Ibid., p. 220.

49. Carl Degler, *At Odds* (New York: Oxford University Press, 1980), p. 323.

50. See, for example, Boston *Evening Transcript,* June 26, 1923.

51. Letter from Miss Plug [Boston], *UTO,* December, 1921, p. 7.

52. "Some Observations," *UTO,* December, 1921, p. 8; Howler [pseudonym], "New Year's Resolutions and Others," *UTO,* January, 1921, p. 8.

53. Boston *Herald,* June 27, 1923.

54. "Those Startling Styles," *Sacred Heart Review* [hereafter, *SHR*], June 17, 1916, p. 4. See also "Rebuke to the Immodest," *SHR,* June 17, 1916, p. 3; "Clothes Do Not Make the Girl," *SHR,* July 20, 1912, p. 79; and "Slaves of Dress," *SHR,* April 19, 1913, p. 281.

55. "Watch the Dance Programs," *SHR,* April 26, 1913, p. 292; "Is the Younger Generation in Peril?" *Literary Digest,* May 14, 1921, p. 10.

56. "The Religious Press on Youthful Morals," *Literary Digest,* May 21, 1921, p. 52.

57. "The Conspicuous Girl," *SHR,* July 19, 1913, p. 74.

58. In 1900, 83.4 percent of parochial school students in grades ten through twelve were girls. Mary J. Oates, "Organized Voluntarism: The Catholic Sisters in Massachusetts, 1870–1940," *American Quarterly* 30 (Winter, 1978):661.

59. Ida G. Finn Hackett [class of 1919], "Olim Meminisse Iuvabit," in *Academy of Notre Dame, 1854–1954,* Academy of Notre Dame, Roxbury, Massachusetts, 1954, p. 25, Archives of the Sisters of Notre Dame de Namur, Ipswich, Mass.

60. Delia T. Meagher, "Reminiscences of 1890," in *Notre Dame Echoes,* St. Charles School [Woburn, Mass.], 1917, Archives of the Sisters of Notre Dame de Namur; Margaret Doherty, "Class of 1910," ibid.

61. Oates, "Organized Voluntarism," 662.

62. Lois Merk, "Boston's Historic Public School Crisis," *New England Quarterly* 31 (June, 1958):180.

63. Oates, "Organized Voluntarism," 662.

64. Ueda, "Avenues," pp. 339–40.

65. See, for example, *The Pilot,* March 12, 1910; "England's Wild Women," *SHR,* April 12, 1913, p. 259.

66. James J. Kenneally, "Catholicism and Women's Suffrage in Massachusetts," *Catholic Historical Review* 53 (April, 1967):47.

67. Donna Merwick, *Boston's Priests, 1848–1910* (Cambridge, Mass.: Harvard University Press, 1973), p. 128.

68. Ibid., p. 175.

69. Aileen Kraditor, *The Ideas of the Woman Suffrage Movement,*

1890–1920 (Garden City, N.Y.: Anchor Books, 1971), p. 233; Kenneally, "Catholicism," 47, 50.

70. Kenneally, "Catholicism," 51.

71. John Boyle O'Reilly, editor of *The Pilot* until his death in 1890, signed the first male anti-women's-suffrage petition submitted to the Massachusetts legislature in 1885. Boston suffragists claimed that O'Reilly "will soon enjoy the distinction of having called women's suffrage more bad names than any other man of his day and generation." Ibid., 45; quote from Hasia Diner, *Erin's Daughters in America* (Baltimore: Johns Hopkins University Press, 1983), p. 148. *The Pilot*, which became the official archdiocesan newspaper in 1908, continued to oppose women's suffrage until 1920.

72. Diner, *Erin's Daughters*, pp. 99, 102.

73. Ibid., p. xiv.

74. Ibid., p. 25.

75. Mary Kenney O'Sullivan (1864–1943) was a long-time labor organizer in Chicago and Boston and one of the principal founders of the National WTUL in 1903. Leonora O'Reilly (1870–1927), a garment worker and leader of the New York WTUL, was a labor organizer, women's suffragist, peace activist, socialist, and a founder of the National Association for the Advancement of Colored People. Elizabeth Gurley Flynn (1890–1964) was a leader of the Industrial Workers of the World and later of the Communist party. Mary Donovan Hapgood's career is discussed in chapter 6.

1

The Work Experience, 1878–1923

Telephone operating became a woman's job during the 1880s and was part of the trend toward the feminization of lower-white-collar work. Since 1870, when the majority of women in the paid labor force were domestic servants, an increasing number of women had entered new, low-paying jobs in light manufacturing, offices, and department stores. These jobs had grown out of the massive industrial expansion and bureaucratization of the late nineteenth century. In factories, mechanization reduced the need for heavy physical labor and created a variety of light, unskilled jobs for which women were deemed especially suitable. The rise of large offices resulted in a transformation of clerical employment, and large numbers of women were drawn into new positions at the bottom of this increasingly elaborate bureaucratic hierarchy.

Until the late nineteenth century, offices had been small, staffed by two or three male clerks. The skills required in clerical work had tended to be specific to a particular firm, and the clerk derived a sense of importance because of his "indispensability."[1] In many firms, clerks were promoted to managerial positions. As a result, employers preferred to hire men, who could be expected to remain with the firm for a long period, rather than women, who were regarded as transient workers.

The administration of the large corporations emerging in the late nineteenth century, however, required a vast bureaucratic hierarchy in which clerical workers occupied the bottom rungs. There was not a sufficient supply of literate male labor to meet the great demand for office workers. By 1890, more women than men were graduating from high school, so the ever-increasing demand for clerical workers could be met by women. Men moved into the new middle-level management positions while clerical work, which now involved the performance of narrowly defined menial tasks offering no opportunity for advancement, became feminized.[2] Unlike the male clerks of the earlier period, who had aspired to be businessmen themselves, female clerks might hope at best to rise to a lower-level managerial position, such as supervisor of a typing pool. Nearly all of them would perform routinized, low-wage clerical labor for the entire duration of their working lives.[3]

The most common way women entered clerical work was by mastering the typewriter, which was widely introduced as offices expanded enormously in the 1880s, and then finding a job as a typist. Typing involved no initiative, only copying, and women were considered especially suitable because they were assumed to possess superior manual dexterity. Furthermore, as a new machine, the typewriter was not associated with male operators, and women were therefore not seen as displacing men.[4] The Bell Telephone Company identified typing as the work most closely resembling that of the telephone operator: "The telephone operator's work . . . is reasonably comparable to that of a copying typist. As the typist must learn the typewriter keyboard, so the telephone operator must learn the switchboard multiple. Each, by practice and experience, develops dexterity, accuracy, and speed in performing simple manual operations."[5]

Other lower-white-collar positions for women also emerged during the late nineteenth century. Nursing and schoolteaching in the lower grades were service occupations which involved tasks traditionally associated with women in the home: tending the sick and caring for children. The department store, which proliferated in the 1890s, preferred to hire women as clerks, opening yet another poorly paid service position. The old dry-goods stores had given their clerks—mostly men—a wide range of responsibilities, including purchasing merchandise as well as selling it. The department store, however, employed a specialized buying staff and reduced the job of clerk to a menial position offering little possibility for advancement. Viewing women as less ambitious, easier to discipline, and more willing to work for low wages than men were, the department stores hired them in large numbers; about three-quarters of department store employees were female.[6]

The first telephone operators employed when the telephone was introduced in the 1870s were teenage boys, a carry-over from the telegraph industry. The first commercial telephone exchange was opened in 1878. Early exchanges were located in the corners of offices, the back rooms of stores, attics, and railroad stations rather than in separate buildings. Telephone switchboards and other operating equipment also differed widely, as the Bell Company initially lacked facilities for manufacture and exchanges were supplied by a multitude of small producers.[7] The completion of a telephone call usually involved the cooperation of two to four operators, who had to shout to each other and run from board to board to make connections.[8] Busy exchanges therefore tended to be extremely noisy. One of the early boy operators in Boston described the operating room in which he worked in the late 1870s: "A number of boys, wearing carpet slippers to deaden the noise of their feet, running up and down before a switchboard twenty feet long, three or four of them sometimes making a jump to answer the same drop that had fallen and yelling their lungs out through a hand telephone."[9]

Because the pace of work was unhurried for much of the day, the boy operators were assigned a wide range of tasks in addition to operating. There was far less business traffic than in the 1890s, and the paucity of residential subscribers meant that few calls were placed in the evenings and on Sundays. Calls at night were almost always of an emergency nature.[10] Boy operators did janitorial work, ran errands, collected bills from subscribers, and sometimes performed minor repair work on outside telephone lines. These responsibilities often allowed them to be free of direct supervision. One former boy operator recalled that continuous trouble with outside wires resulted in his spending much of his work time alone outside the exchange:

> Because of the small amount available for the purchase of poles . . . the construction gang in planting the poles made the distance between them as great as a strand of wire would permit. It was only natural, therefore, that two parallel lines swinging between poles 300 feet apart would become "crossed" by every strong gust of wind. When that happened, I followed the course of the line out of town with a wagon spoke in my hand, and on reaching the point of trouble, a well-aimed throw of that wagon spoke knocked out the "cross." Then, walking back to town, I would resume my business.[11]

Believing boys temperamentally unsuited to telephone operating, telephone companies switched to female operators in the 1880s. The companies objected to the boys' boisterous behavior, inattention to instructions, and insolence toward subscribers, including the use of profane language. They assumed that young women and girls were capable of greater civility and could more easily tolerate monotonous work and low wages. The hiring of women operators initially encountered opposition from managerial officials who feared that they would prove inefficient because of an alleged tendency to engage in prolonged conversations and that male supervisory personnel, who predominated in the telephone exchanges until at least 1890, would "form preferences" on the basis of sexual attraction rather than merit.[12] Some officials also objected to employing women on the grounds that such sophisticated mechanical instruments as telephone switchboards required men to operate them.[13] Nevertheless, by the late 1880s, nearly all the daytime telephone operators in the Bell System were young women and girls. Boys remained as night operators, even in the larger cities, until as late as 1903 or 1904.[14]

It appears that the first women telephone operators viewed the work as "white collar," similar to schoolteaching or clerking in a store, and had not considered factory jobs. Katherine Schmitt, who became a telephone operator in New York in 1882, recalled, "At the time I was waiting for an appointment as a teacher in the public school, but the vacancies were few and the appointments were as a rule political preferments. There were but a few other lines of work open to young women and these were not appealing, as, for example, sales clerks in 'dry goods' stores (department stores were not then in vogue)." Another woman, explaining why she sought employment as an operator in St. Louis in 1883, stated, "The only positions open to women on the outside were as salesladies or schoolteachers, and I did not want to be either."[15]

During the 1880s, telephone operators continued to enjoy a relatively unhurried pace of work, few standardized procedures, and limited supervision. A single operator regularly served the same small group of subscribers. As a result relations between operators and subscribers tended to be very informal. Operators were often on friendly terms with subscribers and at times engaged in lengthy conversations. They also sometimes took messages and provided callers with information about sporting events, election returns, fires, and accidents.[16] Giving presents, including money as well as such items as flowers and candy, to operators was common, especially during the Christmas season. Operators sometimes received cash presents of as much as $50 from banks and other frequent users of the telephone. Because this practice encouraged the operator to favor particular subscribers in placing telephone calls, it was either prohibited or severely restricted by nearly all telephone companies by 1910.[17] No standard method of answering telephone calls existed prior to the 1890s; an operator might say "Hello," "Number," "What," or the name of the exchange.[18] The asymmetry between operators and supervisory personnel was reduced by the latter's frequent assistance at switchboard work and janitorial duties. Training new operators was unsystematic until the first decade of the twentieth century. It usually consisted only of the recruit's observing an experienced operator for a day or two before being placed at the switchboard.[19]

While telephone operating was much less monotonous and exhausting in the 1880s and 1890s than it became under the intense pace, strict supervision, and standardized procedure of the early twentieth century, it nevertheless had many unpleasant features. Although telephone operators always earned poor wages, the pay ceiling was much lower in the late nineteenth century. There was no regular system of pay increases based on length of service. The maximum wage for operators in Boston in the 1880s and early 1890s appears to have been $6.50 to $7.00 a week.[20] New operators were not paid during training.[21] There was no compensation for sickness or disability. Operators usually worked ten or eleven hours a day without specified relief periods, although they had far more control over their pace of work than they did later and were able to intersperse some play and socializing with work. Many women operators complained that they often had to work additional hours because the boy operators assigned to relieve them at night were irresponsible and failed to appear on time or at all.[22]

The physical surroundings of the exchanges were far inferior to those of the early twentieth century. An exchange might be situated in a dingy loft at the head of six or seven flights of rickety stairs. Room stoves sometimes ceased to function during the winter, forcing operators to work at below freezing temperatures.[23] There were no exchange retiring rooms or cafeterias, and operators often ate their lunch at the switchboard. The facilities in the early years were generally less clean and less safe than they later were. Fire danger was much greater than in the early twentieth century, when telephone exchange buildings were provided with fire escapes and the Bell companies introduced regular fire drills. In the era of the Triangle Fire, no loss of life occurred as a result of fire in any of the exchange buildings constructed by the Bell companies in the early twentieth century.[24]

Early twentieth-century operators benefited from improvements in telephone equipment. The operators' headsets in use in the 1880s were much heavier and less comfortable than those of the early 1900s. The common battery switchboard, which replaced the magneto-type by 1900, reduced noise in the exchange and eliminated one task operators had found annoying, although it created a faster pace of work. The magneto switchboard had required that each subscriber's telephone contain a dry battery. Subscribers generated the current necessary to call the central exchange by turning a crank attached to their telephone each time they wished to call. This attracted the attention of the operator at the exchange by causing an annunciator drop—a small metal bar—to fall on the switchboard. The central battery switchboard instead contained a centralized battery for the whole exchange. All the subscribers had to do to reach the exchange was to take down the receiver. Common battery switchboards contained electric light signals that permitted the operator to see at a glance whether a subscriber was on the line. The adoption of the common battery switchboard eliminated the hand labor required to place the annunciator drops back into position, which the operators had viewed as a considerable irritation.[25]

The Emergence of the Bell System

The telephone service was dominated from the beginning by the Bell Telephone Company, which was first organized in Boston in 1877 by Alexander Graham Bell, who had received the basic telephone patent the year before, and Thomas Sanders and Gardiner Hubbard, who financed Bell's telephone experiments. To obtain the capital required to develop the telephone commercially, Bell, Hubbard, and Sanders in 1879 joined with a group of Boston merchants and financiers to organize a new company with a larger capitalization, the National Bell Telephone Company.[26]

Because the telephone was a relatively simple and easily duplicated instrument, the Bell Company in its early years had to defend its patents against a flood of imitations. Between 1877 and 1894, when its original patents expired, the Bell Company prosecuted over six hundred infringement suits. By far the most important test involved the giant Western Union Telegraph Company. In 1878, it had entered into direct competition with the Bell Company, after taking over the patent claims of Elisha Gray and Amos Dolbear, inventors whose work it believed constituted a valid challenge to the Bell patents. After a bitter court fight, Western Union agreed in November, 1879, to give up the telephone business and assign all its telephone patents to the Bell Company in return for 20 percent of telephone rental receipts over the next seventeen years.[27]

During the last two decades of the nineteenth century, a national "Bell System" emerged consisting of numerous subsidiary corporations directly controlled by the Bell Company in Boston. Each of the subsidiaries supplied telephone service to a specific region of the country; all of these were connected with each other through a rapidly expanding network of long distance lines. By 1900, these regional subsidiaries, known as the "associated Bell companies," included the New England, New York, Chicago, Southern New England, Chesapeake and Potomac, Southern, Southwestern, and Rocky Mountain telephone companies. By acquiring control of the Western Electric Manufacturing Company in 1882, the Bell Company was able to assume a dominant position in the manufacture of telephone equipment. This allowed Bell to make telephone equipment uniform in design throughout its system.

Because a larger capitalization was required after the settlement with Western Union, the American Bell Telephone Company was created by a special act of the Massachusetts legislature in 1880. American Bell formed the American Telephone and Telegraph Company (AT&T) as a subsidiary long distance company in 1885. American Bell, however, was too small and too restricted by Massachusetts laws governing ownership of stock in associated companies to serve as the parent company for the rapidly expanding Bell System. The Massachusetts legislature was extremely reluctant to allow increases in capitalization. As a result, in 1900 the directors of American Bell made the subsidiary AT&T, which had been incorporated in New York, the parent company. In 1907, AT&T's headquarters were transferred from Boston to New York.[28]

The Elaboration of a Work Hierarchy

During the 1890s, an elaborate system of hierarchical relationships developed in the larger telephone exchanges of the Bell System. A federal investigation of the telephone industry in 1910 noted that it "has developed a scheme of administrative organization the perfection of which is to be found in few of the older industries."[29] By the early twentieth century, female supervisory personnel had entirely replaced males within the exchanges. This appears to have resulted in part from pressure by the telephone operators themselves. One of the principal demands in the San Francisco telephone operators' strike in 1907, discussed in the next chapter, was the removal of male supervisory personnel from the exchanges. The position of supervisor was created in the mid-1890s.[30]

A supervisor had charge of six to fifteen operators (generally eight or nine) and was directly responsible for their work; she reported to a chief operator. The larger exchanges also had one or more assistant chief operators. The supervisor stood behind the operators, who since the 1880s performed their work seated rather than standing at the switchboard. She observed their work, assisted and instructed them when necessary, enforced discipline, and handled difficult and irregular traffic. She also assigned her operators to particular positions on the switchboard and scheduled their lunch breaks and relief periods. Supervisors were drawn from the more proficient and experienced operators, who were known as "senior operators." The chief operator, the head of an exchange, was responsible for the work of the entire operating force, the recording of traffic fluctuations at her exchange, and promotion of operators.[31]

The position of chief operator represented the highest level a woman could attain in the telephone service, except in extremely rare instances. The normal line of advancement was student operator, operator, senior operator, supervisor, assistant chief operator, chief operator. A further advancement was the selection of toll operators, who were drawn from the ranks of experienced local operators because their work was more complex.[32] Only a small proportion of operators attained even the rank of supervisor. A study of the employees of the New England Telephone Company in Boston conducted by the Women's Educational and Industrial Union in 1916 estimated that the chances for promotion of a woman employee of the Traffic Department, which was responsible for telephone operating, to a position above the rank of operator was about one in a hundred. Nor did telephone operating prepare a woman for any other occupation.[33] In 1917, the New England Telephone Company reported that the work force of a typical telephone exchange was composed of 75 percent operators, 3 to 4 percent student operators, 12 percent supervisors, 2 percent clerks, an assistant chief operator, and a chief operator.[34]

The positions in the Traffic Department above the rank of chief operator were held by men. The territory served by an associated Bell company was split into divisions, each managed by a division superintendent of traffic and subdivided into districts managed by a district traffic chief. Every chief operator made a brief report to the district traffic chief early in the morning concerning the conditions at her exchange. This official was responsible for the quality of operating service in his district and reported to the division superintendent.[35]

In the Plant Department, which employed only male workers responsible for the construction and maintenance of lines and installation and repair of telephones, the opportunity for advancement was much greater than in the Traffic Department. According to the Women's Educational and Industrial Union study of 1916, of the 490 female employees in the Traffic Department aged twenty-one years during the period from July 1, 1915, to July 1, 1916, only 4 had advanced to the rank of supervisor. However, the 77 twenty-one-year-old males in the Plant Department were employed in fifteen different positions: 27 percent were laborers, the lowest position, while 73 percent had already advanced to positions as wiremen, installers, trouble clerks, and foremen, all of which required some skill. Even the laborers received higher wages than the telephone operators.[36]

Scientific Management and the Routinization of Work

By the first years of the twentieth century, the telephone operator had lost any autonomy she had possessed in the 1880s and 1890s, and her work had become highly routinized. The vast expansion of telephone service, the standardization of equipment, and technological advances in telephony, which greatly increased the speed with which calls could be handled, allowed the telephone companies to introduce scientific management procedures into the exchange. These permitted management to dictate precisely how the operating was to be performed and to regulate more strictly the pace of work.

The ideas of Frederick Winslow Taylor, the leading proponent of scientific management, attained wide influence in large-scale industry during the first two decades of the twentieth century, although few corporations implemented all the elements of his system. For Taylor, efficiency in production required systematic management control over all aspects of production. By carefully analyzing each task involved in production, one could determine the "one best way" to perform it. Taylor relied primarily on the stop watch, which he used to time every motion required in the task. Each worker could then be carefully instructed in the correct performance of her/his task and closely supervised. An incentive wage, "scientifically" determined by efficiency experts employing time and motion study, would be assigned to each task. There was no room in Taylor's system for worker initiative. As Taylor himself put it, "Under our system the workman is told minutely just what he is to do and how he is to do it; and any improvement which he makes upon the orders given him is fatal to success."[37] All of the above features, except the incentive wage, were applied to telephone operating. In fact, the degree of supervision exercised over the telephone operator was unparalleled in any other occupation.

Despite her street clothes, the telephone operator on the job resembled a machine attendant in a light manufacturing establishment. Forming a semicircle around three sides of the room, the operators were seated beside each other on high chairs opposite a switchboard. The bottom of the switchboard was about level with the operator's elbow, while the top was considerably above her head. Each hole in the lower section of the switchboard was the terminal of a subscriber's telephone; the holes were distributed such that each operator had before her a certain number of telephones for which she was directly responsible. Over each hole (or answering jack) a tiny electric light glowed whenever subscribers lifted their receiver from the hook. An operator could connect a caller with any of the telephones in the exchange, whose terminals were repeated over and over ("multiplied") throughout the upper section of the switchboard ("the multiple"). Over her ear, the operator wore a receiver that was attached to a metal band around her head; a transmitter into which she could speak directly was suspended on her chest.[38]

From the moment the operator donned her headset, her attention had to be focused entirely on the switchboard. The "A" telephone operators, who spoke to the subscriber and directly transmitted calls within the same exchange, handled from two hundred to three hundred calls an hour, while the "B" operators, through whom the "A" operators transmitted calls between exchanges, were expected to handle as many as six hundred calls an hour.[39] The English author Arnold Bennett, on a visit to a New York telephone exchange in 1912, described the operator as working at a breakneck pace so totally determined by the switchboard machinery that she seemed a mere appendage of it: " . . . a long row of young women seated in a dim radiance on a long row of precisely similar stools, before a long apparatus of holes and plugs and pieces of elastic cord, all extremely intent, that is the first broad impression. One saw at once that none of these young women had a single moment to spare; they were all involved in the tremendous machine, part of it, keeping pace with it and in it, not daring to take their eyes off it for an instant. . . . "[40] Scientific management intended, as Taylor put it, for every worker "to become one of a train of gear wheels."[41]

As local operating became highly routinized, however, toll work retained much of the variety and slower pace of operating in the late nineteenth century. Toll calls were those placed beyond the locality and required an extra charge. Because several steps were involved in a toll call, necessitating cooperation among as many as seven operators, the pace of work could not be as fast as in local operating. Toll operators, the elite of the operating force, were divided into several specialties, the largest being the recording and the line operators. Toll operators were able to alternate among several tasks, making the work much less monotonous than local operating. A subscriber wishing to place a toll call was connected by the local operator with a recording operator. This operator entered on a ticket the party and number desired by the subscriber and informed him/her, "Thank you, we will call you." The recording operator then sent the ticket to a distributing operator. The distributing operator took it to a line operator at a toll switchboard, who contacted the party or station desired and called back the subscriber. The length of the conversation was timed by a "calculograph," which stamped the time at the beginning and end of it on the ticket. After being examined by still another operator for irregularities, it was placed in a cabinet until the next morning, when it was forwarded to the auditor's office for billing.[42]

The local operator's relationship with the subscriber was formalized as her conversation was restricted to set phrases memorized from an instruction manual, which were supposed to cover all possible contingencies. By 1912, operating phraseology was uniform throughout the Bell System; management believed it to be "so skillfully worded as to meet all operating situations with the brevity and clearness of meaning necessary to the speed of the service."[43] As the representative of the company most frequently in contact with the public, the operator was expected to display a "courteous and ladylike" manner.

Since the operator and subscriber did not meet face-to-face, the operator had to make her impression through her voice. The company expected her to speak in "the cheery tones of a Polyanna."[44] The operator was required to answer a call by asking "Number, please?" and to repeat separately, with clear enunciation, each digit of the number the subscriber requested. All questions were to be posed with the rising inflection on the last word. The operator was to use a falling inflection for the "busy" and "do not answer" reports:

> The meaning to be conveyed is not merely that the line of the called subscriber is already in use, but that the operator is *sorry* to have to report that such is the case. . . . "Line *busy*" (which is the busy report) should be said with the same emphasis on the first syllable of the word "busy" and with the same tone of sympathetic concern, as one would employ in saying "I am *sorry* Mr. Smith, but I cannot give you what you want." . . . Practically the same ideas apply in the "don't answer" report. (They don't *answer*.)[45]

The instruction books specified the exact enunciation of numbers: " . . . '2' is to be spoken as 'TOO'—with a strong T and long OO.

'3' is to be spoken as 'TH-R-R-EE'—with a slightly rolling R and long E."[46]

Under no circumstance was an operator permitted to talk back to a subscriber, even when insulted. An operator confronted by an irritated subscriber demanding an explanation for a delay in answering could only repeat "Number, please?" until the subscriber gave the number. If anything beyond the set phrases was required, the operator was to connect the subscriber with the information desk.[47] As a result, the operator seemed "strangely impersonal . . . an automaton, wound up always to say the same things over and over again."[48]

Scientific management practices introduced after 1900 greatly increased the supervisory personnel's scrutiny of the telephone operator. Management believed scrutiny of the operator's performance to be "analogous to the inspection of the product of the factory, telephone service being the product in our case."[49] Engineers responsible for methods and standards devised operating rules and techniques "to give the best possible service with maximum efficiency . . . under all conditions." To determine "proper standards" for operators' work loads—that is, the number of calls an operator was to handle each hour—the engineers used stop watches to time each step of a call "to the exact second."[50] The companies established strict standards of operating efficiency for which the chief operators were held accountable. The chief operators in turn applied pressure to the supervisors to ensure that the operators in their charge met these standards.

The New England Telephone Company in 1912 had a "standard speed of answer" of four seconds; on no more than 3 percent of the calls could the answering time exceed ten seconds. The "standard for irregularities" was 10 percent, "irregularities" indicating failure of operators to conform to the company's operating practices and instructions. The New England Telephone Company's magazine for employees noted that there were over a thousand manual or verbal operations that an operator could perform incorrectly, several of which could occur on the same call. Many errors occurred in the area of operating phraseology, where the company had restricted the operators to 115 specific expressions.[51]

A system of double supervision allowed the telephone companies to maintain continuous surveillance of their operating forces. In no other job could management so closely observe its employees without their being aware of it. An observation board, controlled by a woman known as a "monitor" and connected with each switchboard position in the exchange, was situated in the center of the operating room next to the chief operator's desk. The monitor could plug in on any operator without her knowledge and study her work in detail.[52] By 1912, the Main exchange in Boston had been equipped with an observation board by which monitors were able to "listen in" on any operator in the seven central exchanges in the Metropolitan District. In addition, most telephone companies employed men known as "service testers," who tested both the condition of the lines and the service rendered by placing calls from various public and private telephones as though they were subscribers. Errors recorded by service testers were listed in monthly service reports, which management used to evaluate the performance of each operator.[53]

The application of scientific management practices made it impossible for the telephone operator to exercise even the slightest initiative and placed her under enormous strain. The New England Telephone Company regarded the work of the telephone operator as "necessarily routine": "She has neither time nor training to deal with the unusual. She is not asked to. Demands above or beyond the ordinary are promptly taken off her hands by supervisory people."[54] Management expected the operators to work continuously at a rapid pace. As a Bell official explained, "The underlying reason for this is [that] good work is done under steady pressure. . . . Idleness would result in inattention and that would lead to mistakes."[55]

Since operating was restricted to the repetition of a few simple motions and approved phrases, skill came to be equated almost entirely with speed. Many operators took pride in the number of calls they could crowd into a few seconds; they were urged on by supervisors and chief operators intent on establishing a speed record for the exchange. This sort of competition between exchanges was no doubt also encouraged by the operators' high school experience of inter-class and inter-school rivalry. Efficient performance, however, often caused traffic engineers to increase the number of calls the operators were expected to handle per hour.[56]

Abuse from subscribers, often impatient when placing a call, contributed to the strain on the telephone operator. Unlike the telegraphist who interacted with a fellow operator, the telephone operator interacted with the public, which possessed little understanding of the methods involved in operating and the pressures under which the operator worked.[57] During periods of heavy traffic, with several lights on the switchboard glowing simultaneously, it was difficult for the operator to determine the order of calls. Subscribers who did not receive prompt answers often indicated their impatience by moving the hook of their telephone receiver up and down, which caused the operator to hear a clicking or banging sound and made the light on the switchboard flash on and off. The operator's awareness of subscribers, including perhaps a service tester, signaling their displeasure and of the supervisor standing behind her added to the strain of the rapid work pace.[58]

The telephone companies enforced compliance with work-speed and efficiency standards through strict discipline and the system of double supervision. Nelle Curry, assigned to investigate the working conditions of telephone operators for the U.S. Commission on Industrial Relations in 1915, asserted, "There is possibly no woman in any industry whose remissness is more instantly checked by the incisive action of an overseer than the telephone operator."[59] Curry reported that operators in Los Angeles exchanges received "punishment hours," assignment to an undesirable work shift for a certain period, for committing such errors as "slow answers" (over ten seconds), a "slow disconnect" (over ten seconds), or an "unanswered flash" (call).[60] Operators were not allowed to speak to each other or read at the switchboard, even during slack periods.

Operators were as physically restricted as the assembly-line workers of a later era or high school students forced to sit rigidly at their desks and unable to leave the classroom without a hall pass, almost never granted by teachers. An operator had to get a supervisor's permission, which was not easily obtained, to go to the bathroom or get a drink of water. Mary Quinn, an operator in Springfield, Massachusetts, who became the first vice-president of the Telephone Operators' Department, left the employ of the New England Telephone Company for six months in 1911 because a supervisor refused to let her go to the bathroom.[61] According to Julia O'Connor, president of the Telephone Operators' Department who began work as an operator in Boston in 1908, "Inside the central office an operator is supervised, tested, observed, disciplined, almost to the breaking point. It is scarcely possible for her to obey any natural impulse without breaking a rule. She must not move her head to the left or right; she must not indulge in social conversation, by which may be construed her 'hello' and 'goodbye' to the adjacent operator; she must sit, even when not engaged in operating, if such a moment ever comes, with plug in hand ready to answer. . . . "[62]

In its insistence on strict adherence to rules of conduct, the telephone company closely resembled the high school, as did many of its punishments, such as detention hours and suspension. Rose Finkelstein, who worked as an operator and supervisor in Boston exchanges from 1907 to 1921, recalled that "they were constantly punishing a girl for some slight infraction." For tardiness, which Finkelstein claimed the company defined as being "one minute late," an operator was forced to sit for a time in a punishment room and was docked pay.[63] To a young woman in her teens or twenties this was undoubtedly demeaning, as though she were a child being made to stand in the corner. Operating errors or insufficient speed could result in suspension from work for several days without pay or dismissal.

High school students of the early twentieth century often complained about the schools' excessive attention to enforcing silence and decorum. An editorial in the April, 1906, issue of the *Cambridge Review*, the student magazine of Cambridge High School, near Boston, declared that "something is wrong" when one-third of the seniors in the school's Latin division were censured for conduct, as had happened the previous month. According to the *Cambridge Review*, the majority of the offenses were not deliberate acts of misbehavior but rather "little careless whisperings and communications that are bound to take place in a class whose members have had 5 years to get acquainted." Much of this "unintentional rule-breaking" had occurred in the school corridors between classes: "In our opinion it would be almost impossible to have perfect order and quiet at such times." The school board had overreacted in giving detention to the offending students: "It is not pleasant to carry home a 'censured for conduct' on one's report card, it is not pleasant, for either teacher or scholar, to remain in the close air of the school room until 2:00 doing penance for one's sins, when the warm, fresh air of spring is calling to the woods and the fields."[64] It is likely that having resented this in high school, the telephone operators were not keen on experiencing it in the workplace.

The Telephone Operators' Union strongly opposed the system of double supervision and urged that the position of monitor be abolished, but management never made any concessions on this issue. The union's national president Julia O'Connor, asserted in 1920 that

> head tests on an operator's position have neither morale nor service justification. . . . If the chief operator would occasionally listen in on an operator with a view to ascertaining her tone, her courtesy to subscribers, etc., and then take up the matter in the proper way with the operator it might not be so objectionable, but this person constantly on the job to discover your faults, whose stock in trade is your mistakes and who isn't making good unless she can get something on you, is one of the meanest elements in the telephone service.[65]

The union leadership believed that organizing supervisors was important not only to promote labor solidarity in the exchanges, but because improvements in their working conditions would also benefit the operators. The most unpleasant feature of the supervisor's job was that, like the sales clerk, she was never permitted to sit down. According to Julia O'Connor, "The supervisor . . . is as much a victim of petty, unintelligent exchange administration as is the operator. . . . Standing on one's feet all day is not conducive to good spirits and good disposition. Supervisors ought to have a chance to sit down and most decidedly her hours should be less than eight hours a day."[66]

Recruiting and Training the Operating Force

Recruiting and training new operators in the Bell System were standardized during the first decade of the twentieth century. Beginning with the National Cash Register Company in 1901, many large corporations that could afford the investment established centralized personnel departments to control hiring, transferring, and promoting workers. These were previously the responsibilities of individual foremen—the telephone company's equivalent being the chief operators. The larger corporations, however, had come to believe that their method promoted inefficiency, because the foremen had often given preference to friends and members of their own ethnic groups.[67] Centralizing hiring and transfers gave the telephone company far greater ability to place operators where traffic required, thus providing more efficient service across a city. In most cities, women seeking employment as telephone operators no longer applied to the chief operator at the exchange but at the company's central personnel office, which was often combined with the company's training school.

The telephone companies established very strict age, physical, and educational qualifications for operating positions. An applicant was required to be between the ages of seventeen and twenty-six, unmarried, with at least a grammar school education and preferably two years of high school. Management exercised more flexibility in hiring in the smaller towns and rural areas. A woman with work experience in several other occupations who applied for a position as a telephone operator in Chicago in 1920 emphasized that she had never before encountered such a "complicated and systematic procedure" in being hired: "Some places, like laundries and packing houses, didn't care who or what you were as long as you could stand up nine hours a day. Other places, like department stores, put you through a mild grilling, looked at your vaccination, and required a couple of references. But to become a telephone operator was almost as bad as the preliminaries incidental to getting a passport in wartime."[68] Because it was necessary for an operator to speak clearly and use proper English, management believed education to be essential. Education was also important because the operator interacted largely with people who were relatively affluent; most subscribers were middle or upper class. As a Bell official explained, "Telephone users are mostly the better educated, hence the necessity of these qualifications that she may cope with them on an equal plane."[69]

The applicant was subjected to a stringent physical examination, in part to determine her "nervous endurance and nervous adaptability." The physician administered a blood test and checked for evidence of heart disease and tuberculosis. The applicant had to have an arm stretch of at least five feet and a sitting height of at least thirty-two inches to reach the higher sections of the switchboard, which generally disqualified women less than five feet tall. Good eyesight and unimpaired hearing were also necessary.[70]

Telephone company interviewers closely examined the speech of the applicant and sought to determine whether she was capable of displaying the necessary patience and courtesy with subscribers. To qualify for consideration an applicant had to speak English without an accent, which eliminated nearly all immigrants.[71] Women with poor enunciation or "harsh or displeasing" voices were also rejected.[72] Considerable attention was devoted to the applicant's "general appearance of alertness and neatness."[73] According to Mary E. Harrington, who had charge of hiring and training new operators for the New England Telephone Company in Boston from 1906 until about 1930, "A slovenly girl is, as a rule, careless about detail and rarely, if ever, develops into an accurate operator. Exaggerated dress is another evidence of poor surroundings, and indicates a person of too light a mind to apply herself well."[74]

The telephone companies specified that prospective operators must be between seventeen and twenty-six years of age because they believed younger women were more amenable to work-discipline and better able than older women to withstand fatigue and nervous strain. Girls younger than seventeen lacked the necessary "physical strength and mental poise."[75] According to Julia O'Connor of the Telephone Operators' Union, the telephone companies wanted their operators to be "girls fresh from school discipline."[76]

The policy in the Bell System was to hire only unmarried women as operators, and operators who married were expected to leave the telephone service. The general superintendent of traffic of the New

England Telephone Company explained in 1916: " . . . we do not encourage the girls to stay after marriage. Their interest is divided between their domestic duties and their work, consequently they are apt to be tardy and . . . unpunctual in their attendance. While we do not actually require an operator's resignation when she marries, we regard her continuance as temporary, and reserve promotion . . . for those whose devotion to telephone work is more single-minded."[77] The New England Telephone Company gave strong preference to applicants who lived with their parents, "as they are more carefully guarded, and are generally surrounded by wholesome influences."[78]

By 1910, the New England Telephone Company had discontinued direct advertising for new operators, relying instead on personal referral by school officials and clergymen (particularly Catholic priests). Mary E. Harrington stated that advertising had attracted "foreigners, illiterate and untidy," while the new method produced "young ladies of refinement." Harrington also noted that the referral method saved the company a considerable amount of preliminary work, since the applicants usually had been screened as to their age and educational background. She claimed in 1910 that 50 percent of the applicants were accepted in Boston where no advertising was done, whereas only 10 percent to 28 percent were accepted in cities where the Bell companies relied upon advertising.[79] More important, the company could more easily discourage members of groups it held in disdain from applying, particularly Jews and blacks.

The New England Telephone Company maintained a policy against hiring Jews and blacks as telephone operators until the 1940s. Blacks were not hired in any capacity higher than janitor anywhere in the Bell System until the late 1930s.[80] In 1923, the *Labor News*, Massachusetts's statewide labor newspaper published in Worcester, tried to learn why not a single Jewish woman was employed in the Worcester telephone exchange: " . . . upon investigation it was found that the local management objected first, because of the many holidays which Jewish girls are compelled to observe . . . and second, that Jewish girls are slow workers, and consequently do not make good operators; and third, Jewish girls employed in trades where their sex predominates are known as agitators of the highest type. . . . "[81] Rose Finkelstein, one of the few Jewish operators in Boston, who was hired in 1907, emphasized that the New England Telephone Company barred Jews and blacks from employment as operators until the establishment of the Fair Employment Practices Commission (FEPC) in the 1940s:

It so happened that there was a man relieving when I applied for the job. But they had a hiring plan, they had a couple of sisters named Harrington, and they had the entire say of the employment. And you just couldn't get by them. . . . only two or three Jewish girls, maybe, throughout the whole system. They never took in Jewish girls, they never took in black girls. . . . if you didn't come with a recommendation from the Church you couldn't get by. . . . it took a long time before— it was after the FEPC that the Telephone Company, the employment division, changed their tune.[82]

Schools to provide systematic training of new telephone operators were established by the Bell companies in many of the larger cities during the first decade of the twentieth century. This made it much easier to promote uniformity in operating practices. The first training school opened in New York in 1902, and within a few years formal training programs lasting from three to four weeks were instituted in such cities as Boston (in 1906), Chicago, Philadelphia, Houston, and Denver.[83] In Boston, the telephone company employment bureau was combined with the training school, under the direction of its principal Mary E. Harrington, previously chief operator at Boston's Main exchange.[84]

The training schools combined classroom lectures and demonstrations of operating methods with practice at dummy switchboards connected to the instructors' desks. Oral quizzes and written examinations were frequently administered, and each student received a daily grade for her work. The course of instruction included such topics as the functions of the various telephone company officials and departments; the rules governing the conduct of operators in their relations with the public and with their superiors; the construction of the telephone instrument and switchboard; operating phraseology; and the handling of various types of telephone calls. The instructors simulated the sorts of calls operators could expect to encounter.[85]

The training schools devoted considerable attention to enunciation and voice modulation. The program of the Chicago Telephone Company, for example, included a half hour a day of "voice training" under the direction of an "accomplished singer and elocutionist." The points emphasized were "proper breath control, deep breathing, proper position of the body, a loose and free movement of the tongue, the proper placing of the voice, and the importance of tonal resonance." Recitation work by the students consisted of breathing and syllable exercises and singing scales.[86]

Student operators were treated as though they were pupils in a public school. They filled out their applications in a room which the Pacific Telephone Company compared to a homeroom.[87] In the lecture rooms, the student operators were seated alphabetically at their desks. A New York State Department of Labor investigation of the telephone industry published in 1920 stated that, in the New York Telephone Company training school in Manhattan, "the atmosphere and discipline is that of elementary school rooms."[88] A woman who entered the training school of the Chicago Telephone Company in 1920 declared, "It was a shock to have a lesson suddenly interrupted by a teacher's stern voice saying, 'Miss Green, are you chewing gum?' And when Miss Green with a guilty expression nodded her head, to have teacher continue in sepulchral tones, 'Come in front then and put it in the waste basket.' "[89] Training school instructors also impressed upon the students "the necessity of simple dressing." One recruit to the New York Telephone Company recalled her instructor's objecting to students' wearing white shoes.[90] According to the 1910 U.S. Senate investigation of the telephone industry, the proportion of student operators who failed to graduate from the various training programs across the country ranged from 25 percent to 40 percent.[91] Upon the student's completion of the training course, an envelope known as the "Employees' Service Record," containing the student's application blank, letters of reference, and a report of her work at the school, was sent to the chief operator at the exchange to which she was assigned.[92]

Telephone Operating as a Vocation

Vocational counselors in the early twentieth century viewed telephone operating as white-collar work similar in status to clerical employment. It was recommended for young women who did not desire factory work but could not afford business college and were therefore unable to acquire the skills of a typist or stenographer.[93] Student operators were paid from the time the training schools were established. The wages received by telephone operators were low and did not permit them to be self-supporting, but they still compared favorably with those of women workers outside the clerical sector because the operators were not subjected to seasonal unemployment.[94]

According to a U.S. government investigation in 1909, the average weekly earnings of women employed in Boston's eleven largest department stores was $7.46, while telephone operators received $7.62. Women in Boston employed in factories, mills, and "miscellaneous establishments" earned an average of $6.53 a week. Of course, more of the telephone operators' wages was consumed by carfare, since they usually worked in downtown districts a considerable distance from their homes. Factory women, if not department store clerks, often worked within easy walking distance of their homes.[95]

While vocational counselors viewed office employment as the most attractive of the women's occupations, they considered telephone operating to be among the relatively small number of jobs open to women that could be classified as "ladylike." Counselors warned the woman who had to work outside the home that jobs requiring manual labor, personal service and deference, interaction with persons of lower social standing, or familiar contact with strange men would undermine her status as a "lady." She must above all be concerned with avoiding any appearance of sexual impropriety. It was also important to maintain a neat and clean appearance.[96] The telephone operator's work was physically arduous to be sure, but she at least kept her hands clean.

Since she repeated only prescribed phrases to subscribers with whom she never came into direct contact, she escaped the feeling of being at their service. The subscribers were usually upper or middle class, so the operator was not interacting with persons "beneath her." The telephone operator was protected from sexual harassment; unlike women working in offices and stores, she never came into face-to-face contact with men in the workplace. In most cities after 1900, and everywhere after 1910, operators worked exclusively under female supervision in the exchange. In a study of women workers published in 1909, which formed part of the *Pittsburgh Survey*, Elizabeth Beardsley Butler stressed that "the stores are avenues through which any who will may come. . . . without attracting attention, men can come into the stores and talk to the girls."[97] Because it offered seclusion from the public, the position of telephone operator was better suited than any other woman's job to "the girl of natural refinement and reserve who dreads personal contact with all sorts of men and women."[98] Telephone company management always claimed that its operators were "selected from the best class of young women seeking employment," and it emphasized, "We advertise for 'young *ladies*,' as operators. . . ."[99]

Vocational counselors generally identified the major disadvantages of telephone operating as low wages and frequent evening, night, Sunday, and holiday work, which resulted from the need to provide telephone service twenty-four hours a day, every day of the year. The only other occupations employing young women in which the worker

was assigned such irregular hours were telegraph operating and domestic service. The telephone operator shared with the domestic servant the feeling of being almost always on duty. She not only worked
at all hours of the day and night, Sundays, and holidays, but was
generally "on call" on her day off, because the company might need
her in the event of a sudden increase in telephone traffic resulting
from an emergency such as a fire, flood, a particularly bad storm, or
major interruption of streetcar or subway service.[100]

Night work was highly disruptive, particularly for young women
drawn to the new nighttime commercial amusements and dance halls.
Socializing with men was sharply restricted, since most men worked
during the day when the night operators were free. Night operators
were also seriously inconvenienced because they could not conform
to meal hours, whether at home or in a boardinghouse.[101] Since most
considered it "natural" to work during the day and sleep at night,
night work could be disorienting in a larger sense. The night telephone
operator might feel cut off not just from the rhythms of family and
community life but from what seemed like the rhythm of nature
itself.[102]

Night operating was also far more stressful than work during
the day. Travel to and from work not only was inconvenient but also
could prove dangerous. In most city neighborhoods, it was difficult
to sleep during the day. Although traffic was light at night, most of
the calls were of an emergency nature, which produced considerable
nervous tension. Many women left Bell Company employ for lower-
paying jobs as private branch exchange (PBX) operators in stores or
offices, which did not involve evening, night, Sunday, or holiday
work.[103]

The Bell companies did make some effort to protect the safety
of their night operators, although they never heeded reformers' suggestions to substitute men operators for women at night, as had been
done in the late nineteenth century. Night operators all reported to
work and left work at the same time, whereas day operators came to
work in small groups at different hours, ate their lunch at different
times, and stopped work at different hours.[104] The prohibition of night
work became a favorite issue of reformers after the 1908 Supreme
Court decision in *Muller v. Oregon,* which upheld maximum hours
for women on the basis of arguments that women's inferior physical
capacity and their role as propagators of the race required that they
be protected.[105] While not going so far as to suggest outright prohibition of night work, the secretary of the Employers' Welfare Department of the National Civic Federation, who advised the American

Telephone and Telegraph Company (the parent company of the Bell System) on working conditions, recommended that the use of women under twenty years of age be discontinued on the night shift. The advisor justified this because she considered young women physically weaker and also because "the character of many night calls is such that young women should not have to be concerned with them."[106] While Bell management presented an image of paternalistic concern for its operators, allegedly weak and in need of its protection, it continued to employ younger women at night work.

The daily pattern of telephone traffic resulted in the company's establishing the most undesirable work shift, which was known as the "split trick" (*trick* was the term used in the Bell System for a set of working hours). Split trick operators were assigned to two separate sets of working hours during the day, with several hours off in between. While the volume of traffic varied considerably over the course of the day, it generally followed a regular pattern known as a "traffic curve." In most exchanges located in business districts, the volume of calls increased gradually from about 7:00 A.M. until 11:00 A.M., when the busiest hour or "morning peak of the load" was reached. The volume of calls then declined until 2:00 or 3:00 P.M. and then began to rise, reaching the "peak of the afternoon load" between 4:00 and 5:00 P.M. Traffic in exchanges serving wholesale marketing districts, such as the Richmond exchange in Boston's North End, did not follow the usual pattern at business district exchanges but reached peak volume during the early morning hours. The traffic curves in exchanges serving residential districts differed significantly from those in business district exchanges. The peak loads in residential exchanges generally occurred during the evening and on Sundays and holidays, when the volume of calls in the business district was at its lowest. Because of the traffic curve, the telephone companies preferred part of the operating force to work only during the periods of heaviest traffic.[107]

Although generally grouped with lower-white-collar occupations, telephone operating cannot be strictly classified as either white-collar or blue-collar work. As has been pointed out, telephone operators resembled clerks or other lower-white-collar workers in several ways: (1) because the job required proficiency in speaking English, telephone operators, like most white-collar workers, were generally native-born and of British or Irish ancestry; (2) the telephone companies required a higher level of education—at least grammar school—than was needed for factory employment; (3) the physical surroundings of the telephone exchange were cleaner and more com-

fortable than the factory; (4) unlike most factory workers, the telephone operator was not subjected to seasonal unemployment; (5)
because the telephone operator in the early twentieth century interacted primarily with subscribers who were upper or middle class, she
could to some extent, like a department store clerk, borrow prestige
from the customer; and (6) the white-collar worker's claim to prestige
was expressed, as the label implies, by style of dress. While the standardization and mass production of fashionable clothing eliminated
many distinctions important during the nineteenth century, significant
differences in style of dress continued to prevail between white-collar
workers and factory workers. Factory workers might wear standardized street clothes off the job, but white-collar workers wore them
on the job as well.[108] The telephone operator's style of dress was
clearly that of the white-collar worker.

However, the actual work performed by the telephone operator,
which involved the continuous repetition of a few simple motions at
high speed under extremely close supervision, did not differ appre-
ciably from factory work. Like the factory worker, the telephone
operator received low wages, was subjected to harsh discipline, was
assigned to work at night and on Sundays and holidays, and had little
prospect for advancement.[109] The telephone operator had even less
control over her pace of work than did most factory hands.

Company Paternalism and the Operating Force

Presenting itself as the operator's guardian, Bell management
encouraged dependency in its young and relatively inexperienced operating force. It continually referred to the Bell Company as the "Bell
family." Company literature portrayed the telephone exchange as an
extension of the home. A recruiting brochure of the Chicago Telephone Company, for example, announced that it provided "the parental care of a far-seeing monopoly," and it emphasized the
"protection" afforded the operator by seclusion from the public, the
"self-control" of supervisory personnel, and the "wholesome and refined" work atmosphere.[110] Magazine feature-writers might describe
the supervisor as the "sergeant" of the exchange, but Bell management
referred to her as the operator's "older sister."[111] A study of the
telephone industry by the New York Department of Labor in 1920
stated that telephone company management allowed the operator
little or no initiative and compared the operator to a "schoolgirl,"
who was expected to display "obedience, loyalty, and appreciation."[112] Until at least the 1940s, the telephone company had a cus-

tom, known as "Parents' Night," which reinforced the image of the telephone operator as a schoolgirl; on Parents' Night, it invited the operators' parents to visit the telephone exchange and meet their daughters' supervisors and chief operator.[113]

To promote employee loyalty and increase work efficiency, Bell management established retiring rooms and cafeterias for telephone operators during the early twentieth century. As the operators' pace of work intensified, many of the Bell companies instituted morning and afternoon relief breaks of ten or fifteen minutes, which were established as a right after unionization. The retiring room, generally containing a piano or Victrola and magazines, was made available for the operators' use during the relief periods. An effort was made to create a "restful atmosphere" in the room through "soft colors" and "low lights."[114]

Cafeterias were opened in the larger urban exchange buildings and provided what management claimed were nutritionally balanced meals at or near cost. Operators employed in these exchanges generally lived too far away to return home for lunch and as a result ate hurried meals in cheap restaurants. Management believed the "nutritionally balanced" cafeteria meals contributed to greater work efficiency, particularly in the afternoon.[115] The New York Telephone Company described the exchange cafeteria, whose supervisors were usually trained in domestic science, as an "indoor garden of delight."[116] The New England Telephone Company claimed that the cafeteria in Boston's Main exchange compared favorably with the dining room of a "high-class" hotel: " . . . the color scheme of the walls, which are in shades of buff and dull yellow, is pleasing and in harmony with the natural oak finish of the furniture. The crockery is a good quality of porcelain and tastefully decorated. The napery is of unusually fine quality. . . . "[117] Surroundings of this sort helped disguise the routinized, low-wage nature of the work. Management believed that operators would regard the comfortable retiring rooms and eating facilities as privileges bestowed by a "benevolent" employer and would therefore develop a stronger attachment to the company.

A telephone exchange retiring room was supervised by a woman known as the "matron" or "operators' quarters supervisor." Bell management, intent on presenting the company as a "family," envisioned her as a "mother-substitute" who typified the "human side of the telephone business." Unlike the chief operator, who had to consider the interests of both the subscribers and the operating force, the matron was concerned only with the welfare of "her girls." The matron greeted the new operator when she arrived at the telephone exchange and introduced her to the other operators. According to the New England Telephone Company's magazine, "From that moment the new recruit is one of the girls—one of that mother's girls." The matron advised the operators on personal hygiene and attended to operators who became sick during the workday. Management believed that the matron's interest in the health of the operators helped to increase work efficiency: "It is not a little precaution for her to discover the wet shoes or damp clothing of the girl who comes to work through a beating storm; and the drying of those clothes or shoes means the ounce of prevention which assists in keeping the ranks at the switchboard full at all times."[118]

The Bell companies also developed elaborate athletic programs to increase employee identification with the company. Since the 1890s, large corporations had viewed organized sports as a means of promoting physical fitness among workers and harmonizing labor relations. Sports provided a safety valve for industrial discontent by diverting workers' attention from job grievances and political issues and blurring the line between labor and management. Steel magnate Andrew Carnegie was prominently involved in the formation of baseball and football teams near the Bessemer works in Braddock, Pennsylvania, after a violent strike had occurred there. The wealthy mill owner and Republican politician Garrett Hobart established a baseball team at Paterson, New Jersey, in 1896 after a strike.[119] After 1900, the Bell companies sponsored baseball and bowling leagues for their employees across the country. Bell teams competed not just in major cities like New York, Boston, and San Francisco, but in small towns such as Boise, Idaho, where Bell employees played in a twilight baseball league.[120] Managerial officials often participated in league contests, such as the New England Telephone Company's bowling league in Boston, where teams composed of wire chiefs, engineers, and division foremen competed with plant maintenance and plant accounting teams.[121] Mixed teams composed of both workers and managerial officials were also formed. Bell teams were entered in innumerable corporation leagues where they competed against teams of electric company workers, bank tellers, drug store clerks, and so on.

The Bell Company athletic programs were mostly set up for the male employees, with women involved in a supporting role, as spectators. The New England Telephone Company, however, did participate in a "Ladies' League," in which its women employees bowled against teams from Filene's clothing store, the Columbia National

Life Insurance Company, the United Stationery Company, and the like.[122] At an indoor track meet for employees, organized by New England Bell in Boston in 1914, one of the ten events—a forty-yard dash—was for women.[123]

Bell management's paternalism was further reflected in the uniform, noncontributory employee benefit plan introduced throughout the Bell System in 1913, which provided retirement pensions and accident and disability payments. The plan, regarded by American Telephone and Telegraph Company officials as "strictly a business proposition," was motivated by management's desire to "maintain freedom from labor unions," increase worker efficiency, and attract more employees.[124] AT&T officials also hoped the benefit plan would instill a greater sense of being part of the Bell System: "To a large majority of the workers . . . the AT&T Company is a myth, they feel no interest in it. . . . They feel their loyalty to the company which pays their wages, but most do not feel their loyalty to the system as a whole. . . . If every Bell employee is made to feel that the central organization takes an interest in him, he in turn will take an interest in securing greater harmony in the working of the system as a whole."[125]

The only part of the plan of real significance to the operating force was the sickness disability program. Beginning on the eighth day of absence, it provided full or partial payment of wages, depending on length of service, to operators employed for at least two years.[126] Few operators worked the twenty years required to qualify for a pension, since the average term of service for operators in the associated Bell companies was about three years, and the accident disability program was designed primarily for the telephone linemen, whose work was relatively dangerous.

Management allowed the employees no voice in the administration of the benefit plan, which it viewed as a "privilege" it could withdraw at any time. The New England Telephone Company warned its unionized employees in 1917 that it would discontinue the plan rather than allow worker participation in its administration: "Each employee should impress upon himself the fact that the Companies in the Bell System have established this plan voluntarily. This is mentioned because if any group of employees not duly authorized attempted to dictate how the Plan should be administered, it might mean the withdrawing of these benefits."[127]

The paternalism of the Bell System in the early twentieth century was not inconsistent with its emphasis on scientific management in the telephone exchanges. Bell management had grown increasingly concerned that the faster pace of work required of telephone operators and the impersonal nature of their relations with supervisory personnel might undermine employee identification with the company. The introduction of exchange cafeterias, retiring rooms, company-sponsored athletics, and the benefit plan were all intended to generate a sense of belonging and a devotion to the company in telephone operators seemingly lost in the anonymity of mass industry. The retiring room matron was supposed to "humanize" the telephone exchange by providing the operator with personal access to management available only to those employed in small shops. Cafeterias, retiring rooms, and recreation programs were also designed to promote work efficiency by reducing the fatigue and nervous irritability produced by the faster pace of telephone operating made possible by scientific management.

Early Investigations of the Telephone Service

The working conditions of telephone operators received widespread attention as a result of an investigation into the causes of the 1907 strike of over four hundred Bell Company operators in Toronto, Canada. The strike was precipitated when the Bell Telephone Company of Canada announced on very short notice that the workday for telephone operators would be extended from five hours to eight hours, with a wage increase that was not proportionate to the increase in hours. The extended workday drastically reduced the income of the self-supporting operators by depriving them of the overtime work on which they depended. The operators ended the strike, which did not result in unionization or achieve any concrete gains, after the intervention of the Canadian Department of Labour led to the appointment of a special Royal Commission to conduct hearings and make recommendations concerning the operators' working conditions.[128]

The Royal Commission concluded in its report that the strike had been justified and sharply criticized the Bell Company for its lack of concern for the health of its operating force. Julia O'Connor later described the report of the Royal Commission as "alive, human and . . . the only investigation on record in which the operators have had their say."[129] The Royal Commission's report particularly emphasized the physical and nervous strain to which the telephone operators were subjected. In no other occupation employing women were "the senses of hearing, speech, and sight . . . called into play simultaneously to

Boy telephone operators, New York, 1879. (Courtesy of the Boston Public Library, Print Department.)

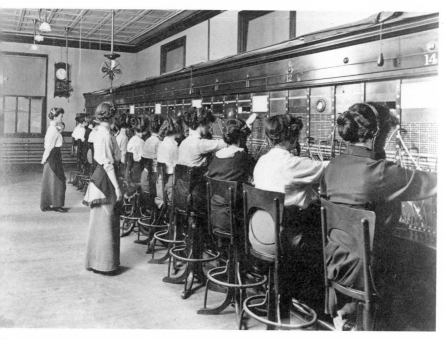

Telephone operators at the switchboard, with supervisors standing behind them, New England Telephone Company, Boston, 1915. (Courtesy of the Boston Public Library, Print Department.)

Telephone operator at the switchboard, New England Telephone Company, Boston, ca. 1915. With her right hand she pushes the plug into the jack to connect the lines of the person calling and the person receiving the call; with her left hand she operates a key that rings the bell of the receiving party. Note how well she is dressed—in embroidered linen and lace. (Courtesy of the Boston Public Library, Print Department.)

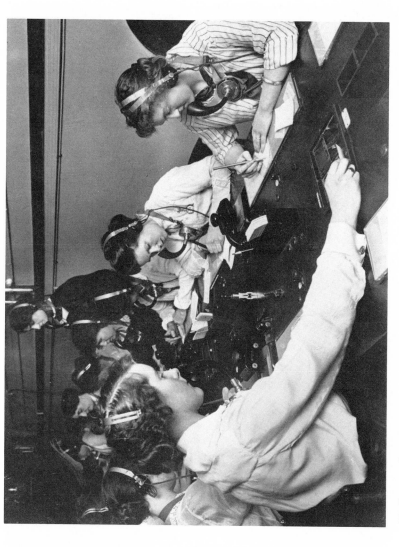

Toll recording operators, with supervisor standing in the rear, New England Telephone Company, Boston, ca. 1915. (Courtesy of the Boston Public Library, Print Department.)

Lecture room of the training school for operators, New England Telephone Company, Boston, ca. 1915. (Courtesy of the Boston Public Library, Print Department.)

Training school for operators, New England Telephone Company, Boston, March 1922. (Courtesy of the Boston Public Library, Print Department.)

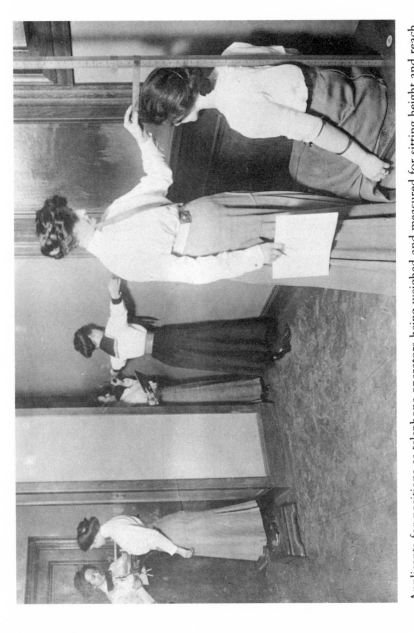

Applicants for positions as telephone operators being weighed and measured for sitting height and reach, New England Telephone Company, Boston, ca. 1915. (Courtesy of the Boston Public Library, Print Department.)

Telephone operators in an exchange retiring room, New England Telephone Company, Boston, 1916. Note bell in background which summons operators back to work. (Courtesy of the Boston Public Library, Print Department.)

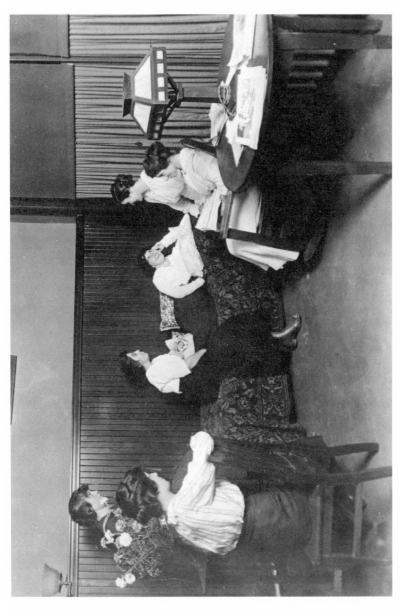

Telephone operators in an exchange retiring room, New England Telephone Company, Boston, 1916. (Courtesy of the Boston Public Library, Print Department.)

the same extent or required to be so constantly on the alert." Operators testified that the pace of work caused them to become "exceedingly nervous" and led to fainting and "overexcitability."[130] The Royal Commission subpoenaed twenty-six physicians, nearly all of them from the medical faculty of the University of Toronto, to give evidence concerning the impact of telephone operating on a woman's health. Believing young women were especially susceptible to nervous disorders, the physicians agreed the eight-hour day was much too long. Many of them warned that the existing working conditions could disqualify a telephone operator for motherhood, since they might cause her to produce children with "epilepsy and all sorts of nervous diseases."[131] The Royal Commission recommended a workday for telephone operators of six hours at the switchboard with frequent relief breaks, but it added that "medical men favour a still shorter time."[132] The company, refusing to be bound by any of the Royal Commission's recomendations, would only agree to a seven-hour day spread over nine hours.

After 1907, government investigatory commissions and reformers in the United States demonstrated increasing concern over the operators' low wages, long hours, and nervous strain. Federal and state government investigations of the telephone industry were strongly influenced by the Royal Commission's report. The U.S. Senate investigation of 1910, which implied that wages were too low and hours too long, contained a lengthy summary of the physicians' testimony before the Royal Commission.[133] Nelle Curry, field investigator of the U.S. Commission on Industrial Relations, stated in her 1915 report on telephone operators' working conditions that her interviews with operators across the country "amply supported" the findings of the Royal Commission. She strongly recommended a maximum workday of six hours and higher wages for operators. Curry claimed that management showed little concern for the health of operators, despite their frequent "nervous collapses" and "hysterical attacks" at the switchboard.[134] The New York State Department of Labor's 1920 report on the telephone industry, which criticized the low wages paid to New York telephone operators, also referred to the Royal Commission's findings.[135] Such reformers as Elizabeth Beardsley Butler in her study *Women and the Trades* (1909), Josephine Goldmark in *Fatigue and Efficiency* (1912), and Mary Caroline Crawford in the first article supporting the cause of unionizing telephone operators published in a national magazine, relied heavily on the Royal Commission's report in arguing for better conditions for telephone operators.[136]

Conclusion

Significant numbers of telephone operators experienced intense job dissatisfaction stemming from the contradiction between their self-image and the nature of their work. Telephone operators saw themselves as white-collar workers, with status similar to or even higher than office or department store clerks. By working-class standards, operators were well educated. Most attended high school, and, like office clerks, they received several weeks of training in a special school. They interacted primarily with subscribers who were affluent and well educated. Their employer continually emphasized that they were not ordinary girls but "young ladies of refinement." Telephone operating also commanded prestige because it excluded immigrants and blacks, whom many viewed as socially undesirable. The job, while for the most part routine, did involve significant responsibility in emergency situations.

Nevertheless, telephone operating more closely resembled the factory assembly line than white-collar work. Telephone operators, working under the system of double supervision, were unable to develop informal mechanisms of control over the work process. Their situation was in sharp contrast to department store clerks, for example. Store clerks, who spent relatively little time with customers and were allowed to move about their departments, could socialize with each other. Staffing policies that assumed certain types of women were appropriate for each department—for example, younger women on the first floor, more mature women in the higher-priced departments—solidified bonds among clerks within each department while dividing them from the clerks outside. Store departments comprised not only administrative but social units, and management often complained about the clerks' boisterous sociability. According to Susan Porter Benson, limited supervision and emphasis on worker initiative in selling created "an atmosphere highly congenial to workers' attempts to impose their own ideas about the proper way to run a department." Clerks exercised significant control over their pace of work and developed procedures for selling within their "informal work group" that were distinct and often in conflict with those of management.[137] At the same time, the autonomy the clerks enjoyed working as part of a small and relatively isolated group served to inhibit unionization.[138]

The telephone operator, by contrast, was as powerless on the job as the factory assembly-line worker of the middle and late twentieth century. The sociologist Robert Blauner has identified several individual task-related freedoms which together comprise control over the immediate work process: control over pace of work, freedom from pressure, freedom of physical movement, and the ability to control the quantity and quality of production and to choose the techniques of work. According to Blauner, "When rationalized technology and work organization do not permit the active intervention of the worker at any of these points, the alienating tendencies of modern industry, which make the worker simply a responding object, an instrument of the production process, are carried to their furthest extremes."[139]

While the secretary, office clerk, and even typist had some ability to control work pace and output and had some ease of physical movement in the workplace, the telephone operator enjoyed none of these task-related freedoms. She had absolutely no control over the pace of work. Just as the auto worker has to work at the speed of the assembly line, the telephone operator was required to handle calls as fast as they were placed. The system of double supervision subjected her to constant pressure and did not allow her a moment's rest. Like the auto assembly line, telephone operating represented an extreme example of restricted physical movement. The telephone operator could not leave the switchboard without her supervisor's permission, which was often denied. Nor did telephone operators have any control over the quantity of production. Workers must always meet a minimum level of production, but many jobs allow them to vary hourly and daily output greatly. Operators had no choice but to respond to every light on the switchboard as it appeared. The standardized phraseology and intense pace of work did not permit the operator any control over the quality of her work—all calls were the same. Good work was defined as fast work. Finally, the choice of techniques—formulating the methods of telephone operating—was entirely in the hands of supervisory personnel and time-study men. Telephone operating lacked the "team production" which permitted work crews on factory assembly lines some opportunity to fraternize. Only through unionization could the telephone operator end her isolation and attain some satisfaction in work.

NOTES

1. David Lockwood, *The Blackcoated Worker* (London: Allen and Unwin, 1958), p. 83.

2. Margery Davies, *Woman's Place Is at the Typewriter* (Philadelphia: Temple University Press, 1982), pp. 58–59.

3. Elyce Rotella, *From Home to Office* (Ann Arbor, Mich.: UMI Research Press, 1981), p. 161; Davies, *Woman's Place,* pp. 54–55.

4. Davies, *Woman's Place,* p. 58.

5. "Statement Submitted by the New England Telephone and Telegraph Company to the Subcommittee on Telephone Service of the Committee on Public Utilities of the Boston Chamber of Commerce," May 7, 1924, File 311–219, Boston Chamber of Commerce Papers, Baker Library, Harvard School of Business Administration, Boston, Mass.

6. Lois Scharf, *To Work and to Wed* (Westport, Conn.: Greenwood Press, 1980), pp. 5–8; Sheila Rothman, *Woman's Proper Place* (New York: Basic Books, 1978), pp. 52–53.

7. Marion May Dilts, *The Telephone in a Changing World* (New York: Longmans, Green, 1941), p. 105; Brenda Maddox, "Women at the Switchboard," in Ithiel de Sola Pool, ed., *The Social Impact of the Telephone* (Cambridge, Mass.: MIT Press, 1977), p. 265; R. T. Barrett, "The Changing Years as Seen from the Switchboard," Part 4, *New England Telephone Topics* [hereafter, *NETT*], April, 1935, p. 6.

8. Maddox, "Women at the Switchboard," p. 265.

9. "Emma Nutt, First of Our Thousands of Operators, Dies at 77," *NETT,* July, 1926, p. 120.

10. "Old Timers' Edition," *NETT,* March, 1915, p. 362.

11. Barrett, "Changing Years," Part 2, *NETT,* February, 1935, p. 4.

12. Maddox, "Women at the Switchboard," p. 266; Barrett, "Changing Years," Part 3, *NETT,* March, 1935, p. 5.

13. Herbert Law Webb, "Soft Answer to Hello!" in Grace Dodge et al., *What Women Can Earn* (New York: Frederick A. Stokes, 1899), p. 163.

14. Barrett, "Changing Years," Part 2, p. 4.

15. Ibid., Part 3, p. 5.

16. Susannah F. Lange, "Those Good Old Days When Operators Received $6.50 a Week," *NETT,* October, 1929, p. 289; Dorothy Thorne, "Bayonne—Old Days and New," *Telephone Review,* March, 1917, p. 75.

17. By 1910, the New England Telephone Company had prohibited operators from accepting gifts in Boston exchanges and probably throughout the entire system; other companies permitted operators to give their names to subscribers only during the ten days prior to Christmas. U.S. Congress, Senate, *Investigation of Telephone Companies,* 61st Cong., 2d sess., 1910, S. Doc. 380, pp. 76–77.

18. Lange, "Those Good Old Days," p. 289; Dilts, *The Telephone,* p. 102.

19. Barrett, "Changing Years," Part 5, *NETT,* May, 1935, p. 7.

20. Lange, "Those Good Old Days," p. 288; "Old Timers' Edition," p. 360.

21. "Training Operators—Past and Present," *NETT,* December, 1908, p. 2.

22. Thorne, "Bayonne," p. 76; Lange, "Those Good Old Days," pp. 288–89.

23. Katherine M. Schmitt, "Woman's Contribution to the Bell System Heritage," *Telephone Review,* December, 1923, p. 366.

24. "Welfare Work on Behalf of Telephone Operators," *Pacific Telephone Magazine,* May, 1913, p. 5; Mary Mahan, "Impressions of a Telephone Afternoon," *NETT,* October, 1914, p. 184.

25. U.S. Congress, Senate, *Investigation of Telephone Companies,* pp. 15–16; "General Questions and Answers" (for employees of Commercial Department, New England Telephone Company), 1912, pp. 26, 37, AT&T Archives, New York, N.Y.; Katherine M. Schmitt, "I Was Your Old Hello Girl," *Saturday Evening Post,* July 12, 1930, p. 19; U.S. Department of Labor, *Effects of Applied Research upon the Employment Opportunities of American Women,* Bulletin of the Women's Bureau, no. 50 (Washington, D.C.: Government Printing Office, 1926), p. 38.

26. Horace Coon, *American Tel & Tel: The Story of a Great Monopoly* (New York: Longmans, Green, 1939), pp. 19, 36, 78–79.

27. Robert W. Garnet, *The Telephone Enterprise* (Baltimore: Johns Hopkins University Press, 1985), pp. 11, 15, 24, 53; John Brooks, *Telephone* (New York: Harper and Row, 1975), pp. 61–64; Coon, *American Tel & Tel,* pp. 38–42, 51.

28. N. R. Danielian, *A.T.&T.: The Story of Industrial Conquest* (New York: Vanguard Press, 1939), pp. 39–41; Coon, *American Tel & Tel,* pp. 61, 78, 120; Maurine Weiner Greenwald, *Women, War, and Work* (Westport, Conn.: Greenwood Press, 1980), p. 187.

29. U.S. Congress, Senate, *Investigation of Telephone Companies,* p. 17.

30. According to the *Telephone Review,* a publication of the New York Telephone Company, the position of supervisor was established in New York "about 1893." *New England Telephone Topics,* another publication of the New England Telephone Company, states that in Boston the first supervisors were appointed in April, 1895. "Supervisor's Instruction Course," *Telephone Review,* April, 1915, p. 136; W. E. Lockwood, "The First Time," *NETT,* December, 1908, p. 2.

31. "Organization of the Traffic Department," *NETT,* May, 1909, p. 6; "Chief Operator—Some Job!" *NETT,* August, 1916, pp. 97–99.

32. Laura Smith, "Opportunities for Women in the Bell System," *Bell Telephone Quarterly,* January, 1932, pp. 37–38.

33. "Organization of the Telephone Industry," 1917, Box 8, Women's Educational and Industrial Union Papers, Schlesinger Library, Radcliffe College, Cambridge, Mass.

34. "Promotion in the Central Office," *NETT,* January, 1917, p. 284.

35. "Organization of the Traffic Department," p. 6.

36. "Organization of the Telephone Industry."

37. Daniel Rodgers, *The Work Ethic in Industrial America, 1850–1920* (Chicago: University of Chicago Press, 1978), p. 55.

38. U.S. Congress, Senate, *Investigation of Telephone Companies,* pp. 39–40; Bernard Muscio, *Lectures on Industrial Psychology* (New York: E. P.

Dutton, 1920), p. 120; Nelle B. Curry, *Investigation of the Wages and Conditions of Telephone Operating* (Report submitted to U.S. Commission on Industrial Relations, Washington, D.C., 1915), p. 27; Josephine Goldmark, *Fatigue and Efficiency* (New York: Russell Sage Foundation, 1912), p. 46; *NETT,* March, 1914, p. 344.

The telephone operator performed the following routine in handling a call originating and terminating in the same exchange (for example, Main exchange): (1) After the subscriber removed his/her telephone from the hook, causing a tiny electric light to glow on the switchboard, the operator took a brass-tipped cord, inserted the tip or "plug" into the hole, or "jack," just below the light, at the same time throwing a key with the other hand in order to switch her transmitter line into direct communication with the caller, and said, "Number, please?" (2) The caller replied by giving the name of the exchange and the number he/she wanted, for example, "Main 1268." The operator repeated the number 1–2–6–8. (3) The operator then took up the cord which was the teammate or "pair" of the one with which she answered the caller, located the jack numbered 1268, and "tested" the line by tapping the tip of the plug for a moment on the sleeve of the jack to ascertain whether the line was busy. (4) If no click sounded in her ear, she pushed the plug into the jack and with her other hand operated a key on the switchboard desk. The first action connected the line of the subscriber called; the second rang his/her bell. When either party hung up the receiver, a light glowed on the switchboard desk, indicating to the operator that the connection was ended.

A call originating in one exchange (for example, Main) and terminating in another exchange (for example, Dorchester) required the cooperation of two operators: (1) After following the first two steps listed above, the "A" operator connected with her transmitter by pressing a button with her left hand. She then repeated the number desired (say 1–9–4–2), while holding the plug opposite the jacks connecting the Dorchester trunk lines. (2) The Dorchester "B" operator assigned to the "A" operator at the Main exchange a trunk line by calling its number, for example "5," whereupon the "A" operator at once completed her part of the operation by inserting the plug in trunk 5. (3) The Dorchester "B" operator, at the same time she assigned trunk 5, picked up the plug of the cord connecting with that trunk and tested (as described in step 3 above) to ascertain whether the line was busy. (4) If the busy click did not sound in her ear, she inserted the plug in the jack of Dorchester 1942 and rang the Dorchester subscriber by depressing a key with her thumb. *NETT,* March, 1914, p. 344.

39. Curry, *Investigation,* pp. 25–26.

40. Arnold Bennett, *Your United States* (New York: Harper and Brothers, 1912), pp. 75–76.

41. Rodgers, *Work Ethic,* p. 55.

42. Ned Loud, "A Glimpse of the Boston Toll Office," *NETT,* September, 1919, pp. 105, 108–9; "Will You Hold the Line Please?" *Southern Telephone News,* August, 1926, p. 7.

43. "Making Expert Operators," *NETT*, May, 1912, p. 19.

44. "The Speech Weaver's School," *Pacific Telephone Magazine*, December, 1916, p. 10.

45. J. L. Turner, "Work of the Telephone Operator: The Art of Expression as Applied to Switchboard Operation," *NETT*, February, 1912, pp. 5–7.

46. John Bradshaw, "Operators' Voices, Their Importance, and the Method of Their Cultivation," *Journal of Ophthalmology, Otology, and Laryngology* 22 (April, 1916):341.

47. U.S. Congress, Senate, *Investigation of Telephone Companies*, p. 56.

48. Sylvester Baxter, "The Telephone Girl," *The Outlook*, May 26, 1906, p. 231.

49. "General Questions and Answers," p. 57.

50. Ibid.

51. "Standards of Operating," *NETT*, June, 1912, p. 44.

52. U.S. Congress, Senate, *Investigation of Telephone Companies*, p. 55; State of New York, Department of Labor, "The Telephone Industry," Special Bulletin 100 (n.p., July, 1920), pp. 51–52.

53. "General Questions and Answers," p. 57; U.S. Congress, Senate, *Investigation of Telephone Companies*, p. 55.

54. "Statement Submitted by the New England Telephone and Telegraph Company to the Subcommittee on Telephone Service."

55. "The Busy Operator Is the Best Operator," *Southwestern Telephone News*, November, 1907, p. 5.

56. *New York Times*, January 13, 1907.

57. "The Health of Telephone Operators," *Lancet* 2 (December 16, 1911):1716.

58. Canadian Department of Labour, *Report of the Royal Commission on a Dispute Respecting Hours of Employment between the Bell Telephone Company of Canada, Ltd. and Operators at Toronto, Ontario* (Ottawa: Government Printing Bureau, 1907), pp. 55–56; Muscio, *Lectures*, pp. 123–24.

59. Curry, *Investigation*, p. 33.

60. Ibid., p. 40.

61. Mary Quinn Wynne, interview by Stephen H. Norwood, Springfield, Mass., June 28, 1974.

62. Julia O'Connor, "The Blight of Company Unionism," *American Federationist*, May, 1926, p. 544.

63. Rose Finkelstein Norwood, interview by Stephen H. Norwood, Boston, Mass., July 18, 1974. Elizabeth Cleary, president of the Lynn Telephone Operators' Union, stated in 1923, "If an operator is sixty seconds late, even though there be a foot of snow on the ground, she is marked tardy." Lynn *Telegram-News*, July 6, 1923.

64. "Editorial," *Cambridge Review*, April, 1906, p. 3.

65. Julia O'Connor to Marjorie White, December 2, 1920, Julia

O'Connor Parker Papers, Schlesinger Library, Radcliffe College, Cambridge, Mass.

66. Ibid.

67. David Gordon, Richard Edwards, and Michael Reich, *Segmented Work, Divided Workers* (New York: Cambridge University Press, 1982), p. 137.

68. The Pilgrim [pseudonym], "Pilgrim's Progress in a Telephone Exchange," Part 1, *Life and Labor*, January, 1921, p. 11.

69. P. M. Grant, "The Selection and Training of Operators," *Southwestern Telephone News*, August, 1908, p. 2.

70. Quote from Anna G. Richardson, "Telephone Operating: A Study of Its Medical Aspects with Statistics of Sickness Disability Reports," *Journal of Industrial Hygiene* 1 (May, 1919):57; U.S. Congress, Senate, *Investigation of Telephone Companies*, p. 17.

71. U.S. Congress, Senate, *Investigation of Telephone Companies*, p. 103.

72. LeRoy Thompson, "The Telephone Operators' Throat," *Journal of Ophthalmology, Otology, and Laryngology* 22 (April, 1916):346.

73. Anna Steese Richardson, *The Girl Who Earns Her Own Living* (New York: B. W. Dodge, 1909), p. 117.

74. M. E. Harrington, "The Training of Operators in Boston," *NETT*, June, 1910, p. 18.

75. Richardson, *The Girl Who Earns*, p. 116.

76. O'Connor to White, December 2, 1920.

77. "Why Telephone Operators Make Good Wives," *NETT*, February, 1916, p. 266.

78. Harrington, "Training," p. 18.

79. Ibid.

80. Brooks, *Telephone*, p. 29.

81. *Labor News*, July 13, 1923.

82. Rose Finkelstein Norwood, interviews by Stephen H. Norwood, Boston, Mass., January 28 and July 18, 1974; Rose Finkelstein Norwood, interview by Brigid O'Farrell, [1977], Rose Finkelstein Norwood Papers, Schlesinger Library.

83. Barrett, "Changing Years," Part 5, p. 7; Commonwealth of Massachusetts, Bureau of Statistics of Labor, "New England Telephone and Telegraph Company," *Labor Bulletin of the Commonwealth of Massachusetts*, no. 44 (December, 1906):462; "Telephone School in Houston," *Southwestern Telephone News*, November, 1907, p. 5.

84. "Making Expert Operators," p. 15.

85. Ibid., pp. 18–19; Commonwealth of Massachusetts, Bureau of Statistics of Labor, "New England Telephone and Telegraph Company," p. 462.

86. Richardson, *The Girl Who Earns*, p. 118; quotes from Bradshaw, "Operators' Voices," 339–40.

87. "The Speech Weaver's School," p. 10.

88. State of New York, Department of Labor, "The Telephone Industry," p. 21.

89. The Pilgrim [pseudonym], "Pilgrim's Progress," p. 12.

90. Eleanor V. Foley, "My Experiences and Impressions as a Student," *Telephone Review*, May-June, 1915, p. 163.

91. U.S. Congress, Senate, *Investigation of Telephone Companies*, p. 24.

92. "Making Expert Operators," p. 19.

93. Richardson, *The Girl Who Earns*, p. 113; Mary A. Laselle and Katherine E. Wiley, *Vocations for Girls* (Cambridge, Mass.: Riverside Press, 1913), p. 26; E. W. Weaver, *Profitable Vocations for Girls* (New York and Chicago: A. S. Barnes, 1916), p. 115.

94. Alexander Keyssar, in his study of unemployment in Massachusetts, reports telephone operators had the second lowest unemployment frequency (2.8 percent) of trade union members in fifty-eight occupations in the period 1908–22, behind the railway telegraphers. Unemployment frequency is defined as the percentage of labor force members who were unemployed at some point during the year. Alexander Keyssar, *Out of Work* (New York: Cambridge University Press, 1986) pp. 325–26.

95. U.S. Congress, Senate, *Report on Condition of Women and Child Wage-Earners in the United States*, Vol. 5, *Wage-Earning Women in Stores and Factories*, 61st Cong., 2d sess., 1910, S. Doc 645, pp. 84, 91.

96. Sarah Eisenstein, *Give Us Bread but Give Us Roses* (London: Routledge and Kegan Paul, 1983), pp. 73, 83, 86.

97. Elizabeth Beardsley Butler, *Women and the Trades* (New York: Charities Publication Committee, 1909), p. 295.

98. Richardson, *The Girl Who Earns*, p. 121. This point received considerable emphasis in Bell Company literature. See, for example, a pamphlet issued by the Chicago Telephone Company, "Why a Telephone Operator?" 1918, p. 1, Julia O'Connor Parker Papers.

99. Chicago Telephone Company, "Why a Telephone Operator?" p. 2; Turner, "Work of the Telephone Operator," p. 5.

100. General Supervisor of Traffic, New York Telephone Company, to J. L. R. Van Meter, June 17, 1912, Box 121, National Civic Federation [hereafter NCF] Papers, New York Public Library, New York, N.Y.; Sadie Cameron, "Sadie, the Switchboard Girl, Speaks Her Mind," *Journal of Electrical Workers and Operators*, January, 1928, p. 13; Dilts, *The Telephone*, p. 132.

101. U.S. Congress, Senate, *Investigation of Telephone Companies*, p. 34.

102. Kai Erikson, "On Work and Alienation," *American Sociological Review* 51 (February, 1986):5.

103. *New York Times*, July 16, 1899; Bennett, *Your United States*, pp. 78–79.

104. U.S. Congress, Senate, *Investigation of Telephone Companies*, p.

28; State of New York, Department of Labor, "The Telephone Industry," p. 25.

105. Alice Kessler-Harris, *Out to Work* (New York: Oxford University Press, 1982), pp. 186–87, 191.

106. Gertrude Beeks to Harry R. Barber, July 23, 1912, Box 121, NCF Papers.

107. Canadian Department of Labour, *Report*, pp. 2–3; Dilts, *The Telephone*, p. 132; U.S. Congress, Senate, *Investigation of Telephone Companies*, pp. 28, 98.

108. C. Wright Mills, *White Collar* (New York: Oxford University Press, 1951), pp. 173, 241.

109. A federal investigation of the telephone industry in 1910 determined that the average monthly wage of telephone operators in the Bell System was $30.91, with over 90 percent earning between $20 and $45 a month. The highest average monthly wage was paid in New York City, where the operators received $36.96. The lowest average monthly wage for a large city in the Bell System in 1910 was $22.40 in Nashville, Tennessee. Wages tended to be somewhat lower in the smaller towns and rural districts and for operators employed by the independent telephone companies. U.S. Congress, Senate, *Investigation of Telephone Companies*, pp. 93–94.

110. "Why a Telephone Operator?" p. 1.

111. Baxter, "The Telephone Girl," p. 238; "Supervisors' Instruction Course," p. 137.

112. State of New York, Department of Labor, "The Telephone Industry," p. 17.

113. See, for example, "Parents' Night at Newport," *NETT*, July, 1922, p. 119, and "Parents' Night," *NETT*, November, 1944, p. 11.

114. "Life in Our Operators' Quarters," *NETT*, June, 1916, pp. 33–36.

115. "Employees' Lunches for Health and Efficiency," *NETT*, March, 1913, pp. 319, 322.

116. Dorothy Thorne, "Where the Genial Rest Time Goes," *Telephone Review*, July, 1917, p. 190.

117. "Lunches by the Thousands," *NETT*, December, 1914, p. 245.

118. "Life in Our Operators' Quarters," pp. 33–36, quotes on p. 35.

119. Robert F. Wheeler, "Organized Sport and Organized Labour: The Workers' Sports Movement," *Journal of Contemporary History* 13 (April, 1978):194–95.

120. *Idaho Daily Statesman*, March 28, April 2, April 12, and May 3, 1908.

121. "New England Tel & Tel Bowling League," *NETT*, March, 1912, p. 29.

122. "Ladies' League," *NETT*, January, 1916, p. 248.

123. "Indoor Athletics and Dance," *NETT*, February, 1914, p. 311.

124. J. D. Ellsworth to Theodore N. Vail, April 6, 1910, Box 47, AT&T Archives.

125. Walter S. Allen, "Provision for Employees," July 20, 1910, submitted by J. D. Ellsworth to Theodore N. Vail, July 25, 1910, Box 47, AT&T Archives.

126. Richardson, "Telephone Operating," 56.

127. "The Employees' Benefit Fund," *NETT*, September, 1917, p. 146.

128. Joan Sangster, "The 1907 Bell Telephone Strike: Organizing Women Workers," *Labour/Le Travailleur* 3 (1978):113, 116.

129. O'Connor criticized the U.S. Senate *Investigation of Telephone Companies* of 1910 and the special bulletin of the New York State Department of Labor on the telephone industry issued in 1920 for analyzing the working conditions of telephone operators without having interviewed the operators themselves. O'Connor stated that the 1910 Senate investigation "was made during the two preceding years, the exchange in which I was working is one of the exchanges which formed a part of the investigation and neither I nor any other operator employed there knew that an investigation was going on. If any operator was interviewed, which I doubt very much, she was not informed as to the purpose of the interview and certainly did not know that the government was making an investigation."

O'Connor described the New York State Labor Department special bulletin as "interesting and valuable as a cross-section of contemporary telephone conditions" but complained that "it does not go half far enough": "A series of sporadic strikes occurred while this investigation was going on. In one exchange after another the girls quit their boards for varying periods of time to protest against unsympathetic treatment by supervisors, and low wages. No mention of this occurs in the report, deleted apparently to soothe the feelings of the telephone company. Likewise I am convinced that little serious attempt was made to get the point of view of the operators, and if any interviewing was done it was done under company auspices and is therefore valueless. I venture to say that not 2 percent of the operating force of the New York Telephone Company knew that an investigation was made. . . ." O'Connor to White, December 2, 1920.

The third major report of telephone operators' working conditions published during the period 1910–20, written by Nelle Curry, field investigator for the U.S. Commission on Industrial Relations, and published in 1915, did include information secured through personal interviews with telephone operators in their homes.

130. Canadian Department of Labour, *Report*, pp. 60–63.

131. Sangster, "The 1907 Strike," 122; quote from Canadian Department of Labour, *Report*, p. 75.

132. Canadian Department of Labour, *Report*, pp. 97, 100.

133. U.S. Congress, Senate, *Investigation of Telephone Companies*, pp. 69–76.

134. Curry, *Investigation*, pp. 30, 33.

135. State of New York, Department of Labor, "The Telephone Industry," pp. 8–9, 36; *New York Times*, June 8, 1920.

136. Butler, *Women and the Trades*, p. 289; Goldmark, *Fatigue and*

Efficiency, pp. 48–49; Mary Caroline Crawford, "The Hello Girls of Boston," *Life and Labor*, September, 1912, pp. 260–64.

137. Susan Porter Benson, " 'The Clerking Sisterhood': Rationalization and the Work Culture of Saleswomen in American Department Stores, 1890–1960," in James Green, ed., *Workers' Struggles, Past and Present* (Philadelphia: Temple University Press, 1983), pp. 108–10; Susan Porter Benson, " 'The Customers Ain't God': The Work Culture of Department Store Sales Women, 1890–1940," in Michael Frisch and Daniel Walkowitz, eds., *Working-Class America* (Urbana: University of Illinois Press, 1983), pp. 190, 192 (quote on p. 192).

138. Benson, "Customers," p. 204.

139. Robert Blauner, *Alienation and Freedom* (Chicago: University of Chicago Press, 1964), pp. 21–22.

2

Women Follow Men
Telephone Operators
in the West, 1902–8

Telephone operators first organized in the West during the early years of the twentieth century—in Montana towns, where a tradition of labor militancy in the dominant mining industry provided a favorable climate for unionization, and in San Francisco, where labor was stronger than in any other American metropolis. These efforts, which were directed not by women but by male trade union officials under the auspices of central labor bodies, failed to eventuate in permanent organization. It was an inauspicious time for women to attempt unionization. Since the collapse of the Knights of Labor in the late 1880s, labor organization among women had all but disappeared. The skilled craft-oriented unions of the American Federation of Labor (AFL), which had supplanted the Knights as a national labor organization, showed no interest in women workers. As a result, the telephone operators' unions which were formed were entirely local in character and were not affiliated with any international. They were thus without the financial backing and prestige that came with membership in a nationwide trade union.

Their problems were compounded by the absence of a women's movement in the areas where they organized, which might have provided leadership training, encouragement, and financial support. This was a period of relative inactivity for the women's movement, which was predominantly middle class and was focusing its efforts almost exclusively on attaining the suffrage. The suffragists enjoyed so little success during the first decade of the twentieth century that the period came to be known as "the doldrums." The movement devoted very little attention to working women until 1909, when a wave of women's strikes erupted in the garment industry.

The American Telephone and Telegraph Company (AT&T), which became the parent company of the Bell System in 1900, and its subsidiaries from the start vigorously disrupted any attempts at organization. Frederick Fish and Theodore Vail, who succeeded Fish as president of AT&T in 1907, firmly opposed unionization among their employees. They both belonged to the National Civic Federation (NCF). The NCF, a group dominated by large-corporation heads and supported by conservative labor leaders like AFL president Samuel Gompers, encouraged labor-management conciliation. It promoted contacts among employers, labor officials, and representatives of the "public" to prevent strikes, undermine labor radicalism, and stabilize the emerging system of large corporations. Like Fish and Vail, many of the employer members accepted conservative unionism in principle or for public relations purposes, but they opposed it in their shops. Cyrus McCormick, George Perkins, Elbert Gary, Henry Phipps, and Henry Davidson of the United States Steel and International Harvester corporations were among the most generous contributors to the NCF, but their companies became increasingly anti-union between 1904 and 1910.[1]

The AFL expressed much concern during the early years of the twentieth century about Bell Company discrimination against male telephone workers who attempted to unionize. Referring to the Bell System as a whole, Samuel Gompers complained to President Vail in 1907 that "a systematic espionage is established over the men for the purpose of ascertaining who are members of the organization, and then upon such information, to either discriminate against the men in their employment, or refuse to employ or discharge if they are found to be members of a union."[2] Few organizing ventures in the telephone service succeeded during the first decade of the twentieth century, even among the skilled linemen, cable splicers, repairmen, and installers, who had AFL support.

Unlike the male telephone workers, telephone operators did not have the AFL's support, which severely hindered their organizing efforts. As semiskilled women workers, they were deemed poor candidates for organization. The International Brotherhood of Electrical Workers (IBEW), the AFL affiliate with jurisdiction over the telephone workers, made no effort to organize telephone operators during the first decade of the twentieth century.

Organizing in Montana

Telephone operators first began to organize in 1902 in Montana, the leading mining state, where conditions had proved quite favorable for men's trade unionism. Rapid technological advances in the mining industry, which diluted skills and disrupted established work patterns, and the dangerous and unpleasant nature of the underground work produced intense labor unrest in the late nineteenth and early twentieth centuries. The relative ethnic homogeneity and absence of language barriers in the major mining districts, where the majority were native-born and the foreign-born came largely from the British Isles and Scandinavia, facilitated union organization.[3] In 1893, Montana's miners were instrumental in forming the Western Federation of Miners (WFM), a militant industrial union which united mine workers across the Rocky Mountain region.

Workers in Montana's mining towns had wide public support during strikes, which is consistent with Herbert Gutman's argument that the social environment of small one- and two-industry towns was often very favorable to labor. During the period of rapid economic and social change when industrial capitalism was still relatively new— as it was in Montana in the early twentieth century—large corporations entering already established communities were perceived by many as alien and disruptive. The headquarters of the large mining corporations were often located in distant cities and allowed local managers little control over labor policy. This made the mining corporations vulnerable to charges of insensitivity to local needs. AT&T, headquartered in first Boston and later New York, and Rocky Mountain Bell, its regional subsidiary headquartered in Salt Lake City, were seen as similar to the mining corporations. The foreign nature of the mining corporations was dramatized when they imported strikebreakers from distant cities, a practice also employed by Rocky Mountain Bell.

Because workers comprised a large proportion of the town electorate, they commanded significant political influence, which could translate into police support during strikes. This greatly inhibited the power of the industrialists, forcing them at times to appeal for assistance to state and even federal troops. Workers also exercised great influence as consumers, since merchants, professionals, and farmers were dependent on their patronage.[4] As the mining industry increasingly came under absentee ownership, miners' strikes took the form of community struggles in which local business and professional people allied with workers against powerful "foreign" corporations. The same pattern of "community" versus "outsider" emerged in Montana's telephone strikes.

Independent telephone companies, aggressively competing with the Bell System in the Rocky Mountain region, strengthened the operators' prospects for organization in Montana. The Bell Company had enjoyed a virtual monopoly from its establishment in 1877 until its basic patent protection expired in 1894; Bell's conservative Boston owners had been able to restrict the extension of telephone service through a policy of high rental charges.[5] By the turn of the century, however, key patents were no longer in effect, and Bell faced intense competition from a multitude of independent companies, particularly in the rural areas and Western states, where it had not yet penetrated or it had established service at relatively high rates.[6] The independent companies proliferated so rapidly that by 1907, their peak year of strength, they had in service nearly half the nation's telephones.[7] The independent companies' share of the telephone market diminished rapidly after that as AT&T gained access to new sources of capital and obtained control of independent companies by merging with them. But for a time, the presence of an independent telephone alternative gave trade unionists, who were able to draw on wide community support, a critical weapon which they used with great effectiveness during telephone strikes: a boycott of Bell telephones, which could cause severe damage to the company's business.

The highly traditional views about gender relations that prevailed in the Montana mining towns also affected the organization of telephone operators. The work structure of the mining economy allowed few opportunities for female employment, forcing virtually all adult women into economic dependency on men. Mine workers' wages were usually high enough in any event to keep women out of the workplace. The labor movement assumed that women's place was in the home and considered it a major achievement that men's union wages kept women in the domestic sphere, uncorrupted by the workplace. That miners worked in an all-male environment deepened the sense of difference between the sexes. As Elizabeth Jameson points out in her study of Cripple Creek, Colorado, miners' lives revolved around work and work associations. Much of their leisure time was spent not at home but in such male institutions as bars, gambling houses, and lodges.[8] Because of the paucity of jobs for women and the physically exhausting nature of mine work, women were expected to devote themselves to servicing male wage earners.

Women were viewed as delicate and submissive and as the morally superior gender. For Montana trade unionists, organizing telephone operators meant protecting the "weaker sex," whose virtue was threatened by an unscrupulous employer and degrading work conditions. Given this attitude, it is not surprising that organizing campaigns and strikes among telephone operators were largely directed by male trade unionists associated with the central labor bodies and the state labor federation.

The first union of telephone operators in the United States was organized in December, 1902, at Butte, a major copper-mining center known as the "Gibraltar of unionism" because of the high degree of organization among its workers and the closed shop in the mines. Nearly all of Butte's craftsmen and laborers were represented in a strong central labor union, the Silver Bow Trades and Labor Assembly. The Butte WFM local was at the time the largest union local in the country, with a membership often as high as five thousand.[9]

Hoping to reduce twelve-hour workdays and to gain a "living wage," Butte's telephone operators organized as a local of the American Labor Union (ALU). The ALU, headquartered at Butte and largely composed of WFM members, was formed after the State Trade and Labor Council of Montana in 1898 withdrew from the American Federation of Labor in protest against its inattention to unskilled workers and the special needs of the West.[10] Male unionists provided considerable assistance to the operators in organizing; the ALU's journal stated that "the work was done wholly from the outside" to protect the operators from company reprisals.[11]

The Butte telephone operators were quickly forced into a strike by the Rocky Mountain Bell Company, whose management was committed to the open-shop policy of the parent corporation, AT&T. AT&T President Frederick Fish adamantly refused to concede the right to organize in the telephone service and would not sign contracts with labor unions. Fearing unionization would precipitate a sympathetic strike that could interfere with service across its entire territory, Rocky Mountain Bell wholeheartedly agreed with Fish's policy. But George Y. Wallace, president of Rocky Mountain Bell, was also well aware of the power of Montana's labor movement. As he informed President Fish, "The labor leaders of Montana are using every effort to get us in their clutches so that they can call a strike at any time. . . . The great trouble . . . is that the people seem to be with the laborers."[12] Wallace told local officials that if they must accede to the operators' demands, they should do so without any contract.[13] In Butte, the company began to disrupt the Telephone Operators' Union almost immediately after it was formed by discharging both chief operators and announcing that they would be replaced by women from Salt Lake City. At least three other operators were also dismissed.[14]

The Butte operators' union appealed to ALU President David MacDonald for assistance and placed leadership of their movement in his hands. MacDonald informed the company that, if it brought the Salt Lake City women into the Butte exchange, he would call the Butte telephone operators out on strike. Negotiations between MacDonald and the Bell management quickly collapsed, and the company then issued a notice that women had been shipped from Salt Lake City to take the positions of the Butte operators. A strike was immediately ordered, both by a motion of the operators' union and by President MacDonald. On April 16, 1903, twenty-two of the twenty-five operators at the Butte exchange left the board.[15] The strikers announced they might call for a boycott of Bell telephones at any time.[16] The Butte *Miner* reported considerable involvement by male unionists in directing the strike, and the city's labor movement provided strong backing for the operators: "As soon as it became generally known that the strike was on, hurried conferences were held among union men in the city. Members of the various labor organizations gathered at union headquarters, and a plan of action was mapped out. Delegations were soon on the ground and advising the strikers."[17]

The Butte Telephone Operators' Union was able to command considerable support by portraying the strike as a conflict with a giant foreign corporation insensitive to the rights of local workers. The alien nature of the company was underlined by its unfortunate choice of strikebreakers: members of the despised Mormon church from Utah's "City of Saints."

From the beginning, it was clear the residents of Butte solidly backed the strikers. After the first day of the walkout, George Wallace, in daily correspondence with AT&T President Fish in Boston, complained, "You cannot picture Butte. They are all owned, body and soul, by the unions."[18] The company's plan to move bedding into a dormitory for the strikebreakers was thwarted by a "jeering crowd of several hundred," which prevented the company's wagons from unloading furniture.[19] The Butte police refused to intervene when asked to by the company's manager, who feared the "mob" planned to "gut the building."[20] The local manager and eight strikebreakers imported from the Montana towns of Missoula, Great Falls, and Helena barricaded themselves in the exchange building, but they were soon forced to shut down the switchboard and leave. None of Butte's 1,200 subscribers received telephone service for the duration of the strike. In the meantime D. S. Murray, general manager of Rocky Mountain Bell and escort for the eleven strikebreakers from Salt Lake City, received word of the "state of siege" in Butte and stopped at Dillon, Montana, where the strikebreakers remained for several days.[21]

Because the Rocky Mountain Bell Company believed the Butte police and county sheriff were in sympathy with the strikers, it sought to appeal to federal troops to crush the strike. George Wallace informed President Fish, "That gang of irresponsible villains need a file of U.S. troops in front of them to make them hide and run to their holes like whipped curs."[22]

On April 20, 1903, the company reached agreement with representatives of the ALU, the Silver Bow Trades and Labor Assembly, and the strikers. The settlement was highly favorable to the operators. It allowed all strikers to resume their former positions at wages of $50 a month, a $15 increase, and accorded union recognition and the nine-hour day. The union shop was established, and all operators were to become members of the union after their first payday.[23]

By early 1907, an organizing drive directed by the Montana Federation of Labor (formerly the Montana Trades and Labor Council) had resulted in the establishment of telephone operators' unions in many of the state's principal cities. These took the form of locals affiliated with the state federation of labor. They did not become part of any international, even though the male telephone workers had for several years belonged to the AFL's International Brotherhood of Electrical Workers. In February, 1907, the operators at Helena, headquarters of the Montana Federation of Labor, won a strike to increase wages to the rate received by Butte's operators, $50 a month.[24] The federation's executive board then submitted demands to the company on behalf of the locals at Great Falls, Billings, Red Lodge, Livingston, and Lewistown for the wages and working conditions that prevailed in Butte and Helena, where union contracts had been signed. The principal demands were for an increase in wages to $50 from $35 a month, the nine-hour day rather than the current nine to twelve hours, time-and-a-half pay for overtime work, two fifteen-minute relief periods a day, and the reinstatement of the union telephone operators at Billings, who had walked out on strike after the company fired their president and vice-president.[25] The company refused to consider the demands, and in March, 1907, the Montana Federation of Labor called out on strike the telephone operators at Lewistown, Red Lodge, Great Falls, and Livingston. The Butte and Helena operators walked out in sympathy.[26]

Presenting itself as the chivalrous defender of "young ladies" abused by an avaricious foreign corporation, the Montana Federation of Labor assumed charge of the strike from the beginning. It condescendingly portrayed the telephone operators as "helpless beings" in need of protection "on account of the weaker nature of the sex." To generate the widest possible base of support, the federation sought to identify the strikers with Christian values and the community itself. In an appeal for a boycott of Bell telephones, addressed to the "Citizens of Montana, Christians of this Great Commonwealth," it emphasized that the Rocky Mountain Company was not a "home institution." Exploiting the religious idiom, the federation denounced the telephone company as "soulless" and its managers as "unscrupulous" and "degenerate," and it described labor's organizing drive among the telephone operators as a "mission" to "uplift" the "unfortunate." Condemning the corporation as totally corrupt, the labor body argued that its failure to pay a "moral wage" forced the telephone operators into prostitution to survive: "Citizens . . . Christians . . . do you want conditions to exist in Montana such as those in the underpaid department stores and factories of the east, where the poorly paid girls must . . . get some 'friend' to pay their board and room rent? . . . It is an insult to womanhood."[27]

The striking telephone operators commanded considerable support throughout the state. They received favorable newspaper coverage and benefited from the rivalry of the other Montana cities with Butte and Helena, where operators enjoyed higher wages and better working conditions. In Great Falls a public mass meeting, at which the mayor presided, demanded that the company accede to the operators' demands and recognize the union. Broad community support for the operators was reflected in the large numbers of business and professional men who attended the meeting. Speeches supporting the strike were made by a lawyer and a doctor.[28] President George Wallace of the Rocky Mountain Bell Company was greatly distressed that most Montana newspapers supported the union demands. He found this "incomprehensible" since, as he informed President Fish, "we have always endeavored to be very good to all newspapers. We give them a 50% rebate on their tolls and advertise largely with them." Wallace believed one newspaper, the Great Falls *Tribune*, was motivated by an interest in the Montana Independent Telephone Company.[29]

No settlement could be reached for over a year in most of the cities because the Montana Federation of Labor ordered the operators to stay out in sympathy with a strike for a $.50 wage increase by male telephone linemen, cable splicers, repairmen, and installers. The strike began in May, 1907, and affected the entire territory of Rocky Mountain Bell, which provided telephone service to Montana, Utah, Idaho, and Wyoming. The telephone men were affiliated with the Rocky Mountain District Council of the International Brotherhood of Electrical Workers, which had about three hundred members in the four states. The IBEW, which until this time had ignored the telephone operators, showed no interest in chartering the operators' locals in Montana or in organizing the operators in the other three states.

In Montana, the prospect of competition from independent telephone companies and extensive community support for the strikers allowed the boycott to be instituted on a wide scale. In September, 1907, the labor movement demonstrated its power in Helena, where the Trades and Labor Assembly called a general strike after business leaders refused to stop using the Bell telephone. The business community immediately capitulated. The Streetcar and Electrical Light Company announced it would cease using the Bell telephone only two minutes after the streetcar and electrical workers went on strike. A two-hour strike by men in the livery barns brought the same promise from their employers. The union carpenters had already compelled most of the building contractors to remove the Bell telephone.[30] The boycott was also effective in Billings, where what President Wallace called "an excellent opposition plant," the Independent Telephone Company, existed; Butte, where the Retail Merchants' Association announced that its members would not use the Bell telephone; and Livingston, whose Businessmen's Association also stated that its members would observe the boycott.[31]

The settlement which ended the one-year strike in May, 1908, provided the desired wage increase for the male workers, but the operators did not realize their demands. More important, the telephone operators' unions emerged from the strike badly damaged. The long strike had inflicted a severe financial burden on the locals, and many operators had left the telephone service to take other positions. The striking operators in Montana were reinstated, but many strikebreakers were retained since the open shop prevailed in most cities. By 1910, all the operators' locals except Butte's had disbanded.

Given the cultural norms in the Montana mining towns which strongly emphasized female dependency, and the absence of a women's movement, the telephone operators were in no position to develop the self-confidence, assertiveness, and leadership necessary for women's unionism to survive. Montana's male trade unionists, who saw themselves as protectors of the "weaker sex," dominated the operators' locals, directing organizing efforts, negotiations with management, and strikes. They viewed the operators as marginal to the labor movement, and they largely ignored them except when company bullying became excessive. Nor was there any youth culture in Montana, like that emerging in the big cities, which would allow the operators to view themselves as a distinct group with interests different from those of older adults in management or in the male labor movement. As a result, telephone operators' unionism in Montana all but disappeared until the woman-led operators' movement in New England began national organizing several years later.

Telephone operators' unionism in Montana did revive during the next decade, although not on as wide a scale. Butte was the first local outside New England to affiliate with the telephone operators' national union movement, which began in Boston in 1912, and three other Montana cities were organized by 1920. When efforts to organize telephone operators resumed in Montana cities outside Butte during 1917–18, the operators appear to have had little or no knowledge of the labor militancy among operators in 1907–8. Beatrice Coucher (b. 1901), a member of the executive boards of the Telephone Operators' Department and its Rocky Mountain District Council in the 1920s, knew of no labor union activity among telephone operators anywhere in Montana prior to 1918, when the operators of Missoula walked out on strike. Coucher was from a trade union family; her father was a carpenter active in the Missoula Trades and Labor Council.[32] Missoula, a railroad town and the home of the University of Montana, was not affected by the 1907–8 operators' strike, even though it was a strong union town and the telephone company had expected trouble there.[33] According to Coucher, the Missoula operators first learned of the telephone operators' national union movement when organizer Rose Sullivan came to Missoula from Boston to form a local during a strike there in 1918.[34]

Organizing in San Francisco

The first union of telephone operators in a large city was formed in 1907 in San Francisco, the West's leading metropolis and a stronghold of organized labor. As in Montana, organizing efforts were directed by male trade unionists who failed to encourage operator initiative. The union was quickly put to the test by the Bell Company and proved unable to survive a strike. Here, as elsewhere, the operators' union was not affiliated with any international; instead, it was chartered by the AFL as a federal union. The IBEW, the AFL international with jurisdiction over the male telephone workers, showed no interest at this time in the telephone operators, and its leadership actually helped undermine the operators' strike by actively discouraging the male telephone workers from walking out in sympathy. Lacking the financial backing of an international, federal unions were relatively weak organizations. They usually were composed of unskilled and semiskilled workers, as was the case with the operators, and therefore considered of dubious legitimacy by a labor movement largely organized along craft lines.[35] The operators also remained isolated from the city's women's organizations, which had yet to show much concern for the problems of wage-earning women. San Francisco's settlement houses had abandoned social reform activities for charity and relief after the earthquake and fire of 1906.[36] Shortly before the strike, Bay area trade unionists had issued a stinging denunciation of the Young Women's Christian Association for proposing charity and moral uplift, rather than union organization, as solutions to the problems of the woman worker. Labor men found these solutions condescending.[37] The San Francisco Equal Suffrage Association gave verbal support to the union's organizing campaign, which was directed by the city's Labor Council, but provided no other assistance.[38] Overall control of the strike was maintained by the Labor Council, although the operators were able to exert more influence than in Montana, especially in formulating demands. While unable to sustain organization, the San Francisco telephone operators did force important concessions from the telephone company. Their 1907 strike was important in combining both trade union and women's issues, in particular a demand for an end to sexual harassment of operators in the exchanges.

By 1903, San Francisco had acquired a reputation as America's closed-shop city. While this description somewhat exaggerated the power of the city's labor movement, a significant proportion of not just skilled but unskilled workers were organized, and collective bargaining had been introduced on a wide scale. Labor was scarce because of San Francisco's relative isolation, and employers were not able to undermine organization by drawing on a cheap labor pool. The city absorbed few of the immigrants from Southern and Eastern Europe who arrived in massive numbers in the East after 1880. The restriction

of Chinese immigration had greatly reduced San Francisco's traditional body of cheap labor. At the same time, the past threat of low-
wage Chinese labor competition still served to unite white labor. In
addition, the mountain barrier and distance from the East greatly
reduced the threat to manufacturers of competition from outside the
region. As a result, many employers believed they could pay union
wages without damaging their competitive position.[39]

Since 1900, the San Francisco Labor Council had devoted some
attention to organizing women workers, and several trade unions with
predominantly female memberships had been formed, including locals
of laundry workers, garment workers, waitresses, bindery workers,
and tobacco workers. Most of these, however, appear to have been
under male leadership. In the laundry workers' local, by far the largest
of these new unions, women outnumbered men by five to one, but
they always elected male delegates to represent them at conventions
of the State Federation of Labor. The tobacco workers had a male
president, even though twelve of the local's fourteen members were
women. A San Francisco reformer reported that women were discouraged from participating in the affairs of the city's unions: "[At
meetings] men are inclined to assume a domineering attitude, making
it unpleasant for women to speak freely."[40]

In 1907, rising prices and rents, resulting from shortages of
commodities and housing caused by the fire, and the tight labor market led to an upsurge of labor militancy, of which the telephone
operators' strike was a part. Several San Francisco unions, backed by
the Labor Council, demanded higher wages and the eight-hour day.
The strike wave began in April, when over 1,500 laundry workers,
mostly women, walked out in San Francisco, Oakland, and San Jose.
On May 1, the metal trades unions called out over 4,000 men in the
first general strike in the industry since 1901. Only a few days later,
the carmen began the most violently contested streetcar strike ever to
occur in San Francisco or probably in any American city. Including
the telephone operators, about 10,000 San Francisco workers were
on strike during 1907, a level not again approached until World
War I.[41]

The telephone operators walked out on strike in May, 1907,
only three weeks after their 500–member union had received a federal
charter from the AFL. The operators' union had been organized by
the San Francisco Labor Council and was under its direct supervision.
The Labor Council reviewed the operators' demands before they were
presented to the Pacific States Bell Telephone Company, headquartered in San Francisco.[42] As in Montana, these included a wage in-

crease, union recognition, and an end to the company's policy of discharging operators for union activity.[43]

The operators also demanded changes in working conditions. They called for a revision of the company's dress code, a rearrangement of the switchboard so that operators would no longer have to "stretch painfully" to reach numbers at the ends of their section, and the replacement of male chief operators by women to eliminate sexual harassment. The operators were also apparently annoyed by the rowdy and even violent behavior of some male chief operators, one of whom used a pistol to shoot an exchange cook in a dispute that occurred close to operators at the switchboard. It is not clear from newspaper accounts or company records what the company dress code required for operators. Operators likely resented the expense involved in purchasing prescribed clothes and possibly the discomfort of overly formal wear. As young, high-school-educated women, they also may have objected to older management telling them what to wear and choosing their styles. The operators also complained that the company did not supply enough chairs in the exchanges, forcing many to use stools that led to backstrain. The work itself they termed "nerve destroying."[44]

Fearing that the operators had the public's sympathy, the company tried to direct attention to its "welfare" program.[45] It particularly emphasized that it provided the operators with retiring rooms, each with a matron "to look after their wants," and served free lunches in the exchanges. According to the union, however, the company had eliminated the operators' rest breaks since the fire, and they thus had no opportunity to use the retiring rooms. Union president Alice Lynch angrily rejected the suggestion that the free lunches indicated the company's generosity to its operators: "Lunch! Do you call a scrap of bologna sausage lunch? Or a spoonful of beans? Or a cup of cheap tea? Or an invisible slice of cold ham?"[46]

The Labor Council had urged the operators to avoid a strike, despite the company's adamant refusal to consider any concessions. The operators were angered, however, by the company's attempts to intimidate them. When the operators assembled for payday at the end of April, they had been taken into a room twenty at a time by company officials, who gave them their pay envelopes with a printed resignation from the union that they were asked to sign. Nearly all had refused.[47] Against the advice of the Labor Council, which believed the new union could not defeat the well-financed Bell Company, the operators at their next meeting voted unanimously to strike. According to the San Francisco *Chronicle*, "The spirit of revolt was rampant in the closely packed gathering of femininity, and one might as well have tried to stem a hurricane." Much stamping of feet and waving of handkerchiefs accompanied this display of militancy, yet the operators agreed to place leadership of the strike in the hands of a committee of Labor Council leaders. The Labor Council the next day voted down a proposal to boycott the Bell telephone. The male telephone workers decided against a sympathy strike, although they did vote the operators some financial support.[48]

The male telephone workers' refusal to engage in a sympathy strike proved an important factor in the operators' defeat. The operators could be replaced with new recruits if the company was willing to tolerate inefficient service until they became adept at the work. Skilled linemen and cable splicers, however, were far more difficult to procure. Without the ability to make repairs, particularly in the event of a severe wind or rainstorm, the company would be unable to provide service, no matter how many strikebreaking operators it managed to recruit. The male workers finally walked out after the strike had been in progress for two months, but by then it was too late. The company had trained a large body of strikebreakers and was providing what it considered adequate service. Even then, the men's strike action appears to have been forced by the votes of unemployed linemen, who comprised a sizeable proportion of the local's membership. The IBEW Pacific District Council refused to sanction the sympathetic strike and proceeded to revoke the local's charter and establish a new organization.[49]

In August, 1907, the striking operators voted to return to work after the company had agreed to some concessions, although they had to apply for their positions as individuals. Few operators had deserted the ranks during the strike. Yet neither their enthusiasm nor the financial donations of the Labor Council had been sufficient to win. The company granted a small wage increase and two fifteen-minute relief periods a day. Most important, it agreed that only women would be employed in the exchanges, eliminating the male chief operators. However, less than half of the strikers were reemployed by the company, and the Telephone Operators' Union was broken. San Francisco's operators would not organize again until 1917.[50]

Unequal Partners in the Labor Movement

No telephone operators' union established during the first decade of the twentieth century survived for more than a brief period, with the exception of the local at Butte, Montana. A 1910 report to the United States Senate, based on an investigation directed by Commissioner of Labor Statistics Charles P. Neill, concluded, "Practically no organization exists among operators. Only five local federal unions of telephone operators are affiliated with the American Federation of Labor. None of these are large or are located in cities of considerable size. One or two of these when visited seemed to be more like social clubs than trade unions."[51]

Montana operators possessed little influence in a labor movement that did not accept them as equal partners but viewed them as weak and defenseless girls in need of its protection. This was less the case in San Francisco, where the size of the operators' local—five hundred members—made it a more formidable presence and allowed the operators to include a specific women's issue in their demands: the end to sexual harassment in the exchanges. Even so, the San Francisco operators' union, lacking the assistance of feminists and the financial backing of an international union, had no choice but to accept the leadership of male trade unionists in the Labor Council.

Although Montana's telephone operators strongly backed the male telephone workers in a long sympathy strike, San Francisco's operators did not receive the support of the telephone men when they walked out in 1907. The refusal of the male telephone workers in San Francisco to join the operators' strike presaged serious difficulty in the future—a lack of solidarity between men and women that eventually proved fatal to telephone operators' unionism. Male and female telephone workers ultimately were unable to unite even in Boston, the bastion of telephone unionism, where strong support from both feminists and male trade unionists led to the formation of the nation's largest and most influential union of telephone operators in 1912.

NOTES

1. James Weinstein, *The Corporate Ideal in the Liberal State, 1900–1918* (Boston: Beacon, 1968), p. 11.

2. Samuel Gompers to Theodore Vail, June 25, 1907, Box 1365, AT&T Archives, New York, N.Y.

3. Melvyn Dubofsky, *We Shall Be All* (Chicago: Quadrangle Books, 1969), p. 24.

4. Herbert Gutman, "The Workers' Search for Power," in H. Wayne Morgan, ed., *The Gilded Age* (Syracuse, N.Y.: Syracuse University Press, 1963), pp. 33, 35, 37–38.

5. N. R. Danielian, *A.T.&T.: The Story of Industrial Conquest* (New York: Vanguard Press, 1939), p. 46.

6. Ibid., p. 46; Gabriel Kolko, *The Triumph of Conservatism* (Chicago: Quadrangle Books, 1967), p. 47.

7. Kolko, *Triumph,* p. 48.

8. Elizabeth Jameson, "Imperfect Unions: Class and Gender in Cripple Creek, 1894–1904," in Milton Cantor and Bruce Laurie, eds., *Class, Sex, and the Woman Worker* (Westport, Conn.: Greenwood Press, 1977), pp. 166, 169–73.

9. William D. Haywood, *Bill Haywood's Book* (New York: International Publishers, 1929), p. 83.

10. "American Labor Union," in Gary M. Fink, ed., *Labor Unions* (Westport, Conn.: Greenwood Press, 1977), pp. 19–21.

11. *American Labor Union Journal,* April 23, 1903.

12. George Y. Wallace to Frederick P. Fish, March 18, 1907, Box 1314, AT&T Archives.

13. George Y. Wallace to Frederick P. Fish, March 15, 1907, Box 1314, AT&T Archives.

14. *American Labor Union Journal,* April 23, 1903.

15. Butte *Miner,* April 17, 1903.

16. *American Labor Union Journal,* April 23, 1903.

17. Butte *Miner,* April 16, 1903.

18. George Y. Wallace to Frederick P. Fish, April 17, 1903, Box 1314, AT&T Archives.

19. Ibid.

20. George Y. Wallace to Frederick P. Fish, April 18, 1903, Box 1314, AT&T Archives.

21. Butte *Miner,* April 17, 1903; Wallace to Fish, April 17, 1903.

22. Wallace to Fish, April 18, 1903.

23. *American Labor Union Journal,* April 23, 1903.

24. Great Falls *Tribune,* February 19–24, 1907.

25. Executive Board of Montana Federation of Labor to H. L. Burdick, Superintendent of Montana Division of Rocky Mountain Bell Company, March 11, 1907, Box 1314, AT&T Archives.

26. Great Falls *Tribune,* March 13, 1907.

27. Montana Federation of Labor, "Some Reasons Why You Should Support the Telephone Girls' Strike," March 12, 1907, Box 1314, AT&T Archives.

Elizabeth Beardsley Butler in her study of women workers conducted during 1907–8 and published as part of the *Pittsburgh Survey,* identified the "moral jeopardy" of the shop girl as one of the most serious and widespread problems of the trades employing women: "Some employers . . . assume that their women employees secure financial backing from outside relationships, and knowingly pay wages that are supplementary rather than large enough to cover the cost of a girl's support." Elizabeth Beardsley Butler, *Women and the Trades* (New York: Charities Publication Committee, 1909), pp. 305–6.

28. Great Falls *Tribune,* March 17, 1907.

29. Wallace to Fish, March 18, 1907.

30. Butte *Miner,* September 22, 1907; *New York Times,* September 23, 1907; Helena *Independent,* September 24, 1907.

31. George Y. Wallace to Theodore N. Vail, June 13, 1907, Box 1314, AT&T Archives; Great Falls *Tribune,* May 27 and August 1, 1907; Helena *Independent,* September 5 and October 13, 1907; Butte *Reveille,* September 6, 1907.

32. Beatrice V. Coucher, telephone interview by Stephen H. Norwood, August 29, 1982.

33. Wallace to Fish, March 15, 1907; Anaconda *Standard,* August 9, 1907; Great Falls *Tribune,* August 8, 1907.

34. Beatrice V. Coucher, telephone interview. Coucher began work as an operator at Missoula in 1918, shortly before the strike. After leaving high school, she had worked briefly as a soda jerk and in a candy factory before becoming a telephone operator. During the early 1920s, she became the first woman president of the Missoula Trades and Labor Council.

35. Robert E. L. Knight, *Industrial Relations in the San Francisco Bay Area, 1900–1918* (Berkeley: University of California Press, 1960), p. 63.

36. Allen Davis, *Spearheads for Reform* (New York: Oxford University Press, 1967), p. 23.

37. San Francisco *Chronicle,* April 8 and 9, 1907.

38. San Francisco *Examiner,* April 9, 1907.

39. Knight, *Industrial Relations,* pp. 41–42, 377.

40. Lillian Matthews, *Women in Trade Unions in San Francisco* (University of California Publications in Economics, Vol. 3, No. 1, June 19, 1913), pp. 38, 53.

41. Knight, *Industrial Relations,* pp. 185–87, 198.

42. San Francisco *Chronicle,* April 14, 1907.

43. San Francisco *Examiner,* May 2, 1907; San Francisco *Chronicle,* May 2, 1907. The wage scale presented was $30 a month for student operators and for the first three months of service, $35 for the next three months, $40 after nine months, $60 after one year, and $75 for supervisors. Until a month before the strike, operators were not guaranteed increases based on length of service. The current scale paid students $20 a month, operators $25–48, and supervisors $60. The majority received $25–35. Operators worked six days a week and every other Sunday with no vacation. San Francisco *Examiner,* April 1 and May 2, 1907; San Francisco *Chronicle,* May 4, 1907.

44. San Francisco *Examiner,* April 1 and May 4, 1907; San Francisco *Chronicle,* August 11, 1907; Matthews, *Women in Trade Unions,* p. 87.

45. E. J. Zimmer, vice-president of the Pacific Telephone Company, informed AT&T's Boston headquarters, "The girls . . . have the sympathy

of the public, who feel that we should have made a general increase in salaries because everybody else has done so." E. J. Zimmer to F. A. Pikernell, assistant to the president, AT&T Company, Boston, April 5, 1907, Box 1365, AT&T Archives.

46. San Francisco *Examiner*, May 2, 1907.

47. San Francisco *Chronicle*, May 2, 1907.

48. Ibid., May 3, 4, and 7, 1907.

49. Ibid., June 4 and 5, 1907.

50. Matthews, *Women in Trade Unions*, p. 87; Walton Bean, *Boss Ruef's San Francisco* (Berkeley: University of California Press, 1967), p. 234; San Francisco *Examiner*, August 3, 1907.

51. U.S. Congress, Senate, *Investigation of Telephone Companies*, 61st Congress, 2d sess., 1910, S. Doc. 380, p. 79.

3

Protest and the Networks
of Class and Gender
Boston, 1900–1913

Boston in the second decade of the twentieth century provided a social environment highly conducive to the development of telephone operators' unionism. The operators' local formed in 1912 was easily the largest and most dynamic in the nation. It contributed most of the leaders of the Telephone Operators' Department and never constituted less than one-fifth of its total membership. Like San Francisco, Boston was a strong labor city, but it was also the center of a vigorous organized women's movement, which had existed since the founding of the American Woman Suffrage Association in 1869. During the early twentieth century, many Boston feminists, based in the city's numerous settlement houses and colleges, became concerned with the plight of wage-earning women. Their eagerness to assist women workers in their organizing efforts and to train women for trade union leadership allowed the Boston local not only to emerge as a powerful and independent force within the city's labor movement but to supervise the organizing of telephone operators across the United States and Canada into what was in effect the only woman-led international union on the continent. Women telephone operators, not male trade unionists, formulated the union's strategy and led it to victory in major confrontations with management and government in 1913 and 1919. The local itself became a major component of the women's suffrage movement and provided women with the opportunity to shoulder important political responsibilities in an era when they were denied the vote in the larger society. While male unionists rarely viewed women workers as anything but auxiliaries in the labor movement, the Boston telephone operators' local commanded such influence that it boasted its annual election was the most important political event in the city's labor circles, with a turnout consistently larger than that of any other trade union, male or female.[1]

To understand the militancy of the Boston telephone operators and their ability to sustain organization for eleven years, attention must focus not only on working conditions but on regional and local mentalities and traditions of struggle, both labor and feminist. As Edward Shorter and Charles Tilly observe in their study *Strikes in France, 1830–1968*, "If people strike, it is not solely because they are boilermakers or machine-assemblers or masons. . . . It is also because they are enmatrixed in a certain kind of community with certain acquired habits of joint action." Labor militancy was more likely to develop when the workers' parents and grandparents had engaged in labor struggles.[2] Organizing campaigns and strikes had a far greater prospect of success in communities where long-standing labor institutions were drawn together by a strong central labor union. Local trade unions were rarely able by themselves to extract concessions from employers, since this usually required the threat of strike. Few locals could survive a strike, given the employers' vastly superior financial resources. When confronting semiskilled and unskilled workers, such as the telephone operators, employers in almost every city could draw from a large reservoir of potential strikebreakers, even in periods of relative prosperity. Only trade unions working in concert afforded workers any chance of success. Labor's most powerful weapons were the sympathetic strike and boycott. Neither could be employed without a central labor union to coordinate the actions of the individual unions.[3]

Extensive cooperation developed among Boston's trade unions during the first decade of the twentieth century. The Boston Central Labor Union (CLU) had been established in 1878, antedating the American Federation of Labor (AFL) by three years. Boston's trade unions grew rapidly as its diversified commercial and industrial economy experienced relative prosperity after the end of the depression of the 1890s. The considerable progress of the Boston labor movement prompted the AFL to hold its national convention in the city for the first time in 1903. Nearly two-thirds of the union locals in Boston in 1909 had been established since 1900. In 1913, when the newly organized Boston telephone operators threatened to strike in their first major confrontation with the New England Telephone

Company, they were backed by a central labor union with a membership of 96,621 workers in 350 affiliated AFL locals.[4]

The Central Labor Union gave delegates from the various trade union locals in Boston a sense of being part of a larger labor movement with common problems and goals, encouraged trade unionists to cooperate, provided strike support, and assisted in the conciliation of strikes. The representatives of the affiliated unions, most of them Irish-Americans like the telephone operators, attended meetings of the CLU every two weeks. Extensive coverage of trade union affairs was provided by Boston's many newspapers, and the *Globe* and the *Post* ran a column of Central Labor Union news each week.

At the state level, an association of trade unions and central labor bodies was formed in 1887. Known as the Massachusetts State Federation of Labor, it was the fifth oldest such organization in the United States and among the first to be represented at an AFL convention.[5] Its annual convention provided an important meeting-ground for trade unionists from across Massachusetts. The state federation experienced its greatest expansion from 1901 to 1913, with nearly two hundred trade union locals and central bodies affiliating during this period.

Despite its rapid expansion, the labor movement in Boston and the state as a whole remained largely indifferent to women workers in the first decade of the twentieth century. Male trade unionists were formally committed to unionizing women, but they were not prepared to accept them fully in the labor movement, since they viewed them as temporary workers whose primary role was in the home as mother and wife.[6] The Massachusetts State Federation of Labor at its first convention in 1887 unanimously voted to support the organization of women workers, and a resolution calling for equal pay for equal work was "the most heartily endorsed of any acted upon." But considerable attention was also given to "the case of the wife at work in the factory, while the husband walked the streets in idleness."[7] The opposition to discriminatory pay was partly motivated by a desire to deprive women of their jobs, since equal compensation for women generally meant that employers would just as soon replace them with men.[8]

The occupational structure of the telephone industry, with its sharp division between male and female jobs, made it easier for telephone operators than for other women to gain the support of male trade unionists in their organizing efforts. Repair, cable-splicing, and installation jobs in the telephone companies were for men only, whereas only women could be hired as operators; the sexes did not mix in the workplace. There was a fundamental and easily discernible difference in the nature and skill level of the work performed by men and women in the telephone service. Distrust of women workers in such industries as boot and shoe, garment, and telegraph, based on the fears that they might replace men in their jobs or undermine them by offering low-wage competition, did not exist in the telephone industry.[9] Male trade unionists were thus more sympathetic to the telephone operators than to many other women workers. The sexual division of telephone work was clear, and no one could fail to grasp that telephone operators should be organized as *women,* which was hardly the case in most other industries.[10] While male telephone unionists wished to dominate the operators within the International Brotherhood of Electrical Workers (IBEW), none ever suggested that the operators should be organized in locals with men. The establishment of separate women's locals made it possible for the operators to exercise considerable control over their organizing efforts and ultimately to gain autonomy within the IBEW.

In the early years of the twentieth century, women workers received far more assistance from middle- and upper-class women reformers than from male trade unionists. Having served as the nineteenth-century headquarters of the American Woman Suffrage Association, Boston had a long tradition of women's political activism. Although this was a period of stagnation for the suffrage movement nationally, three major Boston-based suffrage organizations—the Massachusetts Woman Suffrage Association, the College Equal Suffrage League, and the Boston Equal Suffrage Association for Good Government—worked vigorously to promote suffrage in Massachusetts after 1900.[11] In an effort to broaden the base of suffrage support, these organizations gave increasing attention to drawing working women into the movement. Their associations with women workers led many suffragists to become interested in helping them improve their conditions at work.

The settlement house movement, in which women were heavily involved, was even more important for women workers because it sought to draw reformers into direct contact with the working class. Boston ranked with New York and Chicago as the nation's principal centers of settlement work. Most of the important settlement houses were very sympathetic to organized labor. In Boston, Denison House and South End House were especially close to the labor movement and provided meeting space for trade unions.[12]

Settlement house workers joined with progressive labor leaders in 1903 to establish the National Women's Trade Union League (WTUL), the organization most active in promoting the unionization of women workers during the first half of the twentieth century. Without the support of the Boston WTUL, the telephone operators could not have organized in 1912. The League's first chapters were formed in Boston, Chicago, and New York, where the settlement house movement was most strongly entrenched.[13] In 1908, a chapter was also organized in St. Louis. Membership was open to "any person who will declare himself or herself willing to assist those trade unions already existing, which have women members, and to aid in the formation of new unions of women wage earners."[14] Rejecting the prevailing view of women as temporary workers, the WTUL attempted to convince trade unionists that women were in the labor force to stay.

The AFL gave formal support to the League once it was established, allowed the WTUL to hold its national convention at the same time as its own, and accepted nonvoting delegates from the WTUL. The League won grudging acceptance from male trade unionists as a result of its early organizing and strike support efforts, although according to one leader of the WTUL, AFL presidents Samuel Gompers and William Green always regarded it as a "joke."[15] The AFL was never comfortable with the League's feminism or the upper-class background of many of its leaders, and it remained largely unresponsive to the needs of women workers.[16]

Women workers faced other obstacles in organizing besides AFL indifference. Many working women were burdened with household chores during their leisure time, which restricted their participation in social activities with other workers off the job. Such activities facilitated discussions of job grievances among workers that could encourage organized protest. Drawn as they were to the flapper lifestyle and the new "cheap amusements" of the consumer culture, the telephone operators undoubtedly were more successful in evading these household chores than were other women workers. The home also was not always a conservative influence, as other family members with pro-labor views might instill union consciousness. Women did lack the more formal institutions like the tavern or ethnic club, which promoted sociability among male workers. One of the WTUL's contributions was to offer a convenient and "respectable" place where women workers could meet.[17]

Women, particularly telephone operators, usually worked in environments dominated by the very young. They thus had more difficulty than men in acquiring information about the past normally communicated by older workers, although many were influenced by older relatives. The telephone operators also worked in a new industry, without a tradition of labor struggle. Even in Massachusetts, the first state to establish a bureau of labor statistics, relatively little published information was available in the early twentieth century on women's unions, organizing efforts, and strikes. Sue Ainslee Clark, at the time the president of the Boston WTUL, complained in 1911 that "one finds great difficulty in getting any consecutive history of women's trade unions, and still greater difficulty in getting adequate statistics about them." She noted that the 1903 book *Organized Labor* by John Mitchell, whom the labor historian Philip Taft called "next to Gompers the most eminent labor leader of the time," contained only a brief chapter devoted to women and children: "There is not even a chapter devoted to women alone."[18]

The WTUL also had to overcome the barrier of social class that separated the upper- and middle-class reformers (or "allies" as they were called), who led the organization in its early years, from the working women they sought to unionize. Most of the allies in the Boston chapter were wealthy and highly educated, and they could trace their ancestry to seventeenth-century Massachusetts. Feelings of inferiority that discouraged women workers from associating with the allies, however, were less of a problem among the telephone operators, since they had more schooling than most in their social class and were viewed by their employer as "young ladies of refinement." They also interacted in their work with telephone subscribers who tended to be upper or middle class. Unlike the New York WTUL, which after 1906 focused on the garment industry dominated by Yiddish and Italian-speaking workers, the Boston WTUL had no language barrier to overcome in organizing the Irish-American telephone operators.

The wave of strikes by women workers in the garment industry in the period from 1909 to 1911, of which New York's "Uprising of the 20,000" was the most prominent, brought the Women's Trade Union League national attention and greatly improved the prospects for organizing women workers. The "Uprising of the 20,000," which the WTUL was involved in from the beginning, was the largest strike of women workers in the United States until that time and virtually stopped production in New York's garment industry. Its outcome represented an important victory for the supposedly unorganizable unskilled and semiskilled women workers, who had unionized at their own initiative, displayed impressive spirit and solidarity during the strike, and won significant concessions from the employers. The strike, which occurred over the objections of the union's male leadership, demonstrated that young, unmarried women could often surpass men in strike militancy. They were less likely than men to be the family's primary income earner and could therefore more easily rely on other members of the family for support during a strike.[19]

In Boston, the WTUL proved it could provide women workers with effective support when it intervened in a strike by Roxbury carpet weavers against a wage reduction in 1910. After the WTUL organized them as a local of the United Textile Workers' Union, the strikers gained a settlement viewed as "a victory for the weavers on every point." Their employer restored the previous wage scale and accorded union recognition. Boston WTUL ally Elizabeth Glendower Evans believed that the Roxbury strike, while much smaller than the "Uprising of the 20,000," shared with it "many important elements" and "may equally be counted as the opening of a new era for women in industry."[20]

Boston's trade unionists devoted increasing attention to women workers after this strike, and WTUL membership grew significantly. When the National WTUL convention met in Boston in 1911, the Boston chapter claimed eleven union affiliations and 425 members, of which 275 were trade unionists and 150 allies.[21] An indication of the increasing prestige of the WTUL in the labor movement was the seating for the first time of a League representative, Mabel Gillespie, as a fraternal delegate at the convention of the State Federation of Labor, a practice continued into the 1940s.

In 1912, when the Boston telephone operators began to organize, major strikes occurred among the city's trans-Atlantic longshoremen and the motormen and conductors of the Elevated Company. Like the telephone operators, these workers were predominantly Irish-American; many of the strikers had telephone operators in their families. The militancy of these strikers undoubtedly helped to instill a sense of trade union consciousness in many telephone operators in the year of their organization. That the Elevated Company, described by the State Federation of Labor as "one of the largest corporations in America" commanding "almost unlimited capital," was forced to recognize the streetcarmen's union reflected the growing strength of Boston's labor movement. The state federation's officers announced at the annual convention in 1912, "Probably no event has stood out with such prominence in the history of labor during the past score of years as the victory of the street railwaymen of Boston."[22] The heavy financial losses suffered by the business community as a result of the interference with Boston's port and streetcar system in 1912 made many of its more influential members amenable to mediation in labor disputes during the next few years.

The telephone operators who organized in 1912 came of age in a period of great expansion for Boston's labor movement, with trade union affairs receiving continuous newspaper coverage. Although the city's male trade unionists were relatively indifferent to women workers, the women's movement devoted much attention to assisting them in the first decade of the twentieth century. The Women's Trade Union League had become a significant force in Boston by 1912 and provided the operators with major assistance in their organizing effort. When the operators faced their critical test in 1913, they had the backing of a strong network of trade unions, many of which were ready not only to provide considerable financial assistance but to strike in sympathy. Concerned about further business losses after the highly disruptive dock and streetcar strikes, Boston's business leaders were prepared in 1913 to pressure the telephone company to negotiate with the telephone operators.

The Formation of the Boston Telephone Operators' Union

A small group of Boston telephone operators initiated the movement to form a union in March, 1912, but its success required the intervention of the Women's Trade Union League and major assistance from the Central Labor Union, impressed by the recent militancy of women workers. Nearly the entire operating force in Boston was organized within a year, despite severe intimidation from a management determined to defeat the first union drive by either male or female workers in the thirty-year history of the telephone company. Continued dismissals for union activity and the refusal of company officials to entertain seriously the operators' demands led the Telephone Operators' Union to poll a strike vote in April, 1913, raising the prospect of an even more devastating interference with business activity than occurred during the Elevated strike of the preceding year. The threat of sympathetic strike action by other trade unions and the prospect of a "titanic battle" between the American Federation of Labor and the parent corporation of the New England Telephone Company, the American Telephone and Telegraph Company (AT&T), forced management to accord union recognition.[23]

The immediate impetus for the union movement came from the erosion of already low wages by rising prices after the depression of 1907–8 and the introduction of new work schedules, in particular the split trick, in 1910. Julia O'Connor, a charter member of the

Boston Telephone Operators' Union and later president of the national union of telephone operators, recalled that the "Boston organization came into existence almost entirely as a result of the hardship and burden imposed by the long and irregular working hours, particularly the then infamous split trick. . . . the chief grievance and slogan of the new union was 'abolition of the split trick.' "[24]

The New England Telephone Company introduced the split trick in an effort to make more efficient use of its operating force. On the split trick, the operator's day was divided into two separate work tours, with several hours off in between. This allowed management, aware that a traffic curve existed at most exchanges, to assign more operators to work during periods when calls were more frequent and to reduce greatly the number at times when fewer calls were placed. Previously, there had been three work shifts in the Boston Metropolitan District: a day shift of nine and a quarter hours, with an additional forty-five minutes for lunch; an evening shift from 5:00 P.M. to 11:00 P.M., to which many operators who attended high school in the daytime were assigned; and a night shift from 11:00 P.M. to 7:00 A.M. Evening and night operators ate their "lunch" at the switchboard. In 1910, the company abolished the evening shift, instituted the split trick to cover both day and evening hours, and added an hour to the night shift so that it started at 10:00 P.M. rather than 11:00 P.M. without extra compensation.[25]

The operators complained about the excessively long workday and constant travel required by the split trick, in which the nine and a quarter hours of work extended over a period of usually fifteen hours. A split trick might begin at 7:00 A.M. and not terminate until 10:00 P.M. Much of the free time between the two sets of working hours was consumed by the operator's travelling to her home and back to the exchange, at her own expense.[26] Mary Quinn, later the first vice-president of the Telephone Operators' Department who worked the split trick in Springfield, Massachusetts, during the period 1910–13, explained: "You had no life of your own because you had three hours off in the afternoon—if you had to go home you'd no more than get home than you had to come back."[27] Although the company had introduced the split trick to increase work efficiency, the union argued that excessive fatigue engendered by the long workday and its four streetcar trips reduced the operator's speed and level of concentration during her second set of hours.

However burdensome for the operator, the split trick facilitated unionization by creating a space in which the operators could fraternize and exchange ideas away from company supervision. The company maintained strict control over its operating force in the workplace. Each group of eight or nine operators was closely watched by a supervisor, and the intense pace of work did not permit conversation among the operators at the switchboard. Company regulations forbad talking at the board, even on the rare occasions when the level of calls was low enough to make it possible. Management also maintained close supervision during leisure hours; retiring rooms and cafeterias were administered by a company matron. But the split trick allowed operators to congregate in small groups around the city during the intervals between work tours and thus to escape company scrutiny. After they organized, many operators could spend their time between shifts at union headquarters.

In a larger sense, the split trick enhanced the prospects for organization by contributing to the peer orientation and feeling of youthful independence many operators had developed in high school. Since most operators viewed travelling home and back again as simply too inconvenient, they spent their leisure time with their workmates rather than family, whether their parents liked it or not. Because little sociability was possible at work, the strong peer attachments formed from constant association at leisure were especially important in drawing the operators together as a group.

Determined to effect changes in their working conditions, a group of twenty toll operators gathered on Boston Common after work on March 26, 1912. It was no accident that they were toll operators. Their work, conducted at a slower pace than that of local operators and involving close cooperation among several women, provided ample opportunity for group cohesion. This may explain why the toll operators not only initiated organization but dominated the Boston local during its first six years.

The young women who had gathered on the Common knew little about trade unionism. They wandered up Boylston Street looking for the office of a labor organization where they could get advice and assistance, until they noticed the sign of the headquarters of the Women's Educational and Industrial Union, an organization that sponsored programs of domestic and vocational training for women. The people at that office referred them to the Women's Trade Union League at 7 Warrenton Street.[28] Upon entering the WTUL office, the operators informed the WTUL secretary, Mabel Gillespie, that they would no longer submit to split-trick assignments, excessive hours of work, unpaid overtime, and a petty system of penalties, and they announced they planned to strike that night.[29] Gillespie argued strongly against this course, and after a long conference she persuaded the operators that the most effective results could be obtained by organizing a union and presenting carefully formulated demands to the company. The WTUL officers decided that the telephone operators logically belonged to the AFL's International Brotherhood of Electrical Workers (IBEW) since the mechanics, cable splicers, and linemen employed by the telephone company were already members of that union, although not in Boston. The general organizer of the IBEW, Peter Linehan, was summoned from New York to organize the operators.[30]

That the IBEW responded so readily to this request by the WTUL is an indication of the WTUL's growing influence in the labor movement. Mabel Gillespie (1877–1923) in particular provided an important link between male unionists and working women. Although Boston's labor men were not entirely comfortable with the WTUL allies, they did hold Gillespie in high esteem. She was elected a vice-president of the Massachusetts State Federation of Labor in 1919, and at that organization's convention in 1921 she was almost elected president. Many believed that had she not been a woman her election would have been unanimous.[31] A resident of Denison House, Gillespie had worked briefly in a cannery and a tin factory in an effort to gain greater knowledge of working conditions, and she had been arrested in 1910 while attempting to organize women workers at the Gillette Razor plant in Boston.[32] She formed lifelong friendships with several telephone operators and other young workers close to the League. She lived for a time, for example, with the Scottish-born jute spinner Mary Gordon Thompson, who became president of the Boston WTUL in 1925.[33]

Although the IBEW focused primarily on skilled electricians in the building trades and had done little organizing among women, Peter Linehan (1879–1914) took his assignment seriously and proved highly effective. Considered by the IBEW leadership as one of the union's most valuable organizers, he left a lasting impression on the telephone operators, despite his sudden death only two years after the establishment of the Boston union. Julia O'Connor noted his "magnetism" and "charm" and wrote, "In so far as the success of any movement . . . can be credited to an individual, the sure and steady progress of trade union organization among New England telephone operators can be attributed to him."[34]

Directing the organizing campaign along with Gillespie and Linehan were Anne Withington, Susan Grimes Walker Fitzgerald, and Sarah McLaughlin Conboy of the Boston WTUL organizing committee. The backgrounds of Withington and Fitzgerald, on the one hand, and Conboy, on the other, reflected the vast differences between the allies and the working women active in the WTUL. Withington, like Gillespie a resident of Denison House, had served as secretary to the muckraker Henry Demarest Lloyd and had edited with Jane Addams a collection of his writings entitled *Man, the Social Creator*. Fitzgerald (1871–1943), a member of the Boston WTUL executive committee in 1909 and from 1913 to 1920 and a nationally known suffragist, was also active in the settlement house movement. The daughter of a rear admiral, she graduated in 1893 from Bryn Mawr College, where M. Carey Thomas, a noted feminist, and other students inspired her to think of becoming something other than a society girl. After leaving Bryn Mawr, she married a wealthy, Harvard-trained lawyer and served as head of the West Side Branch of the University Settlement House in New York from 1901 to 1904. Moving to Boston in 1904, she became involved in the women's suffrage movement and was secretary of the Boston Equal Suffrage Association for Good Government and corresponding secretary of the National American Woman Suffrage Association. During the period from 1912 to 1916, she campaigned for women's suffrage throughout New England, Ohio, Michigan, Pennsylvania, New Jersey, and Iowa.[35] Conboy (1870–1928), who later served twelve years as secretary-treasurer of the United Textile Workers of America, came to the WTUL from the factory rather than the settlement house movement. She began work at age eleven in a candy factory after the death of her father. After working for a time in a button factory, she became a carpet weaver and came to the attention of the WTUL when she led a strike of 680 women against a wage reduction at her Roxbury factory.[36]

The WTUL's organizing drive met with an enthusiastic response from the operators. So many turned out for the first meeting that Linehan had to find a larger hall. A few days later, a charter was issued by the IBEW to the new Boston Telephone Operators' Union. Since the IBEW constitution contained no provision for telephone operators' locals, the union was organized as a sub-local of the Boston linemen's local 104. Only two weeks after the drive began, a union meeting drew over six hundred operators.[37] Rose Finkelstein, a charter member of the Telephone Operators' Union, recalled, "The organization came easy because conditions were so bad it was practically spontaneous. . . . As soon as exchange by exchange they heard they were forming a union and meeting, they came from every exchange in hordes. We hired a hall at Washington Street near Dover called Wells Memorial. There we met and they came in from everywhere to join the union."[38]

Under the influence of the WTUL and IBEW organizers, the union formulated standard trade union demands, including establishing a formal mechanism for collective bargaining, handling grievances, and improving wages and hours. There was no direct appeal by the union for a restructuring of the work process—for example, by reducing excessive supervision or the pace of work. The union sought to introduce the seniority system as the basis of promotion and a standardized wage scale based on automatic time increases in pay.[39] An operator's promotion depended on the decision of the chief operator, often based on personal preference rather than merit. The union proposed that an adjustment board, composed of representatives of both the operators and the company, be established to hear worker grievances and to serve as an organ of collective bargaining.

The adjustment board would remove the confusion engendered by the prevailing method of handling grievances, called the "right of appeal." The right of appeal required an operator to present her grievance individually to a series of company officials, beginning with her chief operator and then proceeding to the next level in the hierarchy if the decision was unfavorable to her. Theoretically, she could continue to appeal to a higher level until she had either achieved satisfaction or reached the president of the company. An aggrieved operator thus might appeal a chief operator's decision to the district traffic chief, from the district traffic chief to the division superintendent of traffic, from the division superintendent of traffic to the general superintendent of traffic, from the general superintendent of traffic to the general manager, and then through two vice-presidents to the president. In each case, the operator was required to make her appointment with the next higher official through the official whose ruling she was appealing. The operators knew of no case in which an employee had ever successfully negotiated this formidable stepladder of interviews.[40]

A conference committee of telephone operators, representing the seven metropolitan and forty-five suburban exchanges in the Greater Boston district, worked with Gillespie and Linehan to draw up a formal list of demands that was submitted to the company on April 15, 1912. The demands included the reduction of the workday from nine and a quarter hours to eight hours; the abolition of the split trick; a wage increase and a standardized wage scale with automatic time increases in pay, beginning at $6 a week for the first six months and ending at $12 a week for the sixth year; time-and-a-half pay for overtime work; a full hour for lunch instead of forty-five minutes;

and the establishment of an adjustment board composed of an equal number of representatives of the company and representatives chosen by the Telephone Operators' Union.[41]

The management of the New England Telephone Company had long sought to discourage workers from organizing on their own behalf by implying an association between criticism of work conditions and deficiency of character. The company's attempt to fashion inner-directed, work-driven employees who scrutinized their performance in the interest of self-improvement contrasted sharply with the trade union conception of work as alienating and the resulting aim of reducing work hours to expand workers' leisure. The union portrayed telephone operating as tedious and unrewarding work, causing enormous fatigue and nervous tension.

As models for its work force, the company's monthly magazine for employees, *New England Telephone Topics,* established in 1907, featured profiles, accompanied by cover photographs, of the company's leading executives. Every issue from August, 1907, to November, 1908, carried a lead article on a high management official. To encourage personal achievement, all promotions were listed in *Telephone Topics.* The magazine honored telephone operators of long service in articles praising their diligence in performing assigned tasks, suggestions for helping the company save money, punctuality, attendance, service to the public, and faithfulness to the company. Considerable emphasis was placed on "hello heroines," who risked physical injury or death by remaining at their posts during serious emergencies, such as fires and floods. In the interest of operators' self-improvement, the magazine each month printed a list of operators' mistakes that had inconvenienced subscribers during the previous month.

The company continually insisted that all criticism of the company was destructive and that success came to those employees who displayed the qualities of hard work, thrift, sobriety, ambition, and loyalty. The desire for more leisure time was merely an expression of laziness. Elbert Hubbard, in a 1908 article in *Telephone Topics,* contrasted the "two distinct classes of employees" in every business house. One class is called "the Bunch," suggesting a combination of workers, as in a trade union. These workers "are out for a maximum wage and a minimum service"—trade union demands for higher wages are associated with an aversion to hard work—and "plot and plan for personal gain—for ease and a good time." They regard their employer as an enemy and "persistently knock." The better sort, those workers who advance in the company, are highly disciplined individualists who "get their sleep, take their cold baths, do their Emersonians, join no cliques, and hustle for the house."[42] In another article frequently reprinted in *Telephone Topics* between 1907 and 1930, Hubbard described all criticism of working conditions as malicious and asserted it had no place in the telephone service: "If you must vilify, condemn, and eternally disparage, resign your position, and when you are outside, damn to your heart's content."[43] Harland Reed in the September, 1913, issue was even more explicit: "If you can't be loyal to a man, don't work for him. Resign. Quit. Get your time. Disappear."[44]

The telephone operators' demands were rejected by the superintendent of traffic, F. P. Valentine, but the union appealed to the president of the company, Jasper N. Keller, who asked for time to conduct a careful investigation of conditions. In the meantime, the operators worked to solidify their organization, adding over two hundred new members at meetings during the latter part of April, 1912.[45]

During May, 1912, the operators initiated a campaign to organize the male employees of the New England Telephone Company. May Matthews, an officer of the Boston Telephone Operators' Union, later informed the national convention of the Women's Trade Union League: "We started and got the men. That is the time we led and the men followed."[46] For women workers to organize men was highly unusual if not unprecedented and reflected their growing confidence in the wake of the "women's strikes" in the garment industry and the recent upsurge of female trade union membership in Boston. At a meeting at Wells Memorial Hall at which Peter Linehan presided, over four hundred male telephone workers applied for a union charter from the IBEW. The men cheered a committee of twelve young women from the Telephone Operators' Union who described their organization and its growth to over a thousand members within two months.[47]

Fortified by its daily increasing membership and organizing progress among operators in other New England cities, the Boston Telephone Operators' Union threatened to strike after the company announced in June that it would not grant the eight-hour day before January 1, 1913. As a result, the company promised the eight-hour day on July 15 and agreed to several other concessions, including a fifteen-minute rest break for every four hours of work. Operators who had served eighteen months or more were not to be assigned to the split trick.[48]

Alarmed by unionizing progress in Boston, the AT&T management in New York sent a circular letter to the presidents of the

associated companies asking them to report on "any recent agitation among your operating forces" and to detail any conditions
about which operators might have cause for grievance.[49] AT&T Vice-
President H. B. Thayer travelled to Boston in July to investigate the
labor situation.

Another major source of dissatisfaction among the telephone
operators, night work, was discussed in the September, 1912, issue
of the National WTUL organ *Life and Labor*, which presented the
case of the telephone operators to a national audience for the first
time. The author of the article, Boston WTUL ally Mary Caroline
Crawford (1874–1932), a Radcliffe graduate and writer of historical
romances, charged that night work subjected young women to sexual
harassment by men. Crawford noted that many exchanges were located in unsavory neighborhoods, where it was dangerous to walk at
night, and claimed that the company subordinated the safety of its
work force to a desire to economize on rent. Expressing an upper-
class distrust of working-class forms of leisure, she cited the warnings
of social workers about the "very real danger" for split-trick operators
in "killing time" at the moving pictures. The article also repeated the
union's complaints about fatigue, nervous tension, and inefficiency
caused by overwork; poor ventilation in the exchanges; regimentation
that made it difficult to get a drink of water or go to the lavatory
when necessary; management's insistence on the use of exact phrases
prescribed by company instruction manuals in conversations with
subscribers; and discrimination against operators for their union
activity.[50]

Crawford's opposition to night work for telephone operators
had long been shared by the state's male trade unionists. In 1911, the
State Federation of Labor supported for both "moral" and economic
reasons a bill introduced in the Massachusetts state legislature that
would have prohibited women under twenty-five years of age from
working in telephone exchanges between the hours of 10:00 P.M. and
6:00 A.M. The *Labor News,* Massachusetts's statewide labor newspaper, asserted that young women on their way to and from the
exchanges were "at the mercy of roughs and thugs" and claimed that
by employing female labor at night the company could pay 50 to 75
percent less wages than male labor would command.[51]

Leaders of the Telephone Operators' Union also indicated that
night work for younger telephone operators was improper. They dis-
puted the company's claim that the operators enjoyed "every possible
protection." May Matthews, a member of the union executive board,
described the plight of the teenage night operator: "She's on the street

at 10:30, and exchanges are often in isolated places, and it isn't good for her."[52] Many younger operators objected to night work and demanded that they not be assigned to it. The union leaders sensed this was an issue that could help them win the sympathy of the public, eager to protect the safety of young women. The Boston Telephone Operators' Union, however, did not refer to its younger members as "defenseless girls," as male trade unionists often did. Unlike the male trade unionists, who proposed to replace women operators with men at night, the Boston operators favored substituting older women for younger.

Inspired by the growth of the Boston Telephone Operators' Union, the IBEW initiated organizing campaigns in nearby Lynn, one of the country's major shoe-producing centers and a strong union town, and in Springfield, the largest city in western Massachusetts. The organizing in Lynn, where all 105 operators were concentrated in one exchange, was managed by Boston operators who visited Lynn after their working hours. The IBEW sent one of its international officers from New York to direct the drive in Springfield. Mary Quinn, later president of the Springfield Telephone Operators' Union, described her impressions of the campaign as a young telephone operator in 1912:

> I'll always remember the name—Vice-President Bugniazet of the International Brotherhood of Electrical Workers, who organized us. The chief operator and other officials of the company would find out where we were having the meeting, and they would hide behind trees, and telephone poles, and get our names, and the next morning we'd be called up to the desk and we'd be told the advantage and disadvantage of joining a union and what would happen and what wouldn't happen. But it didn't deter any of us. . . . We were all young girls, and most of us still in our teens.[53]

The organizing progress in Boston, however, was interrupted by a change in the management of the New England Telephone Company. President Jasper N. Keller was replaced by Philip L. Spalding, a vice-president of the Bell Telephone Company of Pennsylvania known for his strong anti-union views. Spalding, who had taken a leading role in breaking a strike of male telephone workers in Pennsylvania, New Jersey, and Delaware in 1907, refused to honor the concessions granted by Keller. In March, 1913, the Telephone Operators' Union—now boasting 2,200 members and representation in the Boston Central Labor Union, the Massachusetts State Federation of Labor, and the New England Council of Electrical Workers, a regional federation of IBEW locals—again presented its demands to the company. Making use of contacts among Boston's middle-class reformers, the Telephone Operators' Union received expert legal assistance in formulating its petition to President Spalding. Boston WTUL allies Mabel Gillespie and Elizabeth Glendower Evans secured the services of their friend, the noted "people's attorney" Louis Brandeis. The union asked Spalding to reply to its demands by March 31, 1913.[54]

Unwilling to negotiate with the union, President Spalding issued an "indirect reply" on March 26 in the form of a letter posted in the various exchanges. It referred the demands to the superintendent of traffic and included instructions that he inform the operators of the "properly defined way in which complaints or requests should be taken up": they must be presented to the chief operator, with the right of appeal to the next highest official. Spalding warned that the company would never recognize the union: "The Company . . . must deal with its employees only as employees." He refused to accede to any changes in wages or working conditions: "The present conditions of work are fair and reasonable, and . . . the Company is facing all the expenditures it can assume." Spalding also stated that the labor movement's traditional concern for improving job security could not be reconciled with management's need to regulate expenses: "The Company . . . reserves the right to dispense with the services of any of its employees at any time."[55] The operators derided Spalding's instructions on grievance procedure as a "Guide to Heaven," because higher officials would remain remote and inaccessible to the workers.[56]

Amid a clamor by many operators for an immediate strike, the Telephone Operators' Union, at a mass meeting held to plan a response to the company's decision, voted to demand a conference between President Spalding and the union's nine-woman arbitration committee. The telephone operators appealed to the Boston Central Labor Union, the WTUL, the Chamber of Commerce, and Mayor John F. Fitzgerald to pressure the company to reopen negotiations, and the IBEW leadership sent Vice-President Gustave Bugniazet to Boston to help the operators formulate their strategy. At WTUL headquarters, a joint committee of the three Boston IBEW locals of male telephone workers—Linemen's 104, Cable Splicers' 396, and Inside Telephone Men's 142, which now boasted about a thousand members among them—promised a sympathetic strike in the event of an operators' walkout. Because the operators had helped the male telephone workers unionize soon after they formed their own local, there was a common bond between them, which had not existed in San Francisco, where the men's organizations had long preceded the operators' union. The operators' position was further strengthened when several hundred delegates at the meeting of the Boston Central Labor Union unanimously voted to endorse their cause.[57]

The "Uprising of the 2,200"

On April 7, 1913, the union polled a strike vote following a conference that President Spalding had treated as a "joke," according to the telephone operators' committee.[58] The operators' representatives claimed Spalding had done nothing at the meeting but reiterate his refusal to consider the demands. The Telephone Operators' Union, in a statement to the mayor and President James Jackson Storrow of the Boston Chamber of Commerce, announced that it had exhausted all honorable means to arrive at a settlement. Accusing Spalding of having withdrawn concessions granted by his predecessor, the union drew particular attention to the split trick, which it termed one of the major points of contention. President Keller had promised that no operator with over eighteen months experience would be asked to work divided hours, but Spalding had declared to the union committee that there was "no such word as 'exempt' in the Company's rules of conduct, that its rules are compulsory and must be obeyed."[59] The company braced for a strike by sending its managers about the city in taxicabs to visit the homes of former employees for the purpose of recruiting them to replace operators who left the boards. One newspaper, however, noted that the company appeared to be experiencing considerable difficulty in this endeavor.[60]

The pervasive fear of the consequences of a telephone operators' strike, reflected in the editorial columns of Boston's newspapers and Boston business leaders' frantic appeals to the mayor to conciliate the differences between the company and union, demonstrated the highly important role the telephone had attained in commerce and society generally. The Boston *Post* declared, "Twentieth century living has made 2,000,000 of Greater Boston people absolutely dependent on the telephone. . . . [A strike] would frightfully cripple the stock exchange, the railroad systems, in fact every form of business. The inconveniences which would result are almost impossible to conceive."[61] Predicting that a telephone operators' walkout would prove even more disruptive than the Elevated strike of the preceding summer, the Boston *Herald*, a conservative newspaper with a wide circulation in the business community, warned of "enormous money loss and menace to life and property." Because the telephone operators wielded a "powerful club"—the ability to inflict serious damage on business by withdrawing their services—"a club such as is in the grasp of almost no other group of workers," the *Herald* urged the company to compromise: "Both [sides] no doubt should make concessions."[62]

As the mayor and leading businessmen initiated steps to bring about arbitration, the 2,200 members of the Telephone Operators' Union voted to strike by a resounding nine-to-one margin. Newspaper reporters who watched the operators file in to vote at the Women's Trade Union League headquarters commented on their youthful appearance. The Boston *Globe* stated that "hardly one in ten seemed twenty years old,"[63] and the *Herald* observed that "a noticeable fact . . . was the extreme youth of the vast majority and their extreme nervousness, due to the tension of their work."[64] The *Globe* also mentioned the "elegance" of the operators' attire, unusual for such low-paid workers; the operators wore "furs, hats of chic design, and smart-looking and expensive-looking shoes."[65] Reporters also noted that private branch exchange operators were among those voting, the first indication that such operators belonged to the union.

While the balloting was in progress, Gustave Bugniazet, representing the operators, and telephone company attorney Samuel Powers appeared separately before the State Board of Arbitration in an effort to avoid a strike.[66] The union agreed to postpone action for forty-eight hours while the two sides attempted to reach a settlement. However, no sooner had this understanding been reached than the telephone company began to import hundreds of strikebreakers from across the country to take the places of the Boston operators.

The first group of strikebreakers from New York, escorted by detectives, arrived at Back Bay Station on the night of April 7. Peter Collins, a former president of the Boston Central Labor Union and former secretary-treasurer of the IBEW who was a passenger on the train, learned the group's purpose and alerted the Telephone Operators' Union. The union was also informed that the company had contracted for several hundred automobiles to be ready on short notice to transport strikebreakers.[67] Hundreds more strikebreaking operators poured into Boston the next morning.

When the Boston Central Labor Union received word from union railroad telegraphers that trainloads of strikebreakers had left various southern and midwestern cities, the Telephone Operators' Union leadership had great difficulty holding its members at the boards. Alice Donovan, the union's press secretary, recalled that when the day operators came off their shift, large numbers of them gathered at union headquarters "and all I could hear was the word 'strike.' "[68] The numerous business concerns calling the Telephone Operators' Union office to determine whether there would be a strike all received the following reply: "Have the operators on your private switchboard join the union and then you can learn from them what they intend to do."[69]

By April 8, it was evident that the telephone company was preparing for the strike with the most lavish expenditure of money in the history of Boston industrial disputes.[70] The arrival of six hundred telephone operators from New York, Jersey City, and Philadelphia and an announcement from the AT&T headquarters that the entire Bell System would assist its subsidiary company in breaking a strike surprised and disappointed the Telephone Operators' Union, which had expected the New England Telephone Company to fill strikers' positions by recruiting new employees in the Boston area. H. B. Thayer, vice-president of AT&T, announced that not only New York and its suburbs but Chicago, Washington, Baltimore, and Pittsburgh had been asked to send to Boston what operators they could spare. The company soon expected to have assembled in Boston between one and two thousand strikebreaking operators: "We asked for volunteers in the various New York exchanges and more girls offered to go than we could send. We expect no trouble in getting plenty of volunteers from other offices. The AT&T is satisfied that the demands of the Boston operators are unjustified."[71]

A special train carried over three hundred telephone operators from New York, accompanied by detectives and twelve "elderly matrons." In a separate car were about seventy linemen and "troublefinders," sent in anticipation of possible sympathetic strike action and sabotage by Boston's male telephone workers. The Philadelphia train brought 175 telephone operators from Philadelphia, Washington, and Pittsburgh, among whom the company had distributed bundles of magazines, boxes of candy, and baskets of fruit. Most of the operators appeared to regard the trip as a "joy ride at the expense of the Telephone Company."[72] The operators were to receive their regular wages in Boston, a bonus of $25, a room in a modern hotel, and all expenses paid, including laundry. The company arranged for the New York operators to be taken to Boston's most luxurious hotel, the Copley Plaza, where the best apartments were placed at their disposal. When off duty they were promised sight-seeing tours of Boston.[73]

Even under the supervision of the matrons and detectives, the New York operators, the first to arrive, displayed the exhibitionism and desire for excitement associated with the "new woman" of the

1910s. The Boston *Globe* reported that the strikebreakers, scarcely any of whom seemed over twenty years old, "all acted as though they thought themselves on a lark . . . they showed no signs either in their faces or in their costumes of being in need of employment."[74] One of the imported operators told a reporter, "We are real fly operators, the very smartest in New York. The Company gave us a chance to come over here and is going to give us an extra $25 for a week and let us have all the fun we want. Say, we won't do a thing but eat, sleep, and have a good time. Are there any shows in town? Say, where is the nearest movie?"[75]

The newspaper commented that the New York operators were noticeably well dressed. So concerned were they about their appearance that many carried hatboxes, "since it would never do to appear on every occasion in the same hat."[76] Students from the nearby Massachusetts Institute of Technology building on Trinity Place, who gathered to watch the procession of New York operators from the railroad station to the hotel, were so impressed by the ornateness of their attire that they addressed them as "Oh you show girls!" Even the Boston *Post* remarked that the strikebreakers "looked more like chorus girls from some high-class theatrical show than they did telephone operators."[77] As the young women passed in review, they bantered with the college students. "Be good, you, and maybe we'll invite you to the dance in the gilt ballroom tonight," called out an eighteen-year-old operator in a blue suit and pudding-bowl hat with a green feather.[78] It is not likely that young factory women would have attracted such interest from college students, much less be put up by an employer in a luxury hotel, even as strikebreakers.

The strikebreakers appeared to have little understanding of the issues involved in the controversy in Boston, but they were grateful for the diversion from their usual routine. Many expected to be rewarded with a promotion for accepting the company's offer. Union telephone operators who attempted to engage the strikebreakers in a dialogue about their dispute with the company as they were marched double file to the hotel met with little success. Those who tried to talk with the arrivals were rudely shoved away by company detectives. One union operator who managed to slip by the detectives asked a strikebreaker whether she was aware there might be a strike in Boston. The strikebreaker informed her, "Oh yes we were told you were talking of striking, but most of us do not intend to stay more than a week. We just came over for a good time." Another, when asked if they were experienced telephone operators, reported: "We have all worked either in the exchanges or the pay stations. . . . Of course none of us left good jobs in New York. . . . we thought if we came over here the Company might give us better jobs when we went back."[79]

Never in the history of Boston, or probably any other city, had strikebreakers been housed in such magnificence as were the New York operators at the Copley Plaza Hotel. That evening, the hotel held a costume ball attended by some of the most prominent persons in Boston, Brookline, and New York society, including members of the Gould family and Charles M. Schwab, the first president of the United States Steel Corporation. As the men and women of wealth pirouetted about in the grand ballroom of the hotel at the most elaborate and exclusive function of the closing social season, the telephone operators chatted in their rooms above or walked about the lobby purchasing candy and souvenir postcards. Young women who lived in $3–a-week bedrooms in Hoboken now enjoyed at their employer's expense the Copley Plaza's great Jacobean sleeping rooms, each with deep velvet carpets, mirrored doors, and luxurious baths.[80]

By the evening of April 9, the management of the New England Telephone Company was confident it had imported sufficient numbers of operators from other cities to maintain adequate service in the event the Boston operators left the boards. Company officials announced they were prepared to spend $800,000 to maintain service should a strike occur. Over a thousand strikebreakers from Baltimore, Washington, Pittsburgh, Philadelphia, various New England cities, and as far west as Chicago and Madison, Wisconsin, had joined the New York area operators in twelve Boston hotels. A trainload of strikebreakers had also left Indianapolis, and company officials continued their efforts to recruit former Boston operators, precipitating the first violence in the controversy, when boys stoned company vehicles in Malden.[81] The company indicated it was prepared to wait out a long strike when it leased the Hotel Bartol in the Back Bay. Formerly an apartment hotel occupied by retired business and professional men and vacant for over a year, the Bartol contained enough room for six hundred operators.[82] The company could draw no strikebreakers from Lynn or Springfield, where the telephone operators were fully organized and prepared to strike in sympathy with the Boston operators.

Labor officials attempted to influence public opinion in the union's favor by implying a connection between strikebreaking and prostitution and thus calling into question the integrity of the telephone company. Bringing to mind the recently passed Mann Act, they denounced the company's transporting of its employees across state lines as "girl traffic" and prepared to introduce legislation in Congress to render such practices illegal. John B. Colpoys, secretary of the Washington, D. C. Central Labor Union, who announced the drafting of such a bill, impugned the morality of the telephone company in referring to the "indignities" inflicted on those who formed a part of what the Washington *Post* called the company's "shipment of girls" to Boston.[83]

The Telephone Operators' Union leadership faced great difficulty in keeping its membership at work in the face of company provocations, which included not only the massive importation of strikebreakers but harassment and intimidation of the operators in the exchanges. A large group of operators gathered at union headquarters demanding a strike, and only an enormous effort from IBEW Vice-President Bugniazet, who argued that a walkout would play into the company's hands, induced them to return to work in the morning. Operators at the Back Bay exchange, asked to sign a statement that they would remain loyal to the company, immediately called the Women's Trade Union League for instructions. They were told to remain at the switchboard until they received a signal from union officers to walk off the job.[84] Each operator in the Newton unit, comprising the three Newton exchanges and those of Wellesley and Needham, was summoned individually to the office of the traffic manager and asked whether she belonged to the union. The cable splicers and linemen were also called in and questioned as to what action they would take in the event of an operators' strike. They were unanimous in declaring they would strike in sympathy. Operators who were questioned disclosed the manager had warned that anyone who participated in a strike would never again be employed by the telephone company.[85] Mary Quinn recalled that the operators in Springfield closely followed the situation in Boston and were called in and questioned individually by management: "We were interviewed and asked if we'd go out on strike if the Boston operators went out, we said surely we would. We'd support them."[86]

Strengthening the hand of the Telephone Operators' Union was the promise of sympathetic strike action by not only the male telephone workers' locals but many other Boston trade unions. The Boston *Evening Transcript* remarked, "Were it to be a fight alone between the Telephone Company and its 2,200 girls in Greater Boston, there would be no question about the outcome. . . . It is the union affiliations, however, that the girls count on to support them in a contest."[87] It was expected that if the sympathetic movement were extended, the telegraphers would be the first group not connected with the IBEW to be called out.[88] In New York, four hundred women members of the AFL's Commercial Telegraphers' Union of America met to denounce the strikebreaking of the New York telephone operators and voted to offer financial support to the Boston operators.[89]

Both locals of the Boston Hotel Workers' Union, 6 and 80, each with a membership of between six and seven hundred, voted to strike rather than serve the imported operators should the Boston operators walk out. John Kearney, business agent of Local 80, had great difficulty dissuading his members against an immediate strike in hotels where the strikebreakers were quartered.[90] The cooks and waiters voted to instruct the hotel managers to pin badges on the imported operators so they could be distinguished and refused service in the event of a strike. The Engineers' Union, whose members controlled the heating systems in the hotels, also voted to join a sympathetic strike if the operators went out.[91] The Boston Central Labor Union appointed a special committee headed by its president to assist the Telephone Operators' Union in planning its strategy.[92]

The telephone company's enormous expenditure of money to import hundreds of strikebreakers from around the country and house them in luxurious hotels caused public sentiment in Boston to shift in favor of the operators. The Telephone Operators' Union estimated that the company's contract with detective agencies alone cost $80,000 for two weeks, as opposed to the $300,000 required to readjust the wage scale to meet the operators' demands.[93]

On April 9, the Massachusetts state legislature ordered the appointment of a committee of five members to study the telephone situation. A substitute motion, empowering the committee to investigate not only the current controversy but also company earnings, the quality of service provided the public, and wages, which would have compelled company officials to testify before it under oath, was defeated in the most vituperative party fight of the legislative session. Representative Giblin of East Boston, who favored putting the legislature on record as in sympathy with the telephone operators, opened the fight against the order and was followed by Martin Lomasney, who declaimed, "Let us adopt an order with some teeth in it. The Telephone Company can't stand a real investigation. Give the people a chance to get at the books of the Company." The substitute motion was voted down 128 to 95 on strict party lines, with Democratic, Bull Moose, and Socialist party members in favor and all but three Republicans opposed. The original order then passed unanimously.[94]

The prospect of serious business losses from a telephone operators' strike and a possible citywide general strike prompted the Boston Chamber of Commerce to offer its services as a mediator between the telephone company and the union. It succeeded in bringing about a conference on the evening of April 8 at Young's Hotel. The directors of the Chamber of Commerce appointed a three-man committee, headed by President James Jackson Storrow (1864–1926), to participate in the negotiations.

Storrow was not in a position to be entirely objective as a mediator, as he long had had close connections with the telephone company and undoubtedly harbored antagonism toward Irish-Americans, whom he blamed for his narrow defeat in the 1910 Boston mayoralty election. Storrow's father, James Jackson Storrow, Sr., had been the Bell Telephone Company's leading patent lawyer, serving the company from 1878 until his death in 1897. After graduating from Harvard Law School in 1888, the junior Storrow had joined a law firm headed by Frederick P. Fish, later president of AT&T, who had worked for the Bell Company on numerous telephone patent cases. In 1900, Storrow left his law practice to take a position with the investment banking firm of Lee, Higginson, and Company, which had long advised the Bell Company on financial matters.[95]

In 1910, Storrow ran for mayor as the candidate of the Good Government Association against John F. "Honey Fitz" Fitzgerald, a product of the Irish Democratic machine of the North End, and lost by a margin of only 1,402 votes out of over 90,000 cast. Storrow believed that solid Irish-American support for his opponent had caused his defeat. Shortly after the election, he wrote to a supporter, "Few people realize that the political limits of Boston only include a limited section of the whole city, and that in this limited section there is such a racial predominance that it permits a straight appeal to racial ties—. . . . Neither in New York nor in any large city in this country does sixty percent or even one-half of the population belong to one racial stock, emphasized still further by social conditions and religious sympathy."[96]

The conference at Young's Hotel represented the first formal negotiating session between the New England Telephone Company and a union committee. The Telephone Operators' Union committee was composed of President Annie Molloy, Vice-President Mary Meagher, Secretary Mary Mahoney, Treasurer Melena Godair, Mary F. McCarthy, Bessie S. Shilladay, Alice M. Keating, Mary F. Murray, and Julia S. O'Connor, nearly all of whom were in their early twenties. Molloy at thirty-two was an exception. At least three of the four officers—Molloy, Meagher, and Mahoney—were toll operators, the group which had started the union in March, 1912.

Negotiations were resumed on April 9 as the New England Telephone Company's representatives, President Philip Spalding, Vice-President E. K. Hall, and company attorney Samuel Powers, were joined by Union N. Bethell of New York, vice-president of AT&T. His appearance was taken to mean that the controversy no longer involved only the telephone operators of Boston and the New England Telephone Company but had become a national issue affecting the parent company and every operator in the United States.[97] The committee of nine operators handled all the bargaining on the labor side. During intervals in the conference, it conferred with IBEW Vice-President Gustave Bugniazet and the presidents of the Boston IBEW linemen's and cable splicers' locals.

As negotiations proceeded, the imported operators grew increasingly resentful of their treatment by the company, which did not want to risk any fraternization between the strikebreakers and trade unionists. Termed "prisoners in a gilded cage" by the newspapers, they were not permitted to leave their hotels and were under constant scrutiny by telephone company matrons and detectives. The imported operators, who had arrived in Boston rollicking and out for a good time, were not only deprived of their promised sight-seeing tours of the city but could not even walk about the hotel lobbies and corridors. The young women were rebuked for even smiling at other hotel guests, not to mention talking to them.

Although they had come to Boston eagerly expecting a break from their usual work routine, the imported operators at the Copley Plaza experienced the same strict supervision and regimentation as in the exchange. Like schoolchildren, they descended to breakfast in a double line with a monitor behind every tenth couple. After the meal, a New York Telephone Company division superintendent, acting as a sort of "head chaperone" for the over three hundred operators housed at the hotel, explained that "certain opposition" rendered it impossible for them to leave the premises. The young women, greatly disappointed, were then formed into a double line and marched upstairs to the grill room, where they were permitted to play the piano and dance the "Grizzly Bear" and the "Bunny Hug" with each other. In the afternoon, they played such children's games as tag, puss in the corner, and hide-and-seek on the hotel roof. After supper, the company substituted "vaudeville entertainment" for the promised outing: a prestidigitator performed tricks and Vice-President E. K.

Hall of the New England Telephone Company sang to piano music by the hotel's publicity agent.[98]

Many operators were enraged because they had been assigned to hotels older and less ornate than the Copley Plaza, opened in 1912, and were thus deprived of the oriental rugs, silken hangings, scented baths, and the novelty of living in rooms where the heat could be controlled to the degree by turning a thermostat.[99] Several of these operators, whose evening's entertainment consisted of looking, chaperoned, over a hotel balustrade at a clerk informing late arrivals that there would be no more vacant rooms, were so angry they refused to speak with reporters.[100]

In contrast to the childlike dependency of the imported operators, Boston's union operators confronted the company's negotiators as equals and impressed observers with their maturity and confidence. Although the operators were new to the labor movement, their sophistication was evident in their first picket line, established while negotiations were still in progress. Over two hundred telephone operators surged out of a union meeting at 11:00 P.M. and marched to the Hotel Thorndike, where strikebreaking operators from Chicago were expected. Walking in pairs, arm in arm, the operators formed a picket line around the hotel and were cheered on by passing cabmen and chauffeurs. Soon the sidewalk before the hotel entrance was entirely blocked, although the operators, careful to observe the law, moved along in regular procession, "as orderly and well-behaved as the most decorous of school-ma'ams." A detail of police was assigned to observe what the Boston *Globe* called "an exhibition of splendid picket work."[101] The operators dispersed when they learned the strikebreakers would not arrive until the next day.

After a conference lasting fifteen consecutive hours, the telephone company and the operators' union in the early morning hours of April 10 reached an agreement which, while embodying significant concessions from the company, fell far short of the union's demands. Instead of gaining an increase in weekly wages, the operators were given "anniversary payments," that is, annual bonuses: "After two years an operator would receive a bonus at the end of the year of $25. Operators with between three and nine years of service would receive $50. After ten years of service, and each year thereafter, an operator would receive $100." A permanent adjustment board, composed of an equal number of management and union representatives, was established to confer on "all matters requiring discussion." Through the adjustment board, the operators expected to shorten the work day to eight hours and extend the lunch period from forty-five

minutes to one hour. While no mention was made of the split trick—
one of the major points of contention—the company apparently had
promised that it would not be compulsory for an operator after eighteen months of service. The operators assumed that the company had,
by accepting the adjustment board, recognized the union.[102]

Certain that the agreement would be ratified by the members of
the Telephone Operators' Union, the company began to send home
its 1,200 strikebreaking operators, and AT&T Vice-President Bethell
returned to New York. Boston's newspapers also declared the controversy to be entirely settled because, according to the Boston *Evening Globe,* "there is no doubt in anybody's mind that the union will
accept the terms." To the *Herald,* ratification by the rank and file
was "practically assured," and the *Christian Science Monitor* went
even further, predicting that the terms would be "accepted by a big
majority." The *Post* headline read "Girls to Accept Pact Today," and
Hearst's *Daily Advertiser* reported "general satisfaction" by all parties
over the agreement, with "no doubt" that it would be ratified. Only
the conservative *Evening Transcript,* fearing that manipulative labor
leaders had inculcated a "strike mentality" in the younger operators,
hinted at possible trouble. The newspapers were all favorable to the
terms; even the *Evening Transcript,* never friendly to labor, praised
the agreement because, by establishing an adjustment board, it reduced the possibility of future strikes. As a result of the settlement,
the state legislature called off its investigation of the controversy.[103]

The telephone operators, however, were more strongly committed to the demands than the company and the Chamber of Commerce mediators had assumed, and bitter argument ensued in the
ranks over the agreement. The operators were angered by continued
harassment for union membership in the workplace, and they were
deeply suspicious of the Chamber of Commerce, although many believed that, since it represented the company's most important customers, it was the only body that could have influenced management
to negotiate at all. One union operator expressed the prevailing distrust: "The Chamber of Commerce people are all representatives of
invested money, none of them naturally on the side of labor. They
wanted the strike kept off, of course, but that was their own selfish
hunt. They had to have the phones in order to do business; they didn't
care whether we got a square deal or not, so long as they prevented
a strike. And when it came to arguing which side should give up a
point, they argued stronger against the girls than against the company."[104]

The telephone operators voted in three shifts, with a few hundred casting their ballots in the morning at union headquarters in the Women's Trade Union League office at 7 Warrenton Street, a few hundred more in the afternoon at Wells Memorial Hall in the South End, and then 1,800 operators, comprising most of the day force, at an evening meeting at Wells Memorial presided over by Gustave Bugniazet and Annie Molloy. The real fight began in the evening, as operator after operator denounced the terms as unfair. For a time it seemed as though the settlement would be completely repudiated. The operators were almost unanimously opposed to the bonus plan, which implied a pay raise was a favor that could be granted or withheld at the pleasure of the company and which ignored the operators with less than two years of service, who many felt worked for less than a living wage.[105]

Although some argued that the adjustment board would make it possible to effect the desired changes in the near future, the operators refused to ratify much of the agreement. Immediately after the evening meeting, Vice-President Bugniazet announced:

> The report as submitted by the arbitration committee was divided. The portion providing for an adjustment committee was unanimously adopted.
>
> The balance of the report, with the exception of the yearly bonus system, was accepted under protest.
>
> The bonus plan was unanimously refused, as the operators have decided that they do not desire to receive any money from the company except in the form of weekly wages which they rightfully earn, and do not desire any donations, presents, or bonuses from the company.[106]

The union then declared that existing differences would be taken up by the new adjustment board. It became apparent, however, that while the union envisioned the adjustment board as an organ for collective bargaining, the company had no such understanding, insisting that it was to be restricted to handling grievances of individual employees only.[107] As a "ludicrous expression of astonishment" spread through company headquarters at 50 Oliver Street, management was again forced to sit down with the telephone operators.[108]

As a result of pressure from the Chamber of Commerce mediation committee, the company finally decided to discard the bonus system in favor of increases in the weekly wages. The wage scale demanded by the union, beginning at $6 a week on assignment as operator to a maximum of $12 a week at the end of six years, became effective on June 1, 1913.[109] When the settlement was reached, the remaining strikebreakers were sent home. In one of the most massive and expensive importations of strikebreakers in the history of the United States, the company had drawn on Bell System operators from the New York area, Philadelphia, Pittsburgh, Washington, Baltimore, the New England states, and forty-one cities in Illinois, Ohio, Wisconsin, and Indiana.[110]

The elections for the three operators' positions on the new adjustment board precipitated new controversy. The union insisted that only its members be allowed to vote, at the Women's Trade Union League headquarters. The company, however, planned for non-union operators, about 5 percent of the total work force, to cast their ballots at the exchanges under the supervision of the chief operator, who would forward them to company Vice-President E. K. Hall. The union's interpretation prevailed, and on April 22 Annie Molloy, Mary Meagher, and Mary Murray were selected from a field of eight candidates. Molloy and Meagher were toll operators, while Murray represented the local exchanges.[111]

The First Step toward a National Union

Having won nearly all their demands, the Boston telephone operators emerged from their confrontation with the telephone company as highly capable and self-reliant trade unionists. As long as it existed, their organization was one of the largest union locals in Boston and the most important source of working-class membership for the Boston WTUL. Two telephone operators, Julia O'Connor and May Matthews, joined the Boston WTUL's executive board in 1913, and O'Connor in 1915 became the first working woman to serve as its president. The strong backing the telephone operators received from the IBEW leadership and the city's trade unions, several of which were prepared to call sympathetic strikes, was a major factor in their success in April, 1913. Yet while they valued this support greatly and consulted throughout the crisis with leaders of the Central Labor Union and IBEW, the telephone operators retained charge of their union's strategy and operations. The operators' self-confidence and determination to control their union was evident when the telephone operators' committee conducted the negotiations alone, face-to-face with leading officials of the Bell Company, men over a generation older and far more educated, even though it could have requested the assistance of more experienced male trade unionists. In both Montana and San Francisco, male unionists had largely directed strike strategy and bargaining for the operators. The long tradition of organized women's activism in Boston, in particular the strong WTUL chapter, and New York's recent garment strike had suggested to the telephone operators the possibilities for independent behavior by women.

While illustrating the telephone operators' potential power to paralyze Boston's economic life, the near-strike of April, 1913, made clear that the well-coordinated Bell System was prepared to use its enormous financial resources to defeat unionization efforts. It could draw upon a huge supply of non-union labor in its employ for strike-breaking. To offset the power of the corporation, the Boston Telephone Operators' Union now turned its attention to organizing telephone operators across the country. The union, with the support of the IBEW, which opened a telephone operators' section in its monthly journal, initiated campaigns in New England that it hoped would spark interest in operators in other regions. Its press secretary, Alice Donovan, stated after the settlement had been reached in Boston, "We regret the telephone operators are not more fully organized for we realized during our recent trouble that we could have demanded much more . . . even if we only had operators in New England or-ganized it would have meant so much."[112] In defeating the Bell System in April, 1913, 2,200 Boston women had taken the first step toward a national union of telephone operators.

NOTES

1. "The Call Circuit," *Union Telephone Operator* [hereafter, *UTO*], July, 1921, p. 12.
2. Edward Shorter and Charles Tilly, *Strikes in France, 1830–1968* (New York: Cambridge University Press, 1974), p. 238.
3. William Maxwell Burke, "History and Functions of Central Labor Unions" (Ph.D. dissertation, Columbia University, 1899), p. 43.
4. Sari Roboff, *Boston's Labor Movement* (Boston: Boston 200 Corporation, 1977), p. 19; James R. Green and Hugh Carter Donahue, *Boston's Workers: A Labor History* (Boston: Boston Public Library, 1979), pp. 72, 87.
5. Ethel M. Johnson, "Labor Progress in Boston, 1880 to 1930," in Elizabeth M. Herlihy, ed., *Fifty Years of Boston: A Memorial Volume* (Boston: Boston Tercentenary Committee, 1932), p. 216.
6. Alice Kessler-Harris, *Out to Work* (New York: Oxford University Press, 1982), p. 153.
7. Albert M. Heintz and John R. Whitney, *History of the Massachusetts State Federation of Labor, 1887–1935* (Worcester, Mass.: Labor News Printers, 1935), pp. 16, 19, 33.
8. Kessler-Harris, *Out to Work*, p. 156.
9. Carole Turbin makes a similar point in explaining how the industrial

structure of Troy, New York, fostered a firm alliance between male iron molders and female collar laundresses in "Reconceptualizing Family, Work, and Labor Organizing: Working Women in Troy, 1860–1890," *Review of Radical Political Economics* 16 (1984):9.

10. The telephone operators did not share the experience of women office workers described by Sharon Hartman Strom in "Challenging 'Woman's Place': Feminism, the Left, and Industrial Unionism in the 1930s," *Feminist Studies* 9 (Summer, 1983):359–86. According to Strom, the Left in the 1930s failed to articulate the sexual division of office work or to grasp that women should be organized as women in an industrial clerical workers' movement.

11. Sharon Hartman Strom, "Leadership and Tactics in the American Woman Suffrage Movement: A New Perspective from Massachusetts," *Journal of American History* 62 (September, 1975):300.

12. Allen Davis, *Spearheads for Reform* (New York: Oxford University Press, 1967), pp. 103, 108.

13. Ibid., p. 143.

14. Gladys Boone, *The Women's Trade Union League in Great Britain and the United States of America* (New York: Columbia University Press, 1942), p. 44.

15. Rose Finkelstein Norwood, quoted in Gary Endelman, "Solidarity Forever: Rose Schneiderman and the Women's Trade Union League" (Ph.D. dissertation, University of Delaware, 1978), p. 119.

16. Nancy Shrom Dye, *As Equals and as Sisters* (Columbia: University of Missouri Press, 1980), p. 7.

17. John Sharpless and John Rury, "The Political Economy of Women's Work, 1900–1920," *Social Science History* 4 (Summer, 1980):318–19; Rosalyn L. Feldberg, " 'Union Fever': Organizing American Clerical Workers, 1900–1930," in James Green, ed., *Workers' Struggles, Past and Present* (Philadelphia: Temple University Press, 1983), p. 163.

18. Sue Ainslee Clark, "Women's Trade Unions in the United States," May 5, 1911, p. 2, Box 7, Women's Educational and Industrial Union Papers, Schlesinger Library, Radcliffe College, Cambridge, Mass.

19. Kessler-Harris, *Out to Work*, p. 160.

20. Elizabeth G. Evans, "The Roxbury Carpet Factory Strike," *The Survey*, May 28, 1910, pp. 337–38.

21. Green and Donahue, *Boston's Workers*, pp. 87–88.

22. Massachusetts State Federation of Labor, *Proceedings of the Twenty-seventh Annual Convention, 1912* (Worcester: Massachusetts State Federation of Labor, 1912), p. 21.

23. The phrase "titanic battle" is from the Boston *Post*, April 9, 1913.

24. Julia S. O'Connor, "History of the Organized Telephone Operators' Movement," Part 1, *UTO*, January, 1921, p. 14.

25. Letter from Alice J. Donovan, *Journal of Electrical Workers and Operators* [hereafter, *JEWO*], September, 1912, p. 550.

26. O'Connor, "History," Part 1, p. 14.

27. Mary Quinn Wynne, interview by Stephen H. Norwood, Springfield, Mass., June 28, 1974.

28. Rose Finkelstein Norwood, interview by Stephen H. Norwood, Boston, Mass., January 28, 1974.

29. "Secretary's Report, Boston Women's Trade Union League," Biennial Convention, National Women's Trade Union League [hereafter, WTUL], 1913, p. 5, Smaller Collections Reel, WTUL Collection, Schlesinger Library.

30. O'Connor, "History," Part 1, p. 14.

31. Boston *Globe*, September 25, 1923.

32. Ibid.; *Labor News*, June 11, 1910.

33. Stephen H. Norwood, "Mary Gordon Thompson," in Gary M. Fink, *Biographical Dictionary of American Labor* (Westport, Conn.: Greenwood Press, 1984), p. 547.

34. O'Connor, "History," Part 2, *UTO*, February, 1921, p. 17.

35. Alice Stone Blackwell, "Mrs. Susan W. Fitzgerald," *Woman's Journal*, February 5, 1910; "Susan Grimes Walker Fitzgerald," in *The National Cyclopaedia of American Biography*, vol. 32 (New York: James T. White, 1945), p. 432.

36. John J. Leary, Jr., "Sarah Agnes McLaughlin Conboy," in *Dictionary of American Biography*, vol. 4 (Charles Scribner's Sons, 1930); *Life and Labor Bulletin*, February, 1928, p. 4.

37. Boston *Globe*, April 15, 1912.

38. Rose Finkelstein Norwood, interview.

39. O'Connor, "History," Part 1, p. 14.

40. Ibid., Part 2, p. 14.

41. "Secretary's Report, Boston Women's Trade Union League," pp. 5–6.

The union's proposed wage scale for telephone operators of $6 to $12 for a proposed forty-eight-hour week can be compared with existing union wage scales in selected trades in Boston in 1912: Male dry-goods clerks received $12 to $15 and female dry-good clerks $7 for a forty-eight-hour week; garment workers $11 to $20 for a fifty-four-hour week; streetcar motormen and conductors $16.10 to $18.55 for a seventy-hour week; and stable and garagemen $13 to $16 for a sixty-five-hour week. Wages for unionized boot and shoe workers in Massachusetts, who worked a fifty-four- to fifty-eight-hour week, ranged from $7 to $10 for tip fixers, $8.50 to $9 for packers, and $10.50 to $14 for stitchers, to about $15 to $22 for cutters. In textiles, across the state, union wages for a fifty-four- to fifty-eight-hour week ranged from $5 to $9 for carders, $3 to $13 for spinners, and $5 to $14 for weavers, to $13 to $18 for mule spinners and $12 to $19 for loom-fixers. A union wage scale for tobacco strippers existed only in Springfield, $7 to $9 for a forty-eight-hour week. Commonwealth of Massachusetts, *Forty-fourth Annual Report on the Statistics of Labor—1913* (Boston: Wright and Potter Printing, 1913), pp. 378–79, 397, 402, 429, 431–34.

42. Elbert Hubbard, "The Two Kinds," *New England Telephone Topics* [hereafter, *NETT*], August, 1908, p. 16. "Cliques" was a euphemism for

trade unions. By "do their Emersonians," Hubbard meant overcoming obstacles through strong character and will.

43. Elbert Hubbard, "Teamwork and the Grumbler," *NETT*, August, 1907, p. 8.

44. Harland Reed, "Loyalty," *NETT*, September, 1913, p. 200.

45. Boston *Globe*, April 26, 1912.

46. National WTUL, "Proceedings of the 1913 Convention," p. 62, Box 13, National WTUL Papers, Library of Congress, Washington, D.C.

47. Boston *Globe*, May 15, 1912.

48. *Christian Science Monitor*, August 3, 1912.

49. H. B. Thayer to presidents of the associated companies, June 14, 1912, Box 47, AT&T Archives, New York, N.Y.

50. Mary Caroline Crawford, "The Hello Girls of Boston," *Life and Labor*, September, 1912, p. 264.

51. *Labor News*, February 4, 1911.

52. Boston *Herald*, April 8, 1913.

53. Mary Quinn Wynne, interview.

54. National WTUL, "Proceedings of the 1913 Convention."

55. Boston *Herald*, March 28, 1913.

56. National WTUL, "Proceedings of the 1913 Convention."

57. Boston *Daily Advertiser*, March 29, 1913; Boston *Herald*, April 5, 1913.

58. Alice J. Donovan, "Description of Boston Telephone Operators' Troubles," *JEWO*, May, 1913, p. 937.

59. Boston *Herald*, April 5, 1913.

60. Boston *Post*, April 7, 1913.

61. Ibid.

62. Boston *Herald*, April 8, 1913.

63. Boston *Globe*, April 7, 1913.

64. Boston *Herald*, April 8, 1913.

65. Boston *Globe*, April 7, 1913.

66. Journal Books of the Massachusetts State Board of Arbitration, entry for April 7, 1913, Massachusetts State Library, Boston, Mass.

67. Boston *Globe*, April 8, 1913.

68. Donovan, "Description," p. 938.

69. *Christian Science Monitor*, April 8, 1913.

70. Boston *Herald*, April 9, 1913.

71. Boston *Globe*, April 9, 1913.

72. New York *Sun*, April 9, 1913; Boston *Evening Globe*, April 8, 1913; Washington *Post*, April 9, 1913.

73. Boston *Evening Globe*, April 8, 1913.

74. Boston *Globe*, April 9, 1913.

75. Ibid.

76. Ibid.

77. Boston *Post*, April 8, 1913.

78. Boston *Globe*, April 9, 1913.

79. Ibid.

80. Boston *Post,* April 9, 1913; Boston *Herald,* April 9, 1913.

81. Boston *Post,* April 9, 1913.

82. Boston *Evening Transcript,* April 9, 1913; *Christian Science Monitor,* April 9, 1913.

83. Washington *Post,* April 10, 1913.

84. Boston *Evening Transcript,* April 9, 1913.

85. Boston *Herald,* April 9, 1913.

86. Mary Quinn Wynne, interview.

87. Boston *Evening Transcript,* April 8, 1913.

88. Ibid., April 9, 1913.

89. Boston *Herald,* April 10, 1913.

90. Ibid., April 9, 1913.

91. Boston *Post,* April 9, 1913.

92. Boston *Herald,* April 9, 1913.

93. Donovan, "Description," p. 939.

94. Lomasney quoted in Boston *Herald,* April 10, 1913; Boston *Daily Advertiser,* April 10, 1913.

95. Henry Greenleaf Pearson, *Son of New England* (Boston: Thomas Todd, 1932), pp. 5, 26, 31.

Over a period of eighteen years, Bell patents were tested in some six hundred cases, of which by far the most important was Bell's suit against Western Union in 1878–79. The suits were brought by the Bell Company against numerous patent infringers, whose object was usually to sell as much stock to the public as possible before being enjoined. Most of the defendants gave up at an early stage. The Bell Company won all the cases that went to a final hearing. Robert V. Bruce, *Bell: Alexander Graham Bell and the Conquest of Solitude* (Boston: Little, Brown, 1973), p. 271.

96. Quoted in Pearson, *Son of New England,* pp. 84, 93.

97. Boston *Globe,* April 10, 1913.

98. Boston *Herald,* April 10, 1913.

99. O'Connor, "History," Part 2, p. 16; Boston *Herald,* April 10, 1913; Boston *Post,* April 10, 1913.

100. Boston *Globe,* April 9, 1913.

101. Ibid., April 10, 1913.

102. Boston *Herald,* April 11, 1913; Boston *Evening Globe,* April 10, 1913.

103. Boston *Evening Globe,* April 10, 1913; Boston *Herald,* April 11, 1913; *Christian Science Monitor,* April 11, 1913; Boston *Post,* April 11, 1913; Boston *Daily Advertiser,* April 11, 1913; Boston *Evening Transcript,* April 10, 1913.

104. Boston *Evening Globe,* April 12, 1913.

105. Boston *Herald,* April 12, 1913; Boston *Evening Globe,* April 12, 1913.

106. Boston *Globe,* April 12, 1913.

107. Boston *Daily Advertiser,* April 11, 1913.

108. Boston *Evening Globe,* April 12, 1913.

109. Commonwealth of Massachusetts, *Twenty-eighth Annual Report of the State Board of Arbitration, 1913* (Boston: n.p., 1914), pp. 73–74.

Senior operators were to receive $10 to $13, supervisors $12 to $15, assistant chief operators $13 to $18, and chief operators, $15 to $25.

110. A. S. Hibbard to E. K. Hall, June 4, 1913, Box 47, AT&T Archives.

111. Boston *Herald,* April 23, 1913.

112. Donovan, "Description," p. 942.

4

Women in a Men's Union, 1913–18

Although the International Brotherhood of Electrical Workers (IBEW) formally committed itself to a national organizing campaign among telephone operators as a result of the victory of the Boston Telephone Operators' Union in 1913, it provided very little assistance, and operators' unionism remained largely confined to Massachusetts until the United States entered World War I in 1917. From the time it was founded in 1891, the IBEW had concentrated on organizing skilled electrical workers in the building trades and the craftsmen employed by the telephone companies. During the early twentieth century, it was the second largest of the American Federation of Labor's (AFL) construction affiliates, after the United Brotherhood of Carpenters and Joiners.[1] Although in 1895 it had repealed an amendment to its constitution allowing only men to join, the IBEW had only recently begun to organize electrical manufacturing plants, where the majority of employees were often women. The IBEW was never comfortable with women workers and gave low priority to organizing them, whether in electrical manufacturing or in the telephone service. Most of the organizing of telephone operators before America's entry into the war was thus done in the area immediately surrounding existing locals by union operators. The operators volunteered their services without compensation during what little leisure time they had. During this period, the Women's Trade Union League (WTUL) allies provided them with leadership training and encouraged an interest in women's rights, which made the telephone operators a powerful force not only in Boston labor circles but on the national level in the IBEW itself.

Massachusetts offered favorable prospects for telephone operators' organizing campaigns because of its strong network of central labor unions, the existence of WTUL chapters in Boston and Worcester, and the tradition of labor activism in the state's two dominant industries—textiles and boot and shoe—where the rate of female employment was unusually high. Of the twenty-seven telephone operators' locals established by November, 1916, twenty-one were in Massachusetts. Besides Boston, these included such major shoe and textile centers as Lawrence, Lowell, Haverhill, Brockton, Lynn, Fall River, and New Bedford, as well as the state's two largest centers of diversified manufacturing outside Boston, Springfield and Worcester. At the 1913 IBEW convention, it was decided to charter the telephone operators' unions directly as locals, which were numbered in the order they were organized (the letter "A" after the number identified them as a telephone operators' union; thus, the Boston local became 1A, Lynn 2A, Springfield 3A, and so on).

The IBEW appropriated funds for only one paid organizer for telephone operators. In 1914, IBEW President Frank McNulty appointed a Worcester telephone operator, Mary St. John, as special organizer for the United States and Canada, but she worked primarily in Massachusetts. The president and vice-president of the Boston Telephone Operators' Union, Annie Molloy and Mary Meagher, helped organize the New Bedford local in late 1913, and Molloy spent her two-week summer vacation in 1914 working with St. John on a successful campaign in Fitchburg.

Male IBEW locals, especially in towns where they had been long established, sometimes assisted the operators in their campaigns. According to Mary Quinn, however, the operators often organized the men in Massachusetts. She explained how the Springfield Telephone Operators' Union (Local 3A) carried on organizing drives in western Massachusetts:

> At that time here in Springfield we covered Springfield, Holyoke—which is a city of its own—Westfield, Chicopee, Northampton, Warren—Warren, out on the east side—Ludlow . . . we organized them ourselves, Local 3A. We went out and organized them. And we would go out and hold a meeting probably once a month. The officers from 3A would go to the locals in Northampton where it was difficult for the girls to come in and we'd go out and have a meeting there and have them keep up on affairs, you know.
>
> After the operators were organized the men started to organize, the telephone men—and I think the operators did a pretty good job organizing them. . . . It was the operators who started to organize the men.[2]

Although it was very uncommon for women to organize men in any setting, it was more likely to occur in textile or boot and shoe districts or in centers of diversified industry where there was a high proportion of women in the labor force. The relative importance of women's economic contribution tended to make gender relations somewhat less asymmetric in these places. It was not easy to stereotype women as helpless dependents. Although housework remained primarily a female responsibility, most women were not fully occupied with serving the men in the home, as was often the case in centers of heavy industry or mining; in many households there was probably some sharing of tasks.[3] In Massachusetts, the large local of telephone operators in Boston and the WTUL encouraged operators to organize, even if the telephone men in the locality were non-union, and provided an example close at hand of women who had organized men.

National and International Organizing Efforts

Inspired by the Boston operators' effort, the St. Louis WTUL began a campaign to organize telephone operators in January, 1913. Delegates from the Boston Telephone Operators' Union who attended the National Women's Trade Union League convention in St. Louis in May, 1913, discussed their achievement with working women of that city, and they arranged to mail printed material to St. Louis telephone operators informing them of the improved wages and conditions that had resulted from organization.[4] By June, about six hundred of the nine hundred operators employed by the Southwestern Bell Telephone Company in St. Louis had joined the union, organized as a sub-local of the IBEW. To protect the operators from dismissal by the company, WTUL officers Sarah Spraggon and Cynthelia Knefler, both allies, had been chosen as president and vice-president, respectively, of the operators' union.[5]

St. Louis appeared to offer favorable prospects for organizing because of the IBEW's considerable influence in the city, the strong central labor union, and the recently formed WTUL chapter. The IBEW had been a significant force in St. Louis since 1891, when an "exposition of electrical wonders" attended by electrical workers from across the country had led to the union's founding there. Established in 1908, the St. Louis WTUL only a year later claimed several hundred working women as members and a smaller number of allies. The League's contacts with working women, however, were largely limited to garment and bindery workers and waitresses.[6]

St. Louis telephone operators complained of low wages, long

hours, nervous strain, the necessity of using standardized phraseology, and an arbitrary system of promotion. Although Southwestern Bell claimed that daytime operators handled an average of only 150 to 200 calls an hour, the union insisted the correct figure was 400. A union operator explained to the St. Louis *Post-Dispatch* that promotion was made not according to seniority but on the basis of a system called the "roll of honor." The supervisor assigned each operator a monthly score based on her work performance. Only operators with nearly perfect scores qualified for raises after having served a specified period of time. Supervisors gave demerits for the smallest offenses, which lowered scores and made it impossible for many operators to qualify for raises. One operator reported, "When the subscriber calls I must say 'Number Please,' and if I omit the 'please' the supervisor gives me two demerit points, for a disconnection due to the cords getting tangled I get 5 demerit marks; for smiling, no matter what the provocation might be, 5 demerit marks; unnecessary remarks call for 5 demerits and connecting the wrong number costs 5 marks; repeating numbers too fast or too slow costs 2 points." The operator indicated that a "revision" of the roll of honor would be included in the union's demands, as well as permission for the operators to stand occasionally at the switchboard to allow "muscles to relax."[7]

This first effort to extend organization outside New England ended in failure, however, when Southwestern Bell forced a strike by discharging thirty women operators and twenty-seven telephone men.[8] The main issues in the strike were union recognition and the reinstatement of the workers discharged for union membership.[9] Although the strike, which involved both the operators and the telephone men, lasted seven weeks, the IBEW leadership accepted a settlement on the company's terms and then imposed it on the operators without permitting them to vote on it. In a letter to AT&T headquarters in New York, Eugene Sims, the first vice-president of Southwestern Bell, attributed the company's "complete victory" over the strikers largely to its having granted before the strike the concessions it believed it would be obliged to make if forced into arbitration. Because the company had increased wages significantly and promised the eight-hour day, it was able to convince much of the public, and many operators, that a union was unnecessary. As Nims informed AT&T, "We did not have to grant any concessions which would give the strike the semblance of having succeeded in accomplishing any good results for the operators."[10]

To the union's chagrin it learned, as it had in Boston, that in a strike it confronted not just the subsidiary company but AT&T as well. An AT&T vice-president was dispatched to St. Louis to supervise Southwestern Bell's effort to break the strike.[11] The company's vastly superior financial resources allowed it to present its side of the controversy to the public in large newspaper advertisements and to house strikebreakers in hotels.

After seven weeks, the IBEW leadership reached agreement with the company to end the strike. "Most" strikers, male and female, were to be reinstated without discrimination as to union membership, but the company did not accord union recognition. Although at least half of the striking operators opposed the terms, they were informed by James Noonan, organizer and later president of the IBEW, that there would be no ratification vote, since the IBEW constitution permitted the union executive board, composed of ten men, to settle a strike without one. The operators were irate and "hooted" Noonan when he addressed them, but to no avail. Sarah Spraggon, who claimed the right as president of the Telephone Operators' Union to vote on the executive board, cast the only ballot against the agreement. The telephone men were more amenable than the operators to the settlement, in part because it had been negotiated by their own representatives.[12] Refusing to reinstate a significant number of strikers, the company did not fully live up to the agreement, and many of the more militant operators refused to return to work under the terms of the settlement. The operators were not able to reorganize until 1919, when St. Louis became the first large midwestern city to affiliate with the Telephone Operators' Union.

Although the eight-hour day was introduced throughout the Bell System shortly after being conceded at Boston and St. Louis to inhibit further unionization, the Telephone Operators' Union began to emerge as a national organization during 1915 and 1916. The first operators' local outside Massachusetts was chartered in June, 1914, as Local 9A in Butte, Montana, where the operators had maintained almost continuous organization since 1902. This local was strong enough to win a closed-shop agreement and steady wage increases from the Mountain States Telephone Company (formerly the Rocky Mountain Telephone Company).[13] During 1915, the telephone operators' movement penetrated into the South, a region where trade unionism among women was almost unknown, as locals were formed in the Texas towns of Denison (Local 15A) and Port Arthur (Local 17A). Like Butte, these were towns where the male labor force was almost entirely unionized. According to the Texas State Federation of Labor, Denison, a major railroad center, was 100 percent organized, "both in railroads and other sectors," while Port Arthur, a lumber and oil center and gulf port, was 80 percent organized.[14]

The Texas locals remained isolated in a state where trade unionism was relatively weak and without a women's movement to provide encouragement and leadership training. Only the Denison local lasted for an appreciable length of time. The tiny local at Port Arthur was forced into a strike in November, 1916, when the Texas Long Lines Telephone Company refused to accord union recognition or grant a wage increase, and by 1919 it was disbanded.

The ten telephone operators at Port Arthur had been organized by the four male telephone workers in the town's IBEW local, who had learned through the union journal about the rise of operators' unionism. Until the IBEW men approached them, the telephone operators had been unaware of the struggles of women workers elsewhere in the country, and they had not considered organization as a means of improving their conditions. As Marguerite Weistroffer, the local's secretary, explained, "We did not understand the world as our fellow brothers did. . . . we were girls, and nothing but men in our town belonged to unions."[15]

The Port Arthur operators complained that their wages, which ranged from $18 to $36 a month, were not sufficient to allow them to dress "respectably" or eat properly. The company did not pay the operators for the first two to four months of employment and did not compensate them when they were sick.[16] According to Marguerite Weistroffer, company welfare measures such as the exchange rest room, where books, magazines, and a Victrola were provided for the operators' use, were no compensation for low wages and the fact that the company "worked the sap out of the girls." As in Boston, the operators at Port Arthur wanted no gifts from the company. Weistroffer voiced the position of union telephone operators everywhere: " . . . these are paid for by the profit the company makes out of the girls' low wages, and are really paid for by the girls themselves. Now wouldn't it be better if girls could draw wages that would enable them to have some of these nice things in their own homes, instead of just the privilege of using them as company property."[17]

The Port Arthur telephone operators' strike was directed by D. L. Goble, a male regional organizer for the IBEW. When the company imported strikebreakers from Waco to replace the operators, at $40–a–month wages, the four male telephone workers walked out in sympathy. Although Local 17A received strong backing from Port Arthur's trade unions, its members did not have the financial resources to survive a strike of long duration. Their experience was shared by many other locals during that period: "Local unions sprung up here and there, organized usually by locals of the Brotherhood. Some flourished for a while, improved conditions temporarily, had a strike perhaps, bequeathed us a little history of trade union effort and achievement, . . . and gave up the unequal struggle."[18]

In January, 1917, the telephone operators' movement became truly international when a local was organized at Winnipeg, Manitoba, the first of six to be established in Canada. The Winnipeg organization was one of the largest operators' locals in the IBEW, with 650 members, which it claimed represented 100 percent of the operators in the province of Manitoba. The local was able to maintain a full-time business agent and sent delegates to the 1917 IBEW convention at Atlantic City. In May, 1917, the Winnipeg local (31A) won a sizeable wage increase after a three-hour strike, which its secretary called "the most successful and thorough . . . ever pulled off in Canada."[19]

Despite such occasional successes, little progress was made organizing telephone operators outside New England until American entry into the war produced a climate more favorable to unionization. The IBEW considered organizing telephone operators such low priority that it appointed only one full-time organizer to be responsible for all of the United States and Canada. In much of the country, and not just the South, there was little awareness of women's trade unionism. WTUL chapters, which might provide valuable organizing assistance and help compensate for IBEW indifference, existed in only a handful of major cities. Operators attempting to organize also had to confront the unremitting hostility of the Bell companies. Julia O'Connor, one of the principal leaders of the Telephone Operators' Union, described the Bell policy toward the emerging telephone operators' locals as one of "extermination."[20]

The shortage of women organizers, resulting from the AFL's and IBEW's general lack of interest in women workers, meant that most organizing campaigns among telephone operators outside New England were directed by IBEW men. Men, however, faced serious difficulties in organizing women workers. Male organizers often tended to be condescending toward women, who in turn suspected they were being approached only to strengthen the bargaining position of the male telephone workers. The IBEW, after all, had no women officers and allowed women members little if any voice in the union. In St. Louis, the IBEW had forced striking telephone operators to accept an unfavorable settlement negotiated for them by male officials without permitting them to vote on it. Women were often uncomfortable discussing with men such subjects as sanitary conditions in the workplace or medical and rest-room facilities.

Labor organizers generally believed visiting with the worker at her/his home to be a more effective method of communication than talking at or near the workplace, where the worker was exposed to scrutiny by supervisory personnel or company informants. Yet it was difficult in many cases for a man to call on a woman at her home since she might fear loss of respectability from neighbors misconstruing the visit as a sexual encounter. Or the woman herself might not fully trust the intentions of a strange man. It was particularly difficult for a male organizer to see a woman worker who resided in a boardinghouse, where there were no family members to supervise the encounter or regulations prohibited entertaining guests of the other gender. This often necessitated talking on the street, always inconvenient and particularly so in inclement weather.

Telephone company officials sometimes exploited the qualms experienced by many operators' parents over this sort of male-female interaction. Because telephone operators tended to be very young, generally in their teens or early twenties and living with their families, they were often susceptible to parental influence in this matter. In St. Louis during a strike of operators and male telephone workers in 1919, for example, the Southwestern Bell Company tried to discredit the union leadership by framing male IBEW officials on a charge of sexually abusing female operators. A detective employed by the Bell Company as a labor spy, who had succeeded in establishing a false identity as an IBEW telephone worker, arranged a meeting between three male strike leaders, all in their thirties, and four young telephone operators at a restaurant outside St. Louis to discuss strike issues. While the meeting was in progress, Bell Company attorney Homer Hall appeared at the home of Jefferson Hess, father of seventeen-year-old Marguerite Hess, a member of the St. Louis Telephone Operators' Union executive board and one of the young women at the restaurant, and informed Hess that his daughter had been "abducted" by the union men. Hall then had the father swear out a complaint and the men were arrested, even though Marguerite Hess vehemently denied being abducted. Orville Jennings, one of the arrested IBEW men, angrily declared that the company's purpose was to discredit the union: "If it were shown that I were a bad character, then the mothers of other operators would forbid their daughters to have anything to do with the union."[21] That the encounter had been arranged by the company to defame the union leaders quickly became apparent. Marguerite Hess's father concluded, "I was too hasty. I now see this case as a frameup, made in the interest of the Bell Telephone Company. All I got out of it was embarrassing publicity for my daughter and her friends."[22]

Boston: Toward a Women's Union

The steady growth of the Boston Telephone Operators' Union and the leadership training and organizing experience many of its members gained in the Women's Trade Union League enabled the telephone operators to confront the IBEW leadership over its relative inattention to their needs and its unwillingness to extend to them the same rights accorded the male members. For several years, the operators waged a campaign for "equal rights" within the IBEW, which they consciously modeled on the women's suffrage movement. As a result of their efforts, the IBEW was restructured in 1918 to create a separate department for the telephone operators so that they would have full control over their own affairs. Although affiliated with the IBEW, the Telephone Operators' Department, as it was called, in effect constituted the country's first international union officered and controlled by women.

That the telephone operators could confidently demand equal rights with the men in the IBEW was due in part to the fact that they considered their status to be at least equal to that of the men in their industry. This was exceptional because, in nearly all industries which employed both women and men, women's lesser skill caused them to be perceived as having lower status. Telephone operating, of course, required less skill than the work of the telephone men. Yet it was generally regarded as a white-collar job, performed in street clothes in a clean, office-like environment, whereas telephone men were clearly blue collar, engaged in tasks that often made them dirty. The men worked with objects, repairing lines or splicing cables, while the operators interacted with persons who were usually middle or upper class. While the men were often viewed as uncouth, "cigar smoking" and "tobacco chewing," the telephone operators were portrayed by the telephone companies as "young ladies of refinement."[23] The operators were also more educated than the men. From the very beginning, the Boston operators drew attention to this fact as evidence of the unfairness of the IBEW policy of chartering them only as sub-locals, subsidiary to male locals.[24]

Experience Breeds Confidence

The experience of the Boston telephone operators in governing their huge local prepared them for their "suffrage fight" within the IBEW. Local 1A included nearly all Boston's operators during the first eight years of existence, and its membership increased as the operating force expanded, from 2,200 in 1913 to 3,000 by March, 1914, nearly 3,500 by the end of 1917, and 4,000 in 1919. Local 1A held annual elections to choose union officers, executive board members, adjustment board representatives, and delegates to the Boston Central Labor Union and the Massachusetts State Federation of Labor. Rank-and-file commitment to the local and participation in elections was exceedingly high. As one telephone operator who joined Local 1A in 1916 recalled,

> When you entered the company you were no sooner in than you were approached, either in the locker room, the dining room, the cafeteria, and asked to sign up in the union, and given a card, and paid your dues, and then notified of the monthly meetings. . . . there were very fine meetings, at that time at Wells Memorial Hall . . . and at election times I remember particularly there were so many members they'd be lined up down to the street, for two or three hours, you know, having a chance to vote.[25]

Never again would women workers attain the influence in the State Federation of Labor and the Boston Central Labor Union (CLU) that they possessed during the existence of Local 1A. Telephone operators constituted between 25 and 50 percent of female delegates to the State Federation of Labor conventions each year from 1914 to 1923. In no other industry, with the exception of boot and shoe in 1914 and 1916, did women even remotely approach this level of representation. Female delegates at the conventions ranged from 6 to 13 percent during this period, but they never surpassed 5 percent for the decade after the destruction of the Telephone Operators' Union in 1923.[26] Local 1A was represented at each biweekly meeting of the Boston CLU by a large delegation. Michael Murphy of the Stablemen's Union, a leading official of the CLU, attributed the selection of women to the executive boards of both the CLU and the State Federation of Labor to the power the telephone operators wielded in the labor movement: "The telephone [operators'] union is so strong that it demands attention, and they are going to receive it. There are now two women on the executive board of the Boston Central Labor Union and one on the executive board of the State Branch. . . ."[27]

An important source of strength for Local 1A was the stable

leadership it enjoyed during its formative years. Women's trade unions were seriously disadvantaged because their members' participation in the labor force was usually of short duration. Telephone operators at least did not suffer from seasonal unemployment, which affected most trades in which significant numbers of women were employed. The telephone company's policy of forcing operators who married to resign, however, was seriously disruptive. In June, 1913, only two months after the operators' victory in Boston, the local's press secretary, Alice Donovan, noted, "We are losing many of our members, the majority of which are charter members who have decided to join another union and divert their time to the art of domestic science."[28]

That the union held together in the early years owed much to the toll operators, who dominated its offices from 1912 to 1918. Because toll operators were drawn from among those who displayed particular ability at local operating, they were usually several years older than local operators. They were also more likely to be making telephone operating a career, since they would already have displayed job persistence and been willing to undergo additional training. Women expecting to be employed at telephone operating for a considerable length of time would tend to be more committed to trade unionism than those with only a short-term commitment to the job.

The toll operators were a particularly cohesive force because they were concentrated in a single exchange and viewed themselves as a distinct, highly skilled group. In 1915, the Boston toll exchange was the largest in the country devoted exclusively to handling toll calls, with the single exception of the Chicago Telephone Company's toll office. Boston ranked with New York as the leading center of toll traffic in the world. A staff of 32 supervisors and 281 operators handled 9,500 outbound and 19,000 inbound calls each day. By 1919, there were 50 supervisors and 450 operators.[29] That Boston was unusual even among major cities in having such a large toll office helps explain the almost unique success of its operators in maintaining organization for many years. The toll operators were the "aristocrats" of telephone operating, because their work required greater experience and proficiency than that of local operators and was considered more important by the company. Toll calls produced more revenue than local calls and tended to be made by the wealthier, business subscribers the company particularly valued. Toll operators could also "borrow prestige" as a result of their association with these subscribers.

The toll operators constituted a tightly knit faction during the entire existence of the union, although Local 1A remained relatively free of conflict in its early years. Their position was enhanced by prestige derived from having led the struggles of the first year. The "original twenty" who had gathered on the Boston Common in March, 1912, were venerated as the union's founders. A toll operator served as president from 1912 until 1918 and as vice-president until 1916. As president, Annie Molloy was unopposed in annual elections until 1916, when she was defeated by another toll operator, Mary Mahoney. It is not clear whether there were any issues dividing the two besides personality. The growing influence of operators at the local exchanges was reflected in the 1916 elections, in which Julia O'Connor, a local operator, was elected vice-president unopposed.[30]

Julia O'Connor (1890–1972) was the rising star in the union leadership, soon to head the national Telephone Operators' Department and direct the two major New England operators' strikes, in 1919 and 1923. From the time the Boston operators had first organized, she had been groomed for leadership by the Boston WTUL allies, who were drawn to her by her intelligence, writing ability, and refined manner. Henry Wise, lawyer for the Telephone Operators' Union in the early 1920s, described O'Connor as a "natural aristocrat"; his wife Pearl Katz Wise, office secretary of the Boston WTUL in the 1920s, stated that she "could have been a professor."[31] Born at Woburn, Massachusetts, the daughter of John, a leather currier and member of the Knights of Labor, and Sarah (Conneally) O'Connor, immigrants from Ireland, she became a telephone operator in Boston after graduating from high school in 1908. She joined the Boston Telephone Operators' Union as a charter member in 1912 and almost immediately attracted the attention of the allies who led the Boston WTUL. That year, the allies placed her on their organization's executive board. O'Connor served on the union's nine-woman bargaining committee during the 1913 near-strike, and she was an unsuccessful candidate for the first adjustment board. Her popularity with the allies led her to become the first working woman to attain the presidency of the Boston WTUL, an office she held from 1915 to 1918. The National WTUL, at the recommendation of the Boston chapter, in 1916 awarded O'Connor a scholarship to study at its training school in Chicago, a workers' education project to develop women labor leaders described in chapter 6. The prestige O'Connor gained within the Boston WTUL probably contributed to her narrow victory over Mary Mahoney for the presidency of Local 1A in 1918.

In backing O'Connor for the presidency of the Boston WTUL and favoring her with a scholarship to the training school, the allies ignored several telephone operators more prominent in the union leadership, such as Annie Molloy, Mary Meagher, and Mary Mahoney, who undoubtedly resented this. Molloy and Meagher, president and vice-president of the union respectively from 1912 to 1916, never served on the Boston WTUL executive board. Molloy's absence from the executive board is particularly striking. She was so prominent that she was one of the few working women selected for the U.S. delegation to the International Congress of Women at The Hague in 1915, a conference of women from neutral and belligerent countries called to protest the war and devise a strategy to effect an early peace. Emily Balch of Boston, one of many WTUL allies on the U.S. delegation, noted in 1915 that Annie Molloy was part of a faction in the Telephone Operators' Union opposed to the WTUL.[32] The strain between Molloy and the WTUL was probably due to her discomfort with the allies, who may have rejected her as uncultivated. Henry Wise described Molloy as a "roughneck" and "wildcat" who often "cursed" and "spit."[33]

The Boston telephone operators gained much confidence in the first years after their 1913 victory by effecting significant improvements in their working conditions and gaining wage increases without having to strike. Unionization greatly improved relations between operators and supervisors. Belonging to the same organization drew the two together, while setting both apart from the chief operator and assistant chief operator, viewed as representatives of management and therefore not eligible for union membership. The union, through the adjustment board, was able virtually to eliminate the physical abuse of operators by supervisory personnel, not uncommon in the pre-organization period. Assessing the influence of the adjustment board, Rose Finkelstein commented that "management's supervisors or the assistant chief operator (when you had a grievance they'd shout at you, or sometimes you were treated [roughly]—like they did my sister Anna, pulled the sleeve of her dress, and tear it) . . . were taught to talk in a civilized manner to the workers."[34]

The adjustment board also protected operators harassed by the company because of union activity. In the union's early years, management tried to find excuses to fire the more militant members. The most common excuse was "tardiness." Rose Finkelstein recalled that the company "called up to find out about my record, it seems, and my record had the times you were late."[35] In 1913, the company fired Julia O'Connor for coming in to work late, but the union, in a major grievance action, won her job back through the adjustment board.

The Boston operators also proved competent in collective bargaining. In 1915, they rejected the wage scale drawn up by the New

England Telephone Company, which called for a maximum wage of $12 a week after five years of service. The union, still largely influenced by toll operators concerned with the interests of employees with longer service, claimed that the wage scale discriminated against operators who had been working over five years. It countered with a demand for $13 after five years and $15 after seven years; it compromised at $14 after seven years.[36] In 1917 the union, under growing pressure from the local operators, attempted to reduce the period of service required to attain the maximum level to five years, with a maximum wage of $16. After weeks of bargaining, the company proposed $15 after six years. Determined to enforce the $16 demand, the union took a strike vote and on the eve of the strike settled for $16 after seven years.[37]

Although the union leadership considered the establishment of the eight-hour day to be one of its greatest achievements, it proved unable to reduce it further. One of the union's principal long-term objectives was the six-hour day, since it did not believe the work could be restructured to eliminate the intense nervous strain. This was the workday recommended by the Royal Commission which investigated the 1907 telephone operators' strike at Toronto. The union's press secretary Alice Donovan commented in 1913, "We should be able to secure at least a six hour day with an organization back of us, and even that is too much for an operator to work as statistics show the maximum an operator works is three years, and after that she is a nervous wreck."[38]

The WTUL Provides Support

The Boston telephone operators were prepared for their challenge to the IBEW leadership not only by administering the most influential women's union in New England, but by involvement in the Boston Women's Trade Union League as the largest working-class component. The WTUL provided a forum for leadership training. Local 1A members Julia O'Connor and Rose Sullivan served as president of the Boston WTUL—O'Connor from 1915 to 1918 and Sullivan from 1918 to 1919—and O'Connor, May Matthews, Mary Mahoney, and Rose Finkelstein were all on the Boston WTUL executive board in the 1910s.

No biographical information is available on Matthews or Mahoney, but Sullivan and Finkelstein both came from strongly prounion families. Rose Sullivan (1896–ca.1942), probably O'Connor's closest friend, was the daughter of a molder who was killed in a strike by a "hired thug." Her mother had been a member of a small union of tailoresses in Philadelphia during the 1880s. Sullivan was born in Boston and became a local telephone operator there about 1912.[39] Finkelstein (1891–1980), one of the very few Jewish telephone operators in Boston, was born near Kiev, Russia, and emigrated to the United States as a very young child. She worked the 5:00 P.M. to 11:00 P.M. shift while in high school and became a full-time local telephone operator when she left school in her senior year. A charter member of Local 1A, she attributed her commitment to trade unionism to her father, a tailor who continued to hold strong pro-union views even after becoming the owner of a small shop, and her grandfather. A dramatic confrontation between her grandfather and an uncle, her father's business partner who opposed the unionization of the shop, which occurred when she was a child, left a deep impression on her: "So one day my grandfather, Moshe Yankel, who was a very pious man, came up to the shop. He had heard that his son Louis was anti-labor. Before all the workers, he quoted from the Torah that there should be one day of rest in seven, and that the worker must be treated right, and then he gave his son a good slap across the face. And he told him that he musn't oppose the union. So that's when it became a union shop."[40]

The WTUL introduced telephone operators to women's rights by drawing them into the women's suffrage movement. The WTUL established its own Suffrage Department by 1908 and devoted considerable attention to gaining the vote for women. As the principal liaison between the women's movement and the labor movement, the WTUL induced suffragists to give high priority to recruiting women workers. Dramatizing their new solidarity with the working woman, several prominent middle- and upper-class suffrage leaders openly performed strike support work during New York's "Uprising of the 20,000" in 1909. From 1909, the WTUL and the National American Woman Suffrage Association (NAWSA) exchanged delegates to their national conventions, and the WTUL encouraged working women to participate in NAWSA rallies and parades. Because many working women were uncomfortable in NAWSA, which was dominated by middle- and upper-class women, the WTUL also helped establish independent "wage-earners'" suffrage leagues.[41]

The Boston WTUL allies helped to make the Massachusetts suffrage movement one of the most vigorous in the country during the 1910s. In the years immediately preceding the unionization of Boston's telephone operators, the Massachusetts Woman Suffrage Association (MWSA), one of the largest state suffrage organizations, had begun to employ militant tactics drawn from the English movement, such as open-air meetings and quizzing politicians on their suffrage views at public rallies.[42] Boston WTUL allies Susan Fitzgerald, who led the first open-air meetings in Massachusetts in 1909–10, Anne Withington, Mary Caroline Crawford, Mabel Gillespie, Emily Greene Balch, Ida Ripley, Lois Rantoul, and Elizabeth Glendower Evans were all leaders of the MWSA. Mabel Gillespie and Susan Fitzgerald were also officers of the Massachusetts Political Equality Union, which was organized in 1912 to secure the vote for women and appealed primarily to "working men and women, and those interested in industrial problems."[43] Margaret Foley, a member of the Boston WTUL executive board and an organizer for the MWSA from 1906 to 1915, umpired a baseball game played between rival teams from the Boston Telephone Operators' Union at an outing for the union's Peter Linehan Memorial Fund.[44]

As early as 1913, women's suffragists spoke at Local 1A's monthly business meetings and invited telephone operators to actively participate in the movement.[45] Many telephone operators became prominent in the women's suffrage movement, including Annie Molloy, whose speech at a mass meeting at Faneuil Hall in December, 1913, on "Why the Wage Earning Woman Wants the Vote" was the first of many she delivered in behalf of women's suffrage; May Matthews, a member of the National WTUL's six-woman suffrage committee; and Julia O'Connor, part of the Wage Women's Wedge, a group of working women who toured Massachusetts by automobile campaigning for the suffrage in the week before the state referendum in late 1915.[46]

The WTUL also drew telephone operators into campaigns to organize women in other occupations neglected by male trade unionists, which made them even more sensitive to the treatment of women. During 1913 and 1914, the telephone operators joined WTUL organizing drives among candy workers, women and girls who worked at newsstands, and office-building cleaners. These campaigns sometimes led to friction between the WTUL and male trade unionists, which added to the telephone operators' uneasiness about male domination.

In 1915, the WTUL openly denounced the AFL as condescending and undependable because it had mishandled an organizing drive among women candy workers. After the Boston WTUL had established a local of candy makers following a strike in 1913, the AFL had intervened and insisted that it assume control of organizing. The AFL assigned a male unionist, a cigar maker, to direct all further organizing of candy makers. Even though the WTUL leaders were deeply upset by this action, they did their best to assist the AFL man and turned over their list of members and contacts. While the AFL man depended on the WTUL for advice and assistance with such tasks as addressing notices, he would not hold meetings in the WTUL building and instead used another hall. The drive was a miserable failure. WTUL Secretary Mabel Gillespie bitterly condemned the AFL for its behavior during the campaign: "We could have told them from the beginning it was hopeless. If they had helped us the year before there was a chance of doing something. . . . We organized them, did all the work and the girls won a victory while they [the AFL] looked on. If they had stepped in then we might have had an organization that would have lasted. Then after they failed they said: 'It is no use, we cannot organize women.' "[47]

The Boston WTUL also assisted the telephone operators in advancing their interests as women in the labor movement by sponsoring a broad program of social and educational activities. These activities were designed to teach administrative skills and to overcome feelings of inadequacy in young women having to interact, often in confrontational situations, with more experienced, middle-aged male management and trade union officials. In addition, they generated enthusiasm and drew the operators closer to each other. Membership in the WTUL in itself helped to develop self-assertion in young working women by involving them in a women's organization where they could discuss labor issues, chair meetings, and elect women officers without men assisting them.[48] From 1909 on, working women comprised a majority on the Boston WTUL executive board. Whereas union halls, filled with cigar smoke and spittoons, remained institutions of male culture, the WTUL headquarters provided a space where women could feel comfortable and welcome.[49]

The Boston WTUL expected to give young working women "gay times" as well as to teach them about trade union issues and administration. Referring in its 1913 biennial report to the "festive spirit" which had characterized its activities of the past two years, it commented, "We have danced more and played more of late in spite of the fact that we have had bigger and more engrossing affairs on our hands."[50] The social and educational activities provided by the Boston WTUL included entertainment for working women, lectures and debates on labor issues, and outings to Wellesley College, where allies Emily Balch and Vida Scudder were professors, and to the countryside. Sometimes all these activities were combined in one day, as in September, 1914, when WTUL members followed Paul Revere's route in a caravan of automobiles from Boston to Concord, where they were served tea by a group of suffragists. On the way, they stopped at the Louisa Alcott house, home of the author of *Little Women*, where Mabel Gillespie had lived as a girl. Returning back to Boston by way of Walden Pond, the party assembled for a banquet at WTUL headquarters. Speakers at the banquet included Anne Withington, who, having just returned from the war-torn countries of Europe, described the "horrors of war" and emphasized that "the working peoples of the world have no quarrel"; Annie Molloy, president of the Telephone Operators' Union and Anna Bowen of the Tobacco Strippers' Union, who discussed the need for solidarity among working women; and ally Susan Fitzgerald, who told of the advance of the suffrage movement.[51]

From the very beginning, the Boston Telephone Operators' Union placed heavy emphasis on social activities, although its orientation, unlike the WTUL's, was more heterosocial than homosocial. That the WTUL approach was homosocial was due to the heavy influence of the allies, most of them middle-aged, often unmarried women educated at women's colleges in the 1880s and 1890s.[52] The telephone operators, by contrast, while employed in an all-women's work environment which encouraged homosocial ties, were women in their teens and early twenties, educated in coeducational high schools and drawn to the heterosocial youth culture and flapper pleasure-seeking ethic of the 1910s. Beginning in November, 1912, the Boston Telephone Operators' Union held two meetings a month, the first devoted to union business and the second to social and educational affairs.

That same month, the Boston Telephone Operators' Union put on its first "grand ball," attended by two thousand people. Many of them were prominent in state and city government and labor circles— including the governor of Massachusetts, the mayor of Boston, the entire Boston city council, and several state senators—testifying to the fact that the telephone operators had already become a highly influential and well-publicized force in Boston less than a year after they had organized. The hall was decorated with electric lights set up by male members of the IBEW. In calling their dance a "grand ball," scheduling it in November at the beginning of the Brahmins' social season, and inviting such distinguished guests, the telephone operators were making it clear that working people deserved to share in the "high life" of the consumer-oriented, early twentieth-century metropolis. The grand ball yielded $1,000 for the new union's sick-fund. The union's press secretary, Alice Donovan, summed it up as a "most brilliant and successful social affair."[53] The November grand ball was held again the next year and became an annual event for the Boston Telephone Operators' Union. The union also began an annual "May party" in 1913, which included a dance, with proceeds used to finance sending delegates to the IBEW convention. In addition, it sponsored a midsummer boat excursion "down harbor" to a resort, where the operators held a dance.[54]

As the Telephone Operators' Union expanded and gained experience in trade union administration and negotiations with management, its relationship to the Boston WTUL changed significantly. To be sure, the Telephone Operators' Union continued to rely on the WTUL for leadership training. But the union's victory in the Boston near-strike of 1913 established it as a major presence in its own right in Boston's labor movement; it was no longer the junior partner of the WTUL. The Telephone Operators' Union required no assistance from the WTUL in conducting its two New England strikes in 1919 and 1923. As the largest working-class component of the Boston WTUL, the Telephone Operators' Union exerted considerable influence within it. Most important, it ensured that the Boston WTUL's primary focus always remained union organizing.

The contention of such historians as William Chafe and Nancy Shrom Dye that the WTUL shifted its focus after 1913 from organizing to legislative reform does not hold for the Boston chapter.[55] In fact, the Boston WTUL's emphasis on union organizing increased as the allies began relinquishing control of the League to working women in 1915, when Julia O'Connor became president. Local 1A was primarily responsible for the sharp rise in the Boston WTUL's working-class membership. It brought into the League not only large numbers of telephone operators but also working women in other trades recruited through WTUL organizing drives in which telephone operators participated. It is true the allies placed less emphasis on organizing than the working women did, since the allies generally had no job experience and their education and social position often led them to embrace other reform causes and issues. Most of the allies in the Boston WTUL had travelled extensively in Europe and were very attentive to the peace issue after the outbreak of the European war in 1914. Working-class leaders such as Annie Molloy and Julia O'Connor of the Telephone Operators' Union were also deeply committed peace activists, but their involvement with this cause stemmed, at least in part, from their contact with the allies.

Nonetheless, even during the early 1920s, when union membership in most trades dropped sharply and little organizing took place, the leaders of the Boston WTUL continually reiterated that organizing was their first priority. Mabel Gillespie acknowledged in 1922 that organizing had been difficult since 1918. Noting that the legislature met in Boston, the state capital, she commented, "We have a great temptation in Boston to devote considerable time to legislative work." She stressed, however, that "it was a temptation . . . that must be resisted. . . ."[56] Julia O'Connor vehemently insisted that the National WTUL devote its full energy to organizing and eliminate any activities that interfered with this work: "I refer to legislation, to outlawry of war, to quasi-civic matters generally, and even to education." She declared, "I should like to see the National League eternally concentrating on one objective, trade union organizing among women. . . . Ours is the only machine in existence in America committed definitely to this purpose. . . . we are not being wholly true to our heritage and tradition while we fail to make it the major purpose of our organization existence."[57]

The Struggle for Equal Rights within the IBEW

From the time they were organized, the telephone operators pressed for equal rights within the IBEW and identified their struggle with the larger campaign for women's suffrage. The IBEW had made little attempt to organize women workers until 1911. By that time the IBEW leadership perceived that, if the IBEW were to exercise significant influence in the electrical manufacturing industry, it would be necessary to admit women, since in some plants they constituted as much as 60 percent of the work force. The IBEW, however, restricted the power of women workers in the union by chartering them as sub-locals subsidiary to a male local. The provision for women to be admitted only in sub-locals was originally devised for workers in the electrical shops, but it was applied to the telephone operators when they were organized in 1912. The Boston Telephone Operators' Union was chartered as sub-local 1 of the linemen's Local 104.[58]

The prejudice against women members in the IBEW stemmed not just from sexism and the craftsman's disdain for the unskilled and semiskilled worker but also from concern that they would influence jurisdictional disputes between the IBEW's two major components, the "inside" and "outside" electrical workers, which had long plagued the union. This matter was highly important since awarding jurisdiction over work to one group deprived the other of the opportunity of being employed at it. The intensity of jurisdictional conflict caused the Brotherhood in 1903 to classify the membership into three distinct groups: (1) the "inside" men (also called wiremen), who were employed largely in the building trades and mainly worked inside buildings; (2) the "outside" men (including telephone linemen, cable splicers, installers, and repairmen), who were involved in such tasks as constructing pole-lines for telephone, telegraph, power, and signal purposes and worked almost entirely outdoors; and (3) shop electrical workers, who assembled and repaired electrical machines, switchboards, panel boards, and all electrical apparatus manufactured in the shop.[59]

The suffrage fight within the IBEW began in September, 1913, at the union's twelfth biennial convention in Boston, the first to be attended by telephone operators. Opposition to the admission of the three telephone operators' sub-locals from Boston, Lynn, and Springfield immediately developed, allegedly because they did not belong in an organization of skilled mechanics. More important, however, was the fear that the operators might attain numerical superiority and impose "petticoat rule" or at least interfere in jurisdictional disputes among the male members. Not even a year and a half old, the Boston Telephone Operators' Union had a membership of 2,500. It constituted the third largest local (although technically a sub-local) in the IBEW, and it was four times as large as the linemen's local to which it was subsidiary. Since the IBEW constitution defined the union's jurisdiction as "all persons engaged in the manufacture, installation, and *operation* of all electrical devices," the telephone operators were clearly entitled to membership. The convention therefore decided to seat the telephone operators' delegates but did not permit them to vote, although many male delegates objected that this constituted "taxation without representation" since the operators' locals paid exactly the same per capita dues as the male locals.[60]

The convention further refused to extend equal rights to the operators' locals by granting them only half representation and voting strength for future conventions and referendums. Perhaps impressed that a large proportion of the Boston operators were high school graduates, the convention passed a law providing for the direct chartering of the telephone operators' locals with a per capita tax approximately half that of the male locals. It overwhelmingly defeated a resolution to charter them in an ambiguous auxiliary form under the supervision of a man. Because wages for telephone operators were considerably lower than those for male electrical workers, the operators were satisfied with the dues rate but expressed concern that it appeared to impose a property qualification on voting rights. The operators were irate, however, that the convention prohibited them from holding any office in the international.

The "Votes for Telephone Girls" campaign gathered momentum, and in 1915 the operators emerged from the IBEW's thirteenth biennial convention in St. Paul with full suffrage: "one woman, one vote." However, the entire acts of the convention were defeated in the referendum, although had the members been able to vote separately on the question of voting rights for the telephone operators, the complete enfranchisement of the operators would have been ratified. The operators' locals then initiated a successful campaign for a constitutional amendment granting full representation and full vote, and operators' delegates went to the fourteenth biennial convention in Atlantic City in 1917 with full voting strength. At Atlantic City, the first IBEW convention attended by operators' delegates from outside New England, the operators and women in the electrical manufacturing industry were given representation at large on the union's executive board, but they immediately lost it when the acts of the convention were again voted down by the general membership.[61]

Powerful elements within the IBEW increasingly resented the ascendancy of the telephone operators. In early 1918, the "inside" electrical men, concerned that the operators were supporting the "outside" men in jurisdictional matters, joined with an IBEW leadership agitated about the wartime militancy of telephone operators (discussed in the next chapter) to curtail the influence of the operators in the union. By this time about 10,000 of the IBEW's 85,000 members were telephone operators.[62]

Michael A. Mulcaire, writing from the perspective of the union leadership, stated in his 1923 study of the IBEW, "A large majority of the members were of the opinion that the operators had been casting their votes as a block upon the most serious questions involving the various branches of the trade without regard to the merits of the matters at issue, without even an understanding of the rights of either party, and in such a way as to create confusion, difficulty, and embarrassment."[63] Mulcaire concluded that "it was necessary to take steps whereby the operators would no longer be able to exercise their influence in the IBEW."[64] Mary Quinn, a telephone operators' delegate to the IBEW conventions at Boston, St. Paul, and Atlantic City, agreed that by 1918 the union's leadership had determined to deprive the operators of any influence in the affairs of the international: "They wanted to get rid of us. . . . let's be honest about it!"[65]

As a result, the IBEW leadership in April, 1918, submitted for referendum an amendment to the union constitution that would establish a separate department "under the protection of the Brotherhood" to be known as the Telephone Operators' Department of the

IBEW. This amendment was ratified, and the operators' locals were instructed to send representatives to a convention in Buffalo, New York, scheduled for August 15, 1918.[66] The telephone operators regarded the amendment as divesting them of their right to participate in the deliberations of the IBEW either in convention or referendum while still requiring them to submit to IBEW laws, and they immediately challenged it in court. The powers, functions, and purpose of the Telephone Operators' Department as outlined in a prospectus issued by the IBEW leadership were so ambiguous that the operators feared the leadership planned to retain political and financial control of the Class A locals. Local 1A secured a temporary restraining order from a justice of the Massachusetts Supreme Court, who ruled that the IBEW had no right practically to expel a group of locals who were obeying its laws and whose rights to membership were firmly established in the constitution.[67]

At the Buffalo convention, which the operators' delegates attended under protest, a constitution was adopted providing the Telephone Operators' Department with "full authority for separate self-government" and full control over finances.[68] Acting IBEW President Noonan rejected the constitution on the grounds that it was inconsistent with the laws of the Brotherhood, but he reversed himself after lengthy negotiations and granted complete self-government and financial control to the Telephone Operators' Department. As a result of this action, representatives of telephone operators' locals voted to accept the Telephone Operators' Department and abandon legal action against it. A constitution similar to the one originally rejected by Noonan was ratified by an overwhelming vote of the operators' locals; the result, announced on November 30, 1918, indicated 4,486 were in favor and 95 opposed.[69] The Department could hold its own separate biennial convention, elect its own officers, and conduct its own referendums. The Department could also order telephone operators' strikes and settle them without the approval of the IBEW executive board.[70]

The Telephone Operators' Department of the IBEW began actual operation in January, 1919. It was, in effect, the only international union directed by and composed wholly of women.[71] Exactly a hundred locals had been chartered by the IBEW during a period of nearly seven years.[72] Until 1919, the IBEW had received all dues and other remittances from these operators' locals, but in 1919 the finances were transferred to the Telephone Operators' Department, whose headquarters were established in Boston. Julia O'Connor— who in 1918 had become president of Local 1A, the country's largest operators' local—was elected president of the Telephone Operators' Department, a post she held as long as the Department existed. She did not stand for reelection as president of Local 1A in 1920, but she did remain on its executive board. May Matthews, financial secretary of Local 1A, became the Department's secretary.

Conclusion

The stability of Boston's Local 1A permitted telephone operators' unionism to emerge as a national—even international—movement in the years immediately preceding World War I, and it provided the basis for the operators' successful challenge to the IBEW leadership. Local 1A's ability to secure improvements in wages and working conditions resulted in a marked increase in job persistence; by 1920, the average length of an operator's service in Boston was five years, easily the longest in the country and about two years more than for operators in the Bell System as a whole.[73] Local 1A was thus able to avoid the severe disruption caused by labor turnover suffered by nearly all women's trade unions, even in the telephone service where seasonal unemployment did not occur. The large and well-knit group of toll operators, whose job persistence was the greatest of any in Boston's operating force, provided an additional source of stability. Having established a strong base in Boston, highly motivated operators contributed their free time to organizing in adjacent districts. Their efforts compensated for the lack of assistance from the IBEW, which provided the operators with only one full-time organizer. As a result, by 1917 nearly all of Massachusetts's operators had been unionized, and locals had been formed as well in Maine's three largest cities, Portland, Lewiston, and Bangor. The formidable resources of the Bell System and the IBEW's weak commitment, however, made it difficult to extend organization much beyond New England, although locals were established in the South, the West, and even Canada.

The considerable administrative experience gained by the Boston operators during the prewar years, and the confidence they derived from their successes in collective bargaining, had by 1918 prepared them to lead a national women's trade union. The Boston WTUL and the city's long tradition of women's labor activism encouraged their self-reliance, preventing them from falling into dependency on male trade unionists. Local 1A's social programs stimulated an unusually high level of rank-and-file involvement in the union, and they helped the operators develop a sense of themselves as a group with common interests within the labor movement. The operators' experience in the women's suffrage movement proved especially valuable in enabling them to confront the IBEW leadership and establish control of their own organization. As American entry into the war improved labor's prospects for organizing, the telephone operators appeared to be in a position to establish a truly national union. But the upheavals of war created disorienting new conditions that for a time threatened telephone operators' unionism, even in its Boston stronghold.

NOTES

1. Christopher Tomlins, "AFL Unions in the 1930s: Their Performance in Historical Perspective," *Journal of American History* 65 (March, 1979):1030.
2. Mary Quinn Wynne, interview by Stephen H. Norwood, Springfield, Mass., June 28, 1974.
3. Paul Thompson, *The Edwardians* (Bloomington: Indiana University Press, 1975), pp. 78, 80.
4. Eugene Nims to H. B. Thayer, August 23, 1913, Box 2018, AT&T Archives, New York, N.Y.
5. St. Louis *Post-Dispatch*, May 11 and June 17, 1913.
6. Minutes of Executive Board Meeting, National Women's Trade Union League [hereafter, WTUL], Chicago, March 18, 1909, Box 1, National WTUL Papers, Library of Congress, Washington, D.C.
7. St. Louis *Post-Dispatch*, May 15 and 18, 1913.
8. "Telephone Operators' Strike," *Life and Labor*, August, 1913, p. 239; Nims to Thayer, August 23, 1913.
9. "Telephone Operators' Strike," p. 239.
10. Nims to Thayer, August 23, 1913.
11. Letter from Alice J. Donovan, *Journal of Electrical Workers and Operators* [hereafter *JEWO*], August, 1913, p. 1094.
12. St. Louis *Post-Dispatch*, August 5 and 6, 1913.
13. Julia O'Connor, "History of the Organized Telephone Operators' Movement," Part 2, *Union Telephone Operator* [hereafter, *UTO*], February, 1921, p. 16; "Around the Circuit," *JEWO*, September, 1916, pp. 102–3.
14. Texas State Federation of Labor, *Proceedings of Eighteenth Annual Convention* (Austin: Texas State Federation of Labor, 1915), p. 118, and *Proceedings of Twentieth Annual Convention* (Austin: Texas State Federation of Labor, 1917), p. 107.
15. Letter from Marguerite Weistroffer, *JEWO*, December, 1916, p. 334.
16. Ibid., p. 336.
17. Letter from Marguerite Weistroffer, *JEWO*, February, 1917, p. 460.

18. O'Connor, "History," Part 3, *UTO*, March, 1921, p. 14.

19. Letter from Janet Castle, *JEWO*, October, 1917, p. 144.

20. O'Connor, "History," Part 3, p. 14.

21. St. Louis *Post-Dispatch*, June 24, 1919.

22. Ibid., July 2, 1919.

23. John Schacht, *The Making of Telephone Unionism* (New Brunswick, N.J.: Rutgers University Press, 1985), p. 83.

24. Alice J. Donovan, "Description of Boston Telephone Operators' Troubles," *JEWO*, May, 1913, p. 942; Letter from Alice J. Donovan, *JEWO*, August, 1913, p. 1095.

25. Clare Moriarty [pseudonym], interview by Stephen H. Norwood, Boston, Mass., June 12, 1974.

26. Massachusetts State Federation of Labor, *Proceedings of the Annual Conventions, 1914–1923* (Worcester: Massachusetts State Federation of Labor), on microfiche, AFL-CIO Library, Washington, D.C.

27. Boston *Daily Advertiser*, April 27, 1919.

28. Letter from Alice J. Donovan, *JEWO*, June, 1913, p. 984.

29. "Concerning the Boston Toll Office," *New England Telephone Topics* [hereafter, *NETT*], April, 1915, p. 20; Ned C. Loud, "A Glimpse of the Boston Toll Office," *NETT*, September, 1919, p. 105.

30. Boston *Globe*, June 24, 1916.

31. Henry Wise, interview by Stephen H. Norwood, Boston, Mass., December 4, 1980; Pearl Katz Wise, interview by Stephen H. Norwood, Boston, Mass., September 27, 1980.

32. Emily Balch, "Notes: Journal of a Trip Abroad 1915," April 13, 1915, Box 6, Emily Balch Papers, Swarthmore College, Swarthmore, Pa.

33. Henry Wise, interview.

34. Rose Finkelstein Norwood, interview by Stephen H. Norwood, Boston, Mass., July 18, 1974.

35. Rose Finkelstein Norwood, interview by Brigid O'Farrell, Boston, Mass., [1977], Rose Finkelstein Norwood Papers, Schlesinger Library, Radcliffe College, Cambridge, Mass.

36. Boston *Globe*, December 11, 1915.

37. *Boston Labor World*, January 5, 1918.

38. Letter from Alice J. Donovan, *JEWO*, June, 1913, p. 983.

39. "Address of Miss Rose Sullivan," in Illinois State Federation of Labor, *Proceedings of the Thirty-eighth Annual Convention* (Chicago: Illinois State Federation of Labor, 1920), p. 106; "Address of Miss Rose Sullivan," in Illinois State Federation of Labor, *Proceedings of Thirty-ninth Annual Convention* (Chicago: Illinois State Federation of Labor, 1921), p. 345.

40. Rose Finkelstein Norwood, interview by Stephen H. Norwood, Boston, Mass., May 2, 1975.

41. Robin Miller Jacoby, "The Women's Trade Union League and American Feminism," in Milton Cantor and Bruce Laurie, eds., *Class, Sex, and the Woman Worker* (Westport, Conn.: Greenwood Press, 1977), pp. 214–15.

42. Sharon Hartman Strom, "Leadership and Tactics in the American Woman Suffrage Movement: A New Perspective from Massachusetts," *Journal of American History* 62 (September, 1975):307, 313.

43. Brochure entitled "Massachusetts Political Equality Union," January, 1916, Massachusetts Political Equality Union Collection, Schlesinger Library; *Boston Teachers' News Letter*, January, 1913, p. 12.

44. Boston *Post*, June 13, 1914.

45. Boston *Globe*, December 13, 1913.

46. Ibid., December 17, 1913, and October 25, 1915; Letter from Ethel Hyman, *JEWO*, March, 1915, p. 190.

47. National WTUL, "Proceedings of the 1915 Convention," pp. 185–86, Reel 21, National WTUL Papers.

48. Nancy Shrom Dye, *As Equals and as Sisters* (Columbia: University of Missouri Press, 1980), p. 70.

49. Nancy McLean, "The Culture of Resistance: Female Institution Building in the International Ladies' Garment Workers' Union, 1905–1925," *Michigan Occasional Papers in Women's Studies*, no. 21 (Winter, 1982):42.

50. "Secretary's Report, Boston Women's Trade Union League," Biennial Convention, National WTUL, 1913, p. 8, WTUL Smaller Collections Reel, Schlesinger Library.

51. "Boston," *Life and Labor*, November, 1914, p. 344.

52. For example, of the Boston WTUL allies, Emily Balch graduated with the first class at Bryn Mawr College in 1889; Susan Fitzgerald graduated from Bryn Mawr College in 1893; Mary Caroline Crawford graduated from Radcliffe College in 1898; Mabel Gillespie studied at Radcliffe College from 1898 to 1900; and Sue Ainslee Clark graduated from Wellesley College in 1903.

53. Letter from Alice J. Donovan, *JEWO*, December, 1912, p. 696.

54. Donovan, "Description," p. 942; Letter from Alice J. Donovan, *JEWO*, June, 1913, p. 984; *JEWO*, November, 1913, p. 1133; Boston *Post*, May 21, 1914.

55. Dye, *As Equals*, passim.; William Chafe, *The American Woman* (New York: Oxford University Press, 1972), pp. 70–76.
  Nor does this contention hold for the Chicago chapter, according to Colette Hyman and Elizabeth Anne Payne. See Colette Hyman, "Labor Organizing and Female Institution-Building: The Chicago Women's Trade Union League, 1904–1924," in Ruth Milkman, ed., *Women, Work, and Protest* (Boston: Routledge and Kegan Paul, 1985), p. 25, and Elizabeth Anne Payne, *Reform, Labor, and Feminism* (Urbana: University of Illinois Press, 1988), p. 99.

56. National WTUL, "Proceedings of the 1922 Convention," p. 616, Reel 22, National WTUL Papers.

57. Julia O'Connor to Elizabeth Christman, March 14, 1925, New York WTUL Papers, New York State Department of Labor Library, New York, N.Y.

58. O'Connor, "History," Part 3, p. 15.

59. Michael A. Mulcaire, *The International Brotherhood of Electrical Workers* (Washington, D.C.: University Press, 1923), pp. 27–28.

60. O'Connor, "History," Part 3, p. 15.

61. Ibid., pp. 16–17; "Votes for Telephone Girls," *Life and Labor,* November, 1915, p. 173.

62. *JEWO,* September, 1918, p. 80.

63. Mulcaire, *International Brotherhood,* p. 34.

64. Ibid., p. 35.

65. Mary Quinn Wynne, interview.

66. O'Connor, "History," Part 3, p. 17.

67. Ibid.; *JEWO,* September, 1918, p. 79.

68. "Proposed Constitution of the Telephone Operators' Department," Julia O'Connor Parker Papers, Schlesinger Library.

69. O'Connor, "History," Part 3, p. 19.

70. "Proposed Constitution of the Telephone Operators' Department."

71. Agnes Burns, "Telephone Operators Hold First Convention," *Life and Labor,* November, 1919, p. 286.

72. O'Connor, "History," Part 3, p. 19.

73. Julia O'Connor to Marjorie White, December 2, 1920, Julia O'Connor Parker Papers.

5

The State against the Telephone Operator

The War and Its Aftermath, 1917–19

Telephone operators' unionism attained its greatest strength during and immediately after the period of U.S. participation in World War I. Workers throughout industry gained a new sense of power as wartime full employment greatly increased their ability to win strikes and improve their conditions of employment. The Wilson administration's relatively friendly disposition toward the American Federation of Labor (AFL) and the trade unions' increased leverage due to the tight labor market allowed the AFL to expand considerably during the war. Pledging its assistance to the federal government in the prosecution of the war effort, the AFL gained representation on federal agencies determining and administering national defense policies. As a result of its participation in such agencies as the Council on National Defense and the National War Labor Board (NWLB), the AFL enjoyed an unprecedented level of prestige. Union membership rose dramatically, from 2.8 million in 1916 to over 4 million in 1919, and at least three-quarters of the total affiliated with the AFL. Having entered the work force in unprecedented numbers as a result of the labor shortage created by war mobilization, women participated in this surge of union growth. Major organizing successes among women workers occurred in the garment, textile, and shoe industries as well as in the telephone service. Women's new assertiveness in the workplace was made possible in part by the confidence and self-esteem they derived from the public's unequivocal support for their contribution to the national war effort.[1]

The Wilson administration was the first to maintain a regular and systematic relationship with organized labor, allowing it direct access to the White House and cabinet. Although deeply hostile to the radical wing of the labor movement, the Wilson administration devoted serious attention to the views of the AFL leadership. President Wilson staffed the new Department of Labor, established in 1913, largely with persons sympathetic to labor, many of them drawn from the trade unions. President Wilson appointed as secretary of labor William B. Wilson, a former secretary-treasurer of the United Mine Workers' Union, who considered himself a partisan of trade unionism.[2] The Wilson administration in 1916 supported the Adamson Act, which provided the eight-hour day for railroad workers. Woodrow Wilson addressed the AFL convention at Buffalo in November, 1917, the first president to so honor the labor movement.[3]

Because the government above all needed uninterrupted production during wartime, it often exerted its influence on behalf of wage increases and improved working conditions. It hoped in this way to reduce labor turnover and prevent work stoppages. But despite its relatively congenial relationship with the AFL, the Wilson administration was not prepared to fundamentally alter labor-management relations, since war production would suffer if business were seriously antagonized. While encouraging workers to organize, it did not require employers to bargain collectively. When the government established the National War Labor Board in 1918 to help settle industrial disputes, it made clear that, while management was not to interfere with organizing or to discriminate against union members, trade unions were prohibited from doing anything "to induce employers to bargain or deal with them." The president informed the NWLB that the open shop "shall not be deemed a grievance" where it was already in practice. Nor could trade unions require workers to become members.[4]

The Wilson administration never pursued a consistent labor policy, even during wartime. Wide variations existed in the approaches of different cabinet departments. While the Labor and War departments generally favored trade unionism, the Commerce, Agriculture, Justice, and Post Office departments sympathized with open-shop principles.[5] During the war, the federal government increasingly interceded in labor-management relations, to the great benefit of workers in some sectors of the economy, such as the railroad industry. However, among workers in the telephone service, over which the federal government assumed control in 1918, this intercession created intense discontent. The Post Office Department, which was assigned jurisdiction over the telephone service under government control, not only was completely unresponsive to the telephone operators' demands for wage increases but was strongly hostile to trade unionism. For the telephone operators, according to Julia O'Connor, the period of government control was "literally a reign of terror."[6] In the confusion that prevailed under government control, with telephone workers unable to gain a hearing for their wage demands or other grievances concerning working conditions, large numbers of operators proved receptive to unionization.

Despite the AFL's effort to cooperate with management in the interest of wartime production, the rapid increase in the cost of living after the outbreak of the war in Europe precipitated considerable labor unrest. In 1917, 4,450 strikes broke out, the highest number until then in American history.[7] When the United States entered the war in 1917, prices were about 70 percent above the average of 1913, and they rose another 100 percent over the prewar averages in 1918.[8] Although real wages rose by as much as 20 percent over the prewar levels in the most heavily unionized sectors—coal mining, manufacturing, and transportation—the telephone companies were determined to maintain the prewar wage levels. Labor turnover, always a serious problem in the telephone industry, increased enormously as work became available in the relatively high-wage, war-related industries and as the shortage of male workers created new job opportunities for women.[9]

During 1917, several strikes occurred among telephone operators. The most important involved both male and female telephone workers in the Pacific Northwest. This section had a high rate of unionization and a tradition of labor militancy in its major industries, lumber and shipbuilding. The male telephone workers, organized in the International Brotherhood of Electrical Workers (IBEW), had for several years enjoyed collective bargaining relations with the Pacific Telephone Company. The first telephone operators' local in the Northwest was formed at Aberdeen, Washington, as IBEW local 38A, in the spring of 1917. Within two months, locals were established in the major cities of Washington and Oregon.[10] Although they had not obtained a wage increase since 1913, the male telephone workers held a strong bargaining position when their contract came up for renewal at the end of the year because of the wartime shortage of skilled electrical workers. They demanded a 25 percent wage increase, a closed shop, and recognition of the new operators' locals, which the company viewed as ephemeral wartime organizations. When the company rejected the demands, a strike ensued involving the male telephone workers along the entire Pacific Coast and the operators of Washington and Oregon.[11]

The federal government feared that a tie-up of the telephone system in the Pacific region would interfere with the war effort, and the President's Mediation Commission intervened to effect a settlement. The commission had been originally established by President Wilson to mediate strikes by Arizona copper miners and timber workers in the Pacific Northwest, which seriously hampered the production of ammunition, ships, and aircraft for the war effort. It became involved, however, in a succession of strikes in the trans-Mississippi West, where wartime labor militancy was especially intense. The commission was composed of Secretary of Labor William B. Wilson, two employers' representatives, and two trade union representatives, with Professor Felix Frankfurter, on leave from Harvard Law School, as secretary and counsel.[12]

Because the commission believed the interruption of telephone service "hampered the country's effectiveness at war," it pressured the company to negotiate with the strikers by warning that it might recommend government seizure of the telephone lines. The bargaining sessions, in which the telephone operators were represented by male IBEW officials, resulted in a tripartite agreement signed by the IBEW, Pacific Bell, and the federal government. The terms were relatively favorable for the strikers. Both telephone men and operators gained substantial wage increases, and the company agreed to recognize the operators' locals. The union shop, however, was not established for either the men or the operators. Because the company had hired strikebreakers to replace the operators, it would not reemploy all of them, although the majority were taken back.[13]

The commission did not appear to take the interests of the operators as seriously as those of the men. Felix Frankfurter later declared that the company's objections to operators' unionism were "quite sincere, quite serious." He implied that since they were in the labor force only temporarily—until marriage—they were not as deserving of improvements in wages and working conditions as men were. Frankfurter's condescension toward women workers is apparent in his account of an incident which occurred as he visited towns across the Pacific Northwest in an effort to persuade the telephone operators to accept the terms: " . . . I remember in Aberdeen, Washington having one of the great and also one of the most enjoyable failures of my life. I made a speech to the girls . . . and when I sat down the chairman recognized a young woman. . . . She was a striking beauty. . . . I'll never forget the warm, appealing voice in which she said, 'Do you think it's fair, professor, to have any of us return to work, if all of us can't return to work?' She sat down amid cheers."[14]

Although the company had promised as part of the settlement to recognize the operators' locals, it continued to harass union operators. The tripartite agreement failed to provide a viable method of handling grievances. A complicated and time-consuming procedure was established requiring the aggrieved operator to present her case to a succession of company officials, then to the IBEW district vice-president, and then to a government official. The company was able to destabilize the new locals by discharging many of the operators most active in the union. According to Julia O'Connor, while several of the locals survived, "the vitality of the Unions was crushed, and their spirit broken."[15]

Another major wartime operators' strike occurred at Fort Smith, Arkansas, situated in a militant coal-mining district, an environment similar to Butte in the early years of the century. Sebastian County, where Fort Smith was the principal city, had been a stronghold of the Socialist party for over a decade. Fort Smith's labor movement had attained its peak strength by 1917. That year, the city had a massive Labor Day parade, its largest up to then, in which twenty-five unions from Fort Smith and the nearby railroad shop center of Van Buren participated.[16] As was the case in mining districts, there were few job opportunities for women, and only one women's trade union had existed in Fort Smith—a local of laundry workers. The second women's union established in Fort Smith was the telephone operators' union, organized in 1917 as Local 47A by D. L. Goble, the male IBEW official who had directed the operators' strike at Port Arthur, Texas, the year before.

The strike was precipitated by Southwestern Bell's dismissal of two leaders of the newly organized local, the first two to have signed the union's charter. After a committee representing Fort Smith's Central Trades and Labor Council failed to secure the reinstatement of the discharged operators, the sixty-two members of Local 47A walked out on strike. They charged that, since they had organized, the company had "humiliated and persecuted" them and had used "barbarous third degree methods" to break the union.[17]

The strike received wide community support, allowing the union to institute a boycott of Bell telephones. As in the Montana mining towns, many merchants and professional men were sympathetic to labor, because they depended on the patronage of workers and their families. Although no independent telephone alternative existed in

Fort Smith, the mayor—a strong supporter of the strike—and several businessmen attempted to interest the independent Kinloch Telephone Company of St. Louis in establishing a system in the town. Leading officials of the Central Trades and Labor Council spoke at strike rallies in support of the operators; the town's principal newspaper called one of the rallies the largest labor meeting ever held in Fort Smith.[18] The 3,200–member Sebastian County Federation of Labor paid weekly strike benefits to the operators. Union miners throughout the county's coal belt assessed themselves a dollar a week for the benefit of the strikers, and many of the county's businessmen made contributions to the strike fund. The strikers also received donations from Telephone Operators' Union locals 1A of Boston and 2A of Lynn. The chief of police and county sheriff openly endorsed the strike and refused the company's request for police protection at the exchange.[19]

As they had in Montana, supporters of the strike depicted it as a community struggle to defend "poor, defenseless girls" against a "huge, wealthy corporation." The striking operators identified their struggle with Christian principles and appealed for the support "of all who profess to follow the Lowly Nazarene," whom they, and several of the town's ministers, viewed as a champion of working people.[20]

When the Bell Company refused to negotiate and attempted to resume service using strikebreakers from Little Rock and St. Louis, the Fort Smith Trades and Labor Council ordered a general strike. The strike order affected about 1,100 workers in thirty-four trades, including carpenters, plasterers, bakers, teamsters, paper hangers, painters, laundry workers, retail clerks, barbers, and cigar makers. The most important group to join the strike was the street railway workers, who shut down not only the streetcar lines but the town's only electric power plant, plunging Fort Smith into darkness. The closing of the power plant also stopped production at ten coal mines in the vicinity, several of which supplied army camps in the Southwest.[21] Viewing this as a threat to the war effort, the federal government immediately dispatched a Labor Department mediator to effect a settlement. Pressure was also applied by the parent union of the street railway workers, the Amalgamated Association of Street and Electric Railway Employees, which revoked their charter and ordered them back to work on the grounds that they were violating their contract.[22]

The general strike lasted less than a week and the telephone operators, exhausted after being out three months, returned to work on the basis of a settlement arranged by the federal mediator. The terms, which were not favorable to the strikers, provided for the reinstatement of all but the two discharged operators, who were allowed to appeal their dismissal to the company president.[23] The company did not accord union recognition, and within two years Local 47A had disbanded. In the Fort Smith strike, as in nearly all operators' strikes outside New England, even strong labor and community support was not sufficient to offset the enormous financial resources of a Bell subsidiary.

Government Control and Operation of the Telephone System

Labor relations in the telephone industry deteriorated badly during the period of government "possession, control, operation, and management," which was established as a temporary war measure on August 1, 1918, and continued until July 31, 1919. In the interest of the war effort, the federal government assumed control of the nation's railroads in December, 1917, and seven months later it took over the telephone and telegraph systems, which were placed under the supervision of Postmaster-General Albert Burleson. Although the federal government was in nominal possession of the telephone system and assumed all obligations attendant upon its operation, the officers of the associated companies continued to hold actual control.[24]

Burleson's labor policy differed drastically from that of the Railroad Administration under Director-General William Gibbs McAdoo, in part because trade unions were far stronger in the railroad industry than in the telephone service. The capacity of the nation's poorly coordinated rail network was badly taxed by the economic upsurge induced by war mobilization. Moreover, the powerful railroad brotherhoods had threatened to strike toward the end of 1917, when the Interstate Commerce Commission (ICC) refused to allow substantial rate increases that would have raised the wages of railroad workers. Fearing a collapse of the nation's railroad system in the midst of the war crisis, President Wilson placed the railroads under temporary government control. The railroad corporations were guaranteed a "standard return" equal to average earnings in 1915, 1916, and 1917; this represented, in effect, a government rental payment for using the railroads. Congress effectively abrogated the ICC's power to fix railroad rates by permitting the new Railroad Administration to set rates at whatever level it deemed necessary to keep the railroads running smoothly.[25]

Viewing its major priority as ensuring uninterrupted railroad service and fearing disruptive strikes, the Railroad Administration devoted much attention to establishing harmonious labor relations. McAdoo ordered sizeable wage increases and passed the cost along to railroad users and the general public by raising rates.[26] The Railroad Administration recognized the right to organize and bargain collectively, allowing trade unionism to expand greatly its influence in the railroad industry to include not only the skilled—represented by the "Big Four" brotherhoods of engineers, conductors, firemen, and trainmen—but also the semiskilled and unskilled. By March, 1920, when federal control of the railroads ended, over 80 percent of railroad workers were organized.[27]

In contrast, while operating the telephone service, the Post Office Department demonstrated no concern for improving wages and working conditions and firmly opposed the right to organize and bargain collectively, even suspending it where it had been recognized before the war. By the time government control was introduced in the telephone service, the war was nearly over; as a result, the government was less alarmed about labor disturbances than it had been in the railroad industry. From the standpoint of the federal government, telephone workers appeared far less threatening than railroad workers. The IBEW, which claimed the affiliation of only a small proportion of the nation's telephone workers, had little strength outside the building trades. Postmaster-General Albert Burleson did not share Director-General William McAdoo's sympathy toward the labor movement; rather, he believed the affiliation of government employees with trade unions to be "a menace to the welfare of [the] Republic."

Writing in 1921, Telephone Operators' Department President Julia O'Connor viewed the period of government control as the worst the operators had experienced since they began to unionize in 1912: "Never was the oppressive, anti-union policy of the telephone company so freely and fearlessly exercised as during this period. Unions . . . found themselves fighting, not only the powerful, gigantic corporations, but the prestige, wealth, and the strength of the Government of the United States itself."[28] The Burleson Wire Administration's militant anti-unionism and its failure to provide a method to adjust wage difficulties during the spiralling inflation of the immediate postwar period precipitated strikes in 1919 in New England, along the Pacific Coast, in the Southeast, and in the Midwest.

Burleson, who had served fourteen years as a U.S. representative from Texas and was one of several southerners who dominated the Wilson cabinet, had been deeply influenced by the strong hostility to organized labor that prevailed in his home region. Reputedly the wealthiest man in the cabinet, Burleson had inherited a large quantity of land called the Steiner Valley farm. The sixty families which had rented and cultivated land on the Steiner Valley farm had been displaced without notice when Burleson and C. D. Johns, his brother-in-law, brought convicts to work on the 4,000–acre cotton plantation in 1895.[29] Under the convict lease system in Texas, plantation owners were permitted to employ the inmates of state penitentiaries, who worked under the supervision and were subject to the discipline of prison guards.[30] The Texas State Penitentiary Investigating Committee, which had visited the Burleson and Johns plantation in October, 1909, disclosed that convicts on the plantation were frequently whipped by guards using a short handle of wood to which several straps five feet long were fastened, and that guards had tortured and killed convicts on the plantation.[31]

As postmaster-general, Burleson developed a reputation as the "foremost official enemy of dissidents" in the Wilson administration, and he waged a determined effort to eliminate trade unionism from the postal service.[32] He charged that the wage demands of the organized postal workers were "selfish" since they were "justly compensated, receiving more than three times as much as those fighting in the trenches."[33] Burleson refused to receive representatives of the four postal workers' unions, and he demanded that Congress repeal the law permitting postal workers to join unions; as a result, the AFL convention which met at Buffalo in 1917 denounced him as "autocratic" and "oppressive."[34] Burleson suppressed criticism of the war effort by stripping socialist and antiwar publications of their second-class mailing privileges. Felix Frankfurter considered Burleson's views on labor relations "a little outmoded":

> He understood the movements of the world, of industry and economics on a social and human side about as little as the copper operators of Arizona, and I had very little doubt that if the lines were taken over by the government, even during the duration of the war, the situation for workers would not only not be better but probably worse. . . . He was full of the notion that in war you didn't allow freedom of speech, that everybody who lived in 1917 instead of 1817 was probably un-American. . . . the government did take over the lines . . . and all that I feared about Mr. Albert Burleson turned out to be true.[35]

Insisting that government employees had no right to strike, Burleson notified striking telephone workers that, if they failed to return to their jobs within twenty-four hours, they would not be reinstated. During the first months of government control, Burleson's intervention contributed to the collapse of operators' strikes at Norfolk, Virginia; the twin cities in Minnesota; and Wichita, Kansas. At Norfolk, 170 male telephone workers, joined by an almost equal number of operators in the recently organized Local 81A, ended their strike for higher wages immediately upon receiving Burleson's twenty-four-hour warning. Burleson had also threatened to blacklist from telephone employment anyone who remained on strike. The male IBEW officials directing the strike informed the telephone workers that they had no choice but to send them back to work "since the order came from a high government official."[36]

Although Burleson had justified his action at Norfolk in part by stating that its telephone service was of "vital military importance to the country," he issued the same twenty-four-hour warning when telephone workers in St. Paul and Minneapolis walked out on strike several days after the armistice.[37] In September, 1918, the IBEW had assigned H. H. Broach of its Springfield, Illinois, headquarters to organize the telephone operators of the Northwestern Telephone and Exchange Company, serving Minneapolis and northern Minnesota, and the Tri-State Telephone and Telegraph Company, serving St. Paul and southern Minnesota. Broach's campaign resulted in the chartering of two new operators' locals—88A of St. Paul and 89A of Minneapolis—and a sizeable increase in the membership of the telephone men's locals in the twin cities. When the telephone companies did not accede to the union's demand for wage increases, Broach called both the operators and the telephone men out on strike. Nearly all the telephone men walked out, along with 500 of the 600 operators in St. Paul and about 200 of the 1,000 in Minneapolis.

Because the operators had recently organized locals in cities without Women's Trade Union League chapters, they turned to Broach and other male IBEW officials for leadership. While picketing, the operators were supervised by male strikers.[38] The operators appealed for public support by drawing attention to their wartime purchases of liberty bonds and war savings stamps and to their low wages. They paraded through the streets with banners marked "These are federal employees who quit because they are not paid a living wage" and "Americans cannot live on $1.80 a day."[39]

As it did elsewhere, the telephone operators' fashionable clothing provoked considerable criticism from opponents of the walkout, who questioned whether young women who could afford such clothes were really underpaid. The strikers responded that these clothes were a requirement of the job and were purchased at considerable sacrifice on the credit installment plan at the twin cities' department stores.

As one operator explained, "A girl to hold a position must be decently dressed. To do this sometimes she must do without food that she needs to obtain the clothes to hold a position."[40]

What began as a strike became a lockout when the postmaster-general, citing his twenty-four-hour warning issued at the beginning of the walkout, declared invalid a settlement negotiated by the IBEW, the telephone companies, and the Minnesota Railroad and Warehouse Commission providing for a compromise wage increase contingent on a telephone rate increase. Although many Minnesota trade unions taxed their members to provide a strike fund, the telephone workers were forced to concede defeat after three months. Many of the striking operators were never reinstated; those who were reinstated returned to work under the old wage scale with complete loss of seniority. The lockout nearly destroyed locals 88A and 89A, which were afterwards forced to revert to secret meetings.[41]

The allegation by the secretary of the St. Paul Trades and Labor Assembly that the government acted in the telephone industry as a "strikebreaking agency pure and simple" received further confirmation when telephone operators in Wichita, Kansas, walked out on strike in December, 1918.[42] Wichita's local 85A had been organized by AFL official R. E. Warner in August, 1918, and included 137 of the 231 operators in Wichita. According to its twenty-one-year-old vice-president, Lola Price, the main reason for the formation of the local was the conduct of the chief operator, "who was arbitrary, overbearing, subjecting the operators to innumerable petty annoyances." President Dora Preston also stressed that, prior to unionization, wages had been insufficient to provide proper room, board, and clothing.[43]

The strike was precipitated when the Southwestern Bell Company discharged a twenty-one-year-old supervisor, Lela Phipps, for circulating a petition for higher wages for the operators. Phipps had been employed by the telephone company for four years and lived at home with her mother and sister; two brothers were serving in the U.S. Army in France. Dora Preston stated that the wire chief at the Wichita exchange had intimidated Phipps into asking the union not to protest her dismissal: "I called her and questioned her and found that the girl was very scared and had been scared by the manager until she believed that they would fine and imprison her if she tried to do anything."[44]

The Wichita union telephone operators, however, refused to drop the matter, and they walked out on strike, led by R. E. Warner. Burleson again announced that strikers would be reemployed only if they returned to work within twenty-four hours. Unlike those in Norfolk and the twin cities, the telephone men did not join the strike, although it was endorsed by Wichita's Trades and Labor Assembly and the mayor, who informed the postmaster-general that a general strike might occur if the company did not reinstate Phipps. A Post Office Department inspector who investigated the situation concluded that the dismissal of Phipps was "fully justified," and the company refused to negotiate. The strike collapsed after several months, and only those who could satisfy management that they had been "intimidated and misled" by "ringleaders" were reemployed. Again a telephone operators' strike with strong labor backing had ended in defeat.[45]

Even as the soaring cost of living provoked increasing unrest among telephone workers after the war, the Burleson Wire Administration failed to provide adequate machinery for handling wage adjustments. The Post Office Department established two bodies to administer the telephone and telegraph services under government operation: the Wire Control Board in Washington, chaired by Burleson and composed of two Post Office Department officials and a member of the U.S. Tariff Commission, and an Operating Board in New York, chaired by U. N. Bethell, vice-president of AT&T, and composed of three other members, representing AT&T, the Western Union Telegraph Company, and the independent telephone companies. Responsibility for labor relations was assigned to a special commission of inquiry, known as the Ryan Commission because it was chaired by William S. Ryan, assistant superintendent of the Division of Post Office Service. The duties and jurisdictions of these bodies and of the various telephone companies, however, were never clearly defined during the period of government control, and considerable confusion surrounded negotiations over telephone workers' wages and working conditions.[46]

Labor had little influence on the Ryan Commission, whose function was only advisory. The purpose of the commission, according to Postmaster-General Burleson, was to "investigate the working conditions of and wages paid to employees of the telegraph and telephone companies, and report as to what improvements, if any, should be made in the working conditions, the wages which should be paid the various classes of employees, and the feasibility of standardizing the same."[47] Of the commission's five members, only one—Julia O'Connor—represented the workers, while U. N. Bethell and F. B. MacKinnon, vice-president of the United States Independent Telephone Association, represented the companies and Chairman William Ryan and John B. Colpoys, special agent in the Department of Labor, represented the government.[48] Ryan's views on labor were similar to Burleson's, while Colpoys—formerly an officer of the Washington, D. C. Central Labor Union and later a federal labor mediator—tended to support O'Connor in the meetings.

The government probably selected O'Connor as the labor representative, rather than a male IBEW official, because the operators were the largest group among telephone workers. Equally important, the government was concerned about telephone operator militancy, which it perceived as significantly greater than that of the telephone men. The appointment of O'Connor as "representing the organized telephone workers of the country" was viewed by trade unionists as a significant concession on the part of the anti-union Burleson, since he had refused to appoint women even to clerical positions in some of the divisions of the Post Office Department.[49]

The Ryan Commission, which met infrequently, spent most of its time discussing the need to collect wage data from around the country and devoted little attention to the grievances of telephone workers. On January 6, 1919, O'Connor and Colpoys issued a joint statement to Burleson criticizing the Ryan Commission for its inattention to the nationwide discontent among telephone workers and management's indifference to collective bargaining agreements under government control. A few weeks later O'Connor resigned from the commission, charging that it had no policy but "hostility to the organized telephone and telegraph workers." In her letter of resignation, O'Connor denounced the Post Office Department for its delay of long-needed wage increases and stressed that labor relations in the telephone industry had worsened considerably under government control:

> Repudiation of agreements, breaking of contracts, interruption of friendly relations, destruction of long-established agreements of collective bargaining, persecution and hostility for membership in a union, this has been the unpleasant history of government control of the telephone industry. Methods of discrimination, unparalleled under private control, have been practiced by officials of the Telephone Company upon employees who joined or remained members of a union. . . . [50]

While still a member of the Ryan Commission, O'Connor had been fired by the New England Telephone Company. The company had permitted her to leave work to attend commission meetings in Washington, but it complained of her "long continued absence." Burleson upheld the dismissal, stating to President Wilson that O'Connor had "abandoned her post . . . and attempted to capitalize on her position and unionize the telephone employees of the country."[51]

Burleson angrily rejected O'Connor's charge that unrest among telephone workers was due to the policy of the Post Office Department, claiming that much of the dissatisfaction had been fomented by a "few agitators." In a memorandum to Secretary of Labor William Wilson, Felix Frankfurter sharply criticized Burleson's labor policy, which he charged was "in striking contrast to the general attitude by the Government, and the practices of the Government, in other industries over which it had superintendence." Frankfurter warned that "grievances unredressed for a long time afford growing power to the less patient and more radical among the workers."[52] However, because the telephone service was completely under the jurisdiction of the Post Office Department, neither Frankfurter, William Wilson, nor any member of the administration sympathetic to labor had the power to intervene. President Wilson was preoccupied with the Versailles peace negotiations and could not be persuaded to turn his attention to the telephone situation. The intransigence of the postmaster-general in the face of mounting demands by telephone workers for wage increases precipitated a series of telephone operators' strikes across the United States during 1919.

These walkouts were part of the unprecedented wave of mass strikes that erupted throughout the country in the year after the armistice. Over four million workers, one-fifth of the nation's labor force, were on strike in 1919. Only four days after the armistice, a strike of 50,000 garment workers began in New York. In January, 1919, a general strike of New York's harbor workers and longshoremen stopped all traffic in the country's largest seaport. The next month, a citywide general strike in Seattle lasted five days. Later in the year, a strike of 367,000 steelworkers broke out across ten states, and a strike of bituminous coal miners spread through the nation's coalfields. In Boston, 6,000 carmen on the elevated system walked out in June, and in September even the policemen went on strike. Countless smaller strikes occurred in every region of the country.[53]

The New England Telephone Strike

In April, 1919, telephone operators completely paralyzed service in five New England states in the most massive strike of women workers since the "Uprising of the 20,000" a decade earlier. The strike was the result of the Post Office Department's failure to provide any method for adjusting the telephone operators' wage demands after it had declared invalid the procedure of collective bargaining in force since 1913. Burleson ignored the adjustment board, which was composed of an equal number of representatives from the Telephone Operators' Union and the New England Telephone Company who had negotiated annual contracts. Instead, he substituted a clumsy procedure that did not allow union representatives an opportunity to bargain with management. The procedure was never fully understood by either the company or the union.

General Manager William Driver of the New England Telephone Company informed Local 1A on November 14, 1918, two weeks after the union had submitted its proposed wage scale to the company, that under government control he was not empowered to act upon it.[54] The agreement under which the union was working expired on December 31, 1918. The New England Telephone Operators' Union's wage-scale committee, composed of seven operators from Massachusetts and Rhode Island, then went to Washington in an effort to determine which government body had the authority to act in the matter. On November 20, 1918, the operators' wage scale was submitted to the Ryan Commission based on the unqualified statement of Chairman William Ryan that it had jurisdiction. Ryan assured Julia O'Connor in December that the commission would announce a wage increase retroactive to at least October, 1918.

When the Ryan Commission still had not made any announcement by February, 1919, the union decided to compel action on its wage demands by polling a vote giving the leadership the authority to call a strike. Although the vote showed 95 percent of the operators in favor of a strike, the Post Office Department continued for several weeks to withhold any announcement concerning wage demands.[55]

A strike became inevitable when Burleson outlined a procedure for handling the wage demands that denied the telephone operators their right to bargain collectively. The Telephone Operators' Union's wage-scale committee, which met with Burleson on March 24, 1919, was told that the demands would receive the attention of the Wire Control Board, but on April 10 Mary June of Local 1A, the chair of the wage-scale committee, received a telegram from Burleson contradicting his previous instructions. Burleson now insisted that the demands first be presented to General Manager Driver of the New England Telephone Company who could, if he chose, submit a secret recommendation to the Operating Board in New York, made up exclusively of AT&T, independent telephone company, and Western Union officials. The Operating Board would then submit its recommendations to the Wire Control Board, composed of four government

Julia O'Connor, president of the Telephone Operators' Department, IBEW, 1919–38, and leader of the 1919 and 1923 New England telephone operators strikes. (Courtesy of the International Brotherhood of Electrical Workers.)

Susan Fitzgerald *(right)* with Katherine Tyng, distributing women's suffrage leaflets. Fitzgerald, a leading "ally" in the Boston Women's Trade Union League, helped organize the Boston Telephone Operators' Union in 1912. (Courtesy of the Schlesinger Library, Radcliffe College.)

Rose Finkelstein and Hyman Norwood after a motorcycle trip from Boston to Plymouth, Mass., in 1916. Finkelstein, who served on the executive board of Local 1A, and Norwood, a former streetcar conductor and motorman who participated in the Boston Elevated strike of 1912, were married in 1921. (Author's collection.)

Telephone Operators' Union delegates at the 1917 IBEW convention in Atlantic City. *Front row:* Mary Mahoney, Local 1A, Boston (*far left*); Mary Quinn, Local 3A, Springfield, Mass. (*2d from left*); May Matthews, Local 1A, Boston (*4th from left*). *Middle row:* Julia O'Connor, Local 1A, Boston (*2d from right*). (Courtesy of the Schlesinger Library, Radcliffe College.)

Telephone Operators' Union delegates at the 1917 IBEW convention in Atlantic City. *Front row:* Mary Mahoney, Local 1A, Boston (*3rd from left*); May Matthews, Local 1A, Boston (*4th from left*); Mary Quinn, Local 3A, Springfield, Mass. (*5th from left*). *Back row:* Julia O'Connor, Local 1A, Boston (*2d from left*). (Courtesy of the Schlesinger Library, Radcliffe College.)

Striking Boston telephone operators in the 1919 New England telephone operators' strike. (Courtesy of the Boston *Globe*.)

Telephone Operators' Union strike committee with Boston mayor Andrew Peters during the 1919 New England telephone operators' strike. *Seated:* Mayor Peters and Julia O'Connor. *Standing (left to right):* Bridie Powers, Mary Mahoney, May Matthews, and Mary June. (Courtesy of the Boston *Globe.*)

"Weavers of Speech," a telephone company painting depicting the telephone operator as a central force in the nation's economic life, which the Telephone Operators' Department, IBEW, adopted as its emblem. (Courtesy of the Boston Public Library, Print Department.)

11th Annual Concert and Ball

AUSPICES OF THE

Telephone Operators' Union

L.C.Belden, '21.

AUDITORIUM, SPRINGFIELD, MASS., THURSDAY, APRIL 5th, 1923

21

Program cover of a dance sponsored by Local 3A, Springfield, Mass. (From the Julia O'Connor Parker Papers, the Schlesinger Library, Radcliffe College.)

officials in Washington, after which the matter would go to Post-master-General Burleson for final action.[56]

Although the IBEW leadership was concerned about the attacks on the right of telephone workers to organize and bargain collectively and supported their demands for wage increases, it urged the telephone operators to delay action while it conducted a referendum on whether to call a nationwide general strike of telephone workers. The international's office in Springfield, Illinois, did not expect to complete the referendum until sometime in May, 1919. However, by April the New England telephone operators, who had been working over three months without a contract, lost patience with the Wire Administration. At each union meeting since mid-March, O'Connor and the officers of Local 1A had had great difficulty pursuading the four thousand Boston telephone operators, who comprised about half the operating force in New England, not to declare an immediate strike. Acting IBEW President James Noonan instructed Vice-President Gustave Bugniazet to attend the meeting of Local 1A on April 11 and to make every effort to prevent a strike.[57]

On the evening of April 11, over two thousand Boston telephone operators, along with representatives of every IBEW operators' local in New England, packed Faneuil Hall in one of the most tumultuous labor meetings ever held in Boston. Vice-President Bugniazet, who was the only man in the hall until a committee from the Boston inside men's Local 142 arrived while the meeting was in progress, addressed the operators from the platform and asked that they postpone action for several weeks. He claimed the Brotherhood was sympathetic to the demands of the operators and denounced Postmaster-General Burleson as "worse than the Kaiser." At this point, one of the operators jumped to her feet and yelled, "It took the Yankee Division to lick the Kaiser. Now let the Yankee operators lick Burleson!" According to the Boston *Post,* "The utterance of this operator was like a flame to gunpowder, and any thought that was entertained by the conservatives or by the international officers of restraining the meeting were swept aside, and not until the strike question was put and carried unanimously did the excitement in any way subside."[58]

Julia O'Connor issued orders for the union telephone operators to walk off the job at 7:00 A.M. on April 15. The union demanded wage increases of about 60 percent and sought to reduce the number of years of service to attain the maximum level of pay from seven to four. The current wage scale began at $6 a week for beginning operators and ended at $16 for those with service of seven years or more; supervisors received from $17.50 to $19 a week.[59]

Nearly every telephone operator in five New England states, whether organized or unorganized, came out on strike in probably the most complete response ever to a strike call involving workers across state lines. There was no telephone service in Massachusetts, Rhode Island, Maine, New Hampshire, and Vermont for the duration of the strike. The only New England state not affected was Connecticut, where the telephone operators were employed by the Southern New England Telephone Company. Of the 630,000 telephone subscribers in the four states served by the New England Telephone Company, 500,000 were in Massachusetts—250,000 in the Boston Metropolitan District—60,000 in Maine, 40,000 in New Hampshire, and 30,000 in Vermont.[60]

Like the "Uprising of the 20,000," which it resembled in its spontaneity, the New England telephone strike represented a rejection of male trade union authority by masses of semiskilled women workers. Although this time the telephone operators had the advantage of being solidly organized before the walkout, they were not joined at the outset of the strike by the 4,000 male telephone workers in the five states, who could have considerably strengthened the position of the operators. AFL President Samuel Gompers, who backed the position of the IBEW leadership, sent a telegram to Julia O'Connor which implicitly opposed the strike action of the Telephone Operators' Union: "No one acquainted with the situation can fail to appreciate the grievances which the telephone operators have had to endure and yet in the furtherance of the effort to remove grievances, and for the achievement of rights, I strongly urge that you maintain self-control and give the opportunity to those who are in a position to bring about honorable adjustment."[61] O'Connor also received a request from President Wilson's secretary, Joseph Tumulty, to submit the operators' demands to General Manager Driver, but she refused to do so unless he had full power to negotiate on the basis of collective bargaining. The governors of the five states affected by the strike wired President Wilson in France urging his immediate intervention, but Wilson was preoccupied with the Versailles peace conference and could give the matter no attention.[62]

Nearly all the Boston newspapers strongly opposed the Post Office Department's position and the Burleson procedure for handling the wage demands. An agent of the Post Office Department, reporting from Boston on the strike to the chief post office inspector in Washington, wrote that "newspapers, excepting the *Globe,* appear principally interested in bitter attacks on the Postmaster-General," and added that "public sentiment [is] inclined to favor the strikers."[63]

Even the conservative Boston *Evening Transcript,* a Republican newspaper to be sure, denounced Burleson as a "bumptious bureaucrat" and found much to support in the union's claim that direct negotiation between the union and the company was preferable to "a system of mediation in which they deal with men who have only the power to forward 'recommendations' for the august attention of the Postmaster-General. . . . "[64] The *Evening Transcript* also noted, "There is strong feeling in business and official circles that the course of the strike had been completely dominated by Miss O'Connor, their leader. . . . Feeling is growing that Miss O'Connor has a personal grievance with Mr. Burleson and is determined to make him 'eat out of her hand.' "[65]

The impact of the 1910s youth culture and the enormous energy and brassiness of the flapper were evident in the operators' strike. The operators began the daily mass strike meetings in Boston with a "song and dance prelude." Volunteers from the rank and file took the stage to sing ragtime and other up-to-date songs, while others danced the "Shimmie." Local 1A's secretary May Matthews even became involved in a wrestling exhibition with another operator: "The couple grappled, broke, and clenched again and after separating bowed to an uproarious audience."[66] The telephone operators began twenty-four-hour picketing, probably the first time it had ever been employed by women workers. On the second day of the strike, following a mass meeting of Local 1A at Tremont Temple, the Boston operators took to the streets in an impromptu parade through the downtown business district. Over a thousand operators marched to the Boston Common, where a group of soldiers led cheers for the strikers, and proceeded to the Telephone Operators' Union headquarters at the Old South Building. There the forty-six student operators who that morning had refused to take the places of strikers were enrolled in the union.

As in 1913, the newspapers commented on the operators' attire, noting that many of the strikers had difficulty keeping up with the parade because of the height of their heels and the tightness of their skirts. The *Evening Transcript* described the operators in the parade as a "giggling, silk-stockinged, high-heeled . . . and up-to-the-minute dressed crowd of girls" and complained that "fewer fur coats and quieter styles in headgear would have been more appropriate."[67] The fashionable dress of the striking telephone operators received considerable attention in cities outside Boston as well. In Providence, for example, the press reported Local 65A pickets were ready to exchange their cumbersome high-heeled shoes for "a uniform pair of brannigans" on the second day of the strike[68] Three days later, an angry altercation took place in the downtown business district when a young woman from the city's exclusive East Side section made caustic remarks to several striking operators about their expensive clothes. The young East Sider aggressively asked one picket, a telephone supervisor, how someone striking for a "living wage" could afford to purchase the fur scarf and silk stockings she was wearing. The picket retorted she had paid for the clothes with money she had earned as a telephone operator for the U.S. Army during the war and asked the East Sider whether she could give as good an account of how she had obtained the clothes she wore.[69]

The management of New England Telephone, which was not altogether displeased with the strike because it believed the strike could serve to discredit permanent government ownership of the telephone system, did not attempt to secure permanent replacements for the operating force. Applicants for positions as operators were advised at the company's Boston headquarters that the work was likely to be only for the duration of the strike. The Boston *Post* noted that although some expensively dressed young women from Brookline and other of the more affluent suburbs offered their services without recompense, "the average applicant in appearance and speech did not prophesy well for the future telephone service of Boston."[70]

The company did import some operators from New York, New Jersey, and Philadelphia. At the mass meeting of Local 1A on the second day of the strike, Julia O'Connor ordered the picketing of the Lenox Hotel, the Copley Plaza, and the Hotel Touraine, where the out-of-town strikebreakers were housed. May Matthews, secretary of the Telephone Operators' Department (and also of Local 1A), later told the convention of the National Women's Trade Union League how the union telephone operators reacted when they learned that strikebreakers had arrived in Boston:

> . . . we were so provoked we just surrounded the big hotel where they took them. . . . Two of our girls went to the hotel and registered as guests. We have some very good-looking telephone operators in Boston, and we got the big, stately ones and had them parade through the lobby of the Lenox Hotel. We were sure they could not tell whether they were guests or pickets. The strikebreakers would start down to break-. fast. . . . Immediately those fine-looking guests would go in and surround the strikebreakers. We would have papers telling about the strike and would show them to the strikebreakers. When they went to their rooms, we went on the same elevators, talking about the strike. When they went down to be taken to the exchanges in automobiles we had

a flock of automobiles that went on either side of them, they driving in the middle.[71]

Matthews's statement, which shows a keen awareness of class, appears also to betray an envy of the rich, even a sense of working-class inferiority, in depicting hotel guests as "big," "stately," and "fine-looking." At the same time, it implies a sharp difference between telephone operators and factory women by expressing pride in the fact that at least some telephone operators might be mistaken for wealthy hotel guests.

The importation of strikebreakers led several Boston trade unions to take sympathetic action on behalf of the telephone operators, and for a time the newspapers speculated about a possible general strike across New England. The only unions to take action, however, were those whose members' work brought them into contact with strikebreakers; these workers denied the strikebreakers their services. Strikebreakers arriving at Boston's Back Bay Station had to be driven to their hotels in horse-drawn carriages because no union taxi driver would take them. John Kearney, business agent of the Cooks' and Waiters' Union, addressed the strikers' daily mass meeting on April 17 and announced that the 2,600 members of his union would not serve the strikebreakers at the hotels.[72] Business agent William Timmins of the Boston Carmen's Union issued instructions that members of the union should leave their cars if strikebreakers boarded them.[73] The central labor bodies in the major New England cities pledged full support for the strike. From outside New England, the telephone operators received a message of solidarity from the postal workers; in a telegram to Julia O'Connor, Thomas Flaherty, secretary-treasurer of the National Federation of Postal Employees, strongly denounced Burleson:

> He has attempted to invade every right of postal workers. . . .
> He personally lobbied against wage increases. He brutally characterized our agitation for increased compensation as [a] selfish attempt on [the] part of men already receiving three times wages of soldiers in trenches.
> In six years he has . . . persistently fought every reform we have sought. . . . In behalf of telephone girls now on strike, you are justified in demanding something more substantial than a Burleson promise of future fair treatment.[74]

Early in the strike, Burleson denounced the telephone operators as unpatriotic for striking against the government and threatened to replace them with soldiers. This enraged the members of Local 1A, which had made heavy purchases of liberty bonds, and they responded with a soldiers' demonstration of their own. A hundred men—brothers and boyfriends of the strikers—who had served in the army during the war joined the telephone operators in a parade behind the service flag of the Telephone Operators' Union. The flag had six stars, representing the six members of the union serving with the American Expeditionary Force in France. May Matthews, whose brother had been wounded three times in wartime combat, described the parade to the convention of the National Women's Trade Union League: " . . . every one of the men wore his uniform and had gold braid on his sleeve. . . . The soldiers told them they went across to fight for democracy, but they didn't expect to come home and fight against women."[75]

On the third day of the strike, with public and newspaper opinion overwhelmingly opposed to Burleson's position and the issue nearly decided, the 4,000 male telephone workers in twenty-six IBEW locals in the five states walked out. Because the telephone men had initially refused to demonstrate solidarity with the operators, relations between the Telephone Operators' Union and the male IBEW locals were strained, and they continued to deteriorate in the next few years. May Matthews commented, "The fight had been won, but I guess they had been smoked out by other people in the labor movement." The decision of the telephone men to strike did not surprise company officials, as the operators' walkout had been so complete that there was little work for the men to do.[76] The telephone men were not striking in sympathy with the operators but for wage demands of their own, which they had submitted months before to General Manager Driver, who had failed to act upon them.[77] A delegation from the three male IBEW locals in Boston joined the Local 1A strike committee—consisting of President Julia O'Connor; May Matthews, secretary of Local 1A; Mary June, Local 1A's vice-president; and Bridie Powers, later a member of the Boston WTUL executive board—in a conference with Boston's mayor Andrew Peters, who attempted mediation. The women on the operators' strike committee were all in their late twenties. Throughout New England, the men assumed responsibility for night picketing, indicating that there were limits to how far the operators would challenge conventional gender roles, even in Boston.

A highly unusual feature of the strike was the considerable sympathy shown by the police of Boston and other New England cities toward the striking operators. Since the late nineteenth century, the police had invariably expressed strong hostility toward strikers, even though they themselves had working-class origins. Strike-control activity, including the protection of strikebreakers, had been an important function of urban police departments since the 1880s. Sidney Harring contends in a study of the late nineteenth- and early twentieth-century police that police hostility toward strikers can in part be explained by the fact that patrolmen occupied a relatively privileged position within the working class. Patrolmen were drawn disproportionately from the upper section of the working class and received wages equivalent to those of skilled workers. Patrolmen derived additional income from activities, both legal and illegal, that could be classified as entrepreneurial: taking bribes, receiving a cut of vice activity, providing extra protection for businesses, etc.[78]

The policemen's sympathy for the telephone operators resulted not only from the exceptionally wide support for the strike, but also from their common Irish-American background and their family ties. Moreover, the policemen considered the telephone operators, generally perceived as white-collar workers, to be of higher status than factory hands, whom they viewed with disdain. Striking garment workers, predominantly Jewish or Italian-American, usually were roughly treated by the police during this period. Anna Weinstock, Boston WTUL president in 1919–20, who as an eighteen-year-old neckwear worker led over two hundred women in a nine-week strike in 1917, recalled that she had been arrested merely for calling out to another picket across the street. She described the Boston police as "very unfriendly to labor": "It was our feeling that in almost every instance where women were organizing or any group was organizing, the police were on the side of the employer and would arrest people for loitering."[79] During the 1919 New England telephone strike, however, not a single telephone operator was arrested. The packing of the telephone exchanges with extra policemen after the soldiers' demonstration did not discourage the telephone operators: "The day the extra policemen were put on it rained like the deuce. The policemen took the raincoats they had and gave them to the girls who were picketing. When the girls wanted lunch, we had the police officers go and get it for them."[80]

The 1919 telephone strike helped influence the Boston policemen to organize a union of their own later that year. When the police went on strike in September, 1919, the Boston WTUL and the Telephone Operators' Union gave their full support to the strikers. After the strike was crushed and the entire Boston police force was fired, the Boston WTUL continued to raise money for the discharged men, but Anna Weinstock emphasized that "it was a little bit of a treat to talk to them and remind them of their attitude toward pickets when other groups were striking."[81]

In Providence, telephone company officials complained the police were fraternizing with the telephone operators and allowing the pickets to exceed their rights. As in Boston, both policemen and telephone operators were overwhelmingly Irish-American. Under instructions from the police commission, Deputy Superintendent O'Neil of the Providence police department called all police captains to headquarters and lectured them on the need for "strict neutrality." The patrolmen were then warned by the captains that they were "being watched" and should keep their opinions to themselves. The Providence *Journal* described the ensuing typical encounter between policeman and telephone operator picket, which reflects the strikers' unusually friendly relations with the police:

> . . . a policeman, passing back and forth before an exchange yesterday morning, might be heard to say, without turning his head, to a girl he went to school with: "Sorry but I can't talk to you." And then the next time the picket and patrolman passed: "But it's a fine morning." After more trudging, the operator would get an opportunity to say, "Thought you were getting stuck up." Some seconds later she would venture: "Yes, it's a fine day." More walking, and the guard would risk: "Gotcher Easter bonnet?" And the answer: "No wearing last year's made over."[82]

The depth of public sympathy for the telephone operators was reflected in offers of assistance from lower-middle-class organizations and small businesses, not always favorably disposed toward labor, and mass demonstrations of support in working-class neighborhoods. The Fall River Lodge of Elks announced on the first day of the strike that it would serve lunch to telephone operator pickets. The Lynn Lodge of Elks gave the strikers free use of its offices and meeting hall, and the management of Lynn's Comique Theatre offered the use of the theater for a mass meeting of the telephone operators' locals of the North Shore. An auto accessory dealer in Fall River turned the key of his office over to pickets for the duration of the strike. In Plymouth, businessmen supplied the strikers with chocolate and warm drinks.[83] Merchants in Boston's Chinatown district set up a large table behind the Beach telephone exchange and served food to the exchange's three hundred striking operators. Rose Finkelstein, a striker from the Beach exchange, recalled that the neighborhood's Chinese residents "did the picketing for us at the back door," discouraging strikebreakers from entering.[84] The lone strikebreaker at the South

Boston exchange was followed home by a hissing and jeering crowd of 250, and women in houses along the way made faces at the strikebreaker from their windows.[85]

The widespread participation of young "society women" and affluent college students as strikebreakers provoked considerable violence and rioting by working-class sympathizers of the telephone operators, revealing bitter class antagonisms in the cities of Massachusetts and Rhode Island. The strikebreakers included not only the wives of the New England Telephone Company's general manager and treasurer—Katherine Driver and Katherine Balch, at the time the vice-president of the Massachusetts Anti-Suffrage Association—who worked at the Milton exchange outside Boston, but large numbers of women from Providence's East Side, Fall River's "Hill" section, Worcester's West Side, Brookline, and other exclusive city neighborhoods and suburbs. Although the male college students were the only ones physically attacked, the society women were subjected to jeers and taunts on their way to and from the telephone exchanges and were sometimes pressured by crowds to stop work. In Fall River, a Highland car carrying "Hill" women from the exchange stalled and, while the chauffeur worked frantically to start the Highland, a motorman stopped his streetcar and serenaded the strikebreakers by "beating tatoo with the bell." In Providence, forty operator pickets and a hundred sympathizers followed two East Side "society buds" from the Union exchange through the streets, forcing them to take refuge in the Providence Art Club.[86]

At what the Fall River *Globe* called probably the most enthusiastic labor meeting ever held in Fall River, Monsignor James E. Cassidy gave a thundering denunciation of the city's "idle rich" for taking positions as telephone operators. Cassidy, who later served as bishop of Fall River, had long been committed to the labor movement and was the only Catholic priest in New England to take an active role in supporting the striking telephone workers. Amid deafening applause, Cassidy called for the "branding" of strikebreakers: "In the old days when a woman was crooked she was branded with a scarlet letter. There ought to be another scarlet letter today, it should be 'S' instead of 'A.' " According to Cassidy, the "Hill" women were "breeding more Bolshevism and socialism than the foreigners could make in five years with speeches." The priest criticized the city's trade unions for not offering enough financial support to the telephone operators and announced he would pay for newspaper advertisements so the strikers could present their case to the public. Cassidy closed his speech by proposing that the names of the "Hill" women who were working as operators be inscribed on billboards in large black letters.[87]

Strikebreaking by college students, not uncommon in New England labor disputes, greatly angered the telephone operators and precipitated riots in the streets of Boston, Cambridge, Malden, and Providence. Drawn almost entirely from the upper and middle classes, college students had little sympathy for labor. Few from the working class could afford to attend college in this period. Massachusetts had a state university, but it was located in the western part of the state and served a rural clientele. With an abundance of free time, college students were easily recruited into strikebreaking. They were motivated by a desire to express solidarity with business in its struggle against labor and to earn pocket money for social events. Although college students sometimes took laborers' jobs during strikes, they found telephone operating especially appealing since it was viewed as white-collar work performed in a clean and safe environment.

The college students, dubbed "Lizzies" by the striking operators, were continually subjected to taunts impugning their masculinity. These taunts derived from labor's traditional view of the strikebreaker as servile and the wealthy as soft and decadent; they also possibly stemmed from the fact that the students were males working at females' jobs. Telephone operator pickets greeted MIT (Massachusetts Institute of Technology) students emerging from a telephone exchange in Boston with cries of "Shall I escort you to my car dear?" A jeering crowd of operators and male sympathizers followed the students to a movie theater. When one of the students asked the operators sarcastically, "Will you come in?" they responded, "Yes—when you're a man and grown up."[88] In Providence, a strikebreaker from Brown University called out, "Hello red head!" to a young woman on picket duty, who retorted, "Hello yellow!"[89] When President Julia O'Connor called the roll of pickets at the daily mass meeting of Local 1A and strikebreakers were reported at an exchange, she invariably asked, "Men or boys?" "Lizzies," roared the assembled telephone operators. After a report from the Inman Street exchange in Cambridge that "twenty Lizzies from Harvard" were working there as strikebreakers, Local 1A Secretary May Matthews angrily stormed to the front of the stage and shouted, "How much longer are our institutions like Harvard, Tech, and Tufts going to be incubators for strikebreakers?"[90]

College students were treated roughly and in several cases seriously injured in fights with male sympathizers of the telephone operators, reflecting a deep class animosity between the workers and the students. In Malden, outside Boston, an MIT student was knocked down by a strike sympathizer as he left the telephone exchange and kicked until he had suffered cuts and bruises all over his head and body. Five other MIT students were also "roughly handled" in the fracas. At the Main exchange in Boston, an MIT student working as a strikebreaker lost several teeth in a scuffle with a man sympathetic to the strike.[91] Twelve Harvard students who had relieved women strikebreakers from New York and Philadelphia for the evening shift at the Inman Street exchange in Cambridge were attacked as they were leaving the exchange building about 10:00 P.M., and two were injured. According to the Harvard *Crimson*, the "mob" consisted of "men who apparently were out for a fight against University men rather than in sympathy with the strikers."[92] There are other indications, however, that the opposition to the students represented an expression of worker solidarity for the strikers. When the students attempted to board a trolley car, the motorman—a union member—refused to have them as passengers, and they finally had to be taken back to Harvard in police patrol wagons.[93] The mayor of Cambridge sharply criticized the action of the Harvard students, asserting that the telephone workers were striking for a just cause and that Cambridge had experienced no trouble until the students had interfered in the strike.[94]

At Brown University in Providence, where an article in the Brown *Daily Herald* of April 17 asked undergraduates interested in "the placing of the switchboards on a normal basis" to leave their names at the Brown Union office, a considerable number of students offered their services as strikebreakers. An official of the Providence IBEW, however, gloated that some of the Brown "sapheads" had reconsidered their decision to work as strikebreakers after a "good beating" had been administered by strike sympathizers.[95]

Although strikebreaking by college students was by no means unusual, it proved embarrassing to many New England colleges and universities because the strikers enjoyed the support of most of the public and the press. Many students hastened to register their disapproval of their classmates' strikebreaking. A mass meeting of undergraduates at Brown University, presided over by the president of the student government, passed one resolution affirming the neutrality of the Brown student body in the telephone strike and another declaring that strikebreakers acted as individuals, not as Brown students. The prevailing sentiment at the meeting was that the actions of the strikebreakers were prejudicial to the interests of the university.[96] The

Brown *Daily Herald* apologized for the "misunderstanding" created by its interview with a telephone company official who had denounced the striking operators, which it had published under the title "The Aid of Brown Men Sought to Help Break Strike." The next day it carried a statement by IBEW officials presenting the telephone operators' side of the strike.[97] The latter article was motivated at least in part by a visit from an IBEW committee to the *Daily Herald* office. The union committee also visited Brown's president Faunce, who indicated he was displeased with the strikebreaking by students, although he said he could not prevent it.[98]

A delegation of telephone operators at Northampton, Massachusetts, where Smith College students had "run the gauntlet" of pickets to take positions at the telephone exchanges, fared better in a visit with President William Neilson of Smith College. President Neilson stated that, although there was no college law against it, he did not believe it advisable for the students to interfere in the strike. The students accepted his suggestion to desist.[99]

A Bates College freshman from Rumford, Maine, indignantly denied in the Lewiston *Evening Journal* a report printed in a morning newspaper that he was working as an operator at the Lewiston telephone exchange. He stated his cousin, the chief operator of the exchange, had asked him to work there, but he did not care to be a strikebreaker: "You see, living in a factory town, I know what that sort of thing means."[100]

At Harvard, the strikebreakers received a generally cold reception from the other students and were admonished in class by several faculty members. The Boston *Post* quoted "investigators" as having determined that the strikebreakers included not a single student who had taken part in the "activities of the college" or who wore the letter *H*. Thus, the strikebreakers did not represent "the real Harvard spirit." The Harvard *Crimson*, not usually friendly to labor, published an editorial condemning the Burleson procedure and supporting the telephone operators' side of the controversy. After the incident at the Inman Street exchange in Cambridge, the *Crimson* sharply criticized the strikebreaking by Harvard undergraduates, which it believed injured the reputation of the university: "Harvard all too often is considered reactionary; too often are we named—and wrongly—a breeding place for capitalism. We need not favor the strike, but it is essential that our individual acts do not prejudice the University in the minds of the public." The *Crimson* also published an interview it conducted with the strike leader, Julia O'Connor, in which she denounced the strikebreaking by Harvard students and stated her belief that the conduct of the "few students involved" did not meet with the approval of the university.[101]

A series of disorders occurred on the fourth day of the strike near Boston's Main exchange. Members of a crowd, numbering at least three thousand and including many uniformed soldiers and sailors, beat male strikebreakers leaving the exchange building. Several of the strikebreakers were severely injured. Late in the afternoon, two young men "having the appearance of college students" were accosted by telephone operator pickets, who demanded to know whether they were applying for positions as operators. When they refused to answer, the crowd of strike sympathizers surged toward them, forcing them to flee. One of the young men was cornered in a doorway and left battered and bleeding by the sympathizers.[102] According to the conservative Boston *Evening Transcript*, merely labelling someone a strikebreaker was enough to endanger that person. When the crowd noticed two young men, who had failed to gain entrance to the Main exchange building about 7:00 P.M., a "sailor . . . and several other men" attacked them. The *Evening Transcript* provided the following account of what ensued: "One of the men was beaten until he fell, covered with blood on the sidewalk. His companion was grabbed by a soldier in uniform and other men and pounded unmercifully, until his teeth were knocked out and his clothes badly torn. The girls on hand naturally disclaimed any blame for the affair, but did jeer at the unfortunate victims. . . . " The *Evening Transcript* was sharply critical of the conduct of the Boston police throughout the entire strike: "According to reports in all the newspapers, according to the testimony of many impartial observers, the police did not protect the men and women who attempted to take the place of telephone strikers. . . . They were derelict in their duty."[103]

Three sailors were arrested later that evening after a police officer in plain clothes came to the assistance of a strikebreaker, who had been trapped in a doorway and severely pummeled by strike sympathizers. An eighteen-year-old sailor named Worth Howard, who was leading the assault on the strikebreaker, allegedly struck the police officer on the head with an iron bar when he attempted to intervene. While the policeman arrested Howard, two other sailors—Robert Springer, aged nineteen, and Clarence Christ, aged twenty-one—attempted to interfere and were also arrested. Howard was later found guilty of assault and battery and rioting, and Springer and Christ of rioting.[104]

A Boston IBEW official later noted approvingly in the *Journal of Electrical Workers and Operators* that "a few of the snobveracy of Harvard and Tech had unpleasant experiences, in which some of Uncle Sam's soldiers and sailors, who are always ready and willing to aid beauty in distress, figured prominently."[105] This statement reflected not only the worker's animosity toward the college student but the male trade unionist's condescension toward women workers, viewed as needing protection even when fully managing their own strike and far surpassing the telephone men in militancy.

Burleson came under increasing pressure from the press and Massachusetts politicians to permit direct bargaining between the strikers and the New England Telephone Company. Julia O'Connor stated that the telephone operators would not submit to Burleson's procedure even upon a request from President Wilson. She noted that Wilson had ignored two cable messages from the Telephone Operators' Union and that, before he left for France, he had refused to see the union's committee in Washington on the grounds that he was too busy. Eleven Democratic members of the Massachusetts legislature cabled President Wilson in Paris: "Burleson wrecking party. Remove him and settle this strike." The Boston *Evening Transcript* fumed that New England was "under the yoke of Burlesonism," and it declared that were the president not afraid to call Congress into session, the postmaster-general would be a defendant in impeachment proceedings.[106]

On the fifth day of the strike, Burleson abandoned his opposition to direct bargaining, and First Assistant Postmaster-General J. C. Koons arrived in Boston with full authority to approve an agreement negotiated by union and company representatives. A settlement was reached after an eight-hour conference in which the telephone operators accepted a compromise on their wage demands. The maximum pay was increased from $16 to $19 a week, instead of the $22 demanded, and the operators were granted the beginner's wage of $10 a week they had demanded, a $4 raise. The operators' right to bargain collectively and directly with the company's general manager was recognized. The operators did not win the reduction from seven to four years in the service needed to attain the maximum level of pay. The male telephone workers, who had asked for an increase in pay of $1.40 a day, received instead $.50 a day for those employed in Boston and $.625 for those outside Boston.[107]

Mary Quinn, who was a member of the telephone operators' negotiating committee in Boston, recalled that relations between the committee and the male IBEW negotiators were strained as a result of the men's not supporting the operators at the outset of the strike. The male representatives at first did not want to accept the terms but were persuaded to do so by the operators:

> We knew we would have to dicker on what the terms were, you know, make decisions and concessions and we were perfectly satisfied with it and we . . . had a big meeting of the operators and I was reporting and—which upset me very much—the men didn't want to go back, they brought up some other things they wanted. . . . But we said, "We're very sorry. You didn't come out with us when we first came out. We waited for three days, we made it a successful strike, now you're on your own. We won't scab, we won't try to install telephones. But that's it—we're going back!"[108]

The initial reaction to the terms from the Boston telephone operators' rank and file was not altogether favorable, but the union leadership was able to win acceptance at a mass meeting of over three thousand operators of the Boston Metropolitan District, and the locals elsewhere in New England also ratified the agreement. The Boston *Herald* reported "open signs of revolt" from the rank and file at news of the terms, and it predicted that the union leaders "will have their hands full in bringing about ratification."[109] According to the Boston *Daily Advertiser,* hundreds of operators who went into the meeting in Boston determined to fight for "$22 or Nothing" were swayed by Julia O'Connor to vote for ratification. Some of the operators told a *Daily Advertiser* reporter that Local 1A Secretary May Matthews, later a bitter enemy of O'Connor, had led the fight at the two-hour meeting for "$22 or Nothing," although others said that only members of the operators' negotiating committee had been allowed to speak. A cheering throng of operators followed the automobile which bore O'Connor from the meeting.[110]

The strike settlement represented the first decisive victory for the telephone workers under the Burleson Wire Administration. Julia O'Connor stated the terms were "the best ever put over for the operators."[111] Every telephone operator resumed the position she had vacated at the strike call and all seniority rights were guaranteed, a significant contrast to all other telephone strikes during the period of government operation.[112] The Boston *Post* reported the settlement was widely regarded as a "smashing victory for the girl operators and their men allies."[113] Julia O'Connor ascribed the strikers' victory to the high level of trade union organization the telephone operators had established in New England: "The victory of the New England operators was not accomplished in the few days on the battle line. It had been accomplished in the patient years before, while an organization of character, strength, and of purpose was being built up."[114] Probably never before had an industrial issue so completely penetrated into every village, hamlet, and town of New England.[115]

The major attack on the strike settlement from outside the union came from the Fall River priest James Cassidy, who had delivered a blistering speech on behalf of the telephone operators during the strike. Cassidy (1869–1951), who became bishop of Fall River in 1934 and was active in the National Catholic Welfare Council headed by Monsignor John Ryan, was probably the strongest supporter of the labor movement of any Catholic priest in New England.[116] Fall River was not part of the archdiocese of Boston, and Cassidy was therefore not under the supervision of the anti-labor Cardinal O'Connell.

Cassidy's invocation at the United Textile Workers' Union convention at Fall River in 1922 reflected his deep commitment to trade unionism. He pronounced "against the ever-increasing unification of capital" and against "the enormous fortunes of the few and the utter poverty of the many," pointing out that "in unity and unionism lies the workers' only hope."[117] In his pamphlet "The Saloon versus the Labor Union," Cassidy stressed that "the representatives of the church should ever be . . . side by side and shoulder to shoulder with the representatives of labor." He maintained that "unionism takes the laborer by the hand; it keeps him longer with his family and returns him home earlier at night; it sustains him when he is falling . . . it supports his family when he cannot labor; it educates him; it broadens him; it elevates him; it makes life for him better and brighter and longer and more worth living."[118]

As a priest, Cassidy was uncomfortable with women holding positions of trade union leadership, and this undoubtedly influenced the tone of his correspondence with President Julia O'Connor of the Telephone Operators' Union concerning the terms of the strike settlement. Cassidy's mentor John Ryan believed that work outside the home interfered with what he considered women's primary role of mother and hoped that eventually women could be entirely eliminated from the labor force. According to his biographer Francis Broderick, Ryan had "no truck with the economic independence of women," and he had stated as early as 1910 that the conditions of both women and society as a whole would improve if women ceased to engage in "extra-active" occupations, which left them unprepared for marriage, caused physical damage, and resulted in "injury to the race."[119] Cassidy later assailed the Women's Auxiliary Army Corps when it was formed during World War II, declaring that the enlistment of women into the armed forces was contrary to the teachings of the Roman Catholic church and that Catholic women should not join the corps.[120]

In a letter addressed to the president of the Fall River Telephone Operators' Union with the request that it be forwarded to the strike leadership in Boston, Cassidy demanded to know why the union's negotiating committee had conceded what he considered to be a critical demand: "You . . . would confer a great favor upon me if you could furnish me with the reasons why those who spoke for you at Boston consented to the retention of the conditions requiring you to work seven years before receiving the maximum wage of nineteen dollars a week. To me the agreement is so sinister that it needs the fullest explanation to rescue it from the imputation of dishonesty."[121]

Julia O'Connor, who had served as a representative of the Boston Telephone Operators' Union on every annual wage agreement negotiated during the seven years of organization, found the letter deeply insulting and angrily wrote back, "This imputation [of dishonesty] has been made so freely, so easily, and with, it seems to me, so meager a canvass of the facts, as to scarcely warrant the dignity of a contradiction." Because Cassidy had provided so much assistance to the strikers, however, O'Connor did decide to respond, and in a series of letters she explained the purpose of the strike and the reasons the union agreed to a compromise settlement:

> May I draw your attention to the fact that this strike was called before the wage question was even discussed, and was called for the establishment of a great principle. . . . upon the concession to the unions of the right to bargain collectively the strike was won. A moral victory so complete and sweeping amply justifies itself, and to have been able to secure on top of that a 28 percent increase in pay, and to have it date back to January 1, 1919, does not deserve an unfair and unthinking characterization such as you have placed upon it.[122]

Cassidy, in a rejoinder, charged that the union leadership had ignored the interests of the overwhelming majority of operators. He claimed that in Fall River and New Bedford hardly one-tenth of the operators qualified for the maximum rate of pay.[123] O'Connor did not dispute the figures for those cities, but she argued that the situation there was not typical of New England as a whole. She pointed out that in the Boston Metropolitan District—which employed about four thousand telephone operators, about one-half of the operating force of the New England Telephone Company—one-third of the operators drew the maximum rate of pay.[124] In addition, O'Connor felt the more senior operators were entitled to special consideration: "These operators worked during the early years of the service for starvation wages and the union has always recognized the special claim upon it for consideration of this group in its membership." She noted that the seven-year schedule was introduced in 1915 and "was then, as it is now, unfair, artificial, and reactionary."[125] The union had attempted to reduce the time requirement for maximum pay to four years during the 1918 negotiations, but it was obliged to accept the seven-year period to win better terms for the more senior operators. O'Connor stressed that, in the 1919 strike negotiations, the union accepted the seven-year schedule to add one more dollar to the maximum pay; the choice was between a six-year schedule with an $18 maximum or a seven-year schedule with a $19 maximum.[126]

Cassidy claimed O'Connor had misinterpreted his statement concerning the dishonesty surrounding the strike settlement, which he said he had meant to apply only to the "controlling telephone officials," but his continued insistence on the inadequacy of the terms provoked O'Connor into an impassioned defense of the position of the Telephone Operators' Union leadership. O'Connor argued that Cassidy, in asserting that the telephone operators had been "absolute masters" of the situation, overlooked the danger involved for the union in not accepting a compromise settlement:

> I had before me the picture of a continued series of failures in telephone strikes, both under private and Federal control— . . . furnishing a very vivid and appalling picture of what it is possible for a giant corporation [to do] with unlimited financial and political resources, reinforced in recent cases by all the power and prestige of the Government of the United States. . . . my best judgement . . . dictated the necessity of reaching a settlement with the strike at its highest point of efficiency, with the spirit and faith of the membership completely intact, rather than risking the sacrifice, not only of the principle for which we were contending, but the possible loss of the organization itself.

O'Connor asserted that only a high level of public support for the telephone operators had prevented Burleson from making a concerted effort to break the strike, which could have resulted in the destruction of the union; this support would have dissipated had the operators not agreed to compromise:

> Could we have come out of the conference, having won completely the principle for which we had struck . . . and held the full measure of

public support with which we went into the conference? . . . Failing to reach an agreement with the Company after they had appeared to come halfway would assuredly have caused us to lose to the Postmaster-General this tactical advantage of having the popular issue on our side. Having demonstrated our inability to reach a settlement with the Company on the basis of collective bargaining, he could, with impunity proceed to arrest leaders, indict on charges of conspiracy peaceful picketers, and carry on a campaign of persecution and tyranny which has characterized his previous activities in telephone strikes.[127]

The 1919 New England telephone strike was one of the few in the wave of postwar strikes to end on favorable terms for the workers, and it precipitated organizing campaigns across the country that added thousands of new members to the Telephone Operators' Union in the next few months.

The National Situation

Most of the operators' locals organized after the New England strike were short-lived, unable to withstand the unremitting hostility of the associated Bell companies, which in nearly all cases refused to extend recognition. Most of the newly formed locals could not maintain their organization after being forced out on strike. Of the more than fifty operators' locals chartered outside New England between the end of the strike and the first Department convention in October, 1919, the vast majority had disbanded within two years. Few of the locals had the opportunity to develop any leadership, and none was able to forge an alliance with the women's movement that had done so much to sustain the Boston local. Also contributing greatly to the failure of the new locals was the postmaster-general's policy which, despite an apparent shift caused by a threatened nationwide strike, remained strongly antagonistic to trade unionism.

Conferences with Post Office Department officials failed to end discrimination against union members in the telephone service. In compliance with the nationwide referendum vote completed in May, 1919, the IBEW leadership on June 2 declared a general strike of all telephone workers to begin June 16. This date was selected because the AFL convention was scheduled to be in session at that time, and it would be in a position to render assistance to the strikers. A meeting with a delegation of IBEW and AFL officials in Washington on the eve of the strike impelled an alarmed Burleson to issue Postmaster-General's Order 3209 on June 14. Order 3209 guaranteed telephone workers the right to organize and forbad telephone companies to discriminate against union members. The order provided that "where prior to government control a company dealt with representatives chosen by employees to act for them who were not in the employ of the company, they shall hereafter do so." Companies were to designate one or more officials to whom employees, either individually or collectively, could present grievances. If the employees were not satisfied with the decision rendered, they could then appeal to the Wire Control Board.[128] Order 3209 resulted in the calling off of the general strike, as the IBEW leadership believed that "these rights once established, the question of wages and working conditions are easily taken care of."[129]

Because the postmaster-general's order came less than two months before the restoration of the wires to private control, it did little to improve labor relations in the telephone industry. Management often justified its refusal to recognize or bargain with a newly organized local by citing Order 3209's provision that it need not deal with a union if it had not done so before government control. Low wages and continued discrimination against union members sparked telephone strikes across the country in the summer and fall of 1919. Burleson continued to insist that strikes were not permitted under government control. Most of the companies involved in strikes evaded Order 3209 by declaring that strikers were no longer employees and therefore not covered by the order.[130] During the latter period of government operation, major telephone operators' strikes occurred in the South, the Midwest, and along the Pacific Coast. Undoubtedly influenced by the 1919 strike wave, Sinclair Lewis incorporated a telephone strike in his novel *Babbitt,* published in 1922 and set in the fictional midwestern city of Zenith: "The strike which turned Zenith into two belligerent camps, white and red, began in late September with a walk-out of telephone girls and linemen. . . ."[131]

In the South, where significant organizing progress was made for the first time in the spring and summer of 1919, the principal strikes occurred at Jacksonville, Florida; Atlanta, Georgia; and Columbia, South Carolina. Sixteen operators' locals were established in seven states of the Old Confederacy between May and July, 1919, eleven of them in the Deep South. Julia O'Connor considered the establishment of operators' locals in the South to be a major breakthrough, as "trade unionism in the South is a relatively new doctrine; trade unionism for women an innovation."[132] Unlike in New England, however, the labor movement in the South was weak, and the region was inhospitable to feminism. The South remained to the end almost solidly opposed to the women's suffrage amendment. Settlement houses were far fewer than in the North, and upper- and middle-class women reformers had little contact with working women. The Women's Trade Union League was not a presence in the South, and it did not initiate a major organizing campaign in the region until the late 1920s, when it established a regional office at Richmond to use as a base for unionizing women textile workers.[133] The Telephone Operators' Department could afford to provide only one organizer—Rose Hickey of Boston—for the entire South, and organizing campaigns and strikes among telephone operators were largely directed by male IBEW and AFL officials. Without a trade union infrastructure in the region and a women's movement to provide backing for the telephone operators' locals, the strikes ended in defeat and the operators' movement proved ephemeral.

The Jacksonville strike was called to protest Southern Bell Telephone Company's dismissal of thirty-eight union operators after it had refused to consider a demand for wage increases and union recognition. The Jacksonville operators had organized in 1917 as Local 62A, the first women's trade union in Florida. In a strike in December, 1917, directed by AFL organizer William Pollard, the local had won a wage increase but not union recognition or the end of the open shop. That strike, conducted before the wires came under government control, was settled through the mediation of a Department of Labor official, and it ended with the reinstatement of all the operators to their former positions.[134] Less than half the operating force joined the hastily called strike in 1919. In contrast with 1917, there was no mediation by the Department of Labor, even though the mayor of Jacksonville asked the secretary of labor to send a conciliator. Burleson insisted the Post Office Department had sole jurisdiction over the telephone service under government control, and he refused to allow another department to intervene. The Post Office Department took no action, and the company replaced the operators who had walked out with strikebreakers. The Jacksonville strike was never settled.[135]

The two-month strike of telephone operators in Atlanta also was precipitated by Southern Bell's dismissal of union operators, in this case the local's president, secretary-treasurer, and two members of the executive board. The company refused to negotiate with the local, stating that in dealing with its employees it would never recognize "any outside organization." Burleson again issued his warning that strikers who failed to return to work within twenty-four hours would not be reemployed. The local had been chartered about a month before the strike by the Commercial Telegraphers' Union of America (CTUA) and included about 400 of the 450 operators in the city.

Shortly after the operators went on strike under the leadership of C. F. Mann, the CTUA's organizer for the Southern states, Mann received authorization from the CTUA's national headquarters in Chicago to call a strike of Western Union telegraphers in all of the Southeastern states. The telegraphers' demands included union recognition and a wage increase to meet the rising cost of living, as well as reinstatement of the discharged Atlanta telephone operators.[136] The CTUA was unable to mobilize the majority of telegraphers in the Southeast behind the strike, however, and its national president called it off after a month, leaving the telephone operators to fend for themselves.

About 250 of the 400 telephone operators on strike in Atlanta refused to concede defeat and transferred their affiliation from the CTUA to the IBEW, whose southern organizer, Rose Hickey, had been in Atlanta performing strike support work for several weeks. Under Hickey's direction, the strike continued for another month, but Southern Bell persisted in its refusal to negotiate. When the strike was called off, operators desiring to return to work had to apply as individuals and submit to a hearing where company officials determined whether they should be reinstated.[137]

The strike at Columbia, South Carolina, was called only two days after the IBEW rescinded its order for a national strike—which Columbia's operators, although members of the CTUA, had planned to join—and ten days after the Atlanta operators walked out. Southern Bell had discharged operators active in the recently organized CTUA local, just as it had done in Atlanta. Joined by the male telephone workers, who belonged to the IBEW, the operators demanded their reinstatement, as well as the right to organize and bargain collectively and a wage increase. The strike was directed by male CTUA and IBEW officials. The male strikers viewed themselves as protectors of the "weaker sex," arguing that they contributed far more to the uplift of working women than such organizations as the Red Cross and the Salvation Army, since the union wage was the best protection against "temptation."[138]

Columbia was a strong labor town by southern standards, and the strikers received financial support from the railroad shop workers and streetcarmen, as well as the endorsement of the mayor, who appeared in public wearing a striker's badge. Because the county sheriff also supported the strike, the district attorney urged the judge of the district to send telephone men arrested for wire cutting to a jail outside the sheriff's jurisdiction.[139]

Citing Burleson's twenty-four-hour warning and prohibition of strikes under government control, Southern Bell remained adamant in its refusal to make any concession to the strikers, as it had in Atlanta. The strikers remained isolated; the company reported "no trouble at any other point in North Carolina or South Carolina than Columbia." The company maintained service by importing strikebreakers, and the strike ended without the telephone workers' achieving any of their goals. Strikers were again reemployed only as individuals, and management excluded those it judged to be militants.[140]

Only days after the Columbia telephone operators walked off their jobs, the telephone workers of the Pacific region launched a strike that began in San Diego and spread up the Coast. The principal demands were for wage increases and the establishment of an adjustment board like the one used by the New England telephone operators. The situation was similar to that in New England a few months before in that the Burleson Wire Administration had allowed the tripartite agreement reached in 1917 to expire at the end of 1918 without providing any method for adjusting the telephone workers' wage demands. The agreement, to which the government itself had been a party, had included a provision requiring management to reopen wage negotiations ninety days prior to January 1, 1919. The provision applied not just to the Pacific Telephone Company but to any successor, such as the Post Office Department.[141]

The Pacific strike was initiated by the male telephone workers in open rebellion against the IBEW's cancellation of the nationwide general strike, and it was quickly joined by the telephone operators. While the telephone men were, according to Julia O'Connor, "progressive, well-organized, militant," the vast majority of the telephone operators were not organized. The membership of the Telephone Operators' Union on the Pacific Coast had dwindled greatly as company harassment following the strike settlement in 1917 drove many union leaders and activists out of the telephone service. In following the men, the operators disregarded Department President O'Connor who, believing them to be insufficiently prepared, urged that they postpone strike action for two weeks until she reached the Coast. O'Connor had also wanted the Pacific telephone workers to "try out" Order 3209. Nevertheless, when the operators walked out, O'Connor endorsed the action and ordered Department Vice-President Nellie Johnson to San Francisco, headquarters of Pacific Bell, to take charge of the strike. Department organizer Mabel Leslie, who had just established the first telephone operators' local in Wisconsin at Madison and was working on a campaign at Fond du Lac, was instructed by

O'Connor to proceed to Seattle to build strike support in the Pacific Northwest.[142]

After six weeks, during which about 90 percent of the Coast's operators—mostly unorganized—joined the strike, a settlement was reached. It provided an increase in wages for both the men and the operators retroactive to January 1, 1919, but it did not give them satisfactory adjustment board rights. After returning to work, the strikers rejected the settlement in a referendum requiring them to vote for or against the entire agreement, not each provision. Although the strike produced organization gains in the short run, without an agreement the telephone men and the operators were in no position to withstand continued discrimination against union members. Julia O'Connor, who had regarded the calling of the strike as "very hasty and ill-considered," believed that the telephone workers had dissipated their strength fighting the government for six weeks, only to face a fresh antagonist after the wires were returned to private control.[143]

Telephone strikes also occurred in St. Louis and Cleveland during the summer of 1919, almost immediately after operators' locals were organized. In neither case was the outcome favorable to the operators. Although the IBEW had viewed Order 3209 as a major concession by the postmaster-general, the telephone companies in these cities again invoked it to justify their refusal to recognize the operators' locals. In St. Louis, Southwestern Bell announced only days after the promulgation of Order 3209 that it would not recognize St. Louis operators' Local 116A, chartered in May, 1919. Management also refused to meet with IBEW organizer Orville Jennings, who headed the operators' negotiating committee, on the grounds that he was not an employee of the company. Angered by the IBEW's rescinding of the order for a nationwide strike, which Local 116A had been prepared to join, and by the company's unwillingness to accord recognition and an increase in wages, the St. Louis operators walked out on strike. Southwestern Bell immediately began to import strikebreakers from Little Rock, Chicago, and towns in Missouri and Texas. At the request of Orville Jennings, Telephone Operators' Department Secretary May Matthews came from Boston to take charge of the strike.[144]

As it had done in 1913, the St. Louis labor movement rallied behind the striking telephone operators and telephone men, who joined the walkout, and a boycott of the Bell telephone was instituted, probably the first time it had been attempted in a metropolis. The St. Louis *Post-Dispatch* estimated that between 85,000 and 100,000 workers in St. Louis belonged to trade unions. The boycott was initiated by the 5,000–member streetcarmen's union, whose delegates introduced a resolution before the Central Trades and Labor Council demanding that all union members withdraw their patronage from Southwestern Bell until it came to terms with the strikers. This resolution was unanimously adopted by the council, which also pledged financial support to the strikers.[145] The 10,000–member Building Trades Council endorsed the boycott, and its president accompanied May Matthews on a visit to the governor to protest police harassment of telephone operator pickets. Matthews and ten operators had been arrested earlier in the strike for "peace disturbance." The Central Trades and Labor Council relied on the St. Louis Women's Trade Union League to draw strike support from outside the working class. St. Louis WTUL President Sarah Spraggon, an ally and prominent suffragist, arranged a conference at which representatives of the women's organizations and others interested in "civic, social, and industrial affairs" met to discuss the wages and working conditions of telephone operators.[146]

With the government firmly supporting the company's interpretation of Order 3209—not requiring union recognition or the closed shop—the strikers after six weeks accepted a compromise settlement, which provided for a maximum wage of $16 after four years, instead of the $20 after three years they had demanded. All strikers were reinstated, and the company accepted the right of employees to belong to a union and to bargain collectively. The company, however, announced that it would recognize only one-tenth of its work force as union members and that collective bargaining would be conducted on that basis.[147] This effectively eliminated trade unionism as a factor in the city's telephone service.

The Cleveland strike revealed how Order 3209, purportedly promulgated to protect the telephone workers' right to organize and bargain collectively, could be used not only to maintain the open shop but to promote company unionism (the rise of the company union movement in the Bell System is discussed in chapter 7). Rose Sullivan, a leader of Boston's Local 1A and later vice-president of the Telephone Operators' Department, was dispatched by Julia O'Connor to Cleveland to organize the telephone operators, and within three weeks they had established a local of 1,700 members. Cleveland's Local 134A, chartered by the Department on July 8, 1919, was one of the largest operators' locals in the entire country. The Bell Telephone Company of Cleveland, however, moved quickly to disrupt the organization by pressuring the operators to sign letters of resignation, already prepared by management and addressed to Sullivan, or risk losing their positions.[148] Management officials personally instructed the operators to join a newly formed company association for employees. Cleveland Bell announced that this company association provided a "ready means whereby [employees] may discuss, consider, treat, or bargain with the Company, collectively or individually," and it therefore fully satisfied the requirements of Order 3209.[149]

Having failed to end the company's harassment of union members and believing the formation of a company union constituted a violation of Order 3209, Rose Sullivan led Cleveland's telephone operators out on strike. It appears, however, that only a minority of the operators joined the walkout. It was the opinion of the Labor Department's commissioner of conciliation that Order 3209 had been "flagrantly violated."[150] Burleson as usual announced that strikes were not permitted under government control and upheld the company's position that it was not required to deal with the union. He instructed the operators to present any grievances to the Wire Control Board in Washington.[151] Burleson's conduct angered Department of Labor officials in Cleveland, one of whom bitterly denounced the postmaster-general in a letter to Secretary of Labor Wilson:

> . . . Burleson's statement that [the operators] should take their grievances to the Wire Control Board is all rot, because you know the Wire Control Board was appointed by Burleson . . . without the employees of these companies being consulted in any way, shape, or form. . . . he is using the position of Postmaster-General [as] . . . a strikebreaking agency. . . .
> Yes, he is . . . collecting funds in the name of our government, to pay the strikebreakers, gun men and thugs, for beating up these girls and crushing their organization out of existence.[152]

Although many of the male telephone workers joined the operators on strike, the company remained adamant that it would not recognize trade unions. There was no WTUL chapter to assist the operators, and it appears that trade union support for the strikers was not as strong as in St. Louis. After two weeks, the strikers agreed to return without union recognition on the company's promise that it would reinstate them to their former positions, and that no organization activities were to be permitted for either the company association or the union on the company's time or property.

The company did not live up to this promise, however. It became clear almost immediately that a significant number of the striking operators would not be taken back. Operators accused by strikebreakers of calling them "offensive names" or believed by the company or post office inspectors to have used "immoral language" on the picket line were not reemployed. While this may have just been a convenient way to prevent strikers from returning, it probably reflected the company's concern for punishing conduct unbecoming to "young ladies." The company was much more lenient to the male strikers, nearly all of whom were reinstated. According to the company's traffic manager, there was little prospect that the men's reinstatement would have a "demoralizing effect" on the "loyal" workers, since the strikers could be grouped by themselves and because telephone men often worked alone.[153] Three months after the settlement, Julia O'Connor complained that company association parties were still being held in the exchanges and that all operators were being pressured to attend. The company refused to consider Local 134A members for positions as supervisors and dismissed operators "if they speak the word 'union.' "[154] Like the St. Louis Telephone Operators' Union, the Cleveland local wielded little influence after the strike.

The telephone operators fared better in a strike in Shawnee, Oklahoma, shortly after the wires were returned to private control, although they failed to gain the closed shop. The forty-eight members of Shawnee's Local 94A, one of seven operators' locals chartered in Oklahoma, walked out in September, 1919, demanding a wage increase, union recognition, and the closed shop. The operators abandoned the latter demand after several days in an effort to gain a company commitment to select supervisors only from among union members. The strikers commanded wide community support in Shawnee, a town of 25,000 which served primarily as an agricultural distributing center, probably because of the region's tradition of agrarian radicalism and the distrust of the Southwestern Bell Company, viewed as a "foreign" corporation directed from St. Louis and New York, which exploited local girls and young women. The company's importation of strikebreakers from Oklahoma City and Tulsa was also resented, especially since Shawnee was a small town where a significant proportion of the population knew the striking women. The strike was settled after two weeks, with the operators' winning union recognition. The wage issue was referred for arbitration to the state corporation commission.[155]

The Shawnee strike was followed by another in Palestine, Texas, in October, 1919. In some important respects, this strike closely resembled those which had occurred in the Montana mining towns and in Fort Smith, although it was directed against the independent Palestine Telephone Company rather than the "foreign" Bell corporation.

Palestine, with a population of 11,600, was a shop center for the International Great Northern Railroad and was considered one of the strongest union towns in Texas. Labor leaders held several city offices, and the trade unions ran a cooperative grocery store capitalized at $10,000. The telephone strike, initiated by the five IBEW linemen, was precipitated by the company's hiring a new foreman from outside Palestine, rather than filling the vacancy by promoting the member of the local with the most seniority. The telephone operators, about ten who had organized three months before as Local 147A, walked out in sympathy.[156]

The walkout, which began when the Central Trades and Labor Council instituted a boycott of the town's telephone system, culminated in a general strike. Union waiters refused to serve strikebreakers, forcing the company to establish a special dining room at the exchange. An agent of the Bureau of Investigation stationed in Palestine complained that union telegraphers intercepted messages sent to the telephone company. The agent also reported that the leaders of the Federated Railroad Crafts of Palestine—including the head of the Boilermakers' local, who was a former mayor of Palestine—were taking a prominent part in strike support work. A general strike developed when the Retail Merchants' Association refused to observe the boycott and the company imported strikebreakers. Among those who walked out in support of the telephone workers were the retail clerks, waiters, plumbers, electricians, bakers, and bakery wagon drivers. Even the children at the grammar school demonstrated solidarity with the strikers, threatening to quit school if the telephone at their school building was used. To help enforce the boycott, the pupils also compiled a list of the names of all children whose parents continued to use the telephone at home.[157] Although it is not clear how the strike ended, Local 147A was disbanded by 1921.

Conclusion

Throughout most of the country, telephone operators' unionism remained precarious after the resumption of private control on August 1, 1919, as the associated Bell companies actively disrupted organizing and forced premature strikes which drained the union's meager financial resources. The Wilson administration's toleration of the open shop made it difficult for the operators' locals to bargain effectively or maintain organization. The telephone companies benefited greatly from government control. The postmaster-general intervened to support management's position during strikes and even prevented the reinstatement of strikers after it had been negotiated in Minneapolis and St. Paul. Burleson's Order 3209, which the IBEW had assumed would protect the telephone workers' right to organize and bargain collectively, was easily evaded by the telephone companies. The associated Bell companies emerged from government control financially strengthened, having profited from the high rate increases authorized by the postmaster-general for both long distance and local service. The federal government also absorbed a $13,000,000 deficit that had accrued during the year it had operated the wires.[158]

Only in New England, where wage negotiations had been conducted on the basis of collective bargaining for seven years, did the telephone company regard the union as the legitimate representative of the operating force. The New England Telephone Company, which with AT&T's cooperation had transported 1,200 strikebreakers to Boston from New England, the Middle Atlantic, and the Midwest in 1913 in an effort to destroy the newly organized Telephone Operators' Union, made no attempt in 1919 to secure permanent replacements for the strikers. By contrast, Southwestern Bell in St. Louis and Shawnee; Southern Bell in Jacksonville, Atlanta, and Columbia; Cleveland Bell in Cleveland; and Pacific Bell on the Coast all brought in strikebreakers to displace operators who walked out later in 1919. Except in the smaller towns and in St. Louis, where a boycott was attempted, supportive action by other trade unions was limited to verbal expressions of solidarity and financial contributions; in no city was there a sympathy strike by a group of workers outside the telephone service.

The operators' dramatic victory in New England in 1919 spurred organizing across the country, just as it had in 1913, when the union had achieved recognition in the face of concerted opposition by a management determined to eliminate trade unionism in the telephone service. The 1919 strike, however, also revealed a serious weakness in New England telephone unionism: the male telephone workers refused to demonstrate solidarity with the operators in the early stages of the strike. Relations between the male and female telephone workers became increasingly strained during the next year. The 1919 strike represented the last occasion in which the operators and the male telephone workers participated in joint wage negotiations.

NOTES

1. David Montgomery, *The Fall of the House of Labor* (New York: Cambridge University Press, 1987), p. 6; Henry Pelling, *American Labor* (Chicago: University of Chicago Press, 1960), pp. 132, 135; Maurine Weiner

Greenwald, *Women, War, and Work* (Westport, Conn.: Greenwood Press, 1980), pp. 34, 39.

2. Melvyn Dubofsky, "Abortive Reform: The Wilson Administration and Organized Labor, 1913–1920," in James Cronin and Carmen Sirianni, eds., *Work, Community, and Power* (Philadelphia: Temple University Press, 1983), pp. 199, 203–4.

3. David Kennedy, *Over Here* (New York: Oxford University Press, 1980), p. 259; David Brody, *Workers in Industrial America* (New York: Oxford University Press, 1980), p. 41.

4. Kennedy, *Over Here*, pp. 267–68.

5. Dubofsky, "Abortive Reform," p. 207.

6. Julia O'Connor, "History of the Organized Telephone Operators' Movement," Part 4, *Union Telephone Operator* [hereafter, *UTO*], May, 1921, p. 15.

7. Kennedy, *Over Here*, p. 262.

8. John D. Hicks, *Rehearsal for Disaster* (Gainesville: University of Florida Press, 1961), pp. 36–37.

9. Kennedy, *Over Here*, p. 258; O'Connor, "History," Part 4, p. 14.

10. "Report of First Vice-President Nellie Johnson," in *Proceedings of the First Regular Convention of the Telephone Operators' Department, IBEW*, New Orleans, La., 1919, p. 23, Julia O'Connor Parker Papers, Schlesinger Library, Radcliffe College, Cambridge, Mass.

11. *Report of the President's Mediation Commission to the President of the United States* (Washington, D.C.: Government Printing Office, 1918), p. 11, Chief Clerk's File 20/473, General Records of the Department of Labor, Record Group [hereafter RG] 174, National Archives [hereafter NA], Washington, D.C.; Robert E. L. Knight, *Industrial Relations in the San Francisco Bay Area, 1900–1918* (Berkeley and Los Angeles: University of California Press, 1960), p. 355.

12. Memoranda from William B. Wilson, August 31 and September 19, 1917, Chief Clerk's File 20/473, General Records of the Department of Labor, RG 174, NA.

13. "Report of Vice-President Nellie Johnson," p. 24; Knight, *Industrial Relations*, p. 355.

14. Harlan B. Phillips, ed., *Felix Frankfurter Reminisces* (New York: Reynal, 1960), pp. 121, 127.

15. O'Connor, "History," Part 3, *UTO*, March, 1921, p. 14.

16. Fort Smith *Times-Record*, September 4, 1917.

17. Ibid., September 19 and 20, 1917.

18. Ibid., October 3 and December 4, 1917; *Arkansas Gazette*, December 4, 1917.

19. Fort Smith *Times-Record*, September 20, November 26, and December 2, 1917.

20. Ibid., September 20, 1917.

21. Ibid., December 9, 1917; *Arkansas Gazette*, December 10, 1917.

22. *Arkansas Gazette*, December 11 and 14, 1917.

23. State of Arkansas, *Third Biennial Report of the Bureau of the Statistics of Labor of the State of Arkansas, 1917–1918* (n.p., [1918]), pp. 6–7; *Arkansas Gazette,* December 15, 27, and 28, 1917; Fort Smith *Times-Record,* December 27, 1917.

24. N. R. Danielian, *A.T.&T.: The Story of Industrial Conquest* (New York: Vanguard Press, 1939), p. 249.

25. Kennedy, *Over Here,* pp. 252–55.

26. Ibid., p. 255.

27. Greenwald, *Women, War, and Work,* p. 90.

28. "Report of the Department President," in *Proceedings of the First Regular Convention,* p. 12.

29. U.S. Commission on Industrial Relations, *Final Report and Testimony Submitted to Congress by the Commission on Industrial Relations,* vol. 10 (Washington, D.C.: Government Printing Office, 1916), pp. 9144, 9285–87.

30. Texas Penitentiary Investigating Committee, *Report and Findings of the Penitentiary Investigating Committee,* (Austin, Tex.: Texas Penitentiary Investigating Committee, July 24, 1913), p. 5.

31. Representative Clarence B. Miller, [Speech before U.S. House, 65th Congress, 2d session, September 12, 1918], *Congressional Record* 56, no. 649 (1918):10253–54; see also Joseph Smith, "Burleson and Labor: The Sweater and the Slave-Driver," Box 35, Albert S. Burleson Papers, Library of Congress, Washington, D.C.

32. Kennedy, *Over Here,* p. 75.

33. Boston *Post,* December 6, 1917.

34. Quoted in Miller, *Congressional Record,* 10253; "National Association of Letter Carriers of the United States of America," in Gary M. Fink, ed., *Labor Unions* (Westport, Conn.: Greenwood Press, 1977), p. 182.

35. Phillips, ed., *Frankfurter,* p. 122.

36. N. C. Kingsbury to Albert Burleson, October 31, 1918, and Albert Burleson to C. T. Bonny, October 31, 1918, Box 74, Office of the Solicitor, Records Relating to Federal Operation, Records of the Post Office Department, RG 28, NA; Richmond *Times-Dispatch,* November 1, 1918.

37. Burleson to Bonny, October 31, 1918; St. Paul *Pioneer-Press,* November 15, 1918.

38. Report of Inspectors, February 5, 1919, Case Number 28941–C, St. Paul/Minneapolis File, Box 268, Office of the Solicitor, Post Office Department Records, RG 28, NA; St. Paul *Pioneer-Press,* November 18, 1918.

39. St. Paul *Pioneer-Press,* November 21, 1918; William Hard, "Mr. Burleson Back from Boston," *New Republic,* May 3, 1919, p. 15.

40. St. Paul *Pioneer-Press,* December 16, 1918.

41. "Report of the Department President," pp. 9, 12; O'Connor, "History," Part 4, p. 25; St. Paul *Pioneer-Press,* January 22, 1919; George Lawson to Frank Morrison, February 3, 1919, File 170–148, Records of the Federal Mediation and Conciliation Service [hereafter, FMCS], RG 280, NA.

42. Lawson to Morrison, February 3, 1919.

43. Report of the Inspector, "Statements of Lola Price and Dora Preston," December 26, 1918, Case Number 30866–C, Wichita File, Box 268, Office of the Solicitor, Post Office Department Records, RG 28, NA.

44. Report of the Inspector, "Statements of Lela Phipps and Dora Preston," December 26, 1918, Case Number 30866–C, Wichita File, Box 268, Office of the Solicitor, Post Office Department Records, RG 28, NA.

45. Albert Burleson to L. W. Clapp, mayor of Wichita, December 16, 1918, Box 268, Office of the Solicitor, Post Office Department Records, RG 28, NA; W. F. Allmon, inspector, Post Office Department, "Report on Wichita Strike," January 8, 1919, Case 30866–C, Box 268, Office of the Solicitor, Post Office Department Records, RG 28, NA; *Proceedings of First Regular Convention,* p. 12.

46. Danielian, *A.T.&T.,* p. 249; Horace Coon, *American Tel & Tel: The Story of a Great Monopoly* (New York: Longmans, Green, 1939), p. 138; Greenwald, *Women, War, and Work,* p. 215; Albert Burleson to William B. Wilson, March 15, 1919, Box 177, Office of the Solicitor, Post Office Department Records, RG 28, NA.

47. A. S. Burleson to W. S. Ryan, September 14, 1918, reprinted in "Minutes of the Meeting of the Ryan Commission," October 24, 1918, p. 1, Julia O'Connor Parker Papers.

48. The United States Independent Telephone Association was made up of independent telephone companies not owned or controlled by the Bell System. At that time in the United States, these companies operated about 15,000 exchanges, under 8,000 separate ownerships. For the most part, these exchanges were located in areas of low population. Three and a half million subscribers were served by independent exchanges that had full connections with the Bell System throughout the country, and about one and a half million subscribers were connected with the Independent exclusively.

49. *Boston Labor World,* September 28, 1918; *Labor News,* September 28, 1918.

50. John Colpoys and Julia O'Connor to Albert Burleson, January 6, 1919, Box 125, Post Office Department Records, RG 28, NA; Julia O'Connor to Albert Burleson, January 28, 1919, Box 125, Post Office Department Records, RG 28, NA.

51. Lamar Whitcher, Division Superintendent of Traffic, New England Telephone Company, to Julia O'Connor, January 17, 1919, Box 6, AT&T Archives, New York, N.Y.; Albert Burleson to Woodrow Wilson, March 28, 1919, Box 177, Post Office Department Records, RG 28, NA.

52. Albert Burleson to William B. Wilson, March 15, 1919, Box 2, AT&T Archives; Memorandum for the Secretary of Labor from Felix Frankfurter, n.d., Box 177, Post Office Department Records, RG 28, NA.

53. Hicks, *Rehearsal,* pp. 36–37, 40; Daniel Bell, *Marxian Socialism in the United States* (Princeton, N.J.: Princeton University Press, 1952), p. 117; Robert K. Murray, *Red Scare* (New York: McGraw-Hill, 1964), pp. 6, 8–9; James R. Green and Hugh Carter Donahue, *Boston's Workers: A Labor History* (Boston: Boston Public Library, 1979), p. 95.

54. Julia O'Connor, "The Truth about the New England 'Phone Strike,' " *Life and Labor*, June, 1919, p. 132; Anne Withington, "The Telephone Strike," *The Survey*, April 26, 1919, p. 146.

55. Withington, "Telephone Strike," p. 146; Boston *Herald*, April 15, 1919.

56. O'Connor, "Truth," p. 132; Withington, "Telephone Strike," p. 146; Boston *Herald*, April 15, 1919.

57. Boston *Post*, April 12, 1919.

58. Ibid.; Boston *Herald*, April 12, 1919; Boston *Globe*, April 12, 1919; Hard, "Mr. Burleson, Back from Boston," p. 15.

59. Withington, "Telephone Strike," p. 146. These figures applied to "Class AA" cities. The New England Telephone Company used six wage scales, depending on the size of the city or town. The operators in the larger "Class AA" cities received the highest wages; the scale decreased somewhat for each category of lesser population, with the smallest "Class E" towns receiving the lowest wages. The "Class AA" cities, in addition to Boston, were Brockton, Fall River, Haverhill, Holyoke, Lawrence, Lynn, New Bedford, Pittsfield, Salem, Springfield, and Worcester.

60. Boston *Post*, April 16, 1919.

61. Boston *Globe*, April 16, 1919.

62. Boston *Herald*, April 16, 1919.

63. Mosby to Chief Post Office Inspector, April 17, 1919, Box 177, Post Office Department Records, RG 28, NA.

64. Boston *Evening Transcript*, April 14 and 17, 1919.

65. Ibid., April 16, 1919.

66. Ibid., April 17 and 18, 1919.

67. Ibid., April 16, 1919. Mosby reported that he was struck by the "good clothes" and "hilarity" of operators in the strike parade. Mosby to Chief Post Office Inspector, April 17, 1919.

68. Providence *Journal*, April 17, 1919.

69. Ibid., April 20, 1919.

70. Boston *Post*, April 17, 1919.

71. National Women's Trade Union League [hereafter, WTUL], "Proceedings of the 1919 Convention," p. 115, Reel 22, National WTUL Papers, Library of Congress, Washington, D.C.

72. Boston *Evening Transcript*, April 17, 1919; Boston *Eveninq Globe*, April 17, 1919.

73. Boston *Herald*, April 19, 1919.

74. Boston *Globe*, April 20, 1919.

75. *Boston Labor World*, April 20, 1918; Boston *Daily Advertiser*, April 17, 1919; National WTUL, "Proceedings of the 1919 Convention," p. 115.

76. National WTUL, "Proceedings of the 1919 Convention," p. 114; Manchester *Union*, April 17, 1919.

77. Boston *Daily Advertiser*, April 19, 1919.

78. Sidney Harring, *Policing a Class Society* (New Brunswick, N.J.: Rutgers University Press, 1983), pp. 27, 42, 141–42.

79. *Life and Labor,* January, 1921, p. 2; Anna Weinstock Schneider, interview by Stephen H. Norwood, August 15, 1974, Sudbury, Mass.

80. National WTUL, "Proceedings of the 1919 Convention," pp. 114–15.

81. Anna Weinstock Schneider, interview.

82. Providence *Journal,* April 20, 1919.

83. Fall River *Globe,* April 16, 1919; Lynn *Telegram-News,* April 18, 1919; Boston *Herald,* April 18, 1919.

84. National WTUL, "Proceedings of the 1919 Convention," p. 115; Rose Finkelstein Norwood, interview by Stephen H. Norwood, July 18, 1974, Boston, Mass.

85. Boston *Herald,* April 19, 1919.

86. Fall River *Globe,* April 18, 1919; Providence *Journal,* April 20, 1919.

87. Fall River *Globe,* April 18, 1919.

88. Boston *Post,* April 18, 1919.

89. Providence *Journal,* April 20, 1919.

90. Boston *Evening Transcript,* April 18, 1919.

91. Ibid.; *New York Times,* April 18, 1919.

92. Harvard *Crimson,* April 18, 1919.

93. Boston *Evening Transcript,* April 18, 1919; *New York Times,* April 18, 1919.

94. Harvard *Crimson,* April 18, 1919.

95. Brown *Daily Herald,* April 17, 1919; *Journal of Electrical Workers and Operators* [hereafter, *JEWO*], May, 1919, p. 520.

96. Providence *Journal,* April 18, 1919.

97. Brown *Daily Herald,* April 17 and 18, 1919.

98. Providence *Journal,* April 18, 1919; Brown *Daily Herald,* April 19, 1919.

99. Boston *Herald,* April 19, 1919.

100. Lewiston *Evening Journal,* April 19, 1919.

101. Harvard *Crimson,* April 16 and 21, 1919.

102. Boston *Herald,* April 19, 1919.

103. Boston *Evening Transcript,* April 19 and 21, 1919.

104. Ibid.; Boston *Herald,* April 19 and 22, 1919.

105. *JEWO,* May, 1919, p. 516.

106. Boston *Herald,* April 18, 1919; Boston *Evening Transcript,* April 18 and 19, 1919. Quoted from Boston *Evening Transcript,* April 19, 1919.

107. Boston *Evening Transcript,* April 21, 1919; Boston *Herald,* April 21, 1919.

108. Mary Quinn Wynne, interview by Stephen H. Norwood, June 28, 1974, Springfield, Mass.

109. Boston *Herald,* April 21, 1919.

110. Boston *Daily Advertiser,* April 22, 1919.

111. Withington, "Telephone Strike," p. 146.

112. O'Connor, "History," Part 5, *UTO*, June, 1921, p. 16.

113. Boston *Post*, April 21, 1919.

114. O'Connor, "History," Part 5, p. 16.

115. Withington, "Telephone Strike," p. 146; O'Connor, "History," Part 5, p. 16.

116. "James Edwin Cassidy," in *Dictionary of the American Hierarchy* (New York: Longmans, Green, 1940), pp. 43–44.

117. "Proceedings of the Twenty-second Annual Convention of the United Textile Workers of America," *Textile Worker*, October, 1922, p. 345.

118. James Cassidy, "The Saloon versus the Labor Union" (Fall River, Mass.: n.p., November 26, 1911), pp. 6–7.

119. Francis L. Broderick, *Right Reverend New Dealer: John A. Ryan* (New York: MacMillan, 1963), p. 59.

120. *New York Times*, May 19, 1942.

121. James Cassidy to Jennie M. Keefe, April 22, 1919, Julia O'Connor Parker Papers.

122. Julia O'Connor to James Cassidy, April 25, 1919, Julia O'Connor Parker Papers.

123. James Cassidy to Julia O'Connor, April 27, 1919, Julia O'Connor Parker Papers.

124. Julia O'Connor to James Cassidy, May 1, 1919, Julia O'Connor Parker Papers.

125. Ibid.

126. Ibid.

127. James Cassidy to Julia O'Connor, April 26, 1919, Julia O'Connor Parker Papers; O'Connor to Cassidy, May 1, 1919.

128. O'Connor, "History," Part 6, *UTO*, July, 1921, p. 15; Cleveland *Plain-Dealer*, July 15, 1919.

129. "Telephone Settlement," *JEWO*, June, 1919, p. 557.

130. O'Connor, "History," Part 6, p. 16.

131. Sinclair Lewis, *Babbitt* (New York: Harcourt, Brace, and World, 1922), p. 249.

132. O'Connor, "History," Part 5, p. 18.

133. William Chafe, *The American Woman* (New York: Oxford University Press, 1972), p. 75.

134. "Telephone Operators in Jacksonville, Florida Go on Strike," *Life and Labor*, January, 1918, p. 20; "Jacksonville Telephone Girls Win Strike," *Life and Labor*, February, 1918, p. 40; *Florida Times-Union*, December 13 and 16, 1917.

135. O'Connor, "History," Part 5, pp. 17–18; *Florida Times-Union*, May 20, 1919; Report of Commissioner of Conciliation F. J. Hawley, August 30, 1919, Case File 170–668, FMCS Records, RG 280, NA.

136. Atlanta *Constitution*, June 1–4, 1919.

137. Ibid., July 3 and 30, 1919.

138. *The State*, June 9, 12, and 22, 1919.

139. Ibid., June 16, 1919; Francis Weston to A. Mitchell Palmer, June 21, 1919, File 16–125–67, Classified Subjects File, Department of Justice Central Files, Box 3365, Records of the Department of Justice, RG 60, NA; Post Office Inspector's Report, A. J. Knight, inspector, June 21, 1919, Case 42380–C, ibid.

140. *The State*, June 28 and July 5, 1919.

141. "Report of the Department President," pp. 8–9; "Report of First Vice-President Nellie Johnson," p. 24; O'Connor, "History," Part 6, p. 14.

142. O'Connor, "History," Part 6, pp. 16–17; Julia O'Connor to Marjorie White, December 2, 1920, Julia O'Connor Parker Papers; "Report of Department President," p. 15; "Report of Organizer Mabel Leslie," in *Proceedings of First Regular Convention*, p. 97.

143. "Report of Department President," p. 14; O'Connor to White, December 2, 1920; "President's Report to Second Biennial Convention of the Telephone Operators' Department," St. Louis, Mo., October 31, 1921, Julia O'Connor Parker Papers.

144. St. Louis *Post-Dispatch*, June 25–27 and 30, 1919.

145. Ibid., July 9 and 14, 1919.

146. F. A. Stevenson to J. C. Koons, July 16, 1919, Box 268, Office of the Solicitor, Post Office Department Records, RG 28, NA; St. Louis *Post-Dispatch*, July 17, 1919.

147. St. Louis *Post-Dispatch*, August 13, 1919.

148. "Report of Department President," p. 14; "Report of Organizer Rose Sullivan," in *Proceedings of First Regular Convention*, p. 97.

149. J. H. Walker to Hon. William B. Wilson, July 15, 1919, File 170–562, FMCS Records, RG 280, NA; Cleveland *Plain-Dealer*, July 13, 1919.

150. Commissioner, Memorandum, July 9, 1919, File 170–562, FMCS Records, RG 280, NA.

151. Cleveland *Plain-Dealer*, July 13 and 15, 1919.

152. Walker to Wilson, July 15, 1919.

153. Cleveland *Plain-Dealer*, July 26, 1919.

154. Julia O'Connor, Memorandum, November 4, 1919, Folder 53341, Post Office Department Records, RG 28, NA.

155. *Daily Oklahoman*, September 1, 2, 11, and 21, 1919; *Labor News*, October 10, 1919.

156. Report of Agent Holman Cook, October 27, 1919, Case 376327, Roll 825, Bureau of Investigation Records, RG 65, NA; Report of Inspectors C. L. Cain and R. L. McManus, December 15, 1918, File 16–113, Department of Justice Records, RG 60, NA; Texas State Federation of Labor, *Proceedings of the Twenty-first Annual Convention* (Austin: Texas State Federation of Labor, 1918), p. 111.

157. Report of Agent Holman Cook, October 27, 1919; Dallas *Morning News*, November 5 and 8, 1919.

158. Greenwald, *Women, War, and Work*, p. 213.

6

Women in Their Own Union

The Making of the
Trade Union Woman

The leadership of the Telephone Operators' Department of the International Brotherhood of Electrical Workers (IBEW) viewed its most important tasks as establishing the union on a national basis and transforming the rank-and-file telephone operator into an assertive and self-confident "trade union woman" who would strongly identify with the working class and would assume a position equal to men in the labor movement. It planned to bring the telephone operator squarely into the center of the labor movement in every section of the country. President Julia O'Connor at the first Department convention stated that it was the "moral duty" of all telephone operators' locals to affiliate with city central labor bodies and state federations of labor and "to support them in every way possible." At the same time, operator unionists were to remain aware of their interests as women and ally themselves "with the women's part of the labor movement." Having witnessed the "unparalleled bravery" of the telephone operators during the strike wave of the preceding months, O'Connor had no doubt that they would increase their already considerable influence in both the workplace and the trade union movement. Yet she knew that the operators were "young, unused to hardships, undisciplined in the administration of organization matters, as well as unschooled in the great traditions of the movement."[1] The survival of women's unionism in the telephone service required the Telephone Operators' Department to move beyond the narrow focus on job issues favored by men's unions and to elaborate social and educational programs that could stir young telephone operators' interest in labor activism and transform their sense of a "woman's place." This chapter explores how the Telephone Operators' Department was administered as an international, woman-led organization as well as the programs it developed in the making of the trade union woman.

Shaping a National Union

The erosion of wages by wartime inflation and the increasing dissatisfaction of large numbers of telephone operators under government control contributed to the considerable organizing success the Telephone Operators' Department enjoyed during 1919. By the time of its first convention, the Department had attained its peak membership of 18,000 across the United States and Canada.[2] Although the Department represented less than 20 percent of the nation's telephone operators, locals had been established in over thirty states, the Panama Canal Zone, and four Canadian provinces. However, even in New England, which according to Julia O'Connor constituted "the financial and moral backbone of the Department," many of the locals were newly established.[3] For example, Providence's 700–member Local 65A, the region's second largest operators' local which had jurisdiction over the entire state of Rhode Island except for Newport, was formed only in November, 1918, when Julia O'Connor and Teresa Sullivan came from Boston to initiate an organizing campaign.[4]

The Department's first convention was held in New Orleans in 1919. Department conventions were held in the same city, though not always the same week, as the IBEW conventions so that Department officers could participate in deliberations with IBEW leaders concerning general telephone matters. Unlike the well-financed craftsmen's organizations, however, most operators' locals could not afford to send delegates to New Orleans. Moreover, the newer ones were not eligible for representation because the Department constitution required that locals be affiliated with the international for six months before they could participate in a convention. Although operators from every section of the country were represented, the first convention was dominated by delegations from New England. Boston's delegation of seven was the convention's largest, and it controlled 45 percent of the vote.[5] Only eighteen locals were able to send delegates, including one from Balboa Heights in the Panama Canal Zone and two from Winnipeg, Manitoba.

President Julia O'Connor, while noting the "splendid progress" of the previous year, reminded the convention delegates of the enormous challenges confronting the union in the "pioneer stage" of its development. O'Connor stressed in her presidential report that, despite the long-standing presence of strong and well-disciplined locals in New England, the right to organize and bargain collectively did not exist for telephone operators in other regions, except in rare instances: "Industrial feudalism flourishes no more vigorously in the coal fields of Colorado and West Virginia, in the steel mill of Pennsylvania, or in any establishment synonymous with industrial servitude than it does in the telephone exchanges of this country."[6] Because the Department had such meager financial resources, it could afford only five organizers for the entire continent and could not respond to the numerous requests for assistance from operators in the South and Midwest. O'Connor therefore proposed that organizing focus on the areas immediately adjacent to union territory, particularly in the Pacific region and Connecticut, the only New England state not yet unionized.[7]

The convention devoted considerable attention to further integrating the affiliated locals in an effort to offset the power of the highly centralized and well-coordinated Bell System. Any associated Bell Company, operating across a vast territory, could easily overwhelm a single telephone operators' local. Realizing that operators required the support of other trade unions to prevail in a strike, the Department also emphasized the importance of translating the particularism of the rank-and-file operator into a broader identification with the labor movement. IBEW Vice-President Gustave Bugniazet, introduced by President O'Connor as "far and away the most popular Brotherhood officer with the Operators," stressed the importance of a national perspective in his address on the opening day of the convention: "You . . . take your little home town and leave it just where it is. . . . You must give consideration to . . . every point within the United States and Canada."[8] The convention began preparations to publish a monthly union journal, which would contribute to the formation of a national identity for the union by facilitating communication among telephone operators in every region and would create links with other internationals. The journal, called the *Union Telephone Operator*, published its first issue in January, 1921. It presented a six-part history of the organized telephone operators' movement by Julia O'Connor, as well as articles on the history of working women and news of the American, British, and Irish labor movements. The Department's administrative structure was also designed to promote interregional contacts. The executive board was composed of a representative from each of seven geographical districts, and the constitution required that one of the three vice-presidents must be from the eastern United States, one from the West, and one from Canada.[9]

Delegates at the first convention were almost completely occupied with administrative matters. Only one political issue was discussed on the floor: the Irish national question, reflecting the union's predominantly Irish-American membership. The convention passed a resolution introduced by several Department officers and delegates from the Boston, Springfield, and Butte locals, which stated, "Ireland has repeatedly by popular suffrage demonstrated its desire for complete separation from the British Empire," and called upon the U.S. Senate to recognize the existence of the Republic of Ireland.[10]

On the last day of the convention, elections were held for the major Department offices, none of which was strongly contested. Julia O'Connor was reelected Department president, defeating Doris Meakin of Winnipeg, while Mary Quinn Wynne defeated Helen Donohue of Worcester for the position of Department treasurer, in each case by a margin of over three to one. The convention minutes do not indicate what issues separated the candidates for president and treasurer. That Mary Meagher, Local 1A's first vice-president and a leader of its toll faction, cast her vote for Meakin suggests, however, that O'Connor continued to be strongly resented by the toll operators of her own city.[11] Mabel Leslie, an organizer based in Boston, was elected Department secretary unopposed after May Matthews of Local 1A declined renomination. Matthews and several delegates, including Meagher, did go on record opposing Leslie's election on the grounds that she was not, and never had been, a telephone operator. Their opposition probably stemmed from the fact that Leslie was close to Julia O'Connor.

Mabel Leslie (1893–1974), a member of the IBEW since 1912, had gained prominence as an activist in the electrical manufacturing industry. Born in Schenectady, New York, she had been employed as a fixture assembler at that city's General Electric plant, the world's largest manufacturer of electrical apparatus. The workers at the plant belonged to twenty-seven different trade union locals, eleven of which were affiliated with the IBEW; each local was represented by five delegates elected to a central body known as the Electrical Trades Alliance. A campaign by the Alliance in 1913 for the eight-hour day and to organize women workers at the plant resulted in the company's firing Frank Dujay, president of the Alliance, and the twenty-year-old Mabel Leslie, chair of the Girls' (Organizing) Committee. This precipitated a strike of 12,000 workers, including 2,000 women and girls, which resulted in the reinstatement of Dujay and Leslie within a week.[12] Leslie served as secretary of the Schenectady Trades Assembly and, after eight years as an electrical worker, received a scholarship to the National Women's Trade Union League Training School in Chicago. She then became an organizer for the Telephone Operators' Department. Leslie was also the editor of the *Union Telephone Operator* for its entire duration (1921–22).

Although organizing gains were negligible during the next two years and the Department's membership declined considerably (the reasons for this are outlined in chapter 7), the existing telephone operators' locals were much more fully integrated with each other by the time of the second biennial convention at St. Louis in October, 1921. This had in part been achieved through the formation in 1920 of two regional federations of operators' locals known as "councils," one in Illinois and Indiana, the other in New England. In 1922, the Butte and Missoula locals in Montana established the Rocky Mountain District Council; its jurisdiction included all the Rocky Mountain states, which with the exception of Montana remained unorganized. The Department believed that by establishing councils it could more easily coordinate the actions of all organized operators employed by a Bell subsidiary or one of the various independent telephone companies, which would enhance their power in bargaining and strikes as well as help them achieve standard wages and working conditions throughout an entire region.

The first federation of locals in the Department, the Central States Council (CSC), was formed largely from locals organized in the central and southern Illinois coal-mining regions in 1919 and 1920. This council, established on instructions from the Department's Boston headquarters, was composed mostly of operators employed by the numerous independent telephone companies in the section rather than by the Bell System. No two locals in Illinois or Indiana contained operators employed by the same telephone company.[13] Similar to the situation in Montana, the heavily unionized Illinois coal fields provided a highly favorable environment for the formation of telephone operators' locals. In the early 1920s, Illinois was not only the largest but the best-organized and most militant district in the United Mine Workers' Union (UMW), which reached its membership peak in 1921. As in Montana, merchants and professionals, depending heavily on the patronage of miners and their families, generally took labor's side in strikes. According to Melvyn Dubofsky and Warren Van Tine, "strikebreakers occupied a lower rung on the moral order than Satan" in most Illinois mining communities.[14] The CSC received strong backing from the mine workers, in part because many telephone operators came from mining families. At least twenty-five Illinois UMW locals made financial contributions to the CSC.[15]

After the establishment of the autonomous Telephone Operators' Department, operators in mining sections were less likely to be forced into dependency on male trade unionists, who had organized and led them in the past. The Department officers maintained close contact with the CSC and provided leadership in the early stages. Department Vice-President Rose Sullivan of Local 1A supervised the initial organizing efforts by the CSC and assisted affiliated locals in contract negotiations. In 1920, Department vice-presidents Rose Sullivan and Teresa Sullivan and organizer Rose Hickey, all from Boston, provided leadership to the operators of the "Egyptian" coal towns of Herrin, Marion, Benton, West Frankfort, and Johnston City, organized as Local 189A. They helped them gain a wage increase in a two-month strike against the Murphysboro Telephone Company.[16] Beatrice Coucher, a member of the executive board of the Rocky Mountain District Council, in which operators from Butte's mining district were heavily represented, recalled that either Julia O'Connor or Rose Sullivan was present at nearly every council meeting.[17]

The presidents of the New England telephone operators' locals, long federated with the male IBEW telephone locals in the New England Joint Council of Telephone Workers, met in Boston in October, 1920, to form a separate council for the telephone operators. Telephone Operators' Union leaders had favored such a council for some time because they had had difficulty eliciting regular attendance from the operators' delegates, many of whom displayed considerable diffidence in speaking and presenting grievances in the presence of the male telephone workers. The secession of the telephone men from the IBEW in May, 1920, (discussed in the next chapter) necessitated the establishment of the New England Council of Telephone Operators' Unions.

Since nearly all the organized telephone operators in New England were employed by the same company, the New England Council had charge of the annual contract negotiations. Three of the council's members, elected at large, constituted a permanent regional adjustment board, which presented to the company's general manager grievances that local adjustment boards had failed to resolve. Nearly every local in eastern Massachusetts and Rhode Island was represented at the monthly meetings of the New England Council in Boston. Mary June, a supervisor at Boston's Back Bay exchange who had succeeded

Julia O'Connor as president of Local 1A by defeating May Matthews in the 1920 election, became the first president of the New England Council.[18]

To more fully integrate the telephone operators of northern New England, where no local could afford to send a regular delegate to the council meetings in Boston, the Department organized special conferences, and its officers regularly visited the three northern states. There were twenty-two operators' locals in Maine, Vermont, and New Hampshire, the majority of which had been organized during and immediately after the 1919 New England strike. The low density of population in northern New England hindered the involvement of many operators in union affairs. The local at Rumford, Maine, for example, contained telephone operators from eleven exchanges, one of which was sixty miles from Rumford. The "foreign" members— the term used by the local's secretary—could participate in the union only by correspondence because weather and transportation conditions permitted them to attend the local's meetings at Rumford only during the summer.[19] To promote solidarity among the telephone operators of Vermont, the state's eight locals each sent two representatives to conferences at White River Junction in May, 1922, attended by President Julia O'Connor and Department Vice-President Rose Sullivan, and at Rutland in July, 1922.[20] These conferences exposed telephone operators to issues of concern to the labor movement and taught skills required to administer union locals in a section where the involvement of workers in central labor bodies and state federations and press coverage of trade union matters were far less pervasive than in Massachusetts and Rhode Island.

The Telephone Operators' Department was one of the least hierarchical organizations in the American labor movement. In no other American trade union was the leadership as accessible to the rank-and-file woman worker. The Department's meager finances, resulting from the inability of the poorly paid membership to contribute much dues and the IBEW's unwillingness to make any but the most minimal donations, inhibited the growth of union bureaucracy. While nearly all national labor officials were far removed from the workplace, at the time of the Department's first convention in October, 1919, all of its officers except the president, secretary, and five organizers were working operators, and even they were "plugging their boards" a year prior to the convention. Compared to other trade union officials, the salaries of the Department officers were low. It was common in 1920 for trade union officials to receive from $5,000 to $10,000 a year. Department President Julia O'Connor in 1919 received as her annual salary $2,500, Department Secretary May Matthews $2,000, and Department Treasurer Helen Moran $200. By contrast, in 1920 the president of the Locomotive Engineers' Union was paid $10,000 a year, the president of the Longshoremen $7,500, and the president of the Typographical $5,000.[21]

The absence of any involvement by the Department's officers in social clubs that included business and professional members provides another indication of the relatively narrow distance between the leadership and the rank and file. Far more labor officials in the early twentieth century belonged to social clubs like the Masons, Elks, Rotary, and Odd Fellows than to reform organizations, suggesting that they were more comfortable with business and professional people than with their own rank and file or even that they aspired to become middle class.[22] Except for Annie Molloy, who after the 1913 near-strike was invited to join the Woman's City Club of Boston, an organization headed by Mrs. James J. Storrow and composed of the wives of financiers and politicians, no leader in the telephone operators' movement belonged to a middle-class social club.[23] All of the Department's leaders, however, were members of the Women's Trade Union League, and most were active in peace and suffrage organizations.

Workers' Education in the Making of the Trade Union Woman

For the leadership of the Telephone Operators' Department, trade unionism was a vehicle not merely for improving wages and working conditions but also for transforming the rank-and-file operator into a "new woman"—self-confident, assertive, and prepared to join with other workers in assuming a far greater role for their class in the shaping of industrial and political life. The Department hoped to undermine the prevailing stereotypes of women as passive and weak, incapable of supporting themselves outside their families, and only marginally important in the labor movement and the nation's political life.

A principal means for effecting this transformation was the workers' education movement. Workers' education received disproportionate attention from women in the labor movement. Women trade unionists had been closely involved with workers' education projects even before World War I. The American Federation of Labor's (AFL's) general lack of support had caused them to turn for assistance to progressive reformers in the universities and settlement houses, many of whom were active in the Women's Trade Union League (WTUL), which placed considerable emphasis on educational uplift to improve the conditions of the working class. Women unionists were also drawn to workers' education because of their pressing need to train leaders. This was a problem peculiar to women in the labor movement. It resulted from the fact that most women workers were very young, lacked work experience, and left the labor force at marriage. The AFL never shared the WTUL's enthusiasm for workers' education, which involved close cooperation with colleges and universities and what Samuel Gompers called "those self-appointed preceptors to the Labor movement known as intellectuals."[24] This stemmed in part from the AFL's fear of upper-class condescension and "dilettantism," as well as anti-intellectualism.

Before the war, the initiative for workers' education had come not from the AFL but from the socialist movement, progressive reformers, and the WTUL. The Rand School for Social Science in New York, the first workers' school to function on a large scale, was founded by socialists in 1906. The most ambitious workers' education program in the trade union movement was sponsored by the International Ladies' Garment Workers' Union (ILGWU), a socialist-led union with a largely female membership. By 1917, the New York locals of the ILGWU operated eight "unity centers." Serving two thousand worker-students, they offered courses in English, labor history, economics, psychology, world history, literature, and health, as well as training in union organizing. Three hundred students pursued more advanced courses at the ILGWU's Workers' University. A major purpose of this program was to enable working women to gain intellectual training, administrative skills, and self-confidence so that they could wield power proportionate to their numbers at work, in the labor movement, and in society. By sponsoring theater, sports, and other recreational events under labor auspices, the ILGWU enterprise sought to overcome feelings of isolation on the part of women members and to provide an alternative to the commercial amusement center, which constricted the intellectual development of the worker. The ILGWU acknowledged the prominence and expertise of women in workers' education at its 1916 convention by appointing as its educational director Juliet Stuart Poyntz, a Barnard history instructor who supervised the educational activities of Waistmakers' Local 25.[25]

In 1913, the Women's Trade Union League established a training school in Chicago, where its headquarters was located, primarily for the purpose of training women labor organizers. This was the first residential workers' education program established in the United

States.[26] Each year from 1914 to 1926, about half a dozen young working women on WTUL scholarships attended the training school. The program combined four months of classroom work in special courses at Northwestern University, the School of Civics and Philanthropy, or the University of Chicago, and eight months of field organizing work. A few students like Julia O'Connor, who had already had considerable organizing experience before she entered the program in late 1916, came for the academic work only. The students had courses in English, economics, and the history of the labor movement. Much attention was also given to more practical matters like parliamentary law, public speaking, the handling of publicity, trade union office administration, and the analysis of union contracts.[27] The League hoped that the students would emerge from the program forceful, self-reliant, and able to manage organizing campaigns and day-to-day union administration without falling into dependency on male unionists. The school was in continual financial difficulty and often had trouble placing its graduates with trade unions, but by 1924 it had trained thirty-seven women.[28] Several leaders of the Telephone Operators' Department attended the National WTUL Training School for Women Organizers besides O'Connor, including Rose Sullivan, Department office secretary Agnes Burns, and Beatrice Coucher, a Department executive board member from Montana.

The Telephone Operators' Department was as deeply involved as any American labor organization in the organized workers' education movement that emerged immediately after the war, when the telephone operators' unions were at peak strength. This movement derived its impetus from the "reconstruction" mood of progressives inside and outside the trade unions, but it included significant AFL participation, resulting from labor's growing disenchantment with public education. The Wilson administration had emphasized that the war was being fought to promote "democracy," and most progressives believed the postwar period offered unusually favorable prospects for reform, particularly in the area of industrial relations. The huge growth of union membership and the unprecedented level of prestige attained by the AFL during the war convinced many progressives that in the near future labor would enter into active participation in the management of industry. The railroad brotherhoods vigorously promoted the Plumb Plan, drafted in 1919, which called for government purchase of the railroads and centralized administration by a tripartite board composed of representatives of management, labor, and the public.[29] Arthur Gleason, a leading figure in the postwar workers' education movement, declared, "Workers' Education . . . presupposes

that labor is gaining power rather rapidly. . . . It is the humanly imperfect effort to meet that situation of responsibility."[30]

By the end of the war, not only progressives in the labor movement but the AFL leadership itself had come to believe it was necessary
to sponsor special educational programs for workers and their families
because of what they perceived as a pervasive hostility toward organized labor on the part of teachers and school boards. The National
Education Association (NEA), the country's leading association of
teachers and school administrators, frequently denounced labor militancy. Its 1894 convention condemned the Pullman strikers for "riot,
incendiarism, and conspiracy" and endorsed President Cleveland's
use of federal troops to crush the strike. In no instance did the NEA
consider the cause of strikes or condemn management's violence.[31]
Most teachers used the social studies courses to inculcate respect for
business and property, and textbooks devoted little or no attention
to the labor movement.

Rose Finkelstein, a member of the executive board of Local 1A
who studied at three of the major postwar schools for workers' education—the Boston Trade Union College, the Bryn Mawr Summer
School for Women Workers in Industry, and Brookwood Labor College—commented, "Most of us became aware of unions because of
conditions that we worked under. Some of us inherited information
through our families. But if you depended on any knowledge that you
got in school—there was *never* anything, in grammar school or high
school the word 'union' was never mentioned. You never got any
information about unions through schools. You'd go through high
school and went into industry—you had no knowledge of what you
were up against."[32]

In 1921, James Maurer, president of the Pennsylvania Federation
of Labor and a leading spokesperson for the workers' education movement, denounced the public school system, from elementary school
to university, as hostile to working people and the labor movement:
"The word 'college' reminds one of the persecution of professors for
showing too much interest in the welfare of the masses and . . . of
college students as strikebreakers. . . . The workingmen's children return from school with accounts of indictments of the labor movement
made by their teachers. . . . " Maurer sneered at the tendency of the
schoolteachers, many of whom believed trade unionism to be "beneath them," to identify with the employing class: "Workingmen have
also observed the snobbishness of the average school teacher. If she
shows any sympathy for workingmen and their families it is the condescending sympathy that is worse than contempt. Her male col-

leagues up in the high school . . . are even worse snobs than she, for they are trying to hobknob with members of the chamber of commerce, rotary clubs, and similar organizations."[33]

Because most teachers were not unionized and thus lacked effective job security, they were easily susceptible to pressure and interference from school boards, dominated by business and professional men. Interests hostile to labor were therefore able to exert strong influence on educational policy and course content in most communities. The 1916 AFL convention complained that state universities could not serve the people if none but captains of industry, bankers, and lawyers controlled them. In 1917, the AFL called for adequate labor representation on all boards of education and demanded that members be paid so that workers could be represented.[34]

The AFL had long urged free compulsory education in the hope that equality of educational opportunity would overcome other inequities of society, but it was increasingly alarmed by developments in the public school system that appeared to reduce the quality of education available to working-class children and to limit their prospects for social mobility. The rise of vocational schools challenged trade union control of apprenticeship and threatened to deprive the worker of the general cultural education which labor believed to be the right of all citizens. Organized labor also opposed the shift away from the traditional division between grammar school (eight grades) and high school (four grades) during the 1910s and 1920s. It charged that the effect and even the purpose of the junior high school was to stop the cultural education of working-class children at the sixth grade rather than the eighth. Labor also feared that intelligence testing, introduced in the public schools after 1910, would be used to channel the working-class child into vocational education. School authorities encouraged pupils scoring high on the tests to enter the academic track and pressured those doing less well to take commercial and vocational courses. Labor resisted the tests, believing the scores were influenced by social and economic status and thus not an accurate measure of "innate intelligence."[35]

By 1921, an organized movement for workers' education had emerged. Its goal was to establish schools and programs outside the system of public education which would provide workers with a broad cultural education as well as more practical skills that would directly benefit the labor movement. Some schools and programs gave more emphasis to cultural subjects, and others to practical subjects; all were to prepare the worker for a coming social order in which labor would participate actively in the management of industry. In 1921, the Workers' Education Bureau (WEB) was established to coordinate the seventy-five workers' schools which had sprung up after the war. Although the majority were night schools administered by trade unions, several permanent resident schools had been or were in the process of being established, including summer institutes for women workers on college campuses.[36] The Telephone Operators' Union was among the most enthusiastic supporters of the WEB. Julia O'Connor served on its national advisory committee and several telephone operators were delegates to WEB conventions.

Long familiar with workers' education as a result of its affiliation with the Women's Trade Union League, the Telephone Operators' Union enrolled its members in significant numbers in the Boston Trade Union College, the most important urban workers' school, and the Bryn Mawr Summer School for Women Workers in Industry, the major residential school for women workers. The Boston Trade Union College was established by unanimous vote of the Boston Central Labor Union (CLU) in February, 1919, and it began classes two months later with 169 students. By the next year the enrollment had reached 400. The telephone operators' union movement benefited enormously from the founding of a workers' school in the city where over a fifth of the nation's organized operators were concentrated.

The plan for such a school was formulated by a group of educators, including Henry Wadsworth Longfellow Dana, Harold Laski, and Horace Kallen, in collaboration with the Reconstruction Committee of the Boston CLU. The Boston Trade Union College announced that its purpose was "to help prepare the workers of New England for the role of increasing importance which labor is to play in the new social order." Not just the "favored youths of our campus colleges" but "the great body of American trade unionists" would now be able to pursue their intellectual interests, without being made to feel uncomfortable because of class background or lack of prior training: "There are no imposing caps and gowns, no dignified president, or pompous list of trustees, and no endowments . . . and 'academic freedom' will not worry instructors; they will have nothing to fear from not pleasing the donors of the college—because it has no endowment."[37]

The Boston Trade Union College was controlled and financed by the trade unionists themselves. The Central Labor Union appointed a governing board of twenty-five members, consisting of fifteen union representatives, five teachers, and five students, thus allowing each of the main groups involved in the school a voice in determining educational policy and course content. The three officers of the school's Board of Control came from the labor movement: Michael Murphy of the Stablemen's Union was chair, Sylvester McBride of the Typographical was vice-chair, and Mabel Gillespie of the WTUL was secretary-treasurer. Mabel Leslie, secretary of the Telephone Operators' Department and editor of the *Union Telephone Operator*, was one of the five student representatives. The school received no financial assistance from the State Board of Education or wealthy benefactors. It had no building of its own but used rooms in a few Boston high schools and the ancient Wells Memorial Building, headquarters of the CLU.[38] Each member of the student body, which was at first restricted to trade unionists affiliated with the AFL and members of their families but later opened to include all wage workers, paid a fee of $2.50 for each course, consisting of one two-hour lesson each week for ten weeks. Funds were also raised from subscription lists passed around in the various trade union locals.

Telephone operators attending the Boston Trade Union College received instruction from perhaps the most impressive faculty ever assembled at a workers' school. It included Roscoe Pound, dean of the Harvard Law School; Felix Frankfurter, a law professor at Harvard and an important adviser on labor matters in the Wilson administration; Zachariah Chaffee, also a Harvard law professor and a leading civil libertarian; William Z. Ripley, professor of economics at Harvard and later president of the American Economics Association; the prominent British political scientist and socialist Harold Laski, at the time lecturing on comparative government at Harvard; Henry Wadsworth Longfellow Dana, recently fired as assistant professor of comparative literature at Columbia because of his opposition to the war (his homosexuality may also have been a factor); and the young Harvard history instructor Samuel Eliot Morison.[39]

The Boston Trade Union College offered courses on a wide range of academic subjects as well as those directly applicable to trade union administration and collective bargaining. There were five academic departments: English, labor organization, government, economics, and science. During the school's first term, April to June, 1919, three English courses were offered—elementary composition, discussion and lecture, taught by Professor Arthur Sheffield of Wellesley College, and "Masterpieces of World Literature," taught by Henry Wadsworth Longfellow Dana. That Dana's course year after year was among those attracting the highest attendance at the college indicates the workers' strong desire for a broad cultural education. The class schedule for the first term also included courses in labor history; collective bargaining; law, taught by Dean Pound of Harvard Law School;

comparative government, British and American, taught by Harold Laski; two economics courses; and courses in elementary physics and psychology. The discussion and lecture course proved particularly valuable at the bargaining table, where workers confronted opponents who were usually far more articulate: " . . . among the students were many presidents and other officials of the labor movement who are eager to hold their own in discussions and negotiations with employing bodies, legislators, and others. They feel that previously, in encounters of this sort, the untrained and uneducated man has been at a disadvantage with the college-bred man who has been accustomed to systematic thinking and precise statement. They want to meet him on more even terms."[40] Henry Wise, the lawyer for the Telephone Operators' Union who helped recruit faculty members for the Boston Trade Union College, recalled that, during the early 1920s, leaders of the faction of Local 1A opposed to Julia O'Connor studied parliamentary law "to see how to handle Julia."[41]

Although telephone operators were more likely to attend night classes at an urban trade union college than a residential school, which required several weeks away from work, the Bryn Mawr Summer School for Women Workers in Industry played a central role in training leaders and organizers for the Telephone Operators' Union. The Bryn Mawr Summer School also provided an important link between telephone operators and middle-class feminists. It exposed the worker-students to highly educated faculty members of their own sex, several of whom held doctorates. These women professors, besides serving as important role models, encouraged intensive study and concentration and forceful speaking, without which women could not exercise effective trade union leadership.

The Bryn Mawr Summer School, which served as the prototype working women's summer institute run in conjunction with American colleges and universities, was established as an eight-week program in 1921 on the campus of the elite "seven sisters" college. Since 1913, the National Women's Trade Union League had urged women's colleges to provide summer programs for women workers. After women's suffrage was obtained, the idea won wide support among those in the universities anxious to prepare women workers for their new political responsibilities. The school's announcement of purpose reflected the "reconstruction" mood of progressive intellectuals and trade unionists in the immediate postwar period: "The object of the School is to offer young women of character and ability a fuller special education and an opportunity to study liberal subjects in order that they might widen their influence in the industrial world, help in the

coming social reconstruction, and increase the happiness and useful-
ness of their own lives." Each student received a scholarship from a
fund provided by trade unions and other benefactors. The Joint Administrative Committee which governed the summer school was composed of representatives of women workers and of the directors,
faculty, and alumnae of Bryn Mawr College.[42]

The telephone operators were among the most heavily represented of any occupational group in the summer school's first class,
with eleven of the eighty-two members. Of the trade unions with
significant female memberships, only the International Ladies' Garment Workers' Union was as committed to workers' education as the
Telephone Operators' Department was. Department President Julia
O'Connor was a member of the school's admissions committee. There
was some controversy among the founders of the school as to whether
telephone operators should be eligible for admission, since they had
defined "workers in industry" narrowly, to exclude white-collar
workers. Yet telephone operators defied classification as either blue
collar or white collar. It was finally decided to admit women "working
with the tools of their trade," including telephone operators but not
sales clerks, office workers, or waitresses.[43] Reflecting a declining
union membership, the number of telephone operators in the class of
1922 dropped to five and in 1923 to four—all from Massachusetts.
Those in the class of 1923 withdrew by the end of the second week
when Julia O'Connor ordered the New England telephone operators
on strike. Participation in the summer school allowed the telephone
operators to establish contacts and friendships with workers in other
trades and regions of the country and to develop a sense of being part
of a national, even international, labor movement. Nineteen states
were represented in the first class.[44]

As they did in the Boston Trade Union College, the summer
school students received instruction in both academic and "practical"
labor subjects, although the former was emphasized. The summer
school expected the students to use their education not for social
mobility out of the working class but for their own personal enrich-
ment and for service to the labor movement. The program included
English composition, literature, political and social history, psychology, art appreciation, public speaking and parliamentary practice, and
economics. There was an "elementary labor course" which focused
on theories of the labor movement, socialism and syndicalism, American and European labor history, and the position of women in the
labor movement. The summer school also presented eight evening
lectures on the "Origin and Evolution of the Earth and Life," covering

such topics as the stellar universe and solar system, matter and its properties, and earth history.[45] The faculty included Paul Douglas, professor of economics at the University of Chicago, a lecturer at the National WTUL Training School for Women Organizers, and later a U.S. Senator from Illinois; Henry Wadsworth Longfellow Dana; Sarah Stites, professor of economics at Mount Holyoke College; and Alice Henry, educational director of the National WTUL and author of *The Trade Union Woman* (1915).[46]

Since relatively few telephone operators were able to arrange leaves of absence from work to attend programs at a resident workers' school, the Telephone Operators' Department developed a "short course" at the National WTUL Training School for Women Organizers in Chicago, which opened in December, 1920. Five telephone operators from Illinois comprised the first group to enroll in the three-week course in "trade unionism, having special reference to women." Alice Henry taught a class on the history of women in the labor movement, and the operators also studied parliamentary law and public speaking. Henry, National WTUL Secretary-Treasurer Elizabeth Christman, and Department Vice-President Rose Sullivan discussed negotiating a trade union agreement and the drafting of resolutions. The operators were also taught how to conduct research at the public library by using the card catalogue and *Readers' Guide*.[47] Rose Sullivan, who had managed organizing campaigns and contract negotiations in Montana as well as in the Midwest, established parliamentary law and public speaking classes for the Butte local, and two Montana telephone operators—Marie King of Butte and Beatrice Coucher of Missoula, a local Sullivan had organized in 1918— attended the National WTUL Training School for Women Organizers in Chicago.

Workers' education projects also helped telephone operators and other young working women become more assertive and self-confident by bringing them into contact with professors and college students who were interested in labor and greatly valued talking to people with first-hand workplace and trade union experience. During the early 1920s, women workers affiliated with the Boston WTUL received numerous invitations to lecture on college campuses. In the spring of 1921, for example, Department President Julia O'Connor spoke on the labor movement before the students of the economics department and the School of Business Administration at Dartmouth College. The lecture was also attended by the telephone operators of Hanover, New Hampshire, who must have been impressed to see their leader address an academic gathering.[48] Boston WTUL Secretary

Mabel Gillespie noted several months after the lecture that Professor Keir of Dartmouth had recently called at the League headquarters in Boston "and said he was never so surprised in his life as when Miss O'Connor presented in a scholarly and philosophical way her subject. . . . "[49]

From a more practical standpoint, the attention the workers' education movement gave to preparing trade unionists to be effective in bargaining sessions led the Telephone Operators' Department to commit itself to sponsoring research on the telephone industry. President O'Connor pointed out that the telephone industry was "almost totally unexplored from the labor point of view" and that this research might provide material the union could use in organizing and strike publicity work. Only the report of the Royal Commission on the 1907 Toronto telephone operators' strike, the 1910 U.S. Senate investigation of the telephone industry, the telephone section of the 1915 report of the U.S. Commission on Industrial Relations, and the New York State Department of Labor investigation of 1920 were available as authoritative studies of telephone working conditions, and the first two of these were badly outdated. O'Connor proposed at the 1921 Department convention that the union sponsor research on all general phases of telephone working conditions, especially on labor turnover and its causes, the wage classification theory of the telephone companies, the various company representation plans offered as substitutes for trade unionism in the 1920s, and fatigue and strain.[50]

As part of its educational mission, the Telephone Operators' Department leadership sought to impart to the rank and file a knowledge of trade unionism and working conditions in foreign countries and to instill an awareness of issues of concern to the international labor movement. President O'Connor took a leave of absence from her post for several months in 1921 to investigate trade unionism and women's working conditions in Western Europe. In a series of articles and letters in the *Union Telephone Operator,* she reported from abroad on British workers' education, the working conditions of British telephone operators, and the Irish labor and nationalist movements. O'Connor, who attended the convention of the Irish Trade Union Congress in Dublin in 1921, was particularly impressed by the influence of women trade unionists in the Irish labor movement:

> The Irish labor movement has given women a more genuine recognition of their place in the movement than has either England or America. No woman has yet gained a place in America on the Executive Council of the American Federation of Labor. In England two women have been elected to the Parliamentary Committee of the Trade Union

Congress by virtue of special legislation reserving two places for women. In Ireland two women have been elected to the National Executive Council of the Trade Union Congress, and elected without qualification or reservation, as trade unionists.[51]

The *Union Telephone Operator* described the purpose of the International Congress of Working Women, which Julia O'Connor had attended as a delegate, and outlined the questions to be discussed at its 1921 meeting in Geneva. This organization had been established in 1919 to familiarize world governments with the views of working women on labor problems.[52] The journal also reprinted the Armistice Day address calling for an end to war and militarism delivered by Julia O'Connor at the Women's Mass Meeting on Disarmament at Washington, D.C.[53]

Social Life and the Youth Culture

Seeing no inconsistency between the flapper's fun-loving, exhibitionistic nature and labor activism and militancy, the Telephone Operators' Department made every effort to draw on her energies as it trained the trade union woman. It strongly encouraged its locals to sponsor social activities that appealed to youth in order to draw the membership closer together, attract new recruits, and raise funds. Such activities generated enthusiasm for unionism among many young women by identifying the local with the excitement of the dance hall and amusement park rather than with the monotony of the business meeting. At the first Department convention, the Committee on Organization emphasized the importance of the "social side of organization work" in its report, noting that "if the social side is kept up, it helps increase the membership." The committee recommended that socials and entertainment be held frequently, with "sufficient variety to keep the membership interested." It advised each local to appoint or elect a social committee at the time of the regular election of officers that would conduct these activities.[54]

Telephone operators' locals held innumerable dances and parties, often in hotel ballrooms or spacious outdoor pavilions. In addition to several smaller dances, many locals held an annual concert and ball, usually in the spring, that was a major event on the social calendar of their cities and towns. Local 71A of Portsmouth, New Hampshire, for example, boasted that its "annual dance is the event of the season in Portsmouth." Brockton's Local 27A reported in 1921 that its fifth annual May concert and ball had been a huge success, attracting over eight hundred dancers in addition to a large balcony attendance. It promised everybody just as good a time at its annual Harvest Ball in October. Over three hundred couples attended Local 5A's dance party in February, 1921, at Worcester's Bancroft Hotel, which included novelty dances, favor dances, and vocal solos. Local 1A's November "grand ball" and big "May party" in Boston were always heavily attended. Masquerade parties and carnivals were also popular among the operators.[55]

Perhaps the most spectacular entertainment sponsored by the telephone operators was Local 1A's two-day "Arabian Nights Bazaar," held in Boston in 1921 and 1922. This appears to have been modeled on major forms of commercial amusement, with which the operators were very familiar, except that this time an entrepreneur did not profit at the workers' expense. The money spent was placed in a fund the local used to acquire a vacation house. From noon until midnight, the operators put on a "continuous program of merriment" that included vaudeville acts, exhibition dancing, motion pictures, and fortune-telling. Each exchange managed a booth with a neighborhood theme: the Beach operators, whose exchange was in Chinatown, were arrayed in "mandarin coats and satin trousers," burned incense, and displayed "jades and jewels of Old China"; the operators from the exclusive Back Bay section, wearing "absolutely the correct thing," conducted a "Country Club Tea House," and so on. The bazaar drew its large attendance from both the operators and the general public; according to the *Union Telephone Operator* it "looked at times like Old Home Week for all the ex-now-married-ops."[56]

As part of its effort to restructure workers' leisure, Boston's Local 1A purchased a vacation house for its members at the seashore at Scituate, Massachusetts. In encouraging its members to spend their Sundays, holidays, and vacations with their fellow workers, the union was strengthening the peer group and favoring the flapper life-style at the expense of family ties. The operators were frequently accompanied on their trips to Scituate by their boyfriends, and the vacation house was the scene of many dances and parties. Many vacation houses had been established for workers by employers and philanthropists—such as Hazelhurst, a country rest home which the Cincinnati and Suburban Telephone Company maintained for its telephone operators—but one owned exclusively by young working women for their own use was highly unusual. Unity House in Pine Hill, New York, set up by the ILGWU's Local 25 of New York City in 1915, appears to be the only other vacation house managed by a women's trade union.[57]

Driftway, Local 1A's "showplace on the South Shore," was opened on Labor Day, 1920, at a housewarming attended by numerous Boston labor leaders and telephone company officials. The *Union Telephone Operator* boasted that the property contained a "broad stretch of white sandy beach" for bathers and "shaded and winding roads" for strollers. The "green shaded lawns with their inviting coolness" provided relaxation for the telephone operator fatigued after six days of nerve-racking work behind a switchboard.[58] Clare Moriarty of Local 1A recalled, "You know when I look back now [on] how well the union was doing, they were able to buy that house at Scituate for a vacation house, and furnish it very nicely and keep a woman employed, especially over the weekends, to cook for the girls—then you only had one day—you worked a full six day week, and so many of the girls would go Saturday night, or if they had a day off—it was a beautiful place. . . . So beautiful."[59]

Social activities and entertainment occupied a prominent place at the second convention of the Telephone Operators' Department, held in St. Louis in 1921. For the delegates, the convention represented an opportunity not only for serious discussion of union business but also for "gay times," both with each other and with men. As one delegate put it, "Did you ever go to a telephone operators' convention? Well if you never ain't then you oughta, that's all. My local sent me to the last one . . . and I had the time of my life."[60]

For many delegates, the fun began even before they reached St. Louis; as one recalled, "We had a circus on the goin' train, an' we had a circus at the destination."[61] The suite of rooms occupied by the Boston, Providence, Newport, and Manchester delegates became notorious for its "any-hour" partying: "It was no unusual sight to see delegations travelling roomward at any time after 12, after having enjoyed themselves at 'headquarters.' " The operators made so much noise that the wife of a sick man occupying the room opposite their suite asked them to be quiet. This seemed unreasonable to the operators ("we couldn't quite figure out why an invalid should interfere with our fun"), and they succeeded in having the man's room changed. Delegates made much of the opportunity to display the brassy and exotic clothes of the flapper. May Brady and Kit McGovern of the Providence local "wore so many different clothes we nearly lost an eye." There was also the "kimona brigade," the "crowd that always wanted to don kimonas as soon as they got in the room just because they had new and pretty ones."[62]

That the operators derived as much pleasure from heterosocial relationships as from partying with each other is made clear in the numerous references in the *Union Telephone Operator* to the delegates' romantic and sexual escapades at the convention. Socializing with men seems to have occurred usually in a group setting. One delegate reported that the "best part" of the convention was the "good time" the IBEW men of St. Louis showed the operators: "They took us to a Hallowe'en Eve Party, sent us to a good vaudeville show, and one afternoon took us all around the city in Ford touring cars."[63] Some operators, however, did slip off with men on dates of their own:

> Annie and Frances in roadsters were seen,
> If we told you any more they'd say we were mean. . . .
> Agnes and Vera from out the great northwest,
> They went to a dance one night,
> Well—we all know the rest.[64]

If we are to believe the *Union Telephone Operator*, these trade union women did not give men the initiative or subordinate their own interests to the men's in dating, contrary to the usual practice in heterosocial relationships. They could be quite responsive to men, but the men had to accept them on their terms. As the following poem, "Meet Me in St. Louis," suggests, men who assumed the operators were waiting passively for them to call were in for a big surprise:

> Young Louis had one aim in life
> To take Ima Plug for a wife, . . .
> One day as he dolled for a date
> He heard a loud knock at the gate,
> And there was a note,
> Which Ima Plug wrote
> That sent anxious Lou in a faint.
>
> (Chorus)
>
> Meet me in St. Louis, Louis, . . .
> Meet me at the Ops' Convention
> Somethin' doin' there
> We will keep the town in tension
> While the Ops sit in convention
> Meet me in St. Louis, Louis,
> Ima' waitin' there.[65]

The dancing and partying, interspersed with the convention sessions and committee meetings, continued to the "witching hour." It was viewed by the delegates not as a distraction from the real business of a union convention but as an integral part of their lives as trade union women. The delegates' raucous behavior and exhibitionism at the convention can be ascribed partly to the exuberance of youth.

But in a deeper sense, these young women were laying their claim to a "good life," to fun and excitement that few working people were permitted to experience. The pride and self-esteem they had gained in building a powerful, woman-led labor organization and fighting their own battles against formidable opponents made them feel deserving of it. The operators' exhibitionism and pride in their achievements are reflected in a delegate's statement equating the Department convention with the simultaneous visit at the same hotel of Marshall Foch, Supreme Allied Commander in World War I: "Wasn't it extraordinary that two such happenings could take place in any hotel in a few days—Our Convention and Foch's visit? The manager certainly should have held one of these headliners for the following week. I'll bet he was wild if he only had a few Kings or something for the next week."[66]

Images of the Trade Union Woman

As a national labor organization controlled by women, the Telephone Operators' Department elaborated a model of the trade union woman at sharp variance with the image held by most male trade unionists, who viewed women workers, even when organized, as relatively weak and defenseless, out of place in the male sphere of work. From the middle of the nineteenth century, the worker in both Europe and North America was depicted in the iconography of the labor movement as a heavily muscled, hammer-wielding male. No trade union emblem portrayed a woman at work; when women appeared, they were only figures of inspiration—goddesses and muses—or figures of suffering and endurance.[67] This was true even of the emblem of the National Women's Trade Union League, which depicted the armored goddess Minerva—symbolizing Victory—clasping the hand of a mother holding an infant in her arms and standing before a factory. Only the emblem of the Telephone Operators' Department presented the woman as worker: the proud "Weaver of Speech" who held in her hands the communication lines of a nation.

The Department portrayed the telephone operator as mature and serious, engaged in the performance of a vital public service. She transmitted messages of great, and often critical, importance to businesses and individuals. The *Union Telephone Operator* continually referred to the composure and dedication of the operator who risked physical injury or death by remaining at her post during public emergencies. It compared her to the soldier under fire: "She has figured gloriously and courageously in the modern annals of heroism."[68] The bravery and quick action of telephone operators during such disasters as fires and floods were credited with saving large numbers of lives.[69] The union also displayed great pride in the skill of its members. Julia O'Connor, for example, took serious exception to the claim of the feminist journalist Marjorie White, who had worked briefly as a telephone operator while conducting research on working women, that she had developed proficiency at operating during her short stint at the exchange: "I absolutely and unqualifiedly dispute your statement that you became an old operator in two weeks. . . . You could not learn the mechanics of operating in two weeks to say nothing of acquiring the knowledge and poise necessary in emergency as well as speed, concentration, and ability to handle choke loads necessary to a good operator."[70]

The union was highly sensitive about the public image of the telephone operator and combatted unfavorable stereotypes in the press and theater. The first issue of the union's journal complained that "the public which thrills and applauds at the story of the union telephone operator who saves a town from fire, risking her own life in the doing, is quite as ready to agree with the funny strip artist's conception of a telephone operator as the living embodiment of careless inefficiency and to laugh at the vaudevillian's time-honored query at the stage telephone: 'Central, what's the correct wrong number to call to get Main 808?' "[71] Asked by Marjorie White to comment on the manuscript of a novel she had written about telephone operators, Julia O'Connor praised its description of the operators' work, " 'the lilt of the game,' the sense of power and exhilaration," but stated, "I object to the mangling of the English language indulged in by most of the operators."[72]

The Department's trade union woman was not only brave and assertive but also deeply committed to the working class and the labor movement. Remaining true to her class, she did not desire social mobility, and she married a working man who shared her love of trade unionism. While rejecting upward inter-class mobility, she claimed the right to enjoy fully the material possessions her class produced. An excellent example of what the Department leadership advanced as a model for the rank and file was "Gwen Marshall," the heroine of a story entitled "Why Not?," published in the March, 1921, issue of the *Union Telephone Operator*. The story begins as Marshall, rebelling against her "conventional and domineering" father, leaves home and moves to an industrial city to take a job in a large printing plant. She is quickly disappointed, however, with the "respectable and proper" lower-middle-class patrons at her boarding house, run by the rigid Mrs. Murdock. At the dinner table Marshall meets "middle-aged spinsters with gushing falsettos" and "bald-headed gentlemen with soft voices who folded their napkins very neatly at the end of a meal and talked at length about their favorite salads." One gentleman is an authority on neckties. Marshall, who had been eagerly following the "daring" and "wonderful" achievements of the modern woman and was fascinated by the "women in industry who figured in picturesque strikes," now finds herself in the same "stagnant, conventional atmosphere" she had learned to hate at home.

There is one boarder, however, who is different from the rest—a "blonde young man, square-shouldered and immaculately dressed," named Mr. Roberts, whom Marshall takes to be "a professional of some sort." The first week Marshall sees little of Roberts, and her after-dinner hours are spent watching the other boarders—she thinks of them as "fossils"—lounge in stiff-backed chairs "endeavoring to create an atmosphere of artificial sociability by lusterless small talk." Much to her dislike, a gentleman "with very elegant manners and very boring conversation" attaches himself to Marshall. But at the end of the week Roberts asks her for a date, and they become increasingly friendly.

One evening, the local newspapers carry "scare headlines" that five thousand women in the city's glove factory have gone on strike for higher wages and shorter hours, and Marshall is forced into a confrontation with the lower-middle-class boarders, all of whom oppose the strike. The ladies assert at the dining room table that joining a union is "shockingly vulgar," while the gentlemen believe the strikers to be manipulated by "criminal agitators." One lady "with a large expanse of chin" is enraged because she has seen some of the glove workers wearing fur coats, reminiscent of the Providence East Siders who taunted telephone operator pickets in 1919; Mrs. Murdock adds that they also carry gold mesh bags on Sunday: "Perfectly outrageous!"

Marshall, having often heard such views expressed at home, cannot control herself and angrily exclaims, "You, you seem to think only those who don't work are entitled to fur coats and mesh bags and all the good things of life. You sit here and rave because they who produce everything, the luxuries and necessities, have warm coats on their backs. . . . These girls must join a labor union if they want protection." Staring fiercely at the boarders, Marshall experiences a sudden desire to laugh when one of the ladies sneers that it appears as though she intends to join the union herself: " 'Intends,' fairly shrieked Gwen in exasperation. 'I've joined the union ever since I worked here and nothing could make me give up my card.' " As a "general murmur of consternation" sweeps the room, Marshall jumps from her chair and rushes out of the house.

In tears, facing the prospect of eviction from the boardinghouse, Marshall runs through the streets, finally stopping to rest on a bench overlooking a brook. She has been there nearly an hour when she feels a tap on her arm and looks up to see Roberts, "his lips puckered into an amused smile, staring at her kindly." Then she makes a wonderful discovery:

> "Mr. Roberts," she began, "I've been wondering all evening what you think of me after the scene I made tonight. I watched your expression but it was so uncommunicative. . . . "
>
> "Can't kick," he answered laconically. He looked down at her and smiled broadly. "I'm business agent for the Machinists' Union myself. . . . "
>
> She looked at him with puzzled eyes. "Not a union like mine, A. F. of L.?" she questioned.
>
> "Ditto," he laughed back.

Roberts then proposes marriage, and the story ends with a display of passion between the two trade unionists: "Gwen felt his strong subtle body against hers and knew that she could lean back with a sense of perfect protection. . . . Just then the moon was hidden by black clouds and everything was enveloped in darkness, and that's how they got away with it."[73]

In the character of Gwen Marshall, the trade union militant and the youthful flapper, rebelling against convention and seeking fun and an exciting heterosexual relationship, are combined. The Department leadership here directly confronted the widely held notion that labor activism, even membership in a union, "de-feminized" women. Instead, it suggested that the trade union woman was more alluring to men, had more "sex appeal." That many telephone operators believed just that became clear during the 1923 New England operators' strike, when pickets in Boston taunted strikebreakers with "Who'd want to marry a girl like you?"[74]

The Trade Union Woman as Independent Wage Earner

Telephone operator unionists rejected the prevailing early twentieth-century view that the role of the woman worker should be that of supplementary income earner in her family. This view stemmed from the notion that a woman's proper place was in the home and that, even as she earned wages outside it, her work should be defined in terms of how it would benefit her as a future wife and mother. Accordingly, ambition and the search for increased income had meaning only for men in the labor force, not women. Only in the 1920s did work-related ambition begin to be legitimated for women, first in the middle class and then in the working class.[75]

Before this shift in attitude became significant, the union telephone operators were arguing that they had a right to be self-supporting outside their families. Julia O'Connor declared at the first convention of the Telephone Operators' Department in 1919 that the telephone operators should be viewed as self-supporting and thus deserving of union organization like men, since "we . . . have the same conditions with which to contend that men have. . . . "[76] By pressing continuously for higher wages, the operators hoped not only to improve their standard of living but also to end their dependency in the family. During the 1923 New England telephone operators' strike, the Telephone Operators' Union publicity committee stated, "We are simply attempting to establish a condition that will make it possible to become self-supporting."[77] The stereotypes of what constituted men's and women's work remained so deeply engrained, however, that the operators never demanded access to male-designated jobs in the telephone service, such as repair, installation, and cable splicing. Nor is there any record of their agitating for the right of married women to retain their jobs as operators in the telephone service, although they may have done so.

The Telephone Operators' Department and the Left

While the Telephone Operators' Department viewed itself as a loyal affiliate of the American Federation of Labor, it did not share the relatively conservative political outlook of most AFL unions, including the IBEW. Although nearly all the Department officers and executive board members belonged to the Democratic party rather than the Socialist party—Beatrice Coucher of Montana was an exception—many of them saw no contradiction between their party affiliation and sympathy for socialism. Department Treasurer Mary Quinn Wynne, a Democrat, voted for Socialist candidate Eugene Victor Debs for president in 1920.[78]

The *Union Telephone Operator* at times made extremely disparaging references to capitalism. An article entitled "Rewards of Capitalism," for example, derided the "capitalist dailies" for praising a telephone operator who made $600 in commissions selling stock in her spare time and dismissed this activity as a "useless vocation peculiar to the profit system." In the same issue, a poem appeared equating profit with theft:

> The merchant calls it profit, . . .
> The banker calls it interest. . . .
> The landlord calls it rent . . .
> But the honest old burglar calls it swag.[79]

The journal also printed highly favorable accounts about the progress of the socialist-influenced labor movements in Britain and Ireland. Department President O'Connor noted approvingly that "[Irish] labor looks to the establishment of the cooperative commonwealth, a workers' republic."[80]

Julia O'Connor and several others prominent in the telephone operators' union movement in Boston were ardent Irish nationalists who appear to have been involved with a socialist and anticlerical, Irish-American organization called the James Connolly Club. O'Connor believed the Irish nationalist and labor movements to be "nearly akin in philosophy and purpose."[81] Named for the martyr of 1916, Connolly clubs had been established in Boston, New York, Philadelphia, Chicago, Butte, and Oakland to familiarize the Irish-American workers with socialism. The clubs emphasized that Connolly "did not die to enable Irish capitalists to grind down the Irish workers under the Iron Heel as the Free State is doing. Nor did he die to see established in Ireland a republic modeled after the American creature of Morgan & Co. He died for what he lived for—a Workers' Republic."[82]

Julia O'Connor had a close friendship for a time with one of the leaders of the Boston Connolly Club, Mary Donovan (1886–1973), who is primarily known for her role in the defense of the Italian anarchists Sacco and Vanzetti between 1924 and 1927. Donovan, who shared an apartment with Loretta Baker, financial secretary of Local 1A who was also active in the Connolly Club, became an adviser to the Telephone Operators' Department and provided a link between the union and the socialist and Irish nationalist movements. Born in North Brookfield, Massachusetts, Donovan was the daughter of a shoemaker and a domestic servant, both immigrants from Ireland. Donovan had worked her way through the University of Michigan, graduating in 1912. While at Michigan, she had been excommunicated by the Catholic church for refusing to resign from the Intercollegiate Socialist Society. She joined the Socialist party in 1911.

Returning to North Brookfield after graduation, Donovan became a schoolteacher and joined the Worcester [Massachusetts] Women's Trade Union League as a charter member in 1915. About 1917, Donovan passed a civil service examination for the post of Massachusetts state factory inspector and moved to Boston, where she met O'Connor and Baker. She walked the picket lines with the telephone operators during their 1919 strike.

During this period, Donovan worked on fund-raising campaigns for the Irish nationalist movement with James Larkin, founder of the militant industrial Irish Transport and General Workers' Union, with whom she developed a close friendship. After the defeat of the Dublin dock strike in 1913, Larkin came to the United States, where he became the leader of the Connolly Club of New York. He was also prominent in the Industrial Workers of the World and later helped form the Communist Labor party. Larkin was sentenced to Sing Sing Penitentiary in 1920 for advocating "criminal anarchy," and, after his release in 1923, he spent time with Mary Donovan in Boston and on her family's farm at North Brookfield; he was later arrested while on his way to see Donovan and deported to Ireland.[83]

In 1921, Donovan travelled with Julia O'Connor to England and Ireland to study their labor movements. In Ireland, O'Connor and Donovan stayed with relatives of Donovan's mother in Dundalk (County Louth), several of whom belonged to the Irish Republican Army (IRA). Donovan's aunt stored dynamite in the cellar and planned to blow up British army barracks nearby; a niece was an IRA messenger. O'Connor and Donovan attended union meetings together in Dublin and met with Larkin's secretary Nora O'Keefe and the Countess Constance Markievicz, Ireland's Minister of Labour, who had worked with James Connolly early in the century.[84] Donovan's friendship with O'Connor ended for personal reasons shortly after their return to the United States. Donovan supported the toll operators' faction in Local 1A which opposed O'Connor. Her close friend Loretta Baker was a leader of the toll faction.[85]

Many leaders of the Telephone Operators' Department and Local 1A patronized a restaurant on Beacon Hill called the "Common Cupboard," which provides another indication of links with radicals. The Common Cupboard was owned by the mother of Department Vice-President Rose Sullivan. Mary Quinn Wynne and Rose Finkelstein both recalled spending much time at the restaurant, which they identified as a popular "hangout" for activists in the Telephone Operators' Union.[86] The Common Cupboard was placed under surveillance during World War I by the Bureau of Investigation, which considered it a meeting place for revolutionaries and draft dodgers. An agent of the bureau reported in May, 1918, that the restaurant was "a rendezvous for socialists and malcontents of every class, from the dynamite anarchists to the 'pink tea' socialists." Socialist literature, including the New York *Call*, was available for purchase. Another agent stated that the patrons stayed until after midnight discussing "many subjects from poetry to economics." The restaurant was situated in a basement and contained four tables seating about twenty persons. According to an agent, "The only illumination is furnished by candles. The place is very weird and grotesque." Young working women who patronized the Common Cupboard reportedly engaged in highly unconventional behavior: " . . . shop girls from the Department stores are being encouraged to frequent this restaurant and are being given cigarettes by the proprietress, who is thus teaching the girls to smoke."[87]

The Telephone Operators' Department was also closely involved with the Brookwood Labor College, a resident workers' school in which socialists had considerable influence. Perhaps the most important workers' education program ever to exist in the United States, Brookwood was founded in 1921 by progressive trade unionists and intellectuals openly critical of the narrow craft unionism and conservatism of the AFL. It offered the most extensive educational program of any workers' school in the country: a two-year course of instruction at its campus in Katonah, New York, combined with field work and strike support. Its purpose was to train workers not for social mobility out of the working class but for effective activity in the labor movement to bring about a more just social order: "Brookwood . . . regards the labor movement, not merely as a machine to secure higher wages, shorter hours, certain improved conditions in the shop, but as the most vital and noble force of our time working to bring a better life to all men. . . . Brookwood is an integral part of the labor movement and exists only to serve it. Its graduates go back to mine, mill, and shop and to their unions, not to get something out of the movement, but to put something into it. . . . "[88] The faculty included several left-wing socialists, such as the school's director A. J. Muste and Arthur Calhoun, a Ph.D. from Clark University and author of a pioneering history of the family. Conservatives in the labor movement were never comfortable with Brookwood, and it was openly denounced as subversive by the AFL in 1928.

Several telephone operators participated in the school's summer institutes. Moira Callahan and Ingrid Mueller, both leaders in the telephone operators' union, attended the regular program at Brookwood Labor College, Callahan from 1923 to 1925 and Mueller from 1924 to 1925. Callahan was president of Local 27A of Brockton, Massachusetts, and secretary of the New England Council of Telephone Operators' Unions. Mueller, originally from Collinsville, Illinois, had worked as an operator in California and had been prominent in the telephone strikes along the Pacific Coast. In 1920, she returned to Illinois to organize telephone operators for the Central States Council. Both women, who had roomed together at Bryn Mawr Summer School, had extensive experience with workers' education projects, Callahan having attended the Boston Trade Union College and Mueller the National WTUL Training School in Chicago.

Callahan and Mueller graduated after the Telephone Operators' Union had for all intents and purposes been disbanded as a result of its defeat in the 1923 New England strike, but as Brookwood had intended, each continued to maintain close contact with the school and the labor movement. It is not clear what Callahan's political outlook was, but Mueller was a committed socialist. Callahan reported a few months after graduating that she and Mueller had had "a rather chequered existence" since leaving Brookwood. They had hitchhiked to Mueller's hometown of Collinsville, Illinois, and then to Chicago, where Mueller was employed for a time at general housework at the Jane Club, a "cooperative housing proposition connected with Hull House," and Callahan worked as a waitress in a tea room. The two women, although happy to be together and looking forward to taking courses at the National WTUL Training School, felt isolated, unable to interest other workers in the labor movement. Callahan wrote to a friend at Brookwood: "I do not expect to remain at the place [the tea room] long. I have fights every day. . . . I want to know all about Brookwood. . . . I feel so shut in and alone here in spite of all the city's activity."[89] By 1927, Callahan was married and living in her hometown of Holbrook, Massachusetts, having spent the previous fall working with Julia O'Connor at the Telephone Operators' Department office in Boston.[90] Mueller joined the left-wing Conference for Progressive Labor Action, established in 1929 by A. J. Muste and other opponents of the AFL leadership (including many Brookwooders) as a "fighting group . . . to revitalize the labor movement," and worked as an organizer for the Amalgamated Clothing Workers in Buffalo, Ontario, and Pennsylvania.[91]

Conclusion

The formation of an autonomous Telephone Operators' Department within the International Brotherhood of Electrical Workers greatly transformed the relationship between the telephone operators and male trade unionists. Having established the Department after a long struggle for equal rights within the IBEW modeled on the women's suffrage movement, the operators continued to assert their independence. In designing their union emblem, they rejected the images of women favored by the labor movement, choosing instead to depict the pride, competence, and strength of the woman worker. They struggled to be self-supporting, rather than remain as supplementary earners within their families. The Department leadership adopted a political outlook considerably to the left of the IBEW and the AFL. Although severely handicapped by lack of funds, the Department undertook an aggressive organizing campaign, hoping to firmly establish the union on a national basis. After 1919, many organizing drives among operators and strikes were led by women rather than men. By leading their own struggles, the operators contributed greatly to undermining the stereotype commonly held by men in the labor movement of women as passive and dependent.

The Department attempted to replace this stereotype with an image of the telephone operator as a trade union woman, self-confident, assertive, a fighter for her class. To realize this objective, it relied heavily on the workers' education movement, which emerged when the Department was at peak strength. Workers' education projects, which frequently drew on the teaching services of college faculties, brought the telephone operators into close contact with middle-class feminists, who as college professors or administrators provided role models of assertive and independent women. The union's involvement in workers' education was facilitated by its strong ties with the Women's Trade Union League, which had operated its own training school since 1914 and helped to administer the Bryn Mawr Summer School, and the Boston Central Labor Union, the first city central labor body to establish a trade union college. In New England, where over half of the Telephone Operators' Department membership was concentrated in the early 1920s, the Boston WTUL, Boston CLU, and Massachusetts State Federation of Labor, all of which provided essential support for the union's workers' education efforts, had attained unprecedented strength. The Boston CLU represented over 100,000 workers in 1919. The attendance at the 1918 convention of the Massachusetts State Federation of Labor was the largest until that time, with 342 delegates representing 203 locals and central labor bodies; during 1918–19, between 500 and 600 locals and central labor bodies were affiliated with the state federation.[92]

The Telephone Operators' Department sought to bring its members squarely into the center of the labor movement while at the same time advancing women's interests within it. As an autonomous body within the IBEW, a major AFL trade union, it could effectively pursue both objectives. The Department's affiliation with the IBEW made it easier for men in the labor movement to accept operators' unionism as legitimate, provided some access to funds, and facilitated the operators' entry into central labor unions and state labor federations. At the same time, as a self-governing, all-female institution, the Department could relate to the needs of its members as women and as youth. Unlike the men's union, it provided social programs and entertainment, which drew the operators together as a group and made them feel that trade unionism was "fun." By appreciating the importance of the "social side," the operators' unions gained the attention of the flapper and drew on her energy and excitement. This focus on social life, along with the narrow distance between the leaders and the membership and the relative homogeneity of the operators in age, ethnicity, and skill level, explains the particularly intense commitment to trade unionism that developed among rank-and-file telephone operators.

NOTES

1. "Report of the Department President," in *Proceedings of the First Regular Convention of the Telephone Operators' Department, IBEW*, New Orleans, La., 1919, pp. 12, 19, 21, Julia O'Connor Parker Papers, Schlesinger Library, Radcliffe College, Cambridge, Mass.

2. "Report of Department Secretary," in *Proceedings of First Regular Convention*, p. 48.

3. "Report of the Department President," p. 8.

4. Letter from May H. Brady, *Union Telephone Operator* [hereafter, *UTO*], January, 1921, p. 8.

5. The vote allotted to each local was weighted according to its membership. Boston's Local 1A, easily the largest in the country, wielded 3,160 votes, with four delegates each having 451 votes and three delegates each having 452. San Francisco's Local 54A had the next largest number of votes, with 567. The top nine locals in voting strength were all situated in New England or on the Pacific Coast. *Proceedings of First Regular Convention*, pp. 64, 67, 89.

6. "Report of the Department President," p. 6.

7. Ibid., p. 8. To help finance organizing, the convention voted to increase the monthly union dues paid by each member from not less than $.50 to not less than $.75. The initiation fee for new members was set at not less than $1.00. The larger locals generally assessed a higher initiation

fee; members of Boston's Local 1A had paid $2.00 as early as 1914. Each local was to pay the Department the per capita tax sum of $.40—raised by the convention from $.25—out of the monthly dues collected from each member, plus the entire initiation fee of each new member. *Proceedings of First Regular Convention*, p. 70; Letter from Alice J. Donovan, *Journal of Electrical Workers and Operators* [hereafter, *JEWO*], February, 1914, p. 85.

8. *Proceedings of First Regular Convention*, p. 63.

9. Ibid., p. 71.

10. Ibid., p. 87.

11. Ibid., pp. 89–91.

12. "Schenectady's Great Strike," *JEWO*, January, 1914, pp. 30–32; Boston *Evening Globe*, November 22, 1913; Boston *Globe*, November 29, 1913.

13. "President's Report to the Second Biennial Convention of the Telephone Operators' Department of the International Brotherhood of Electrical Workers," St. Louis, Mo., October 31, 1921, p. 10, Julia O'Connor Parker Papers.

14. Eric D. Weitz, "Class Formation and Labor Protest in the Mining Communities of Southern Illinois and the Ruhr, 1890–1925," *Labor History* 27 (Winter 1985–86):92; David Montgomery, *The Fall of the House of Labor* (New York: Cambridge University Press, 1987), p. 339; Melvyn Dubofsky and Warren Van Tine, *John L. Lewis* (New York: Quadrangle/New York Times Book Co., 1977), p. 84.

15. Letter from Marguerite McKeon, secretary-treasurer, CSC, *UTO*, May, 1921, p. 9.

16. Letter from Kate Crain, Local 189A, *UTO,* January, 1921, p. 10; Carbondale *Free Press*, July 17 and August 26, 1920; *Daily American* [West Frankfort, Ill.], June 26 and July 15, 1920.

17. Beatrice V. Coucher, telephone interview by Stephen H. Norwood, August 29, 1982.

18. Letter from Margaret B. Hickey, *UTO*, February, 1921, p. 9; "President's Report to Second Biennial Convention," p. 11; Boston *Evening Globe,* June 26, 1920.

19. Letter from Press Secretary, Local 124A, *UTO*, January, 1921, p. 9.

20. Letter from Josephine Hill, president, Local 115A, *UTO*, May, 1922, p. 6.

21. Warren Van Tine, *The Making of the Labor Bureaucrat* (Amherst: University of Massachusetts Press, 1973), pp. 150–51; *Proceedings of First Regular Convention*, pp. 40–45; "Proposed Constitution of the Telephone Operators' Department, IBEW," p. 7, Julia O'Connor Parker Papers.

Nor did the officers of operators' locals receive much pay, if they indeed received any. The only "constitution and by-laws" of an operators' local in the Julia O'Connor Parker Papers, that of Brockton's Local 27A, shows salaries ranging from $3.00 a month for the financial secretary to $.60 a month for the president and recording secretary. "Constitution and By-Laws of Local Union 27A, IBEW, Telephone Operators of Brockton and Vicinity," [1917], p. 10, Julia O'Connor Parker Papers.

A careful itemization of all Department expenses, including officers' salaries, was provided for the rank and file in the published proceedings of the Department convention. "Report of Treasurer," in *Proceedings of First Convention,* pp. 36–47; "Report of Department Secretary," pp. 49–51.

22. Van Tine, *Labor Bureaucrat,* p. 28.

23. *JEWO,* November, 1913, p. 1133.

24. Margaret Hodgen, *Workers' Education in England and the United States* (New York: E. P. Dutton, 1925), p. 193.

25. Workers' Education Bureau, *Report of Proceedings, Second National Conference on Workers' Education in the United States* (New York: Worker's Education Bureau, 1922), pp. 55–56; Nancy McLean, "The Culture of Resistance: Female Institution-Building in the International Ladies' Garment Workers' Union, 1905–1925," *Michigan Occasional Paper in Women's Studies,* no. 21 (Winter, 1982):73–75.

26. Robin Miller Jacoby, "The Women's Trade Union League School for Women Organizers, 1914–1926," in Joyce Kornbluh and Mary Frederickson, eds., *Sisterhood and Solidarity* (Philadelphia: Temple University Press, 1984), p. 6.

27. Letter to National Women's Trade Union League [hereafter, WTUL] Executive Board members, July 10, 1916, Reel 2, National WTUL Papers, Library of Congress, Washington, D.C.

28. Alice Henry, "Trade Union School for Women Labor Leaders," [1921], Box 2, Rose Schneiderman Papers, Tamiment Library, New York University, New York, N.Y.

29. David Kennedy, *Over Here* (New York: Oxford University Press, 1980), p. 256.

30. Quoted in Norman Thomas, "Norman Thomas on Workers' Education," *New Republic,* May 9, 1923, p. 296.

31. Merle Curti, *The Social Ideas of American Educators* (New York: Charles Scribner's Sons, 1935), p. 219.

32. Rose Finkelstein Norwood, interview by Stephen H. Norwood, Boston, Mass., May 2, 1975.

33. James Maurer, "Labor's Demand for Its Own Schools," *The Nation,* September 20, 1922, pp. 276–78.

34. American Federation of Labor, *Proceedings of the 1916 Convention* (Washington, D.C.: Law Reporter Printing Co., 1916), p. 349; Philip Cunroe, *Educational Attitudes and Policies of Organized Labor in the United States* (New York: Teachers' College, Columbia University Bureau of Publications, 1926), p. 113.

35. Cunroe, *Educational Attitudes,* p. 160.

36. Maurer, "Labor's Demand," p. 276.

37. "Records of the Harvard College Class of 1903," entry for Henry Wadsworth Longfellow Dana, Classbook of 1928; first quote from Boston Trade Union College, "The Boston Trade Union College," (Boston: Boston

Trade Union College, 1922); second quote from Boston Trade Union College, "An Educational Institution for Workers" (Boston: Boston Trade Union College, 1920); third quote from *Boston Labor World*, April 12, 1919.

38. Boston *Herald*, October 24, 1920.

39. Henry Wise, who was closely involved with the work of the Boston Trade Union College and for a time served as Dana's lawyer, stated that Dana's homosexuality may have been a factor in his expulsion from Columbia's faculty. According to Helen Norton Starr, Dana's faculty colleague at Brookwood Labor College, Dana's homosexuality was common knowledge to the Brookwood faculty. Henry Wise, interview by Stephen H. Norwood, Boston, Mass., December 4, 1980; Helen Norton Starr, interview by Stephen H. Norwood, New York, N.Y., October 9, 1982.

40. Boston *Herald*, October 24, 1920.

41. Henry Wise, interview.

42. Helen Ferris, "For Women Workers in Industry," 1921, Box 1, American Labor Education Service [hereafter, ALES] Papers, State Historical Society of Wisconsin, Madison, Wis.

43. Hilda W. Smith, "The School for Women Workers in Industry," *Bryn Mawr Bulletin*, May, 1921, Box 1, ALES Papers.

44. Louise Brownell Saunders, "Four Weeks Experience in the Bryn Mawr Summer School for Labor," Box 1, ALES Papers.

45. "Summer School for Women Workers in Industry," 1921, pp. 11–16, Box 1, ALES Papers.

46. Eugene M. Pharo, "Giving the Working Girl a Chance," 1921, Box 1, ALES Papers.

47. Alice Henry, "Report from Secretary of Educational Department," February 11, 1921, Reel 2, National WTUL Papers; "Why a Short Course?" *Life and Labor Bulletin*, April, 1923, p. 2.

48. Mabel Gillespie, "Boston League Gives Service of Many Sorts," *Life and Labor*, July, 1921, p. 222.

49. National WTUL, "Proceedings of the 1922 Convention," p. 618, Reel 22, National WTUL Papers.

50. "President's Report to Second Biennial Convention," p. 14.

51. Julia O'Connor, "Irish Industrial Impressions," *UTO*, February, 1922, p. 20.

52. "The International Congress," *UTO*, October, 1921, p. 13.

53. Julia O'Connor, "An Armistice Day Address," *UTO*, December, 1921, pp. 23–25.

54. *Proceedings of First Convention*, p. 95.

55. Letter from Alice Cooney, press secretary, Local 5A, *UTO*, March, 1921, pp. 7, 12–13; Letter from May Brady, president, Local 65A, May, 1921, p. 8; *UTO*, June, 1921, p. 7; *UTO*, May, 1922, p. 12.

56. "The Story of a Union Bazaar," *UTO*, May, 1921, pp. 18–19, 25; "Bazaar Briefs," *UTO*, June, 1921, pp. 10, 13.

57. McLean, "Culture of Resistance," p. 72; R. T. McComas, "Interest of Employees Constantly Held," *Modern Hospital*, January, 1917, pp. 75–77.

58. Loretta Baker, "Driftway,"*UTO*, February, 1921, p. 19.

59. Clare Moriarty [pseudonym], interview by Stephen H. Norwood, Boston, Mass., June 12, 1974.

60. Letter from Long Answer [pseudonym], convention delegate, *UTO*, January, 1922, p. 9.

61. Letter from Para Cords [pseudonym], *UTO*, January, 1922, p. 10.

62. "Some Observations," *UTO*, December, 1921, p. 8; "Convention Rhymes," *UTO*, January, 1922, p. 20.

63. Letter from Long Answer [pseudonym], p. 9.

64. "Convention Rhymes," p. 20.

65. "Meet Me in St. Louis," *UTO*, October, 1921, p. 10.

66. Letter from Miss Chord [pseudonym], convention delegate, *UTO*, January, 1922, p. 9.

67. Eric Hobsbawm, *Workers* (New York: Pantheon Books, 1984), pp. 87–89.

68. "The Journal and Its Mission," *UTO*, January, 1921, p. 4.

69. See, for example, "Saving Life and Property by Telephone," *UTO*, February, 1921, p. 20; Letter from May Brady, president, Local 65A, *UTO*, February, 1921, p. 8.

70. Julia O'Connor to Marjorie White, December 2, 1920, Julia O'Connor Parker Papers.

Marjorie White (1894–1972) was probably the author of the series of articles about women's work written under the pseudonym "The Pilgrim" which appeared in the WTUL organ *Life and Labor* during the 1920s, including "Pilgrim's Progress in a Telephone Exchange," published in two parts in the January and February, 1921, issues. A member of the WTUL, she began work in 1920 on a novel about telephone operators which she hoped could be used as union propaganda. Her 415–page manuscript, completed by 1927, was never published. White, who was in correspondence with Julia O'Connor between 1920 and 1927, later collaborated with the historian Mary Beard in trying to establish a World Center for Women's Archives and an Encyclopedia of Women, and on projects to revise the coverage and depiction of women in the *Encyclopedia Britannica* and *Colliers' Encyclopedia*.

71. "The Journal and Its Mission," p. 4.

72. Julia O'Connor Parker to Marjorie White, July 7, 1927, Julia O'Connor Parker Papers.

73. Eunice Evelyn Bright, "Why Not?" *UTO*, March, 1921, pp. 21–23, 26.

74. Boston *Evening Transcript*, June 26, 1923.

75. Alice Kessler-Harris, "Independence and Virtue in the Lives of Wage-Earning Women: The United States, 1870–1930," in Judith Friedlander et al., eds., *Women in Culture and Politics: A Century of Change* (Bloomington: Indiana University Press, 1986), pp. 9, 13.

76. New Orleans *Times-Picayune*, October 5, 1919.

77. *Labor News,* July 6, 1923.

78. Mary Quinn Wynne, interview by Stephen H. Norwood, Springfield, Mass., June 28, 1974.

79. "Rewards of Capitalism," *UTO,* February, 1922, p. 25; untitled poem, *UTO,* February, 1922, p. 28.

80. O'Connor, "Irish Industrial Impressions," p. 18.

81. Ibid., p. 16.

82. Quote from *Irish People,* October, 1923; Emmet Larkin, *James Larkin* (Cambridge, Mass.: MIT Press, 1965), p. 244.

83. Stephen H. Norwood, "Mary Donovan Hapgood," in Gary M. Fink, ed., *Biographical Dictionary of American Labor* (Westport, Conn.: Greenwood Press, 1984), pp. 277–79; Richard Caugher, untitled manuscript concerning Mary Donovan and Powers Hapgood, n.d., p. 68 (unpublished), in possession of Hapgood family.

84. Caugher, untitled manuscript, pp. 65–66.

85. Rose Finkelstein Norwood stated that Mary Donovan and Julia O'Connor were no longer on friendly terms when they returned from the trip abroad, and that Donovan immediately "started an anti-Julia move. . . . And Loretta Baker lined up with Mary Donovan to fight Julia." Rose Finkelstein Norwood, interview by Stephen H. Norwood, Boston, Mass., June 12, 1974. Mary Donovan's daughter confirmed that the friendship between Donovan and O'Connor ended during their trip abroad. Barta Hapgood Monro, telephone interview by Stephen H. Norwood, February 6, 1982.

86. Rose Finkelstein Norwood, interview by Stephen H. Norwood, Boston, Mass., July 18, 1974; Mary Quinn Wynne, interview.

87. Reports of Agents Norman Gifford, May 29, 1918, Paul Curtis, April 18, 1918, and John Lyons, April 16, 1918, Roll 643, Bureau of Investigation Records, Record Group 65, National Archives, Washington, D.C.

88. Form letter of recommendation for Brookwood Labor College, 1924, Box 73, Brookwood Labor College Papers, Walter P. Reuther Library, Wayne State University, Detroit, Mich.

89. Moira Callahan [pseudonym] to Lillian, September 14, 1925, Box 85, Brookwood Labor College Papers.

90. Moira Callahan [pseudonym] to A. J. Muste, January 11, 1927, Box 85, Brookwood Labor College Papers.

91. Ingrid Mueller [pseudonym] to A. J. Muste, October 17, 1929, Box 73, Brookwood Labor College Papers; *Brookwood Review,* May, 1933.

92. James R. Green and Hugh Carter Donahue, *Boston's Workers: A Labor History* (Boston: Boston Public Library, 1979), p. 99; Albert M. Heintz and John R. Whitney, *History of the Massachusetts State Federation of Labor, 1887–1935* (Worcester, Mass.: Labor News Printers, 1935), p. 57.

7

The Trade Union Woman
Isolation, Conflict, and Defeat
1920–23

At the time of its first convention in late 1919, the Telephone
Operators' Department was a truly national, even international, labor
organization, boasting locals in over thirty states, in Canada, and in
the Panama Canal Zone. In the preceding nine months, it had recruited
11,000 members and had more than doubled its membership. Inspired
by the spectacular victory of the New England telephone operators
in their strike earlier that year, operators from across the country had
flooded the Department office with requests for assistance in organizing. The Department eagerly confronted the task of bringing into
the union fold the vast majority of operators in the United States and
Canada who remained unorganized. In opening the Department convention, President Julia O'Connor announced to the assembled delegates that she looked forward to the day "when a room ten times as
large as this won't hold our convention."[1]

Instead, the Telephone Operators' Department during the early
1920s suffered a sharp decline in membership, leaving it almost completely isolated in its New England stronghold. The Department leadership had been well aware of the precarious situation of telephone
operators' unionism in most of the country. Much of the new membership had been recruited during what President O'Connor in 1921
called a "period of abnormality," when a severe war-induced inflation
had combined with the disruption of regular bargaining procedures
under government control and the postmaster-general's unwillingness
to grant wage increases to produce intense nationwide discontent

among telephone operators.[2] Despite the impressive organization gains of that period, the telephone companies outside New England remained generally antagonistic to the operators' locals; Julia O'Connor declared at the Department convention in 1919 that they intended to "crush out union organization of their operators at any cost."[3]

The prospects for operators' unionism became increasingly unfavorable during the early 1920s, a period characterized by a pervasive hostility to organized labor. Large corporations, including AT&T, were for the most part successful in their efforts to replace AFL-affiliated trade unions with company unions as the bargaining agents for their employees. The organizing gains of the immediate postwar period evaporated as the masses of both telephone men and operators entered these newly formed "employees' associations." The International Brotherhood of Electrical Workers was eliminated from the telephone service on the Pacific Coast after being defeated in a strike in 1920, called to protest Pacific Bell's requirement that its employees join company unions. Even more damaging for the Telephone Operators' Union was the withdrawal later that year of the male telephone workers of New England from the IBEW and their formation of a company union. Having divided the male from the female employees, the New England Telephone Company repudiated the collective bargaining relationship with the telephone operators that had been in force since 1913 and refused to act on any wage demands.

Motivated at least in part by the desire to disrupt organization among the telephone operators, AT&T began to introduce the telephone dial system in 1920. The Telephone Operators' Union believed that the dial system threatened to eliminate a considerable number of operating jobs. Conversion to dial would also severely reduce the power of a telephone operators' union to interfere with service during a strike. Fearing that company unionism and the dial system threatened the very existence of the Telephone Operators' Union, Julia O'Connor called for a strike of operators in New England in the summer of 1923. By achieving the strike demands for a wage increase and a reduction of the workday to seven hours, O'Connor hoped to restore collective bargaining and to reduce the impact of unemployment resulting from conversion to the dial system. The union's prospects for success in a strike, however, were greatly hindered by bitter factional strife in Boston's Local 1A between the group surrounding O'Connor and the toll operators. A major factor in union politics since at least 1918, this conflict had intensified as the organization declined sharply in strength during the early 1920s.

Labor's Postwar Decline

The artificially tight labor market and the government's need to maintain uninterrupted production, which had allowed labor to exercise considerable influence in industry, no longer existed after the war. The Wilson administration had never intended to permanently alter industrial relations. Because American participation in the war had been so brief, the administration had no difficulty dismantling such agencies as the National War Labor Board, which it had created to oversee wartime labor relations. The administration applied far less pressure on employers to bargain with trade unions after 1918. The massive layoffs caused by the termination of government contracts and the rapid demobilization of troops resulted in a flooded labor market, undermining the power of the trade unions.[4] Trade union membership fell precipitously, from over 5 million in 1920 to about 3.6 million in 1923; among those lost were nearly all the members recruited during the unions' wartime upsurge.[5] The Harding administration consistently sided with employers in labor disputes during the early 1920s. When 650,000 coal miners went on strike in 1922 against a drastic wage reduction, President Harding intervened to reopen the mines. The same year, the federal government broke a strike of 400,000 railroad shopmen, also called to protest a wage reduction, by securing the most severe and sweeping injunction in American history. The railroad workers, who had gained so much from the state's intervention during the war, were now "more tightly strait-jacketed than ever."[6]

No longer benefiting from the government's wartime efforts to effect compromises in labor disputes, trade unions could not maintain organization in manufacturing. The major postwar strikes in this sector, in steel in 1919 and meat-packing in 1921, ended in labor's total defeat. By the early 1920s, the AFL was again almost completely shut out of basic industry.[7] Such important industries as auto, rubber, electrical equipment, cement, chemicals, and food were almost totally devoid of unionization. A campaign to organize steel after the defeat of the 1919 strike was repeatedly postponed and then abandoned entirely in 1923.[8] Two of the previously most dynamic unions—the United Mine Workers and the International Ladies' Garment Workers' Union—experienced a sharp drop in membership during the 1920s. What little organization remained was heavily concentrated in a small number of industries, some of which, like the New England shoe and textile, were in decline as plants relocated to the non-union South.[9]

The rise in real wages after the end of the recession of 1920–21 contributed to organized labor's failure to attract new recruits during the 1920s. The increasing privatization of leisure, resulting from the automobile, radio, and movies, also might have contributed to labor's decline by distracting the worker from union meetings and socials.

The Rise of Company Unionism

After the war, in an effort to discourage unionization and replace existing labor organizations, many of the large corporations—including AT&T—introduced company unions or "employee representation plans" as they were sometimes called. A company union is defined as an organization that restricts its membership to the employees of a particular company or plant and represents these employees in their dealings with management. Company unions, which assume that the interests of labor and management are not opposed, are not affiliated with larger outside trade unions, do not build up strike funds, and are invariably controlled by management. Lower-level managerial officials were sometimes even included in the membership. Company unions existed in only a handful of firms before World War I. Perhaps the best known was the so-called "industrial representation plan" which the Colorado Fuel and Iron Company introduced in its coal mines and steel plants in 1915–16 in an effort to improve its public image after it had bloodily suppressed a strike of miners demanding recognition of the United Mine Workers' Union.[10]

The wartime labor policies of the Wilson administration, while resulting in considerable short-term growth for the AFL, encouraged many corporations to form company unions. To preserve labor peace, the National War Labor Board had pressed many industries to establish machinery that could facilitate the settlement of disputes between labor and management. However, while supporting the workers' right to organize, the NWLB tolerated the open shop and refused to require management to engage in collective bargaining with majority-elected unions. The formation of company unions therefore appeared to satisfy both the government, which desired some sort of employees' organization, and the corporations, which would not accept AFL unionism.

Company unions became increasingly popular after the war among corporate managers in large-scale industry who believed it was in their interest to promote greater employer-employee communication. Such contact might improve employee morale and diminish the attraction of AFL-affiliated trade unions, whose ability to interfere in production was made dramatically evident during the 1919 strike wave. Management also feared that returning to a purely individual basis of bargaining would greatly antagonize workers who had been previously unionized in such industries as railroad and meatpacking.[11] In 1919, at the suggestion of A. C. Bedford, president of Standard Oil of New Jersey, and Owen Young of General Electric, a special conference committee of corporate presidents and industrial relations executives of ten (later twelve) very large firms—including Standard Oil of New Jersey, AT&T, General Motors, and U.S. Steel— was formed to pool information and develop policy concerning employee representation plans.[12]

AT&T management introduced company unionism in the Bell System during the 1919 strike wave. With the approval of Postmaster-General Burleson, it sent letters to the officers of the associated companies urging them to "encourage your employees to form associations which shall appoint representatives to discuss freely and frankly with the officials of the company questions affecting their wages and work." The first associations were established in the departments where trade unionism was most strongly entrenched—the Plant Department, employing linemen, repairmen, installers, and cable splicers; and the Traffic Department, employing operators. Departments usually were organized as separate associations. In a few of the larger subsidiaries, such as Pacific Bell which had jurisdiction over five states, there were further divisions along geographical lines.[13] Company unions were formally established by the Southern Bell Company in July, 1919, a few days before the Atlanta telephone strike was called off. The membership was open to all white employees below the rank of division superintendent, including traffic managers and chief operators.[14] That same month, Cleveland Bell formed a company union to defeat an organizing campaign by the IBEW's Telephone Operators' Department. Southwestern Bell introduced one in St. Louis after the failure of the operators' strike in August.[15]

AT&T Vice-President H. B. Thayer stressed that the major purpose of establishing company unions was to drive the AFL out of the telephone service: " . . . we felt . . . the trade unions were utterly wrong from the fact that . . . the union only thrives on the discontent of its members. . . . The plan we evolved, therefore, was to encourage friendly organizations of the employees. . . . It is our hope that . . . before very long, the employees of the Bell System throughout the country will have no affiliation with any outside labor organization and will cooperate thoroughly with management." Thayer noted in 1922 that "the results have more than met our expectations"; company unions had replaced IBEW locals nearly everywhere except New England.[16]

Contributing to the success of company unionism outside New England was the difficult financial situation of the Telephone Operators' Department, which emerged from the New Orleans convention heavily in debt. Because of "administrative and technical" problems, a $10,000 loan the IBEW convention voted to give the Department in 1919 was never granted. As a result, the Department had to reduce its organizing force to one person, in addition to the vice-presidents. Organizing gains were negligible after 1919, and the Department's membership declined considerably.[17]

The Telephone Operators' Union regarded AT&T's introduction of employee representation plans as merely the latest in a long series of attempts to eliminate AFL influence in the telephone service, and it cautioned that the new associations had nothing in common with legitimate trade unions. At the 1921 convention of the IBEW's Telephone Operators' Department, President Julia O'Connor reported there had been "no change" since 1919 in the telephone companies' "general attitude of antagonism toward organization," and she declared, "I look for union smashing tactics to continue. The byproducts of such a policy are the spy system, company union, and wholesale discriminatory tactics. We must face them all."[18] O'Connor denounced the employee representation plans as "a patent device for the purpose of getting rid of the unions." The associations blurred the distinctions between labor and management, undermined the democratic procedures introduced by the trade union, and increased company scrutinization of the worker: "There are usually no dues; the Company pays all the bills, including the expense of representatives attending district and division conferences. . . . No general meetings of employees are provided for. Elections for representatives are held on the Company's premises, and the voter *must sign the ballot*."[19] Rose Hickey Quinn, the Department's principal organizer in the South, noted that the elective offices of company unions in the Bell System were usually held by management officials with the power to discharge employees, hardly conducive to the free discussion of grievances at meetings. Moreover, company unions for telephone operators were often headed by a male official.[20]

In 1920, Pacific Bell issued an ultimatum that its employees join company unions, forcing a strike which resulted in the virtual destruction of the IBEW locals in its territory. The inconclusive six-week telephone strike in 1919 had seriously weakened the IBEW locals on the Pacific Coast. Many workers had given up their union membership in exchange for a restoration of seniority rights, and management had succeeded in attracting a considerable number of IBEW officers to the company unions. Protesting the company's ultimatum and demanding a $1–a-day wage increase, the IBEW called the male telephone workers out on strike in February, 1920. The strike drew far less support than the IBEW had expected. The majority of workers, motivated in part by management's offer of a wage increase of $.20 to $.50 a day, repudiated the IBEW and affiliated with the company unions. The IBEW officers who had defected to the company union were instrumental in persuading the workers to accept these terms. IBEW President James Noonan later declared that "our members were induced by these men whom they trusted, to accept the Company's proposition and betrayed their fellow workmen by acting as strikebreakers."[21] The relatively small number of operators who remained organized were not asked to join the strike at the outset, although Julia O'Connor was conferring with IBEW officials in San Francisco when the strike began. The strike collapsed within two weeks, before the operators took any action.[22]

Several months after the defeat of the Pacific Coast strike, the male telephone workers in New England withdrew from the IBEW and joined a company union. They were motivated by a long-standing resentment of the IBEW leadership for allegedly consistently favoring the "inside" electrical workers in jurisdictional matters. Three groups within the union—the telephone men of New England, the shop electricians, and the railroad electricians—requested and were denied a department form of organization similar to that of the telephone operators, but only the telephone men refused to accept the decision of the international. The AFL, adhering to its policy of trade autonomy, rejected an application for a separate charter. Representatives of the male telephone locals in New England then met at a convention in Providence, Rhode Island, in August, 1920, and formed the International Brotherhood of Telephone Workers (IBTW).[23] The organization was confined to Bell Company employees, which separated the telephone men from other electrical workers and the rest of the labor movement, and it thus was easily controlled by management. From the beginning, the IBTW operated as a company union.

The IBTW, aware that its survival was problematic without the affiliation of the company's largest group of employees, immediately claimed jurisdiction over the telephone operators and attempted to draw them away from the IBEW. Julia O'Connor responded with a forceful denunciation of the "Secession Movement": "Any division of labor's forces is to be deplored, particularly so in this circumstance since the telephone companies outside New England have not been guiltless of pernicious activity in the organization of company unions sometimes called 'employees' associations' operating under a company-dictated policy."[24] The IBTW nevertheless had considerable success in recruiting telephone operators.

An operator who worked as a Telephone Operators' Department organizer in Vermont in the early 1920s recalled that the Secessionists gave her "a very bad time": "Every time we went into an office—that was during the time just before the election when we were allowed to go into the building to talk to the operators—the telephone men would be sitting in the dining room and you know, they never bothered with the girls about their conditions, they never wanted them in their union anyway, but they were just so sore at the IBEW that they would get the girls all together and talk them out of signing up."[25] The telephone men also took advantage of family ties and friendships to recruit telephone operators to the IBTW. According to Mary Quinn Wynne, who during the early 1920s was business agent of the Springfield Telephone Operators' Union (Local 3A) as well as Department treasurer, "The men started working on the girls to get them out of their Department and into their organization, the IBTW. The men working for the Telephone Company had many friends among the operators, of course, some of them boyfriends, and some of them married afterwards, and were persuading the girls to leave our organization and go in with them. And that was happening in Boston and other places too. . . . Some of the younger girls would probably listen to them—but to their sorrow they found out we were right in the end."[26]

The Secessionists received their strongest support in the northern New England states—Maine, Vermont, and New Hampshire—where commitment to the Telephone Operators' Union and to the labor movement itself had never been as intense as in Massachusetts. Because telephone exchange operating forces were relatively small in the northern states, work was less routinized and relations between operators and supervisory personnel less asymmetric than in the more densely populated sections of New England. Since fewer operators were of Irish-American background, the ethnic antagonism toward telephone company management that was so important in the larger Massachusetts cities was much less of a factor in northern New England. The long-standing association of trade unions at both the city and state levels in Massachusetts, its tradition of labor struggle, and the influence of feminism, especially important in Boston, that had helped sustain the Telephone Operators' Union were absent in the northern states.

The New England Telephone Company signaled a major change in its labor policy during the annual contract negotiations in late 1920. Instead of first informing the wage-scale committee of the Telephone Operators' Union, it announced its rejection of the union's proposals by placing notices on the exchange bulletin boards, as it had before the near-strike of 1913. This action, a clear repudiation of collective bargaining, was bitterly resented by the union. It was plainly motivated by New England Telephone's decision to encourage company unionism.

In late 1919, the New England Telephone Operators' Union had achieved a wage increase of $1.50 to $2.50 a week and a reduction of the length of service required to attain the maximum wage from seven to five and a half years.[27] The next year, the operators advanced the proposals that became the central demands of the 1923 strike: a reduction of the workday from eight to seven hours, substituting a forty-two- for a forty-eight-hour week; a reclassification of wage schedules so that three rather than seven wage differentials would prevail in the New England region; and a wage increase of $5 to $9 a week. All were rejected by the company, which stressed that the operators had not suffered the wage reductions and layoffs imposed in other industries.[28]

The Threat of the Dial

The union leadership had long advocated a shorter workday because of the enormous fatigue induced by telephone operating, but in the early 1920s it was also increasingly concerned about the danger of technological unemployment posed by the introduction of the telephone dial system. Julia O'Connor always maintained that the power the New England Telephone Operators' Union displayed in the 1919 strike strongly influenced telephone company management to introduce the dial system, which it knew would seriously weaken telephone operators' unionism. In hearings conducted by the Massachusetts Department of Public Utilities in 1933 as a result of a suit filed by the Boston Central Labor Union charging the New England Telephone Company with taking excessive profits, Julia O'Connor Parker testified:

Mr. Marshall	[lawyer for Boston Central Labor Union]: Do you know or have you any information as to whether or not this strike [the 1919 New England telephone strike] and the possibility of another strike caused the company to enter upon the policy of machine-switching development?
Mrs. Parker:	It is my opinion that it did affect the policy of the company.
Mr. Marshall:	Because there would be a smaller personnel for the company to deal with?
Mrs. Parker:	Yes.
Mr. Marshall:	And what effect would machine-switching have upon the union organization and membership?
Mrs. Parker:	It would reduce it, of course, and would reduce the importance of the operator as a factor in telephone service.
Mr. Marshall:	And therefore make the union less effective?
Mrs. Parker:	Yes.[29]

The Bell Company had experimented with automatic operation as early as 1889, but it did not begin to open machine-switching telephone exchanges in the United States until after the end of World War I.[30] However, in 1911 Bell's manufacturing subsidiary, Western Electric, had begun producing rotary automatic (dial) exchanges for sale in Europe, where operating agencies were better able to introduce new inventions and improvements in telephony because they did not have the large investments in existing equipment that American companies had and they were not committed to a policy of uniform and universal service. Dial telephones also helped reduce the difficulties caused by language differences, far more serious in Europe than in the United States. Before 1912, German, French, and British firms had acquired manufacturing rights for automatic telephone systems from the Strowger Automatic Electric Company of Chicago.[31] Professor Dugald Jackson, head of the department of electrical engineering at Massachusetts Institute of Technology who went to England in 1912 to assist in the valuation of telephone properties taken over by the British government, reported that automatic systems were giving excellent service in many parts of Europe, particularly Bavaria and Prussia.[32]

Government ownership of the telephone system in such countries as England, where it was adopted in 1912, led AT&T to consider the dial system as a method of controlling and disciplining the labor force. AT&T Vice-President H. B. Thayer in 1912 informed the president of the Bell Telephone Company of Canada: "The situation in Europe is rather different from what it is either in Canada or the United States. Government ownership of the telephone service involves civil service rules with regard to operators which makes the operator question much more serious than with us and therefore the various European governments are looking toward the automatic as a possible relief from trouble."[33]

Influenced by the increasing militancy of telephone operators, the Bell System began preparations to introduce the dial telephone in the immediate postwar period. The first large machine-switching exchange in the Bell System was put into service in November, 1919, at Norfolk, Virginia, where the telephone operators were organized as Local 81A. The telephone company insisted that using the dial required no more effort than winding a watch, but many believed that it would prove too difficult for subscribers. While the Telephone Operators' Union leadership was deeply concerned about the dial threat, publicly it expressed doubt that subscribers would ever master dialling: "Picture your pet Mr. I-Rate Subscriber who now manages to bang his hook for 10 or 12 flashes before your 4 second answer 'dialling' sedately and accurately—3 dials for the exchange wanted, first being sure he has the code correct, then once more for each digit of his number? Well, all we've got to say is better keep the schools equipped they'll have to send the subscribers there."[34]

To teach the public how to use the dial telephone, the telephone company at Norfolk issued special leaflets and placed advertisements in the newspapers. The night before the cutover, stereopticon slides were shown in the city's principal theaters announcing that the dial was coming into use the next day.[35] As the dial system spread during the 1920s, the Bell companies sent "flying squadrons" to visit subscribers in their homes in the cities and towns where cutovers were taking place to give individual instruction in the use of the dial telephone. According to the Southern Bell Company, the task of educating the subscribers was "herculean"; the flying squadrons had to answer over and over such questions as "How is one to dial with hang nails?"[36] Nevertheless, it quickly became clear that subscribers would easily adapt to using the dial telephones.

Dial conversion in New England began in the midst of the 1923 strike, when the Aspinwall machine-switching office was opened, providing service to 1,800 Brookline subscribers. The first New England city to switch entirely to the dial system was Lawrence in December,

1924—not coincidentally, the city with the most complete strike turn-out in 1923. By 1931, the telephone systems of such cities as Worcester, Springfield, and Bangor were entirely dial operated. That dial operation could cause a major reduction in the operating force was already clear by 1920, when less than half the operators at Norfolk were retained after the cutover.[37]

Leaders of the Telephone Operators' Department vigorously opposed the dial system for two decades. As late as 1940, former Department Vice-President Rose Sullivan, testifying at the National Economic Conference of the U.S. Congress, denounced the dial system as "the perfect example of a wasteful, expensive, inefficient, clumsy, anti-social device," which merely transferred the burden of work from the paid telephone operator to the unpaid subscriber.[38] They also advanced the argument that the dial system was useless during emergencies. Department organizer Rose Hickey Quinn asked in 1921, "When the mother sees her child fall into a tub of scalding water . . . can she calm herself and dial the doctor's number, or does she frantically lift the receiver as of old and ask the operator to get her a doctor quickly?"[39] Department President Julia O'Connor Parker stated at national telephone code hearings under the National Recovery Administration in 1934, "You have read stories of the telephone operators sitting at a switchboard until fire burned their fingers, in order that they might serve the public. The dial telephone . . . removes that great human intelligence . . . in time of stress and disaster, and substitutes a little robot of steel and metal, without capacity to respond to a human emergency."[40]

Factional Conflict in Local 1A

The Telephone Operators' Union was also seriously weakened in the early 1920s by factional conflict in Local 1A, which culminated in the revocation of its charter by Department President Julia O'Connor in January, 1923. Two factions—one dominated by toll operators, whose principal leaders were Annie Molloy and Mary Mahoney, the local's first two presidents; the other grouped around Julia O'Connor, a local operator—had emerged as early as 1918, the year O'Connor, in a bitterly contested presidential election, narrowly defeated Mahoney, the incumbent. The Boston *Globe* quoted unnamed union officers who asserted that Mahoney, who had already served two terms, had been prevailed upon to run again by leaders of the toll faction, "although Miss O'Connor, who has been vice-president for two terms, was the logical candidate, according to union ethics."[41]

Company officials closely monitored the factional conflict in Local 1A. A month before the 1919 New England telephone strike, President Matt B. Jones of the New England Telephone Company had informed H. B. Thayer, vice-president of AT&T, that "Miss O'Connor is not popular with our toll office operators who were the dominant element in our operators' union in Metropolitan until Miss O'Connor beat their candidate for the presidency last summer and while they would go out with the bunch they are not likely to be enthusiastic about pulling her chestnuts out of the fire."[42]

Because toll operators were more skilled and more experienced than the local operators and had led the movement to organize back in 1912, they tended to believe that they were the natural leaders of the Telephone Operators' Union. Toll faction leaders often referred to O'Connor's supporters as "youngsters," implying that they should not be taken seriously as trade unionists because they lacked maturity and long-term commitment to the job. The toll operators were also much less concerned about the dial system, since it did not threaten their jobs, only those of the local operators. There was no prospect of introducing direct dialling for toll calls. O'Connor undoubtedly feared that as local operating positions were eliminated by the dial system, power in the union would shift back to the toll operators.

The factional conflict was exacerbated by the deep personal antagonism that existed between O'Connor and Molloy. According to Henry Wise, O'Connor, one of the most talented writers in the American labor movement and a "natural aristocrat," sometimes "let the ordinary Irish of South Boston know she was above them," unlike the less cultivated Molloy.[43] Leaders of the toll faction grew increasingly resentful of O'Connor after her leadership of the 1919 New England telephone strike catapulted her to national prominence.

Many in Local 1A apparently perceived O'Connor as a bureaucrat who had grown too distant from the rank and file and too enamored of herself. These would be viewed as particularly serious offenses in a union led almost entirely by working operators and almost totally devoid of bureaucracy. Henry Wise described O'Connor as "vain" and stated she had let the acclaim she received for her leadership in the 1919 New England strike go to her head.[44] One of her closest friends labelled her "an office type."[45] Another very close friend and former member of Local 1A declared that "Julia never wanted to do anything to push anybody else." She also stated that O'Connor's travelling in Europe was a source of discord in the union: " . . . when you stop and think about it, maybe that was shattering the union a little bit, with the officers goin' off on all sorts of junkets . . . instead of fully explaining it to the membership."[46]

Factional conflict became increasingly serious after the election of Annie Molloy to the presidency of Local 1A in June, 1922. Molloy's candidacy was a response to the challenge of the Secession Movement, which had shortly before the election established a Boston telephone operators' local of the IBTW, led by Mary Mahoney, Local 1A's president from 1916 to 1918. Frances Van Tassel, Local 1A's vice-president who had been the strongest candidate in the field, withdrew from the race in favor of Molloy, who commanded enormous prestige as the union's first president and was considered best able to rally the membership against the Secessionists. Molloy drew an overwhelming majority of the 1,500 votes cast. According to the Boston *Post,* this maneuver "nipped in the bud" the threat of Boston operators' entering the IBTW.[47]

Tensions between the factions increased in October, 1922, when, for reasons which are unclear, O'Connor attempted to expel from the union one of Molloy's chief lieutenants, May Matthews, Local 1A's recording secretary and former Department secretary. Unlike most of those close to Molloy, Matthews was not a toll operator but worked at a PBX board at the Castle Square Hotel. O'Connor filed charges of "disloyalty" against Matthews with the Department executive board. On October 9, board members Agnes Johnson of Portland, Oregon, and Kate Crain of Springfield, Illinois, voted to expel Matthews; the third member—Mary June of Boston—voted against it. Matthews, backed by Local 1A, whose members booed and hissed O'Connor at a meeting held to discuss the issue, responded by seeking a court injunction.[48]

At a union meeting on January 12, 1923, Department President O'Connor, charging administrative and financial irregularities, revoked the charter of Local 1A. O'Connor was seriously concerned about the local's rapidly dwindling membership and treasury, which she believed was in large part the result of Molloy's incompetent leadership. One telephone operator who attended the meeting at Tremont Temple recalled the "tension in the air" as she entered the hall, with the supporters of Molloy and O'Connor urging undecided members to "sit over on our side." She remembered Molloy on the stage, sitting nervously in the president's chair "fumbling with papers" before the meeting began, as though anticipating trouble.[49] The Boston *Post* reported that feelings were "at fever heat" throughout the meeting.[50] According to Molloy's supporters, O'Connor acted to revoke the charter after she twice narrowly lost a vote to grant her the floor to discuss financial matters. After the second vote, President Molloy announced that the meeting would adjourn following the report of the union adjustment board. O'Connor immediately stepped onto the stage. Holding a copy of the union's constitution above her head, she declared, "As Department President I hereby revoke the charter of Local 1A, Boston Telephone Operators' Union."

The Boston *Herald* reported, "The words had barely left her lips when there was a rush to the platform. . . . Cries of 'traitor' and 'We knew you'd come to it' could be heard for blocks. . . . On entering the hall newspapermen found Miss O'Connor the storm centre. She was standing on the platform, holding aloft the constitution. . . . Wildly excited girls and young women surged back and forth, all clamoring to be heard at one and the same time."[51] Only the arrival of a uniformed policeman prevented a physical clash between the supporters of O'Connor and Molloy. Declaring the meeting adjourned, Molloy repaired with her supporters to Local 1A's offices at the Old South Building for an "indignation meeting," leaving O'Connor and her followers in control of the hall, where they began proceedings to establish a new union of telephone operators.[52]

O'Connor prevented Local 1A's delegates from being seated at the next meeting of the New England Council of Telephone Operators' Unions and moved to have the Boston Central Labor Union (CLU) expel Local 1A in favor of a rechartered telephone operators' union controlled by her followers. An irate Molloy denounced O'Connor's "high-handed" action in revoking the charter as "part of her rule or ruin policy to disrupt and tear down where she cannot dictate," and she denied that O'Connor commanded any appreciable support in the Boston local: "She has a blind following of some 25 girls, mostly youngsters. . . . out of a membership of about 4,000."[53]

The Boston CLU meeting of February 4, 1923, one of the largest held in a decade, was attended by some two hundred telephone operators—including representatives from Worcester, Lynn, and other cities outside Boston—who occupied the entire left section of the hall. The huge attendance at this meeting serves as an indication that Boston trade unionists considered the Telephone Operators' Union a highly important part of the city's labor movement. The CLU voted to "take no action" on the seating of delegates from Local 1A until an official communication was received from the IBEW.

At the next meeting of the CLU two weeks later, O'Connor presented a communication from the IBEW supporting the position of its Department president, and the delegates from Local 1A were unseated and replaced by members of the new "Boston Telephone Operators' Union."[54] May Matthews, recording secretary of Local 1A, lost her position as recording clerk of the Boston CLU, and Frances Van Tassel, a member of Local 1A's executive board, lost her position as CLU auditor.[55] A week after the CLU meeting, the New England Council of Telephone Operators' Unions, siding with O'Connor, adopted a resolution calling upon its president, Mary June, who had sided with the Molloy faction, to resign.[56]

Boston's labor movement and the IBEW leadership demonstrated their full support for O'Connor's new local as the legitimate union for the city's telephone operators at the installation of officers in May, 1923, conducted by IBEW Vice-President Frank McNulty. The new local replaced Local 1A as the Boston affiliate of the IBEW's Telephone Operators' Department. Over six hundred telephone operators were present at the exercises and were addressed by Susan Fitzgerald of the Boston Women's Trade Union League, who had assisted in organizing the Boston Telephone Operators' Union in 1912, and E. A. Johnson, president of the Boston CLU. McNulty also read a telegram from IBEW President James Noonan, expressing his regret at not being able to attend. The officers installed were Julia O'Connor as president, Mary I. Brooks as vice-president, Kathryn Tobin as recording secretary, and Cecil Doyle as treasurer.[57] O'Connor's union was known as the "Boston Telephone Operators' Union, IBEW," and Molloy's was branded in labor circles as "Outlaw 1A."

The New England Telephone Strike of 1923

In April, 1923, the New England Council of Telephone Operators' Unions, at a meeting called by Julia O'Connor and attended by delegates representing the forty-nine affiliated locals, voted to again present to the company its demands for a seven-hour day, a wage increase of $5 to $9 a week (with the period of service required to attain the maximum wage reduced from five and a half years to four years), and a reclassification of wage schedules. Having lost its charter, Molloy's Local 1A was no longer affiliated with the New England Council so its representatives were not permitted to attend the meeting. No general wage increase had been granted for four years, and the council declared that operators' wages were far below those paid to women factory workers.[58] On May 26, however, the company rejected the demands as it had done each year since 1920, claiming that the cost of living had declined and reiterating that the operators were not subjected to the seasonal unemployment, layoffs, and wage reductions common in other trades. The New England Council responded by submitting to the rank and file a proposal for a strike referendum.[59] Indicating that the union leadership was fully prepared to call a strike to enforce the demands, the New England Council's wage committee announced that "the fighting spirit of the operators will prove as valiant as in the past, if the arbitrary attitude of the telephone company puts the matter to the test."[60]

Despite the June 8 statement of the old Local 1A, which claimed to represent the majority of Boston's telephone operators, that it would not participate in a strike, O'Connor and the New England Council remained confident the union could paralyze the region's telephone system if its demands were not met. The leaders of the old Local 1A charged that O'Connor's real purpose in fomenting what they termed a "spite" strike was to regain control of the Boston telephone operators, and they declared that, since their local had not been permitted to participate in the referendum, it would not join the walkout. O'Connor dismissed the threat from Molloy's local, claiming that its membership had declined to only 1,788 at the time of the split in January, 1923, and that its powers were "entirely vocal."[61] She believed that in the event of a strike call, most of the rank and file of the old Local 1A would ignore its leaders and join the walkout.

O'Connor was promised strong backing from both the national AFL and Boston's trade union leaders in the event of a strike. Alarmed by the split in the Telephone Operators' Union and the prospect of its being exploited by the Bell System to drive the AFL out of the telephone service, AFL President Samuel Gompers came to Boston to address the Boston Central Labor Union and confer with labor officials. Gompers urged all telephone operators to rally to the IBEW and the New England Council of Telephone Operators' Unions "in order that the movement for higher wages and shorter hours might succeed." The Boston CLU denounced the action of the old Local 1A as "willful and deliberate trade union treason."[62] O'Connor pronounced the charter revocation a dead issue, because her position had been sustained by the Boston Central Labor Union, the president of the IBEW, the executive council of the IBEW, the New England Council of Telephone Operators' Unions, and the executive board of the Telephone Operators' Department.[63]

As the Telephone Operators' Department polled a strike vote, President Julia O'Connor announced that the preservation of the union itself had become the principal issue in the controversy with the company. After receiving the union's demands, the company had instructed chief operators and traffic chiefs to summon the telephone operators to appear before them individually to state whether or not they would participate in a strike. The president of the New England Telephone Company, Matt B. Jones, also sent a personal letter to each of the 12,000 telephone operators in New England asking them not to vote in the strike referendum.[64] On June 18, O'Connor declared, "A war of extermination is on. . . . Following a refusal to improve the inadequate wages of the operators, the Telephone Company launched an offensive against the operators' unions presumably because they dared suggest wage betterments. No other element in the telephone service had the courage to do so, telephone men's organizations being submerged under company control."[65]

It became obvious during the strike referendum that the Telephone Operators' Department was in danger of losing a considerable number of members to the IBTW in northern New England. Several of the Department locals in the northern states—including Brattleboro, Vermont, one of only two IBEW operators' locals remaining in that state, and Dover, New Hampshire—announced that they would not be bound by the strike vote. The company also claimed that, in such Massachusetts cities as Lowell, Haverhill, New Bedford, and Newburyport and in the extreme western part of the state, none of the operators participated in the referendum.[66]

The union's wage-scale committee reported on June 21 that 85 percent of the telephone operators participating in the referendum had voted for a strike, and the next day Julia O'Connor ordered the operators across New England to walk off the job on June 26. It was not clear, however, how many operators would answer the strike call. Of New England's 12,000 operators, 6,100 were concentrated in the Boston Metropolitan District, where both O'Connor and Molloy claimed an overwhelming majority. John J. Dolan, president of the IBTW, boasted that his organization had chartered nineteen locals in New England, and he charged that the IBEW commanded the support of less than 30 percent of the region's operators.[67] O'Connor dispatched Ruth Washburn, a leader of the Brockton Telephone Operators' Union, to appeal for strike solidarity in Manchester, New Hampshire, where Local 66A was threatened by a strong IBTW local.[68] Newspaper editorials almost unanimously opposed a strike, and the Boston and Massachusetts chambers of commerce circulated statements supporting the company's position.[69] The New England Telephone Company in the two weeks before the strike sent letters to about thirty of the leading newspaper editors in New England and officers of the various chambers of commerce explaining its position and informing them "that it is to be a fight to the finish."[70]

As the front pages of newspapers across New England carried huge advertisements presenting the company's position in the controversy, Molloy and her lieutenants toured Massachusetts and Rhode Island campaigning against the strike order. Addressing the operators of Framingham on the night of June 23, Molloy declared that O'Connor had called the strike "to have the girls outside Boston do the dirty work which she knows the girls of Boston will refuse to do." Later that night, Molloy arrived in Providence with fifteen of her followers, and in a speech to the operators there she asserted, "The strike is nothing more than a spite strike to bolster up the waning popularity of Miss Julia O'Connor."[71] Two days later in Worcester, a jeering crowd of fifty operators ejected three representatives of the old Local 1A from their retiring room.[72]

Molloy steered clear of such cities as Springfield, where strike support was strong. Mary Quinn Wynne, business agent of Local 3A, explained, "She knew me better than that. Annie knew me of old, and she wasn't going to battle with me."[73] Local 3A held a meeting on June 23, at which Department Vice-President Rose Sullivan denounced the company's "campaign of intimidation" and John Gatelee, vice-president of the Springfield Central Labor Union, declared that his organization would back the strikers "to the finish." The Springfield *Republican* reported that many of those attending the meeting had at the outset been uncertain about striking, because they feared being replaced by operators in surrounding towns who had announced they would ignore the strike order. In Holyoke, for example, almost the entire force of nearly a hundred operators had transferred its allegiance to the IBTW. The Springfield operators, however, were angered by having been summoned individually before the chief operators and threatened with dismissal if they went on strike, and at the meeting "they listened, and were convinced." The operators left the meeting in a combative mood, "threatening dire injuries to those who remained in and declaring they 'would make applesauce of them.' "[74]

On the eve of the strike, the two major locals of Boston telephone operators exchanged bitter accusations. The IBTW's following was insignificant in Boston. O'Connor labelled the old Local 1A a "strike-breaking machine," and officers of the Boston Telephone Operators' Union warned that Molloy and her followers would be driven from the labor movement for life: "We are not forgetting that the Annie Molloy who is now assisting the company in its union-smashing task, is the same Annie Molloy who went around in 1919 advocating 'no strike at this time.' The delicate line between staying in and being a strikebreaker we will not discuss, because the outcome of such a situation will place outside the pale, now and forever, anyone who tries it out. A strikebreaker on Tuesday is a strikebreaker for life."[75]

A statement issued by officers of the old Local 1A, including May Matthews, Loretta Baker, and Frances Van Tassel, defended "the founder of the union movement among the operators" against O'Connor's attack:

> Will Miss O'Connor deny that in the first uncertain days of the organization it was Annie Molloy who made the sacrifices, worked incessantly, and was successful in preserving the union and establishing it firmly in the labor movement?
>
> Will Miss O'Connor deny that at the most critical period in the union's existence during the 1919 strike, she was comfortably lodged in a suite in the Parker House, while Miss Molloy did almost continuous picket duty at the exchanges . . . ?

The leadership of the old Local 1A declared that it believed the strike demands to be "absolutely justified" but was opposed to the strike because O'Connor had deprived the local of its right to vote in the referendum.[76] Molloy reiterated her accusation that O'Connor's purpose in ordering the strike was to strengthen her control of the union: "In the history of nations, a leader who sees his following to be dwindling has declared a war, feeling that in the emotionalism of the country's crisis all the people will rally to his standard in the name of patriotism. So, in a smaller way, Miss O'Connor has precipitated this strike, without authority from thousands of operators whom she hopes to stampede by 'waving the flag' into an emotional walkout."[77]

In a dramatic show of support for their leader, members of the old Local 1A poured out of an overflow meeting at Tremont Temple and for hours carried Annie Molloy on their shoulders through the streets of Boston, chanting open defiance of O'Connor: "No strike. We work." and "Hang a crepe on Julia O'Connor's door. She's dead but don't know it."[78] Being carried around on the shoulders of her followers was consistent with Molloy's image as a streetfighter; it is unlikely that the refined O'Connor, protégée of the WTUL allies, would have allowed herself to be placed in this position. Nor would O'Connor's supporters, more involved with the WTUL and workers' education, have used such poor grammar when chanting slogans.

The Boston press, which had been relatively favorable to the Telephone Operators' Union during its confrontations with management in 1913 and 1919, was almost unanimously hostile in 1923. The only exceptions were the Hearst newspapers. The Boston *Evening*

Transcript, influenced by Governor Coolidge's stand in the Boston police strike of 1919, denounced the telephone operators' strike as a "crime against the public" and urged that it be "crushed with vigor and enthusiasm."[79] Only two American cities—New York and Chicago—had more telephones in service than Boston did, and the *Evening Transcript* expressed concern that the strikers' refusal to provide telephone service, regarded by the upper and middle classes as an economic and social necessity, might "terrorize" the public "into surrender."[80] O'Connor and her associates, willing to endanger the health of children in the interest of their "self-styled 'grievances' or so-called 'demands,' " had deliberately scheduled the strike at a time when the public was most vulnerable: "They select the summer season when the spectre of homes harassed by illness will make the timid tremble at the thought of being unable to reach a doctor when a little child is ill. They select the post-commencement season, lest the undergraduates in our colleges . . . volunteer to save the public. . . . "[81]

O'Connor attempted to counter the unfavorable newspaper coverage in an emotional appeal for public support on the day before the strike. She focused on the oppressive working conditions of telephone operators, particularly the harsh discipline and brutal pace of work:

> . . . operators are seated so close together that arms and shoulders touch as they reach for subscribers' signals. Electric fans stir the air sluggishly, making it hotter and with their buzzing and humming . . . add to the nervous strain. . . . Signals must burn no longer than ten seconds or the operator will be credited with an error . . . no matter how great the rush or unbearable the heat, she must repeat the subscriber's number with a rising inflection and must not clip an answering phrase lest she be guilty of another error. . . .
>
> As we see the operators who become hysterical or faint, carried from the board . . . we say to ourselves as we go doggedly on, "Well, it's the lucky ones who faint."[82]

Emphasizing bravery, discipline, and endurance, the leadership of the Telephone Operators' Department urged the rank and file to behave during the strike in a manner resembling the soldier in military combat, a drastic departure from the standards for women in any social class. The woman whom newspapers referred to as "Generalissimo" O'Connor praised the "inspiring record of heroism and devotion to duty which has made the telephone operator the modern Joan of Arc." She expected the strikers to display the same "singleness of purpose" as the telephone operator who during a flood remains at her switchboard to provide service to the community while "the rushing waters of flood rise almost level with her keyboard shelf."[83] The O'Connor forces planned to parade with a brass band to the downtown exchanges at midnight on June 26 and begin the strike by posting pickets to the strains of martial music.[84] The appeal issued by the Boston Telephone Operators' Union to the operators' locals throughout New England to join them in common struggle also equated the strike with military combat: "The Boston telephone operators want the seven-hour day and the higher wage schedules as certainly as you do, and they will be found on the firing line making whatever battle is necessary to secure them."[85]

In 1919, the telephone operators had defied male authority to strike against the wishes of the IBEW leadership and the New England telephone men; a Boston operator had openly challenged IBEW Vice-President Gustave Bugniazet during the strike meeting and brought thousands of young women and girls to their feet by comparing the Telephone Operators' Union with the Yankee division that "licked" the Kaiser. In 1923, the Boston Telephone Operators' Union contemptuously dismissed the male telephone workers who had seceded from the IBEW and refused to strike: "We believe that the telephone men will do exactly as they did in 1919—work a day or two and then come out for shame's sake."[86]

As the strike deadline approached, it remained unclear how widespread the walkout would be. The Boston *Evening Transcript* speculated that, since the telephone operators of northern New England and the "suburban districts" presented an "almost solid front against the strike," O'Connor's forces would concentrate on putting the "nerve centres"—the busiest city exchanges—out of commission. The key to the success of the strike was the Boston Metropolitan District, which contained over 35 percent of New England's telephones—352,582 out of nearly 1,000,000—and one-half of New England's telephone operators—6,100 out of 12,000. Massachusetts as a whole had 9,900 operators, Rhode Island about 1,000, Maine 725, New Hampshire 435, and Vermont 350.[87]

Clare Moriarty, who worked in a Boston exchange, recalled that many feared the strike would not succeed:

> I remember being at the meeting and the vote had been taken and the announcement was made, and what we were to do, we were to be out on strike, as of twelve midnight. And the hall was crowded, but there was an undercurrent that it would not be a successful strike. Even when you went out on the street. You had a few policemen out on the line, they were saying, "You're not going to win!" And then of course you'd meet people from the other group saying, "We're not

going out!" And you'd already pledged yourself to go out. And that didn't exist—that feeling—in 1919.

Another operator who planned to strike accompanied her part of the way home from the union meeting. When Moriarty awakened the next morning, however, she considered going to work: " . . . my father . . . said, 'You know, there's a strike on in the Telephone Operators' Union. . . . Are you a member?' And I said, 'Yes.' And he says, 'Well you're out.' And I said, 'Oh, I don't think so, I don't know. I'm not too sure. I don't think everybody's going out.' And he says, 'Well where's your card?' And I went and got my card, and he says, 'Your dues are paid up to date. You're out!' " Her companion of the night before, also confused, changed her mind entirely: " . . . I remember that the other girl with me . . . she went in to work! So you see the feeling the night before, she was going to stay out . . . she went to work the next day."[88]

Since Irish-American Catholics, many of them devout, formed the overwhelming majority of the membership of the Boston Telephone Operators' Union, the leadership appealed openly to the Virgin Mary to support its cause on the eve of the strike. Until her death in 1972, Julia O'Connor retained in her possession a small placard bearing a picture of the Virgin Mary and infant Jesus, inscribed: "This is to certify that *Boston Telephone Operators' Union* has been placed in the Shrine of Our Lady of Perpetual Help, at the Mission Church, Roxbury, Placed by *Themselves*." It is dated June 24, 1923—two days before the operators walked out on strike.[89]

Although Boston's newspapers proclaimed the strike a failure after the first day, it was clear that O'Connor's forces were prepared to put up a determined fight, particularly in the larger Massachusetts and Rhode Island cities where service was badly crippled. Lawrence, Providence, Springfield, Lynn, Brockton, Worcester, and Salem, where nearly all the operators walked out, were the "storm centers" of the strike. The operators in the northern states, except for a few in Portland and Lewiston, remained at work. The outcome hinged on Boston, where the strike turnout fell considerably short of what O'Connor had expected. Although the majority of operators in the Boston Metropolitan District refused to join the walkout, the strikers succeeded in completely paralyzing service at three of Boston's principal exchanges: Main and Beach—the two in which O'Connor had worked before she became Department president—and Richmond, a "day exchange" in the North End handling the calls of the city's major wholesale-marketing district. Service was also seriously impaired at the Back Bay (Boston's largest in number of subscribers), Mystic (Medford), Newton, and Waltham exchanges. O'Connor believed that if the operators of two more Boston exchanges—Congress and Haymarket—could be induced to leave the boards, the strikers would gain the upper hand.[90]

At exchanges across the city of Boston, strikers clashed with supporters of Molloy, who encouraged operators to cross the picket lines. May Matthews, for example, a militant leader of the 1919 strike, now walked back and forth in front of the Haymarket exchange on Chardon Street urging operators to go to work, while the pickets jeered, calling her "strikebreaker" and "scab."[91] Many pickets fainted in the blazing afternoon heat, and some removed their high-heeled shoes and padded around in silk-stockinged feet. The newspapers reported large numbers of strikers deserting the ranks, but O'Connor, heartened by the militancy of the operators in the large cities outside Boston and strong backing from the central labor unions, declared at the end of the first day, "The fight has only begun."[92]

The strikers behaved aggressively, taunting strikebreakers and in some cases surrounding company taxicabs transporting working operators and beating with their fists on the sides of the cars. Each of the taxicabs carried a police guard. In Springfield, an operator slapped a policeman in the face, and when he moved toward her she snapped, "You touch me you bimbo, and I'll knock you for a goal."[93] In Lawrence, telephone operator pickets trapped two male strikebreakers in an alley and administered "some sort of corporal punishment."[94] Hearst's Boston *Daily Advertiser,* the only newspaper to feature personal interviews with the operators on the picket lines, stressed that nothing could subdue the fighting spirit of Helen Colleary, a "pretty, auburned-haired" striker at the Beach exchange, who declared, "We're just like soldiers, patroling in a just cause . . . not one of us will flinch until we have won."[95]

Many of the strikers displayed the enormous energy and need for fun and excitement associated with the flapper. Picketing was enthusiastic, with the strikers often blocking the sidewalks and forcing working operators to walk in the street to pass them; the union had no difficulty maintaining picket lines twenty-four hours a day. According to the Boston *Evening Transcript,* the younger operators picketing at the Back Bay exchange regarded the strike as a "lark": "It was young girls of the flapper type who did most of the jeering. . . . Many were clad as though they were bound for Nantasket Beach or Revere, sporting parasols and enjoying themselves immensely."[96] At the Richmond exchange in the North End, thirty pickets strolled up and down Richmond Street "as cheerfully . . . as if they were on the Charles River Esplanade . . . making a brilliant color picture against the murky grey of the sky."[97] In Brockton, the strikers "made things lively" for the strikebreakers and "gave back better than they received in the way of smart repartee."[98]

The first violence occurred in Boston on the afternoon of the strike's third day, as club-wielding policemen charged a picket line at the Main exchange, knocking down several strikers; eleven telephone operators were arrested on charges of "inciting to riot." After a noon rally, some two hundred operators began a demonstration on the sidewalk in front of the Main exchange, employing the "continuous system train of pickets" that had recently been adopted in garment strikes. Cheered on by a crowd of two thousand sympathizers, the operators paraded back and forth in groups of two and three, making it difficult at times for pedestrians to pass. The pickets jeered the working operators entering and leaving the exchange, calling them "yellow" and "strikebreaker." When the pickets approached a taxicab into which strikebreakers were climbing, the police charged, trying to surround as many strikers as possible and herding them into a doorway. There were reports, denied by the union, that the pickets had become hysterical at the sight of two black strikebreakers entering the taxicab. Four or five of the strikers were shoved by the police to the sidewalk and trampled upon. Eleven strikers, ranging in age from sixteen to twenty-five, were arrested, and police reserves were called out to subdue the angry crowd. When pickets at the Beach exchange learned of the arrests, "the air became electric with trouble," and police formed a solid line around the taxicabs taking the strikebreakers home. The leaders of the old Local 1A responded to the arrests by accusing O'Connor of "bolshevist tactics." Vice-President Rose Collins angrily exclaimed that "Miss O'Connor must be forgetting that we are still living in free America and not in Russia."[99]

The arrests aroused a storm of indignation among the strikers, who charged they were a "frame-up" designed to intimidate pickets. The union also denounced placing patrolmen in each taxicab, a practice followed in all the cities affected by the strike, as an attempt to discredit the strikers by suggesting that they were dangerous and violent.[100] The eleven arrested operators, who appeared in court "dressed in the latest style," all pleaded not guilty to the charges, which had been reduced to disturbing the peace and obstructing a public highway. Judge Abraham Cohen told Department Vice-President Rose Sullivan, representing the arrested operators, that the use of the terms "yellow" and "strikebreaker" by pickets was not permitted. Although the operators testified that the arrests had been indiscriminate and the police unnecessarily violent, the judge found them guilty of both charges and fined each ten dollars.[101]

The Boston policemen were openly hostile to the telephone operators throughout the strike, in sharp contrast to their counterparts in the other Massachusetts and Rhode Island cities. This represented a complete reversal of the attitude shown by the Boston police force in 1919, when patrolmen had been exceedingly friendly with strikers. The change was due to the city's having recruited an entirely new police force; the policemen who had displayed so much sympathy for the telephone operators in 1919 were all discharged after they walked out on strike later that year. Their replacements were men willing to take the positions of strikers and therefore probably not favorably disposed toward trade unionism. Hasty recruiting by the city brought onto the force a large number of men unsuited to police work and less capable than their predecessors of exercising restraint in tense situations.[102] The new force was probably not as overwhelmingly Irish-American as that of 1919, which would also account for the deterioration of relations between the police and telephone operators.

Only hours after the arrest of the Boston operators, an angry crowd of strike sympathizers in Worcester clashed with wealthy supporters of the company in the first of a series of riots outside the Hub. The riot was precipitated when Frederick B. Washburn, president of Worcester's National Bank and a director of the Chamber of Commerce, arrived at the exchange, accompanied by a son, to escort home another son and two other young men who had been working as strikebreakers. The situation at the exchange had been tense since the beginning of the strike, as large crowds had formed to jeer the working operators during the evening shift changes. As the bank president and the four wealthy young men left the exchange, they were followed by an increasingly menacing group of male strike sympathizers. The physical assault occurred in the shadow of Worcester's city hall. According to Washburn, who suffered injuries to his arm, shoulder, nose, and leg, "We had just passed the *Telegram-News* building when one of the crowd said, 'Here's where we'll get them. Jump on them now,' and the crowd came for the boys, slugging right and left. . . . someone from behind struck me an ugly blow and tripped me at the same time. In falling my left shoulder hit the mud guard of an auto. . . . My oldest son lost his hat and umbrella and has a bad blow on his jaw." The victims of the assault finally managed to take refuge in the Bancroft Hotel, where they were provided with a telephone company car for the ride home. The police made no arrests.[103]

Announcing on June 30 that it would reemploy only those strikers who "deserted their post of duty by reason of bad advice," the New England Telephone Company with the cooperation of its parent corporation, AT&T, mounted the greatest intensive training course for new operators in its history.[104] Associated Bell companies throughout the country sent instructors to the New England cities affected by the strike. Raymond Kenney, division superintendent of the Southwestern Bell Company in Dallas, Texas, had charge of training new operators in Lawrence, where 127 of the 130 operators were on strike.[105] By June 30, fourteen instructors from Philadelphia and Albany and traffic engineers and managers from Tennessee and Alabama were at work in the Springfield exchange, and on July 6 the company announced that additional instructors had arrived from Akron, Cleveland, and Columbus in Ohio and Bridgeport, Westbury, and New Haven in Connecticut.[106] In Providence, the company fired the principal of the operators' training school, two chief operators, and two matrons because "they did not appear to be helpful at this time in the effort to restore service," and it imported replacements from outside New England. The new Providence chief operators came from Atlanta (Southern Bell) and Minneapolis (Northwestern Bell).[107]

In Boston, where the company had no trouble recruiting young women to replace the strikers, the principal of the Boston School for Operators, Mary Harrington, implemented a special two-day course for new operators, who were then placed at the rate of a hundred a day on the boards.[108] Since new operators ordinarily studied at the school for three to four weeks, followed by seven weeks of training at the board as a student operator, the service was very poor during the strike and for some time thereafter in exchanges employing large numbers of recruits. The company was willing to subordinate efficient service to the more important goal of destroying the union, and it spent about $1,500,000 for taxi service, protection, housing, and food for the strikebreakers, a newspaper advertising campaign denouncing the strike, and instruction for new operators involving the transfer of high-salaried engineers and technical personnel from outside New England.[109] A plan to pay a $6 weekly bonus to "loyal operators" was cancelled at the request of an embarrassed Annie Molloy.[110]

The massive financial resources of the AT&T and the consistently unfavorable newspaper coverage placed the strikers at a decided disadvantage. The Telephone Operators' Department made an effort to expand the strike by dispatching organizers to the northern states, and it appealed to the labor movement for financial assistance to match what Julia O'Connor called the company's "slush fund of

$2,000,000 to fight us in this strike."[111] The eight operators who went on strike in Lewiston, Maine, where seventy-two remained at work, were joined for a time by Nellie May Smith, vice-president of the New England Council of Telephone Operators' Unions, and Ruth Washburn, both leaders of Brockton's Local 27A. Smith also spent several days in Portland supervising strike activities.[112] On the third day of the strike, twenty-five strikers from Lynn went to Boston and two to Portland, Maine, to help picket.[113]

Boston's trade unionists gave the operators strong verbal support and donated a considerable amount of money to their strike fund. Delegates at the first meeting of the Boston Central Labor Union held during the strike wildly cheered Julia O'Connor, who declared that the company, assisted by "a subsidized press, bought police, and sold-out leaders," was attempting "to tear down the last vestige of trade unionism in its field." Aaron Velleman, a leader of the Cigar Workers' Union, announced the next day that two thousand members of his union had voted to "use their financial resources to the limit" in supporting the striking operators.[114] In Lynn, members of the Amalgamated Stitchers' Union, the largest women's labor organization in the shoe industry, joined the telephone operators in a strike parade.[115] A strike rally on Boston Common on July 1, attended by five thousand people, was addressed by E. A. Johnson, president of the Boston CLU, who denounced Molloy's followers as "strikebreakers," and John Kearney of the Waiters' Union, which donated $1,000 to the telephone operators' strike fund.[116]

Labor, however, would not go so far as to consider sympathetic strikes, although the calling of a citywide general strike was seriously weighed by the Springfield CLU during the third week of the walkout. Boston's union taxi drivers, for example, in early July voted down a proposal for a sympathetic strike and continued to transport strikebreakers to and from the exchanges. They feared possible discharge by their employers, but they were also unwilling to suffer a loss of income during the busy summer season.[117]

Perceiving that the New England telephone operators' strike represented a critical test in labor's struggle against the open shop, Samuel Gompers recalled the AFL's legislative agent, Edward Mc-Grady, from the Pittsburgh steel strike and sent him to Boston to assist O'Connor. McGrady, a former president of the Boston CLU, addressed the operators' mass meeting on July 4, announcing that Gompers pledged the AFL's full support in helping win the strike. He bitterly denounced Molloy and her followers: "It is not the intention of the Federation to allow one of the best organizations in the labor movement to be killed by traitors and treachery." Molloy, who had a few days before cancelled a conference with O'Connor after the latter had declared to the Boston CLU that the operators would "shake the blight of Molloyism off their backs," refused to meet with McGrady to discuss old Local 1A's joining the strike.[118]

During the first two weeks of July, O'Connor spoke at mass strike rallies in Boston, Brockton, Salem, Lawrence, Springfield, Lynn, and Providence. Addressing highly enthusiastic crowds composed largely of workers and their families, she stressed that the telephone operators' strike represented a "war to the death of unionism" and warned that "should the phone operators be beaten, you can count yourselves as the next victims in a labor war."[119] O'Connor compared the labor policy of the Bell System with that of the notoriously open-shop steel industry, but she predicted the operators would not only win the strike but carry the telephone men back into the AFL. She asserted that hiring five hundred new operators in New England would make the seven-hour day possible, but that the company preferred to spend its money "buying mayors and subsidizing newspapers." O'Connor was joined on the speakers' stand in Brockton by Edward McGrady and in Lawrence by Aaron Velleman.[120]

Strike leaders expressed enormous contempt for the male telephone workers, many of whom crossed the operators' picket lines to assist the company at the switchboards. Mary Sands of Local 2A, just returned from the Bryn Mawr Summer School for Women Workers in Industry, ridiculed the telephone men at a strike rally in Lynn:

> They are so yellow that they are not entitled to be known as men. . . .
>   We girls have always carried them on our backs. Every time we start a movement for increased wages or better conditions, they refuse to cooperate with us, but every time we secure more favorable conditions, they benefit. . . .
>   They don't know anything anyway. If they operate a switchboard as fast as they are able to repair trouble with a board, the board will fall over from mildew before they are able to handle calls.[121]

While showing, in the words of their leader, the "determination" of "soldiers in the front line trenches," the strikers much of the time also engaged in boisterous, highly spirited behavior characteristic of young flappers. Two hundred "madly cheering, gaily bedecked" Boston operators, arriving in Brockton with Julia O'Connor in a caravan of trucks and automobiles, turned a mass strike rally into a spectacular demonstration. According to the Brockton *Times*, the Bostonians displayed incredible "pep and spirit," regaling the crowd with songs and cheers all through the rally. They left singing into megaphones, "Hail, hail, the gang's all here. So what the ——— do we care."[122] Strike pickets in Lynn "livened things up" in front of their exchange by singing their "campaign songs." The Lynn strikers also devoted their energies to "decorating" the houses of working operators with "decayed fruit and ancient eggs." Seeking entertainment at a local dance hall, they happened upon four young women who had crossed their picket lines and heckled them mercilessly. Their shouts of "Did you come over in the company's taxis?" were taken up by others on all sides of the hall, causing the strikebreakers' escorts to desert them. The Lynn operators also put on a dance of their own to raise strike funds; it was attended by two thousand people. A strike benefit dance was also held by the Providence operators.[123] In the operators' strike headquarters in Lawrence, a phonograph constantly blaring "up-to-date" tunes like "Yes, We Have No Bananas," the "latest fox trot craze," added to the excitement. At a mass strike meeting in Boston, twenty-three operators from the Mystic exchange in Medford took the platform to entertain their fellow strikers with a song they had written to the tune of "Barney Google," ridiculing the operators of neighboring Malden, who had refused to heed the strike call:

> Raspberries to the Malden exchange, . . .
> They've sold themselves for $6 a week
> Now they're looking just like freaks,
> Raspberries to the Malden exchange.[124]

As in 1919, the telephone operators were incensed at the widespread participation as strikebreakers by what they termed "society queens" (upper-class women) and "rah rah sissies" (college students), reflecting the sharp class divisions in the cities affected by the strike. The company also hired high school students, who were available in large numbers because of summer vacation. The secretary of Providence's Local 65A announced on the second day of the strike that "boys in knee breeches from Technical, English, and Classical high schools" were at work in the exchanges.[125] According to the Worcester *Evening Gazette*, "Are you a telephone operator? is the popular question heard among young women on country club piazzas and at bridge parties." Among the strikebreakers from Worcester's fashionable West Side working in the telephone exchange were young women attending or planning to attend in the fall the Boston Conservatory of Music, Mount Holyoke College, Simmons College, and Wheaton College. The young West Siders were all quick to express their contempt for the telephone operators and their work. "The strikers haven't a chance," stated a student from the Boston Conservatory, adding, "I find the work not hard."[126] The *Labor News*, the statewide labor newspaper published in Worcester, expressed the enormous resentment of many working people toward the "idle rich" in bitter denunciations of the "society queens" at the switchboards:

> Such a jolly lark, you know; gives one a delicious thrill, don't you see, to dare this very venturesome thing. And besides, all the girls who don't need to work for a living feel the same way about it; to become a strikebreaker. Gives one a real tang, a regular jazz feeling to get mixed up in this strike. O dear me yes and all that. It's summertime, don't you see, and we girls simply must have something out of the ordinary. This strike is just heavenly if you know what we mean.
>
> That's the way the society debs spill language when they gush about their saffron hued enterprise.[127]

At the Newton exchange outside Boston, the strikebreakers included Catherine Jones, daughter of Matt B. Jones, president of the New England Telephone Company, and Theda Luddy, a graduate of Cornell; Mrs. Matt B. Jones worked at the exchange preparing dinners for the strikebreakers.[128]

The New England Telephone Company, which had previously refused to hire Jewish women as telephone operators, was now willing to employ them as strikebreakers. In Worcester, for example, fourteen or fifteen Jewish women worked at the telephone exchange during the strike; according to an official of the Telephone Operators' Union, they were for the most part "college girls who, like the West Side society queens, are seeking adventure or extra vacation money."[129] In Springfield, delegates from six Jewish labor organizations formed the "Allied Jewish Conference on the Telephone Strike," with the object of helping the striking telephone operators in every way possible. The participating organizations—boasting a total membership of seven hundred, a majority of the city's Jewish workers—were the Workmen's Circle (two branches), the Jewish Socialist party, the Workers' party, the Jewish National Workers' Alliance, and the Independent Workmen's Circle. A spokesperson for the Allied Jewish Conference announced, "The organizations represented keenly resent the fact that Jewish girls are now acceptable as strikebreakers who before the strike the Company would not hire. An effort will be made to have these girls quit their employment. . . ."[130]

Bitter class resentment was also directed at the male college students who worked as strikebreakers; their masculinity was continually questioned by the striking operators and trade unionists. The

Labor News implied a similarity between the "Rah Rah sissies, back home for the summer" and the World War I "slacker": "In 1913 the slogan used to be this: 'I didn't raise my boy to be a soldier.' In 1923, in some select West Side families, the slogan seems to be this: 'I raised Percy to be a strikebreaker.' " Referring to the incident of June 28 in which male sympathizers of the Worcester telephone operators attacked a bank president and college students working as strikebreakers, the *Labor News* commented, "The rah rah college yap who lost his eyeglasses in his scramble for safety told his pals next day that anyway he didn't lose his self-respect. That's true; the swiftly scooting Willie didn't have any to lose."[131] College students were frequently referred to by the telephone operators in terms suggesting homosexuality, commonly associated in the working class during this period with lack of "manliness" and servility. Boston operator pickets called out to two college boys leaving the Beach exchange: "Oh there go Louise and Eloise. Oh you cute things come over here honey. One of us girls will lend you our powder puffs. I left my sweater upstairs; you can wear it dear."[132] In Brockton, the operators dubbed the male strikebreakers "powder puff boys" and subjected them to applications of powder when they left the exchange.[133]

The attitude of the city government and police force was of considerable importance in determining the strike's effectiveness in particular localities. In Lawrence, one of the strongest union towns in the country with a municipal administration favorably disposed to organized labor, the operators boasted that they could "get away with almost anything"; the four hundred operators in Springfield, continually harassed by a city government which imported state military police reserves to guard the telephone exchange, faced a much more difficult battle.[134] The company abandoned its attempt to provide evening telephone service in Lawrence because it believed that the police deliberately refused to protect working operators from harassment by pickets and strike sympathizers. On July 18, following a "turbulent" evening during which a crowd of several hundred "made things miserable" for strikebreakers leaving the exchange, the company's manager in Lawrence announced, "The disgraceful demonstration of last evening in front of our building, when police refused to disperse a howling mob, making it extremely hazardous to conduct our employees from the building in safety, clearly indicates that the police have no intention of furnishing the protection we are entitled to. . . . We do not intend to jeopardize the safety of our girls in the future, and we decline to furnish more than a restricted evening service from this time on."[135] The police also interfered with the transport of strikebreakers by stopping company taxicabs and arresting drivers for minor license and registration violations. In Lawrence, even the Chamber of Commerce backed the strikers; members refused to sign a petition condemning the strike and demanded a state investigation because the company failed to provide adequate telephone service.[136]

The Springfield city government, angered because the striking operators led by Department Treasurer Mary Quinn Wynne had completely disrupted the telephone service, intervened in the strike to severely restrict picketing, and the operators and their sympathizers were subjected to numerous arrests and beatings by the military police reserves. The Boston *Herald* noted on the first day of the strike that "the Springfield police seemed to resent the presence of . . . the military police reserve . . . [and] the regular bluecoats were noticeably sympathetic with the strikers, and talked amiably with them."[137]

A series of riots in which over fifty operators and strike sympathizers were injured by military police began on the night of July 3–4. From the beginning of the strike the operators had derided the military police as "lollypops," and on July 3 two hundred operators sucking lollypops paraded in front of the telephone exchange. The operators removed the lollypops from their mouths only long enough to impress upon the military police that the candy had been purchased for the purpose of ridiculing them. "Ain't he sweet" and "Pull in your ears, you look like a loving cup" were two of the taunts the operators directed at the military police, who later that night charged the crowd of strike sympathizers in front of the exchange "swinging nightsticks right and left."[138] The next night they charged the crowd again; according to the Springfield *Republican,* "so effectively did the police reserves use their nightsticks that fifty casualties are said to have resulted." The *Republican,* which strongly opposed the strike, claimed that the police reserves had been provoked by a fusillade of bricks, bottles, and giant firecrackers thrown at them by the sympathizers. Four members of the crowd were arrested, including James Gordon, brother of Mary Gordon, president of the Springfield Telephone Operators' Union (Local 3A).[139]

The city government, headed by Republican mayor Edwin F. Leonard, who had defeated the pro-labor candidate George Wrenn in the 1922 election, openly sided with the company in the strike. Mayor Leonard first imported the military police reserves and then on July 6 roped off the street in front of the telephone exchange, forcing union pickets out of the area used by the taxicabs transporting strikebreakers. Not a single member of the city council was willing to sponsor the Central Labor Union's petition for a public hearing on the removal of the military police reserves.[140] The roping off of the exchange, ordered by the chair of the Police Commission, "totally destroyed the effectiveness of the strike pickets," according to the Springfield *Republican*. No vehicular traffic was permitted on the street in the area of the exchange except company taxicabs transporting strikebreakers, and the pickets, forced to the far sidewalk, were warned that shouting or laughing "inordinately" at the "loyal" operators would result in immediate arrest. Previously, it had been necessary for the police to make a lane for the strikebreakers through "howling, hissing" pickets.[141]

Refusing to allow any criticism of public or company officials, the city government also censored banners for the Springfield operators' strike parade held on July 7. The parade nevertheless represented a dramatic display of union solidarity, as thousands massed along the line of march. Even though the city had elected an anti-labor mayor and city council, it was clear that the strikers' cause was supported by a sizeable segment of Springfield's population. At the head of the procession was Local 3A's leader, business agent Mary Quinn Wynne, who was also Department treasurer. She was followed by the local's officers and operators carrying the American flag and then the rank and file four abreast. The strikers stepped to a "stirring march" played by a band from the Musicians' Union. Huge bursts of applause occurred when the band struck up "Hail, Hail, the Gang's All Here" as the strikers passed the telephone exchange, and again as they marched by the CLU hall. The operators carried banners marked "Boys, Don't Forget the Union Telephone Operators Followed You to France," "The Service is Good—Good and Rotten," "Officials and Clerks Work 42 Hours a Week—Why Not Telephone Operators," and "With Wynne We'll Win," and they sang the "war song" of the 1923 strike to the tune of "Yes, We Have No Bananas":

> Yes we have no phone numbers
> We have no phone numbers today;
> We've got pickets and leaders and Julia O'Connor,
> So what can one want today?
> We have these old-fashioned tin soldiers
> And lots of wrong numbers
> But yes we have no phone numbers
> So try and get phone service today.[142]

As the Central Labor Union discussed calling a citywide general strike to protest the roping off of the telephone exchange and ordered three drug stores owned by Mayor Leonard picketed because of his "unfair" attitude toward organized labor, tensions between strike sympathizers and the military police reserves erupted in another major riot. Stirred by Julia O'Connor's speech at a strike rally at Court Square, 350 operators proceeded to the telephone exchange and began mass picketing, cheered on by a crowd of 5,000 sympathizers. Angered by the taunts of "lollypops" and "wooden soldiers" hurled at them by the crowd, the police reserves charged, swinging their nightsticks.

According to the Springfield *Republican,* "Guns glistened in the dim light. A girl picket was pulled under the ropes by police away from friends who were holding her despite the efforts of fifteen officers and finally pushed into the police patrol." As Robert Childs, the captain of the military police reserves, arrested the picket, eighteen-year-old Lillian O'Brien, he struck her over the head with his nightstick: "Cries of 'Captain Childs slugged a girl,' spread like wildfire. Men rushed to the ropes in the street, shouting, 'Show us the guy who hit the girl.' Captain Childs escaped assault only by the presence of other officers. Aged women, many of them mothers of strikers who had come to protect their girls, were jostled and pushed. . . . Julia O'Connor and Mary Wynne were sped away by friends despite their determination to 'stay and see it through.' "[143] O'Brien filed a charge of assault against Captain Childs, who was found guilty in district court on August 6. No penalty was imposed by the judge.[144]

Having been advised by legal counsel that roping off the exchange could not be sustained in court, telephone operator pickets jumped the ropes and began picketing in the prohibited area on July 13. Regular policemen, who had replaced the military police reserves withdrawn only two hours before, made no attempt to stop the pickets. The reserves' violent conduct had seriously embarrassed the city government, and public opinion had forced their removal. The CLU officer who had led the first four pickets over the ropes immediately returned to the CLU hall to report that the roping order had been successfully violated.[145]

Although union solidarity was maintained in the larger cities outside Boston, the company's success in recruiting strikebreakers and the refusal of Molloy's forces, constituting a large majority in the crucial Boston Metropolitan District, to join the walkout resulted in the gradual weakening of the strikers' morale. The strong support for O'Connor among operators outside Boston was due in large part to her standing as president of the national Telephone Operators' Department, a position which allowed her to develop strong ties with the leaders of the more active New England locals during the previous four and a half years, and the prestige she commanded as leader of the 1919 strike. Molloy, who had held only local and not Departmental office, had not established close contacts with locals outside Boston prior to the strike. Many of the rank and file remembered O'Connor's leadership in 1919, but because of the high turnover among telephone operators, relatively few could recall Molloy's during the near-strike of 1913. The Boston newspapers, except for the Hearst entries, had pronounced the strike a failure from the beginning, and each day they reported new desertions from the strikers' ranks.

On June 27, the second day of the strike, two labor mediators from the Federal Mediation and Conciliation Service—Anna Weinstock and John Colpoys—arrived in Boston to confer with O'Connor and company officials.[146] Both mediators had considerable familiarity with labor relations in the telephone industry, Weinstock having served as a vice-president of the Boston Women's Trade Union League during the 1919 New England strike and Colpoys as a member of the Ryan Commission during the period of government operation. According to Anna Weinstock, the company was in too strong a position to show interest in mediation:

> It was apparent from the beginning there wasn't much we could do as mediators. Even though the majority of workers were out on strike there was very little in the way of bargaining that took place because it was apparent that the Company felt it could break the strike. . . . I was part of the Boston situation, knew the people in the Women's Trade Union League very well and knew the telephone operators very well, through close association other than as a mediator and I was aware of what was going on behind the scenes. . . . I was in touch with Julia very often back here in Boston and I was in and out of Washington. But to me that was not too important. Unless we had the employer there in Washington it wasn't going to mean much and we didn't have the employer there.[147]

The demoralization of telephone service in the larger Massachusetts and Rhode Island cities and the company's refusal to cooperate with the federal mediators prompted the mayors of several of the affected cities to intervene in the strike in an attempt to bring about a settlement. Seven mayors met in Providence in mid-July and held two conferences, the first with the nine-woman wage-scale committee of the Telephone Operators' Union and the second with Matt B. Jones, president of the New England Telephone Company, and his legal adviser. The company refused to negotiate directly with the strikers. Mayor James Michael Curley of Boston refused to join the mayors' conference, claiming that the telephone strike was a "New

England" problem and therefore the responsibility of the governors.[148] Curley apparently also feared that a settlement negotiated in Providence would enhance the reputation of the mayor who had organized the conference, Peter F. Sullivan of Worcester, Curley's rival for the governorship.[149]

The union leadership, confronted with daily desertions from the strikers' ranks and the massive hiring of new operators, was by mid-July primarily concerned with preserving its organization. Virtually admitting defeat, the operators' wage-scale committee informed the mayors that the union would drop its demands and end the strike if the company agreed to take the strikers back in a body, with no loss of seniority and benefits, and recognize the union's right to file a claim for arbitration of the demands at a future date. The enthusiastic mayors then presented the union's proposal to President Jones, but they could not persuade him to accept it. The Boston *Post* reported that "bitter disappointment was written on the faces of the seven mayors" as they announced that they "regretted that the Telephone Company did not accept our proposal." According to the *Post,* "While the conference with the company officials was held behind closed doors, it was evident that debate had been long and heated. The mayors seemed careworn when they emerged from the room, where they met a delegation of strikers, headed by O'Connor. . . . Then the girls filed out, their serious faces seeming to indicate the gravity of the situation."[150]

Near defeat and facing the prospect that the strikers would be permanently displaced from the telephone service, the strike leadership reintroduced mass picketing and appealed to the labor movement to back the operators in a "fight to the finish." O'Connor angrily declaimed at the Boston CLU meeting on July 15, "In 1919, when we could have won our fight sitting at home, it was virtually impossible for us to get to our offices, owing to the crowds of labor lights and politicians who wished to offer their services by making speeches and in other ways helping us. Today when these same people believe we have a fight on our hands, not one of them comes near us." Aroused by the company's action at the mayors' conference, trade unions across Massachusetts and Rhode Island responded to O'Connor's call to "furnish a war chest for this fight."[151] In Springfield, for example, the streetcarmen's and carpenters' unions, both of which had already made large donations to the strikers, pledged $900 and $950 a week respectively as long as the strike lasted. The Springfield *Republican* announced that "practically all the other unions are doing proportionately as much." This allowed the union for the first time to pay strike benefits, which were, however, "only a fraction" of the wages ordinarily received.[152] In other cities operators organized tag-day sales to raise funds for the union. In Lynn, 10,000 people purchased tags, providing $1,500 for Local 2A.[153]

On July 19, less than a week after the mayors' conference, O'Connor was forced to concede defeat, although pressure from the Worcester, Providence, Springfield, and Brockton locals led to a prolongation of the strike until July 26. The company announced that it "has stated its determination to carry out the promise which it has made to its new operators that they shall have permanent positions . . . and . . . cannot take back into its employ all the striking operators." Strikers wishing to return to work were required to file individual applications for reemployment. Those who were accepted lost all seniority rights concerning choice of work shifts and vacations—they were considered "junior" to those who replaced them—as well as the right to participate in the company's benefit plan for one year. No supervisors or strike leaders were reemployed.[154]

The Aftermath of the 1923 Strike

Having locked out the strikers, the company proceeded to install company-controlled employees' committees for the telephone operators, over the strenuous objections of the old Local 1A. By assisting the company in breaking the strike and eliminating its rival, the old Local 1A had ironically contributed to its own demise. Fewer than 40 percent of the strikers were reemployed in New England as a whole, and not more than 30 percent in the Boston Metropolitan District.[155] Clare Moriarty, who worked for a year as a PBX operator at several Boston hotels after the strike, described the manner in which she was rehired by the company:

> Well it just happened to be one of those things that some official and manager happened to be at a social function and he had a girl [an operator] that had retired . . . and he said, "Do you know of any girls that would be interested in coming back to work?" Not mentioning strikers, and she did say, "What about some of your strikers?" Well then he was embarrassed and he said, "We've taken all we can get," and she said, "Well I have a couple of names," and she submitted my name and they did call me and interviewed me, but in the interview they were—well I don't say they were insulting, but sort of saying, "Well you look so intelligent" and blah, blah, blah you know about going on strike. . . .
> Of course they did take my rating away—for hours and vacations.

I think I had about six years of service, so I had to start in just as cold. . . . That was the bitter pill, you know. To start from the bottom. . . . It was very humiliating.[156]

The dismissal of the strikers, including the entire supervisory force, and their replacement by new and inexperienced operators caused a serious deterioration of telephone service for several months after the strike. As a result of numerous complaints from individual subscribers and business houses and the passing of orders by the city councils of Lawrence and Lynn demanding a state investigation of the telephone service, the Massachusetts State Department of Public Utilities conducted a survey of the condition of service after the strike. William O'Brien, chief of the Department's telephone division, supervised the survey and stated in his final report, dated January, 1924, "For a while [after the strike] things seemed to pick up a bit, but after Labor Day the general service began to show poorly and by October it was bad . . . we found a consistent high percentage of operating errors, and the same story was heard on all sides, upon the street, the subway, the hotels, the restaurants, clubs, places of business and residence, that service was very poor."[157] Retaining prominent traffic supervisory officials imported during the strike from associated Bell companies across the country, the New England Telephone Company conducted an "intensive drive" to train new operators and restore service to normal conditions. O'Brien reported a "noticeable improvement" in telephone service by January, 1924, but Julia O'Connor, writing in 1926, claimed that service remained "positively inferior" to that provided before the strike.[158]

The old Local 1A was unable to maintain its credibility as a trade union as a result of its conduct during the 1923 strike. Annie Molloy appeared with five of her lieutenants at the convention of the Massachusetts State Federation of Labor at Worcester in August, 1923, presented credentials as delegates from Local 1A, and requested seats. Julia O'Connor, however, immediately objected on the grounds that the local was not affiliated with the AFL. After voting unanimously not to accept the credentials, the convention informed members of the old Local 1A that they were not welcome either as guests or as spectators and instructed them to leave the hall. When they refused to obey, officers of the federation summoned the police and had them ejected.[159] In a gesture of solidarity at the AFL's national convention at Portland, Oregon, in October, 1923, Samuel Gompers called on Julia O'Connor to preside when nominations for president were made.[160] Expressing the disenchantment with Gompers' conservatism shared by Telephone Operators' Department leaders, Mabel Leslie commented to O'Connor that this act was "one of the few nice things I have heard about him."[161]

After the strike, Annie Molloy drew increasingly close to the company. She received several promotions, serving as traffic inspector, assistant to the metropolitan division employment manager, and supervisor of emergency call results. When she died in 1928, the New England Telephone Company's magazine for employees praised her as "a natural born leader and sincere worker." Officials of the company attended her funeral, and Vice-President E. K. Hall of AT&T sent a floral tribute.[162]

Many in O'Connor's faction continued to be active in the trade union and workers' education movements, and several—including Rose Sullivan and O'Connor herself—devoted their lives to them. This was not the case with Molloy's supporters, several of whom remained in the company's employ until they reached retirement age.[163] By 1928, Frances Van Tassel, having been promoted after the strike to chief operator and then to metropolitan division health supervisor, was openly praising the telephone company in its magazine for employees: "The Bell System . . . provides the work for us to do under good working conditions."[164] Among Molloy's followers, only Loretta Baker—who married Michael Flaherty, a socialist and leader of the Painters' Union, and was active in the defense of Sacco and Vanzetti in the years immediately following the strike—appears to have maintained a strong commitment to the labor movement.

The defeat of the 1923 New England telephone strike almost completely eliminated the American Federation of Labor from the telephone service. Abandoned by the male telephone workers and hampered by a sharply divided leadership and a considerably weakened labor movement, the operators were overwhelmed by the highly coordinated Bell System which commanded enormous financial resources. The factional conflict within the Boston operators' local that contributed to the defeat of the strike stemmed partly from the paucity of leadership positions open to women in the labor movement, intensifying the jealousy and competition among the union's officers. It was the declining position of the union, however, which caused the factionalism to become so intense. It is not likely the Telephone Operators' Union could have survived for long in the anti-labor climate of the 1920s, especially without the support of the male telephone workers, whose skills were highly important to the company and who were far less easily replaceable than the operators.

Julia O'Connor appears to have made serious errors in judgement in expelling May Matthews from the union and revoking the charter of Local 1A, and her opponents may have been correct in charging that she was unnecessarily authoritarian. There is no question, however, that the behavior of the leaders of the old Local 1A was far more destructive. They abandoned the union in a critical situation; they not only refused to join the strike but openly encouraged strikebreaking, ensuring the union's defeat. The company had clearly signaled a major change in its labor policy by refusing to bargain collectively after 1920 and had indicated its intention to introduce company unions. O'Connor thus had little choice but to order a strike if she expected the union to retain any power, much less achieve the demands it had been advancing. It is also to her credit that she grasped the threat of the dial and devised a response—the shortened workday—which she hoped would minimize its impact on the operators. Even had the union preserved its organization, however, dial conversion would have greatly reduced its influence by undermining the operators' ability to interfere with telephone service in a strike.

NOTES

1. *Proceedings of the First Regular Convention of the Telephone Operators' Department, IBEW*, New Orleans, La., 1919, pp. 8, 62, Julia O'Connor Parker Papers, Schlesinger Library, Radcliffe College, Cambridge, Mass.

2. "President's Report to the Second Biennial Convention of the Telephone Operators' Department of the International Brotherhood of Electrical Workers," St. Louis, Mo., October 31, 1921, p. 19, Julia O'Connor Parker Papers.

3. *Proceedings of First Regular Convention*, p. 6.

4. David Kennedy, *Over Here* (New York: Oxford University Press, 1980), pp. 250–51, 259; Daniel Nelson, *Managers and Workers* (Madison: University of Wisconsin Press, 1975), p. 160; Melvyn Dubofsky, "Abortive Reform: The Wilson Administration and Organized Labor, 1913–1920," in James Cronin and Carmen Sirianni, eds., *Work, Community, and Power* (Philadelphia: Temple University Press, 1983), p. 214.

5. Irving Bernstein, *The Lean Years* (Baltimore: Penguin Books, 1960), p. 84; David Montgomery, "New Tendencies in Union Struggles and Strategies in Europe and the United States, 1916–1922," in Cronin and Sirianni, eds., *Work, Community, and Power*, p. 97.

6. John Hicks, *Republican Ascendancy* (New York: Harper and Row, 1960), pp. 69–72; Bernstein, *Lean Years*, pp. 211–12; Kennedy, *Over Here*, p. 258.

7. Montgomery, "New Tendencies," p. 97; Nelson, *Managers and Workers*, p. 160.

8. David Brody, *Labor in Crisis* (Philadelphia and New York: J. B. Lippincott, 1965), p. 176.

9. Bernstein, *Lean Years,* pp. 84–85.

10. U.S. Department of Labor, Bureau of Labor Statistics, *Characteristics of Company Unions, 1935,* Bulletin No. 634, June, 1937 (Washington, D.C.: Government Printing Office, 1938), pp. 7, 9.

11. Kennedy, *Over Here,* p. 268; U.S. Department of Labor, *Characteristics,* pp. 2, 12, 20.

12. Bernstein, *Lean Years,* p. 168.

13. John Schacht, *The Making of Telephone Unionism, 1920–1947* (New Brunswick, N.J.: Rutgers University Press, 1985), pp. 40–41.

14. *The State* (Columbia, S.C.), July 29, 1919.

15. Cleveland *Plain-Dealer,* July 13, 1919; St. Louis *Post-Dispatch,* July 30, 1919.

16. H. B. Thayer to Herbert J. Wells, June 2, 1922, Box 1, AT&T Archives, New York, N.Y.

17. "President's Report to Second Biennial Convention," pp. 3–5.

18. Ibid., p. 5.

19. Ibid., p. 15.

20. Rose Hickey Quinn, "Out of the Fog," *Union Telephone Operator* [hereafter, *UTO*], June, 1921, pp. 2–3.

21. Julia O'Connor, "History of the Organized Telephone Operators' Movement," Part 6, *UTO,* July, 1921, p. 18; *Journal of Electrical Workers and Operators* [hereafter, *JEWO*], April, 1920, p. 518, and May, 1920, pp. 600, 613; Noonan quoted in Jack Barbash, *Unions and Telephones* (New York: Harper and Brothers, 1952), p. 11.

22. Los Angeles *Times,* February 14 and 26, 1920.

23. Telephone Operators' Department, IBEW, "A Review of the New England Secession Movement," n.d., pp. 2–4, Julia O'Connor Parker Papers; *JEWO,* July, 1920, pp. 727–29.

24. Telephone Operators' Department, IBEW, "A Review," p. 6.

25. Kathleen Moriarty [pseudonym], interview by Stephen H. Norwood, Boston, Mass., June 12, 1974.

26. Mary Quinn Wynne, interview by Stephen H. Norwood, Springfield, Mass., June 28, 1974.

27. Boston *Globe,* September 12, 1919; *Boston Labor World,* January 31, 1920.

28. "The Revival of the Bulletin Board," *UTO,* January, 1921, p. 17; *New York Times,* December 12, 1920; *Labor News,* February 11, 1921; Boston *Herald,* February 3, 1921.

29. Eye-Witness [pseudonym], "Dials Scrap Labor and Increase Costs," *JEWO,* February, 1933, p. 91.

30. "Bell System Automatic Installations," n.d., Box 1116, AT&T Archives.

31. Marion Dilts, *The Telephone in a Changing World* (New York: Longmans, Green, 1941), pp. 54–55.

32. *Christian Science Monitor,* January 16, 1913.

33. H. B. Thayer to C. F. Cise, May 14, 1912, Box 47, AT&T Archives.

34. Plugan Ansa [pseudonym], "The Automatics'll Get You if You Don't Watch Out," *UTO,* January, 1921, p. 16.

35. *Virginian-Pilot and the Norfolk Landmark,* November 9, 1919.

36. "Flying Squadron," *Southern Telephone News,* September, 1925, p. 8.

37. "Bell System Automatic Installations," n.d., Box 1116, AT&T Archives; Boston *Herald,* July 25, 1923; Rose Hickey Quinn, "Dialling," *UTO,* February, 1921, p. 3.

38. "Statement of Rose S. Sullivan before the Temporary Economic Committee's Hearing on Technology," April 17, 1940, p. 9, Box 3, National Women's Trade Union League Papers, Schlesinger Library.

39. Quinn, "Dialling," *UTO,* p. 3.

40. "Statement of Miss [Julia] O'Connor of the Labor Advisory Board at National Recovery Administration Hearings on National Telephone Code, 1934," p. 3, Julia O'Connor Parker Papers.

41. Boston *Globe,* June 30, 1918.

42. Matt B. Jones to H. B. Thayer, March 7, 1919, Box 4, AT&T Archives.

43. Henry Wise, interview by Stephen H. Norwood, Boston, Mass., December 4, 1980.

44. Ibid.

45. Rose Finkelstein Norwood, interview by Stephen H. Norwood, Boston, Mass., June 12, 1974.

46. Clare Moriarty [pseudonym], interview by Stephen H. Norwood, Boston, Mass., June 12, 1974.

47. Boston *Globe,* June 10, 1923; Boston *Post,* June 25, 1922.

48. Boston *Herald,* October 14, 1922.

49. Clare Moriarty [pseudonym], telephone interview by Stephen H. Norwood, March 10, 1982.

50. Boston *Post,* January 13, 1923.

51. Boston *Herald,* January 13, 1923.

52. Ibid.; Boston *Post,* January 13, 1923.

53. Boston *Post,* January 14 and February 4, 1923.

54. Ibid., February 19, 1923.

55. Ibid., April 2, 1923.

56. Ibid., February 26, 1923.

57. Ibid., May 19, 1923.

58. Boston *Globe,* March 26, 1923; Boston *Post,* April 19, 1923; Boston *Evening Globe,* June 26, 1923.

59. Boston *Post,* May 27 and 28, 1923; Boston *Herald,* June 3, 1923.

60. Boston *Herald,* June 6, 1923.

61. Ibid., June 10, 1923.

62. Boston *Herald,* June 11, 1923.

63. Ibid., June 10, 1923.

64. Ibid., June 18, 1923.

65. Ibid, June 19, 1923.

66. Boston *Herald*, June 20 and 22, 1923; Manchester *Union*, June 26, 1923.

67. Boston *Herald*, June 16, 1923.

68. Manchester *Union*, June 26, 1923.

69. Boston *Evening Transcript*, June 23, 1923.

70. Matt B. Jones to W. Cameron Forbes, June 12, 1923, and E. K. Hall to J. Epps Brown, June 20, 1923, Box 6, AT&T Archives.

71. Providence *Journal*, June 24, 1923.

72. Boston *Daily Advertiser*, June 26, 1923.

73. Mary Quinn Wynne, interview.

74. Springfield *Republican*, June 24 and 25, 1923.

75. Boston *Herald*, June 24, 1923.

76. Boston *Evening Transcript*, June 25, 1923.

77. Boston *Post*, June 23, 1923.

78. Worcester *Evening Gazette*, June 23, 1923.

79. Boston *Evening Transcript*, June 25, 1923.

80. *New England Telephone Topics* [hereafter, *NETT*], January, 1925, p. 431; Boston *Evening Transcript*, June 25, 1923.

81. Boston *Evening Transcript*, June 25, 1923.

82. Springfield *Republican*, June 26, 1923.

83. Boston *Herald*, June 24, 1923.

84. Boston *Post*, June 26, 1923.

85. Mary I. Brooks and Teresa Sullivan, "To All New England Locals of the Telephone Operators' Department," June 11, 1923, Julia O'Connor Parker Papers.

86. Boston *Herald*, June 24, 1923.

87. Boston *Evening Transcript*, June 23, 1923.

88. Clare Moriarty [pseudonym], interview.

89. The placard is in the Julia O'Connor Parker Papers.

90. Boston *Evening Globe*, June 26, 1923; Boston *Herald*, June 27, 1923.

91. Boston *Herald*, June 27, 1923.

92. Boston *Daily Advertiser*, June 27, 1923.

93. Boston *Herald*, June 27, 1923.

94. Lawrence *Telegram*, June 30, 1923.

95. Boston *Daily Advertiser*, July 2, 1923.

96. Boston *Evening Transcript*, June 26, 1923.

97. Boston *Evening Globe*, June 26, 1923.

98. Brockton *Times*, June 26 and July 3, 1923.

99. Boston *Herald*, June 29, 1923; Boston *Daily Advertiser*, June 29, 1923.

100. Boston *Globe*, June 29, 1923.

101. Boston *Evening Transcript*, June 29 and July 3, 1923.

102. Francis Russell, *A City in Terror* (New York: Penguin Books, 1975), p. 232.

103. Worcester *Evening Gazette,* June 29 and 30, 1923; Boston *Evening Transcript,* June 29, 1923. Washburn quoted in Worcester *Evening Gazette,* June 29, 1923.

104. Quote from Boston *Herald,* July 1, 1923; Boston *Post,* June 30, 1923.

105. Lawrence *Telegram,* July 7, 1923.

106. Springfield *Republican,* June 29, June 30, and July 6, 1923.

107. Providence *Journal,* July 1, 1923; "New Chief Operators in Providence District," *NETT,* April, 1924, p. 506.

108. Boston *Post,* June 30, 1923; Boston *Globe,* June 30, 1923.

109. Because of the strike, the New England Telephone Company fell short of earning dividend requirements for the third quarter of 1923 by about $2,200,000. The estimated loss due to strike conditions was about $2,000,000; the other losses were attributable to a seasonal decline in telephone traffic. F. W. Storey, "A Corporate History of the New England Telephone and Telegraph Company," May, 1924, p. 41, Box 1016, AT&T Archives.

110. Boston *Evening Transcript,* June 25, 1923.

111. Lynn *Telegram-News,* July 13, 1923.

112. Lewiston *Evening Journal,* June 27, 1923; *Daily Kennebec Journal* (Augusta, Maine), June 30, 1923.

113. Lynn *Telegram-News,* June 28, 1923.

114. Boston *Herald,* July 2 and 3, 1923.

115. Lynn *Telegram-News,* July 6, 1923.

116. Boston *Evening Transcript,* July 2 and 5, 1923.

117. Springfield *Republican,* July 16, 1923; Boston *Evening Transcript,* July 5, 1923.

118. McGrady quoted in Boston *Post,* July 5, 1923; O'Connor quoted in Boston *Evening Transcript,* July 2, 1923; Boston *Herald,* July 5, 1923; Brockton *Times,* July 6, 1923; Boston *Daily Advertiser,* July 5, 1923.

119. The first O'Connor quote is from the Lawrence *Telegram,* July 9, 1923; the second from the Lynn *Telegram-News,* July 13, 1923.

120. Lawrence *Telegram,* July 9, 1923; O'Connor quoted in Springfield *Republican,* July 12, 1923.

121. Lynn *Telegram-News,* July 6, 1923.

122. Brockton *Times,* July 6, 1923.

123. Lynn *Telegram-News,* July 10, 16, and 23, 1923; Providence *Journal,* July 17, 1923.

124. Boston *Post,* June 28 and July 2, 1923; quote from Boston *Evening Transcript,* June 28, 1923. The "$6 a week" referred to the bonus that the New England Telephone Company had offered to operators who refused to join the strike.

125. Providence *Journal,* June 28, 1923.

126. Worcester *Evening Gazette,* July 6, 1923.

127. *Labor News,* July 20, 1923.

128. Boston *Herald,* June 30, 1923.

129. *Labor News,* July 13, 1923.

130. Springfield *Republican,* July 18, 1923.

131. *Labor News,* July 13, 1923.

132. Boston *Herald,* July 1, 1923.

133. Brockton *Times,* July 5 and 20, 1923.

134. Lawrence *Telegram,* July 2, 1923.

135. Ibid., July 18, 1923.

136. Ibid., June 30 and July 6, 1923; Boston *Evening Transcript,* July 6, 1923.

137. Boston *Herald,* June 27, 1923.

138. Springfield *Republican,* July 4, 1923.

139. Ibid. James Gordon is listed in the 1923 Springfield city directory as a steamfitter.

140. Springfield *Republican,* July 3, 1923.

141. Ibid., July 7, 1923.

142. Ibid., July 6 and 7, 1923; Mary Quinn Wynne, interview.

143. Springfield *Republican,* July 13, 1923.

144. Providence *Journal,* August 7, 1923.

145. Springfield *Republican,* July 14, 1923.

146. Boston *Globe,* June 28, 1923.

147. Anna Weinstock Schneider, interview by Stephen H. Norwood, Sudbury, Mass., August 15, 1974.

148. Boston *Herald,* July 12, 1923; Boston *Evening Transcript,* July 10, 1923.

149. Boston *Globe,* August 15, 1923.

150. Boston *Post,* July 14, 1923.

151. Boston *Globe,* July 16, 1923.

152. Springfield *Republican,* July 15, 1923.

153. Fall River *Globe,* July 18, 1923; Lynn *Telegram-News,* July 18 and 22, 1923.

154. Boston *Evening Transcript,* July 19 and 27, 1923.

155. Julia O'Connor to Massachusetts State Board of Conciliation and Arbitration, 1925, Box 28, Consumers' League of Massachusetts Papers, Schlesinger Library.

156. Clare Moriarty [pseudonym], interview.

157. "Statement Submitted by New England Telephone and Telegraph Company to Subcommittee on Telephone Service of the Committee on Public Utilities of the Boston Chamber of Commerce," May 7, 1924, File 311–219, Boston Chamber of Commerce Papers, Baker Library, Harvard School of Business Administration, Boston, Mass.

158. Ibid.; Julia O'Connor, "The Blight of Company Unionism," *American Federationist,* May, 1926, p. 549.

159. Boston *Globe,* August 14, 1923.

160. Ibid., October 13, 1923.

161. Mabel Leslie to Julia O'Connor, November 5, 1923, New York

Women's Trade Union League Papers, New York State Department of Labor Library, New York, N.Y.

162. "Annie Molloy," *NETT,* May, 1928, p. 37; Boston *Evening Transcript,* March 20, 1928.

163. Besides Molloy, I have been able to find obituaries for only two leaders of the old Local 1A, Frances Van Tassel and Amanda Toohig. Van Tassel, who died at the age of eighty-three in 1976, retired from the New England Telephone Company as a supervisor in 1958, after forty-eight years of service. She was past president of the Dorchester Catholic Women's Club and a member of the Ladies' Catholic Benevolent Association, St. Kevin's Guild, in Dorchester, and of the Telephone Pioneers of America, the company's association for retired employees. Boston *Globe,* September 12, 1976. Amanda Toohig, who along with Molloy was expelled from the Massachusetts State Federation of Labor convention in August, 1923, died at the age of eighty-three in 1981. She retired from the New England Telephone Company in 1963, after forty-eight years of service as an operator and in the personnel department. Toohig was a member of the Maria Asunta Guild of the Immaculate Conception Church in Revere, Massachusetts, and of the Telephone Pioneers of America. Boston *Globe,* July 9, 1981. Both women remained unmarried. Another leader of the Molloy faction, Mary Meagher, who became the first vice-president of the Boston Telephone Operators' Union in 1912, was promoted less than a year after the strike to the position of chief toll instructress in Boston. "New Chief Toll Instructress," *NETT,* July, 1924, p. 128.

164. Frances Van Tassel, "800 Healthier and Happier Girls Get Health Course Certificates," *NETT,* July, 1928, p. 102.

Epilogue

The Telephone Operators' Union declined rapidly in the wake of the company union offensive launched by corporate business in the early 1920s and suddenly collapsed after the 1923 New England strike. During its lifetime, it greatly improved the working conditions of the telephone operator and gave her a new sense of dignity—as the "Weaver of Speech," employed at a task highly important in the nation's business and social life, and as the "Trade Union Woman," struggling for a better world in the labor and women's movements. It did not, however, have the long-term impact on the lives of its members or on the labor movement that its leaders had expected.

The union's contributions in developing social programs and workers' education were largely swept aside in the aftermath of the 1923 strike. The Driftway vacation house, the union's pioneering venture in workers' leisure, was sold to the Catholic church after less than three years of use.[1] Even if the union had survived, its programs probably would have had limited impact because of the short duration of operators' employment, which in 1920 averaged five years in New England and about three years in the rest of the country. The union's principal long-range achievement in workers' education was in training a relatively small number of women who devoted their careers to the labor movement and performed highly important organizing work in the three decades after 1920. These women's lives were forever transformed by their singular experience in workers' education.

The leadership of the Telephone Operators' Union included at least four women who achieved prominence in their careers as labor organizers or administrators in the decades following the destruction of the union: Julia O'Connor (1890–1972), Rose Sullivan (1896–ca. 1942), Rose Finkelstein (1891–1980), and Mabel Leslie (1893–1974), all trained by the workers' education movement. Sullivan and Leslie remained single all their lives, while O'Connor and Finkelstein married after the age of thirty. The latter two, except for a few years when their children were young, remained as active in the labor movement as before, each relying heavily on her mother's assistance in child care.

Julia O'Connor continued to run the Telephone Operators' Department from Boston with a skeletal staff, but only a tiny number of locals remained affiliated, all outside New England. The Department finally disbanded in 1938. In 1925, O'Connor married Charles Austin Parker, a newspaper reporter for the Boston *Herald,* and resigned from the executive board of the National Women's Trade Union League when her first child was born in 1926. O'Connor, however, remained a leader of the Boston WTUL and participated in campaigns to organize women in various trades in Boston during the 1930s. An ardent supporter of Franklin D. Roosevelt, she was also associated with the labor division of the Democratic National Committee in the presidential campaigns of 1932, 1936, and 1940.

In 1939, Julia O'Connor Parker was appointed a general organizer for the American Federation of Labor, a position she held until her retirement in 1957. Placing her two daughters in boarding schools, Parker moved to New York City to work on the AFL's Western Union campaign. She directed organizing drives among chemical workers in New York state in 1943. She then was assigned to the AFL's southern campaign, organizing for the IBEW and AFL in Texas, Mississippi, Georgia, and Florida from 1944 to 1947. Her work in the South included organizing the Peninsular Telephone Company of Pensacola, Florida. In 1947, the AFL transferred her to its Boston regional office, where she participated in campaigns at Bridgeport Brass, General Electric, and the Fore River shipyards. She died in 1972, surviving her husband by twelve years.[2]

Rose Sullivan, who had served as vice-president of the Telephone Operators' Department, remained active as an organizer for the Boston WTUL and various trade unions after 1923. She served as a business agent of the Boston Neckwear Workers' Union local during the 1930s. For a time, she was also a general organizer for the AFL and in this capacity worked with Julia O'Connor Parker in New York City on the drive to organize Western Union.[3] Her career was cut short by her death about 1942, when she was still in her forties.

Rose Finkelstein, a charter member of Local 1A and a member of its executive board, left the telephone service in 1921 when she married Hyman Norwood, a motorcycle racer and owner of a small tire and battery business whom she had met at a motorcycle race in 1916. Hyman Norwood was a former streetcar motorman and conductor who had participated in the Boston Elevated strike of 1912.

During the 1920s, Rose Finkelstein Norwood served on the executive board and as vice-president of the Boston WTUL, and she was active in the peace movement and the campaign to defend Sacco and Vanzetti, two causes in which the Boston WTUL was heavily involved. She attended classes at the Boston Trade Union College from 1919 until its closing in 1931.

Rose Finkelstein Norwood worked as an organizer for a succession of unions, beginning with the Commercial Telegraphers' Union of America from 1933 to 1937, for which she organized the Boston Postal Telegraph Company. She was the business agent for the Laundry Workers' International Union from 1937 to 1939, and led strikes in Boston, Watertown, and Somerville; in the 1940s she was an organizer first for the International Ladies' Garment Workers' Union and then for the International Jewelry Workers' Union. In 1944, she organized the Boston Public Library for the American Federation of State, County, and Municipal Workers, and she participated in campaigns by the Boilermakers' Union among women wartime shipyard workers in Portland, Maine. Joining the staff of the Retail Clerks' International Union in 1949, she organized the Jordan Marsh Department Store in Boston and directed campaigns in Pennsylvania and New Hampshire. She ended her career in the mid-1950s as an organizer for the Building Service Employees' International Union.

A leading figure in the Boston WTUL since the 1910s, Rose Finkelstein Norwood became its president in 1941 and held that office until the Boston WTUL, along with the National WTUL, disbanded in 1950. She also served on the National WTUL executive board from 1947 to 1950. While president of the Boston WTUL, Norwood conceived of the "Books for Workers" plan, through which public libraries supplied books to union halls and factories, and presented a monthly radio program on "Women and Labor." She also maintained close contact with women labor leaders in foreign countries, sponsoring lectures during the 1930s and 1940s by such women as Toni Sender, the exiled German anti-fascist and former Social Democratic Reichstag deputy; Jennie Lee, Scottish Independent Labour party M.P.; and British Labour party leaders Margaret Bondfield and Ellen Wilkinson.[4]

Mabel Leslie left her position as secretary of the Telephone Operators' Department in 1922 and moved to New York City, where she served for many years as the secretary of the New York WTUL. In 1928, she was awarded the first Florence Simms Scholarship, which had been established by friends of the recently deceased industrial secretary of the Young Women's Christian Association to prepare working women who had demonstrated leadership ability "for more effective service in industry." Leslie used the scholarship to study workers' education in Europe.[5]

Leslie was involved with the workers' education movement for the rest of her career, serving as chair of the educational committee of the New York WTUL and director of the Art Workshop, whose purpose was to "provide opportunity for women and girls who work in monotonous occupations to do something creative with their hands and minds." The Art Workshop sought to discourage worker passivity during leisure hours and to provide an alternative to commercial amusement: " . . . Americans are becoming a nation of passive on-lookers. . . . Brains dulled by a day of monotonous machine tending are reluctant to force fatigued bodies further than the radio or the neighboring movie. Life becomes restricted, imagination has no nourishment." The Art Workshop was not organized as a school but offered workers the opportunity for independent study in creative writing, poetry, painting, sculpture, and labor drama. Leslie asked the worker, "What are your secret buried dreams of life? To draw, to paint great sheets of radiant color, to design in forceful black and white, to write all the surging ideas which come as the machinery whirs or the hammers clang, to stir the imagination and paint in telling words the life of labor to those who will not or cannot understand . . . ?"[6] Leslie ended her career as a member of the New York State Board of Mediation.

In New England, the former stronghold of the Telephone Operators' Department, company unionism prevailed for nearly half a century after the 1923 strike. For a decade after the strike, the International Brotherhood of Electrical Workers made no effort to organize telephone workers in any area of the country. In 1927, IBEW President James Noonan stated, "Our experience of the last few years convinces us that were we to attempt to organize the comparatively few in each company who desired organization, it would only result in their being discharged."[7]

Support from women outside the labor movement, highly important in sustaining women's trade unions in the prewar period, almost entirely disappeared in the 1920s. The large and well-organized movement that had been formed around the issue of women's suffrage did not survive the enactment of the nineteenth amendment. The League of Women Voters, which succeeded the National American Woman Suffrage Association in 1919, retained only a fraction of its membership and failed to define new political goals behind which women could unite. Women reformers' influence on male politicians was greatly diminished when it became clear in the early 1920s that women would not vote as a cohesive bloc.[8]

The young women who entered college in increasing numbers during the 1920s did not possess the sense of mission or the drive of the first generation of female college students, many of whom had become allies in the Women's Trade Union League during the prewar period. The prewar allies had attended women's colleges and had formed close ties with other women; about half of those graduating never married. By the 1920s, however, the female college student was no longer regarded by men as a social deviant, and an increasingly large number of women attended coeducational institutions. Whereas the first generation of women college students had emphasized studying and bonding with other women, many women entered college in the 1920s primarily to find a husband. Those few college students interested in social activism found the new opportunities for paid employment in government and social work more attractive than the settlement houses or the declining labor movement.[9] As a result, there were very few young upper- or middle-class women to take the places of the prewar allies who died or drifted away from the labor movement, and women's trade unions lost a major source of support.

Having destroyed the Telephone Operators' Union, the New England Telephone Company in 1923 established committees to represent the operators in each telephone exchange. The committees, each of which consisted of two or three operators elected by the exchange, might present individual grievances to management, but they did not function as bargaining agencies since no contact was permitted among them. According to Julia O'Connor, writing in 1926, the committees were primarily concerned with social functions, such as beach parties; they had failed to confront management on any but the most trivial issues: "It is a matter of record that they once brought about the addition of a water-bottle to an exchange, and on another soul-stirring occasion succeeded in having a dirty electric-light globe washed."[10] During the Great Depression, the committees provided forums in which management justified layoffs and other anti-labor measures. In 1931, for example, the company called the various committees together and secured their consent to the operators' taking a week off without pay and discontinuing wage increases.[11]

When the National Recovery Administration (NRA) blanket code went into effect two years later, the committee system became endangered. Under the NRA code, telephone company employees were paid at an hourly rate for forty hours, instead of a weekly rate for forty-eight hours, resulting in a substantial reduction in earnings. This led to considerable discontent among the operators, and a campaign was begun by Julia O'Connor and others who had been active in the pre-1923 Telephone Operators' Union to establish an AFL-affiliated union of telephone operators. The company resorted to intimidation, subjecting operators suspected of membership in O'Connor's organization to repeated interviews and placing spies in the union's meetings. According to one operator who participated in it, the AFL campaign began poorly: "[At] the first meeting . . . there were so few there that I could name them all off. There was . . . Cecil Doyle, that was a very close friend of all of ours, and of . . . Julia, and everybody; and then Margaret Day, a girl I worked with; and 'Clare' [Moriarty] and I; and Della Foley. Well we were all union people. Then we had two extra women from our office: real spies, real dirty spies."[12] The union's organizing drive drew increasing support, however, and the company was forced to staff its exchange committees with such operators as it could persuade to serve, regardless of whether they had been elected. The company also paid for operators to travel throughout New England campaigning against the AFL and in favor of the committees.

In October, 1933, after the AFL's campaign had collapsed, the company introduced a revised committee system, which was similar to the employee association plans adopted by other Bell subsidiaries during the 1920s. The new exchange committees selected representatives to meet at the district and division levels so they were no longer completely isolated at the local level. They were not, however, affiliated with any outside labor organization. The operators were still represented by a company union. Genuine trade unionism did not return to the New England Telephone Company until 1971, when the telephone operators, along with the telephone men, rejoined the International Brotherhood of Electrical Workers.

Although telephone workers remained quiescent during the 1930s, John Schacht has argued that the Bell employee associations provided a basis for future trade union activity in the telephone service. The associations gave some workers the opportunity to develop organizational skills and experience in conferring with management, usually on minor matters but occasionally on major ones. Meetings of representatives at the district or division levels helped to overcome the effects of geographical dispersion and sometimes drew together members of different departments. Even so, Schacht describes the associations as "languid and toothless."[13] When company unions were made illegal by the passage of the Wagner Act in 1935, the Bell companies transformed the employee associations into formally independent labor organizations but continued to dominate them. The companies helped the new associations, usually led by the former officers, to recruit members, provided free meeting rooms and office equipment, etc.[14]

In 1937, delegates from seventeen Bell company unions met, with the approval of Bell management, to form a national confederation, which they hoped would allow them to exert greater influence over national legislation affecting telephone workers and would make incursions by "outside" trade unions more difficult. This resulted in the formal establishment of the National Federation of Telephone Workers (NFTW) two years later. Twenty-seven company unions affiliated, representing about 37 percent of union-eligible Bell workers. The NFTW was not a national labor organization but a loose confederation; affiliates remained autonomous, and each carried on its own bargaining with its respective company. The NFTW was further weakened by its small budget, which allowed no full-time officers. The telephone operators were vastly underrepresented on the NFTW's executive board; comprising 35 to 40 percent of the NFTW's membership, they never held more than two of the nine board positions. Schacht, however, has argued that the NFTW helped prepare the way for a national trade union by organizing telephone workers on an industry-wide basis and bringing together their representatives in regional and national meetings which emphasized the common concerns of Bell employees.[15]

The absence of militancy among telephone operators during the 1930s can in part be attributed to job insecurity, caused not just by the depression but also by dial conversion. Between 1929 and 1933, the number of workers employed by the Bell System declined by about 40 percent; those who retained their jobs were frequently sent home without pay on what were called "lack of work days." Layoffs were arbitrary, without consultation with the employees' associations.[16] For telephone operators, who had been virtually immune from both cyclical and seasonal unemployment, dial conversion was especially frightening since much of the job reduction occurred during the depression, when those displaced had little prospect of finding other work. By 1930, about one-third of the telephones in the Bell System had been converted to dial, eliminating an estimated 70,000 local operating positions; by 1934, about half of the telephones were dial operated.[17] In the smaller towns, where there was only one telephone exchange, dial conversion occurred suddenly and with devastating effect. For example, in Butte, Montana, a mining town where there were almost no jobs available for women, dial cutover reduced the operating force from 108 to 35 in one day.[18] In the larger cities, the number of local operating positions diminished steadily during the 1930s. The Boston Metropolitan District employed only 3,500–4,000 operators in 1940 as opposed to over 6,000 twenty years earlier, even though the number of telephones in use had increased greatly.[19] Workers who could be so readily replaced were in no position to assert themselves in the workplace.

American entry into World War II caused the wages and working conditions of telephone workers to deteriorate badly, leading to an upsurge of militancy unparalleled since the early 1920s. Bell had subnormal earnings, and, unlike companies engaged in war production, it could not pass wage bills on to the government. For operators particularly, the heavier wartime demand for service increased the workload and required more time on undesirable Sunday and holiday shifts. Increasingly, strike action was considered as a means of pressuring the intransigent Bell companies. As it had in World War I, the war economy tightened the labor market, improving workers' chances of forcing concessions. Telephone companies had difficulty recruiting in all departments, as workers were lured away by higher-paying jobs in defense plants and in other industries.[20]

The Bell companies' refusal to grant wage increases despite the severe wartime and postwar inflation, coupled with the fear that the anticipated mass unemployment would make it exceedingly difficult for labor to achieve any improvements in wages and working conditions, led the NFTW to call the first nationwide telephone strike in April, 1947, involving over 300,000 workers. The strike's effectiveness was greatly reduced by the dial system; local service remained nearly normal for the 65 percent of telephones that were dial operated. With the assistance of managerial officials, nonstrikers, and recalled retirees, the companies were also able to complete a considerable number of nondial calls. Dial equipment did not break down after two or three weeks as the strikers had expected, and strike funds quickly ran out. After six weeks, the strikers settled on relatively unfavorable terms. They gained a small wage increase but no improvements in working conditions.[21]

The defeat of the strike led many telephone workers to conclude that a nationwide trade union was necessary if they were ever to confront successfully the highly centralized Bell management, and the Communications Workers of America (CWA) was formed in June, 1947. The CWA, an industrial union including telephone workers in all departments, affiliated with the CIO in 1949. The telephone operators, however, never regained the influence they had wielded prior to 1923. In part this was due to the diminished importance of telephone operating in the Bell System. By 1970, when nearly 100 percent of local and over 90 percent of long distance calls were direct dialled, telephone operators comprised only 26 percent of Bell Company employees, as opposed to 43 percent in 1950. Even so, the operators were never adequately represented in the CWA and were almost completely absent at the top level of leadership. Women have held none of the major offices and never more than one of the seven to nine district directorships.[22]

The situation was no different in the IBEW, which in the early 1970s organized the New England telephone operators, who had remained outside the CWA. Two veterans of Local 1A claimed that women held as little influence in the IBEW of the 1970s as in the company union of the 1920s:

Clare Moriarty:	I think that's [the situation that prevailed under the company union] pretty well what they've got now. I'm awfully disappointed, they haven't got any department of their own, the operators; they're in with the men now. . . . I was interested to read, they [the IBEW telephone workers' bargaining committee] were just going in for negotiations now . . . and only *two* women [and] it seemed like about fifteen men. And you know it's a majority of women in the company.
Kathleen Moriarty:	They have no . . . leadership among the women. When I think of the old days, what wonderful women they had. And they had the gumption to carry on on their own.[23]

Given women's lack of influence in trade unions today, the Telephone Operators' Union of the 1910s and early 1920s deserves particular attention for making women a powerful presence in the labor movement in several sections of the country. The operators' movement was part of a larger upsurge in women workers' militancy that began with the "Uprising of the 20,000" in New York's garment industry in 1909. Yet the telephone operators were unique in building a national, woman-led labor organization in their industry. The officers, staff, and membership of the IBEW's Telephone Operators' Department, which functioned as an autonomous international trade union, were all women. By contrast, in the garment, boot and shoe, and textile industries, each of which employed sizeable numbers of women, unions above the local level were controlled by men, even when women constituted an overwhelming majority of the membership.

The International Ladies' Garment Workers' Union (ILGWU), for example, became a viable labor organization largely as a result of a strike initiated by women workers, its membership was predominantly female, and many of the leaders of the National WTUL were drawn from it. Despite this, it never had more than one woman on its general executive board prior to 1950. The number of positions on the general executive board, which was composed of the union's president and vice-presidents, ranged from thirteen to fourteen in the 1920s to over twenty in the 1940s. Rose Pesotta, who became a vice-president of the ILGWU in 1934, recalled that she had initially been reluctant to accept a nomination for the position: "It was my contention that the voice of a solitary woman on the General Executive Board would be a voice lost in the wilderness."[24] Women members were also drastically underrepresented at ILGWU conventions, even in the 1910s. Of the 450 delegates elected by the New York City ILGWU locals to the six conventions held between 1910 and 1920, only 25 were women, and few of these attended a convention more than once.[25]

During its lifetime, the Telephone Operators' Union not only significantly improved the wages and working conditions of telephone operators across the country but also encouraged its members to assert forcefully their interests as women in the labor movement. The union telephone operators never hesitated to challenge male trade unionists on issues of union administration or during strikes. Refusing to accept the "second-class" status in the IBEW to which the male members had consigned them, they waged a long campaign for equal rights, modeled on the campaign for women's suffrage. In New England, it was the operators, not the telephone men, who were the first to organize. Their two most important strikes—in New England in 1919 and 1923—were initiated by the operators without the support of the male telephone workers. In 1919, the Boston operators at a mass meeting shouted down an IBEW vice-president who attempted to dissuade them from striking and walked out against the wishes of the IBEW's national leadership and AFL President Samuel Gompers. Remaining loyal to the IBEW when the men seceded from the labor movement in 1920, the operators repeatedly expressed contempt for the telephone men's insufficient militancy. The Telephone Operators' Union also advanced political views which were much to the left of those of the IBEW and AFL.

Combining "homosocial" days in an all-female work environment with "heterosocial" nights in dance halls and amusement parks, the telephone operators were involved in a flapper life-style and consumer culture that had politically ambivalent implications. In the telephone exchange, the operators were not subordinate to men as most other women workers were; they were supervised and disciplined only by women. Nor did the operators continuously have to be attentive to males, for even though most telephone subscribers were men, the operators' contact with them was fleeting and not face-to-face. The operators' homosocial days allowed them to envisage women in positions of authority and made it easier for them to become involved both in women's institutions established within the labor movement and in the women's movement itself.

The operators' heterosocial nights and consumerism involved behavior that was in part liberating, in part constricting. The consumer culture greatly expanded the public space women could enter, bringing them into downtown sections previously the domain of men. It allowed women the opportunity for greater sensual gratification and experience. Operators' promenading the streets in fashionable dress was an assertion that they were deserving of the "better things" enjoyed by the middle class and reflected a heightened self-esteem. The desire to consume led many operators to organize, since the union could increase their purchasing power and offered the prospect of self-support, an end to dependency and oppressive family ties. At the same time, consumerism was part of a masculinist culture, fashioning a "new" but still subordinate woman, who with her careful attention to her physical appearance was increasingly susceptible to being influenced by men's view of her. Women picketing in high heels and fur chokers also might have appeared as frivolous to many—a view which, to be sure, would have been quickly dispelled by observing the operators' behavior in strikes.

A product of developments in politics, culture, and the workplace specific to the 1910s, the Telephone Operators' Union celebrated the strength and dignity of the woman worker while bringing women squarely into the center of the labor movement. It flourished during a decade when both the labor and women's movements were strong, but it proved unable to survive when these movements collapsed in the 1920s. Labor's resurgence in the 1930s was not accompanied by any renewal of women's activism, and it was not possible to organize another women's trade union. Although the Communications Workers of America was established as a nationwide telephone workers' union after World War II, the operators in it were relegated to second-class status. The trade unions had long been quiescent when the women's movement finally reemerged in the 1970s, and they were little affected by it. Having trained some of the principal women organizers of the American labor movement, the Telephone Operators' Union continued to influence workers' lives for decades after its demise in 1923. But telephone operators never regained the influence they wielded in the 1910s, and there has never again been a trade union that did as much to advance the cause of women workers.

NOTES

1. When the author visited the building in 1974 with several of the leaders of the pre-1923 Telephone Operators' Union, it was being used as a residence for priests.
2. Stephen H. Norwood, "Julia O'Connor Parker," in Barbara Sicherman and Carol Hurd Green, eds., *Notable American Women*, vol. 4 (Cambridge, Mass.: Harvard University Press, 1980), pp. 525–26; Stephen H. Norwood, "Julia O'Connor Parker," in Gary M. Fink, ed., *Biographical Dictionary of American Labor* (Westport, Conn.: Greenwood Press, 1984), pp. 454–55; Sally Parker Swerbilov, interview by Stephen H. Norwood, New York, N.Y., February, 1978.
3. *Commercial Telegraphers' Journal*, November, 1941, p. 174.
4. Stephen H. Norwood, "Rose Finkelstein Norwood," in Fink, ed., *Biographical Dictionary*, pp. 438–39.
5. "Mabel Leslie," in Solon DeLeon, ed., *American Labor's Who's Who* (New York: Rand School Press, 1925), p. 135; "The First Florence Simms Scholarship," *Life and Labor Bulletin*, October, 1928, p. 3.
6. Mabel Leslie, "Fatigued Hands Rest with Creative Tasks," *Journal of Electrical Workers and Operators* [hereafter, *JEWO*], November, 1930, p. 623.
7. Quoted in Jack Barbash, *Unions and Telephones* (New York: Harper and Brothers, 1952), p. 11.
8. William Chafe, *The American Woman* (New York: Oxford University Press, 1972), pp. 36–37.
9. Carl Degler, *At Odds* (New York: Oxford University Press, 1980), p. 413; Chafe, *American Woman*, pp. 92–93; Nancy Shrom Dye, *As Equals and as Sisters* (Columbia: University of Missouri Press, 1980), p. 165.
10. Julia O'Connor, "The Blight of Company Unionism," *American Federationist*, May, 1926, p. 548.
11. U.S. Department of Labor, Bureau of Labor Statistics, *Characteristics of Company Unions, 1935*, Bulletin No. 634, June, 1937 (Washington, D.C.: Government Printing Office, 1938), p. 266.
12. Kathleen Moriarty [pseudonym], interview by Stephen H. Norwood, Boston, Mass., June 12, 1974.

13. John Schacht, *The Making of Telephone Unionism, 1920–1947.* (New Brunswick, N.J.: Rutgers University Press, 1985), pp. 43–44, 64.

14. Ibid., pp. 50–51.

15. Ibid., pp. 58–60, 84.

16. Ibid., p. 37; Thomas Brooks, *The Communications Workers of America* (New York: Mason/Charter, 1977), p. 33.

17. Pennell Crosby, "Dials Dock Working Force, Profits Good," *JEWO,* November, 1933, p. 453; Brooks, *Communications Workers,* p. 32.

18. Julia O'Connor Parker, "A Woman Views Girl Displacement by Dials," *JEWO,* January, 1930, p. 13.

19. "Statement of Rose S. Sullivan before the Temporary Economic Committee's Hearing on Technology," April 17, 1940, p. 3, Box 3, National Women's Trade Union League Papers, Schlesinger Library, Radcliffe College, Cambridge, Mass.

20. Schacht, *Making,* pp. 100–103.

21. Ibid., pp. 168–71.

22. Brooks, *Communications Workers,* pp. 162, 204, 238.

23. Clare Moriarty [pseudonym] and Kathleen Moriarty [pseudonym], interview by Stephen H. Norwood, Boston, Mass., June 12, 1974.

24. Rose Pesotta, *Bread upon the Waters* (New York: Dodd, Mead, 1945), p. 101.

25. Roger Waldinger, "Another Look at the International Ladies' Garment Workers' Union: Women, Industry Structure, and Collective Action," in Ruth Milkman, ed., *Women, Work, and Protest* (Boston: Routledge and Kegan Paul, 1985), p. 99.

Bibliography

MANUSCRIPT COLLECTIONS

American Telephone and Telegraph Company Archives, New York, N.Y.
    Records of the American Telephone and Telegraph Company

Schlesinger Library, Radcliffe College, Cambridge, Mass.
    Consumers' League of Massachusetts Papers
    Massachusetts Political Equality Union Collection
    National Women's Trade Union League Papers
    Rose Finkelstein Norwood Papers
    Julia O'Connor Parker Papers
    Women's Educational and Industrial Union Papers

National Archives, Washington, D.C.
    General Records of the Department of Labor, Record Group 174
    Records of the Bureau of Investigation, Record Group 65
    Records of the Department of Justice, Record Group 60
    Records of the Post Office Department, Record Group 28

National Archives, Suitland, Md.
    Records of the General Mediation and Conciliation Service, Record Group 280

Library of Congress, Washington, D.C.
    Albert S. Burleson Papers
    National Women's Trade Union League Papers

Archives of the Sisters of Notre Dame de Namur, Ipswich, Mass.
    Records of parochial schools in Massachusetts administered by the Sisters of Notre Dame de Namur

Baker Library, Harvard Graduate School of Business Administration, Boston, Mass.
    Records of the Boston Chamber of Commerce

Massachusetts State Library, Boston, Mass.
Journal Books of the Massachusetts State Board of Arbitration

State Historical Society of Wisconsin, Madison, Wis.
American Labor Education Service Papers

Walter P. Reuther Library, Wayne State University, Detroit, Mich.
Brookwood Labor College Papers

New York Public Library, New York, N.Y.
National Civic Federation Papers

New York State Department of Labor Library, New York, N.Y.
New York Women's Trade Union League Papers

Swarthmore College Peace Collection, Swarthmore, Pa.
Emily Greene Balch Papers

Tamiment Library, New York University, New York, N.Y.
Rose Schneiderman Papers

BOOKS

Banner, Lois. *American Beauty*. New York: Alfred A. Knopf, 1983.

Barbash, Jack. *Unions and Telephones*. New York: Harper and Brothers, 1952.

Barth, Gunther. *City People*. New York: Oxford University Press, 1980.

Bean, Walton. *Boss Ruef's San Francisco*. Berkeley: University of California Press, 1967.

Bell, Daniel. *Marxian Socialism in the United States*. Princeton, N.J.: Princeton University Press, 1952.

Bennett, Arnold. *Your United States*. New York: Harper and Brothers, 1912.

Bernstein, Irving. *The Lean Years*. Baltimore: Penguin Books, 1960.

Blauner, Robert. *Alienation and Freedom*. Chicago: University of Chicago Press, 1964.

Boone, Gladys. *The Women's Trade Union League in Great Britain and the United States of America*. New York: Columbia University Press, 1942.

Broderick, Francis L. *Right Reverend New Dealer: John A. Ryan*. New York: MacMillan, 1963.

Brody, David. *Labor in Crisis*. Philadelphia and New York: J. B. Lippincott, 1965.

———. *Workers in Industrial America*. New York: Oxford University Press, 1980.

Brooks, John. *Telephone*. New York: Harper and Row, 1975.

Brooks, Thomas. *The Communications Workers of America*. New York: Mason/Charter, 1977.

Bruce, Robert V. *Bell: Alexander Graham Bell and the Conquest of Solitude*. Boston: Little, Brown, 1973.

Butler, Elizabeth Beardsley. *Women and the Trades*. New York: Charities Publication Committee, 1909.

Cantor, Milton, and Bruce Laurie, eds. *Class, Sex, and the Woman Worker*. Westport, Conn.: Greenwood Press, 1977.

Chafe, William. *The American Woman*. New York: Oxford University Press, 1972.

Coon, Horace. *American Tel & Tel: The Story of a Great Monopoly*. New York: Longmans, Green, 1939.

Cronin, James, and Carmen Sirianni, eds. *Work, Community, and Power*. Philadelphia: Temple University Press, 1983.

Cunroe, Phillip. *Educational Attitudes and Policies of Organized Labor in the United States*. New York: Teachers' College, Columbia University Bureau of Publications, 1926.

Curti, Merle. *The Social Ideas of American Educators*. New York: Charles Scribner's Sons, 1935.

Danielian, N. R. *A.T.&T.: The Story of Industrial Conquest*. New York: Vanguard Press, 1939.

Davies, Margery. *Woman's Place Is at the Typewriter*. Philadelphia: Temple University Press, 1982.

Davis, Allen. *Spearheads for Reform*. New York: Oxford University Press, 1967.

Degler, Carl. *At Odds*. New York: Oxford University Press, 1980.

DeLeon, Solon, ed. *American Labor's Who's Who*. New York: Rand School Press, 1925.

Dictionary of the American Hierarchy. New York: Longmans, Green, 1940.

Dilts, Marion May. *The Telephone in a Changing World*. New York: Longmans, Green, 1941.

Diner, Hasia. *Erin's Daughters in America*. Baltimore: Johns Hopkins University Press, 1983.

Dodge, Grace, et al. *What Women Can Earn*. New York: Frederick A. Stokes, 1899.

Dublin, Thomas. *Women at Work*. New York: Columbia University Press, 1979.

Dubofsky, Melvyn. *We Shall Be All*. Chicago: Quadrangle Books, 1969; 2d ed. Urbana: University of Illinois Press, 1988.

———, and Warren Van Tine. *John L. Lewis*. New York: Quadrangle/New York Times Book Co., 1977.

Dye, Nancy Shrom. *As Equals and as Sisters*. Columbia: University of Missouri Press, 1980.

Eisenstein, Sarah. *Give Us Bread but Give Us Roses.* London: Routledge and Kegan Paul, 1983.

Erenberg, Lewis. *Steppin' Out.* Westport, Conn.: Greenwood Press, 1981.

Fass, Paula. *The Damned and the Beautiful.* New York: Oxford University Press, 1977.

Fink, Gary M., ed. *Labor Unions.* Westport, Conn.: Greenwood Press, 1977.

———. *Biographical Dictionary of American Labor.* Westport, Conn.: Greenwood Press, 1984.

Friedlander, Judith, Blanche Wiesen Cook, Alice Kessler-Harris, and Carol Smith-Rosenberg, eds. *Women in Culture and Politics: A Century of Change.* Bloomington: Indiana University Press, 1986.

Frisch, Michael, and Daniel Walkowitz, eds. *Working-Class America.* Urbana: University of Illinois Press, 1983.

Garnet, Robert W. *The Telephone Enterprise.* Baltimore: Johns Hopkins University Press, 1985.

Goldmark, Josephine. *Fatigue and Efficiency.* New York: Russell Sage Foundation, 1912.

Gordon, David, Richard Edwards, and Michael Reich. *Segmented Work, Divided Workers.* New York: Cambridge University Press, 1982.

Green, James, ed. *Workers' Struggles, Past and Present.* Philadelphia: Temple University Press, 1983.

Green, James R., and Hugh Carter Donahue. *Boston's Workers: A Labor History.* Boston: Boston Public Library, 1979.

Greenwald, Maurine Weiner. *Women, War, and Work.* Westport, Conn.: Greenwood Press, 1980.

Hall, Jacquelyn Dowd, James Leloudis, Robert Korstad, Mary Murphy, Lu Ann Jones, and Christopher B. Daly. *Like a Family.* Chapel Hill: University of North Carolina Press, 1987.

Harring, Sidney. *Policing a Class Society.* New Brunswick, N.J.: Rutgers University Press, 1983.

Haywood, William D. *Bill Haywood's Book.* New York: International Publishers, 1929.

Heintz, Albert M., and John R. Whitney. *History of the Massachusetts Federation of Labor, 1887–1935.* Worcester, Mass.: Labor News Printers, 1935.

Hentoff, Nat, ed. *The Essays of A. J. Muste.* New York: Simon and Schuster, 1967.

Herlihy, Elizabeth M., ed. *Fifty Years of Boston: A Memorial Volume.* Boston: Boston Tercentenary Committee, 1932.

Hicks, John. *Republican Ascendancy.* New York: Harper and Row, 1960.

———. *Rehearsal for Disaster.* Gainesville: University of Florida Press, 1961.

Hobsbawm, Eric. *Workers.* New York: Pantheon Books, 1984.

Hodgen, Margaret. *Workers' Education in England and the United States.* New York: E. P. Dutton, 1925.

Janiewski, Dolores. *Sisterhood Denied*. Philadelphia: Temple University Press, 1985.

Johnston, Charles Hughes, ed. *The Modern High School*. New York: Charles Scribner's Sons, 1914.

Kennedy, David. *Over Here*. New York: Oxford University Press, 1980.

Kessler-Harris, Alice. *Out to Work*. New York: Oxford University Press, 1982.

Kett, Joseph. *Rites of Passage*. New York: Basic Books, 1977.

Keyssar, Alexander. *Out of Work*. New York: Cambridge University Press, 1986.

Knight, Robert E. L. *Industrial Relations in the San Francisco Bay Area, 1900–1918*. Berkeley and Los Angeles: University of California Press, 1960.

Kolko, Gabriel. *The Triumph of Conservatism*. Chicago: Quadrangle Books, 1967.

Kornbluh, Joyce, and Mary Frederickson, eds. *Sisterhood and Solidarity*. Philadelphia: Temple University Press, 1984.

Kraditor, Aileen. *The Ideas of the Women's Suffrage Movement, 1890–1920*. Garden City, N.Y.: Anchor Books, 1971.

Krug, Edward. *The Shaping of the American High School*. Vol. 2, 1920–41. Madison: University of Wisconsin Press, 1972.

Larkin, Emmet. *James Larkin*. Cambridge, Mass.: MIT Press, 1965.

Laselle, Mary A., and Katherine E. Wiley. *Vocations for Girls*. Cambridge, Mass.: Riverside Press, 1913.

Levine, Susan. *Labor's True Woman*. Philadelphia: Temple University Press, 1984.

Lewis, Sinclair. *Babbitt*. New York: Harcourt, Brace, and World, 1922.

Lockwood, David. *The Blackcoated Worker*. London: Allen and Unwin, 1958.

Merwick, Donna. *Boston's Priests, 1848–1910*. Cambridge, Mass.: Harvard University Press, 1973.

Milkman, Ruth, ed. *Women, Work, and Protest*. Boston: Routledge and Kegan Paul, 1985.

Mills, C. Wright. *White Collar*. New York: Oxford University Press, 1951.

Montgomery, David. *The Fall of the House of Labor*. New York: Cambridge University Press, 1987.

Morgan, H. Wayne, ed. *The Gilded Age*. Syracuse, N.Y.: Syracuse University Press, 1963.

Mulcaire, Michael. *The International Brotherhood of Electrical Workers*. Washington, D.C.: University Press, 1923.

Murray, Robert K. *Red Scare*. New York: McGraw-Hill, 1964.

Muscio, Bernard. *Lectures on Industrial Psychology*. New York: E. P. Dutton, 1920.

Nelson, Daniel. *Managers and Workers*. Madison: University of Wisconsin Press, 1975.

Payne, Elizabeth Anne. *Reform, Labor, and Feminism*. Urbana: University of Illinois Press, 1988.

Pearson, Henry Greenleaf. *Son of New England*. Boston: Thomas Todd, 1932.

Peiss, Kathy. *Cheap Amusements*. Philadelphia: Temple University Press, 1986.

Pelling, Henry. *American Labor*. Chicago: University of Chicago Press, 1960.

Perrot, Michelle. *Workers on Strike*. New Haven, Conn.: Yale University Press, 1987.

Pesotta, Rose. *Bread upon the Waters*. New York: Dodd, Mead, 1945.

Phillips, Harlan, ed. *Felix Frankfurter Reminisces*. New York: Reynal, 1960.

Pool, Ithiel de Sola, ed. *The Social Impact of the Telephone*. Cambridge, Mass.: MIT Press, 1977.

Richardson, Anna Steese. *The Girl Who Earns Her Own Living*. New York: B. W. Dodge, 1909.

Roboff, Sari. *Boston's Labor Movement*. Boston: Boston 200 Corporation, 1977.

Rodgers, Daniel. *The Work Ethic in Industrial America, 1850–1920*. Chicago: University of Chicago Press, 1978.

Rotella, Elyce. *From Home to Office*. Ann Arbor, Mich.: UMI Research Press, 1981.

Rothman, Sheila. *Woman's Proper Place*. New York: Basic Books, 1978.

Russell, Francis. *A City in Terror*. New York: Penguin Books, 1975.

Ryan, Mary. *Womanhood in America*. New York: Franklin Watts, 1983.

Schacht, John. *The Making of Telephone Unionism, 1920–1947*. New Brunswick, N.J.: Rutgers University Press, 1985.

Scharf, Lois. *To Work and to Wed*. Westport, Conn.: Greenwood Press, 1980.

Sheldon, Henry. *Student Life and Customs*. New York: D. Appleton, 1901.

Shorter, Edward, and Charles Tilly. *Strikes in France, 1830–1968*. New York: Cambridge University Press, 1974.

Sicherman, Barbara, and Carol Hurd Green, eds. *Notable American Women*. Vol. 4, *The Modern Period, 1950–1975*. Cambridge, Mass.: Harvard University Press, 1980.

Spring, Joel. *Education and the Rise of the Corporate State*. Boston: Beacon, 1972.

Tax, Meredith. *The Rising of the Women*. New York: Monthly Review Press, 1980.

Tentler, Leslie Woodcock. *Wage-Earning Women*. New York: Oxford University Press, 1979.

Thompson, Paul. *The Edwardians*. Bloomington: Indiana University Press, 1975.

Van Tine, Warren. *The Making of the Labor Bureaucrat.* Amherst: University of Massachusetts Press, 1973.

Weaver, E. W. *Profitable Vocations for Girls.* New York and Chicago: A. S. Barnes, 1916.

Weinstein, James. *The Corporate Ideal in the Liberal State, 1900–1918.* Boston: Beacon, 1968.

Woloch, Nancy. *Women and the American Experience.* New York: Alfred A. Knopf, 1984.

ARTICLES IN JOURNALS

Bradshaw, John W. "Operators' Voices, Their Importance, and the Method of Their Cultivation." *Journal of Ophthalmology, Otology, and Laryngology* 22 (April, 1916):339–44.

Buenker, John. "The Mahatma and Progressive Reform: Martin Lomasney as Lawmaker, 1911–1917." *New England Quarterly* 44 (September, 1971):397–419.

Erikson, Kai. "On Work and Alienation." *American Sociological Review* 51 (February, 1986):1–8.

"The Health of Telephone Operators." *Lancet* 2 (December 16, 1911): 1716.

Kenneally, James J. "Catholicism and Women's Suffrage in Massachusetts." *Catholic Historical Review* 53 (April, 1967):43–57.

Leach, William. "Transformations in a Culture of Consumption: Women and Department Stores, 1890–1925." *Journal of American History* 71 (September, 1984):319–42.

McGovern, James. "The American Woman's Pre-World War I Freedom in Manners and Morals." *Journal of American History* 55 (September, 1968):315–33.

McLean, Nancy. "The Culture of Resistance: Female Institution Building in the International Ladies' Garment Workers' Union, 1905–1925." *Michigan Occasional Paper in Women's Studies,* no. 21 (Winter, 1982).

Merk, Lois. "Boston's Historic Public School Crisis." *New England Quarterly* 31 (June, 1958):172–99.

Miller, Representative Clarence B. [Speech before the U.S. House, 65th Cong., 2d sess., September 12, 1918]. *Congressional Record* 56, no. 649 (1918):10251–54.

Oates, Mary J. "Organized Voluntarism: The Catholic Sisters in Massachusetts, 1870–1940." *American Quarterly* 30 (Winter, 1978):652–80.

Richardson, Anna G. "Telephone Operating: A Study of Its Medical Aspects with Statistics of Sickness Disability Reports." *Journal of Industrial Hygiene* 1 (May, 1919):54–67.

Sangster, Joan. "The 1907 Bell Telephone Strike: Organizing Women Workers." *Labour/Le Travailleur* 3 (1978):109–30.

Sharpless, John, and John Rury. "The Political Economy of Women's Work, 1900–1920." *Social Science History* 4 (Summer, 1980):317–46.

Strom, Sharon Hartman. "Leadership and Tactics in the American Woman Suffrage Movement: A New Perspective from Massachusetts." *Journal of American History* 62 (September, 1975):296–315.

———. "Challenging 'Woman's Place': Feminism, the Left, and Industrial Unionism in the 1930s." *Feminist Studies* 9 (Summer, 1983):359–86.

Thompson, LeRoy. "The Telephone Operators' Throat." *Journal of Ophthalmology, Otology, and Laryngology* 22 (April, 1916):345–52.

Tomlins, Christopher. "AFL Unions in the 1930s: Their Performance in Historical Perspective." *Journal of American History* 65 (March, 1979):1021–42.

Turbin, Carole. "Reconceptualizing Family, Work, and Labor Organizing: Working Women in Troy, 1860–1890." *Review of Radical Political Economics* 16 (1984):1–16.

Weitz, Eric D. "Class Formation and Labor Protest in the Mining Communities of Southern Illinois and the Ruhr, 1890–1925." *Labor History* 27 (Winter, 1985–86):85–105.

Wheeler, Robert F. "Organized Sport and Organized Labour: The Workers' Sports Movement." *Journal of Contemporary History* 13 (April, 1978):191–210.

MAGAZINE ARTICLES (SIGNED)

Baker, Loretta. "Driftway." *Union Telephone Operator*, February, 1921, pp. 19–20.

Barrett, R. T. "The Changing Years as Seen from the Switchboard." Parts 1–8. *New England Telephone Topics*, January-August, 1935.

Baxter, Sylvester. "The Telephone Girl." *The Outlook*, May 26, 1906, pp. 231–39.

Blackwell, Alice Stone. "Mrs. Susan W. Fitzgerald." *Woman's Journal*, February 5, 1910.

Bright, Eunice Evelyn. "Why Not?" *Union Telephone Operator*, March, 1921, p. 21+.

Burns, Agnes. "Telephone Operators Hold First Convention." *Life and Labor*, November, 1919, p. 286.

Cameron, Sadie. "Sadie, the Switchboard Girl, Speaks Her Mind." *Journal of Electrical Workers and Operators*, January, 1928, pp. 11–14+.

Crawford, Mary Caroline. "The Hello Girls of Boston." *Life and Labor*, September, 1912, pp. 260–64.

Crosby, Pennell. "Dials Dock Working Force, Profits Good." *Journal of Electrical Workers and Operators*, November, 1933, p. 453+.

A Delegate [pseudonym]. "Some Observations." *Union Telephone Operator*, December, 1921, p. 8.

Donovan, Alice J. "Description of Boston Telephone Operators' Troubles." *Journal of Electrical Workers and Operators,* May, 1913, pp. 937–42.

Evans, Elizabeth G. "The Roxbury Carpet Factory Strike." *The Survey,* May 28, 1910, pp. 337–38.

Eye-Witness [pseudonym]. "Dials Scrap Labor and Increase Costs." *Journal of Electrical Workers and Operators,* February, 1933, p. 67 +.

Foley, Eleanor V. "My Experiences and Impressions as a Student." *Telephone Review,* May-June, 1915, p. 163.

Gillespie, Mabel. "Telephone Operators." *Life and Labor,* August, 1912, p. 252.

———. "Boston League Gives Service of Many Sorts." *Life and Labor,* July, 1921, pp. 222–23.

Grant, P. M. "The Selection and Training of Operators." Parts 1–2. *Southwestern Telephone News,* August, 1908, p. 2; September, 1908, p. 2 +.

Hard, William. "Mr. Burleson, Back from Boston." *New Republic,* May 3, 1919, pp. 15–18.

Harrington, M. E. "The Training of Operators in Boston." *New England Telephone Topics,* June, 1910, pp. 18–19.

Hickey, Margaret. "Weavers of Speech." *Brookwood Review,* May, 1925, pp. 6–7.

Howler [pseudonym]. "New Year's Resolutions and Others." *Union Telephone Operator,* January, 1922, pp. 7–8.

Hubbard, Elbert. "Teamwork and the Grumbler." *New England Telephone Topics,* August, 1907, p. 8.

———. "The Two Kinds." *New England Telephone Topics,* August, 1908, p. 16.

Lange, Susannah F. "Those Good Old Days When Operators Received $6.50 a Week." *New England Telephone Topics,* October, 1929, pp. 288–90.

Leslie, Mabel. "Fatigued Hands Rest with Creative Tasks." *Journal of Electrical Workers and Operators,* November, 1930, p. 623.

Lockwood, W. E. "The First Time." *New England Telephone Topics,* December, 1908, p. 2.

Loud, Ned. "A Glimpse of the Boston Toll Office." *New England Telephone Topics,* September, 1919, pp. 105, 108–9.

McComas, R. T. "Interest of Employees Constantly Held." *Modern Hospital,* January, 1917, pp. 75–77.

McGee, Margaret E. "My Duties as a Supervisor." *New England Telephone Topics,* August, 1912, pp. 18–19.

Mahan, Mary. "Impressions of a Telephone Afternoon." *New England Telephone Topics,* October, 1914, pp. 183–84.

Maurer, James. "Labor's Demand for Its Own Schools." *The Nation,* September 20, 1922, p. 276.

O'Connor, Julia S. "Boston Office Cleaners' Union." *Life and Labor*, June, 1915, pp. 100–101.

———. "The Truth about the New England 'Phone Strike.' " *Life and Labor*, June, 1919, pp. 131–33.

———. "History of the Organized Telephone Operators' Movement." Parts 1–6. *Union Telephone Operator*, January-March, May-July, 1921.

———. "The British Telephonist." Parts 1–2. *Union Telephone Operator*, November-December, 1921.

———. "An Armistice Day Address." *Union Telephone Operator*, December, 1921, pp. 23–25.

———. "Labor Education in England." *Union Telephone Operator*. January, 1922, pp. 16–19.

———. "Irish Industrial Impressions." *Union Telephone Operator*, February, 1922, pp. 16–20.

———. "The Blight of Company Unionism." *American Federationist*, May, 1926, pp. 544–49.

Parker, Julia O'Connor. "A Woman Views Girl Displacement by Dials." *Journal of Electrical Workers and Operators*, January, 1930, p. 13.

The Pilgrim [pseudonym]. "Pilgrim's Progress in a Telephone Exchange." Parts 1–2. *Life and Labor*, January, 1921, pp. 11–13; February, 1921, pp. 48–52.

Plugan Ansa [pseudonym]. "The Automatics'll Get You if You Don't Watch Out." *Union Telephone Operator*, January, 1921, p. 16.

Quinn, Rose Hickey. "Dialing." *Union Telephone Operator*, February, 1921, pp. 2–3 +.

———. "Out of the Fog." *Union Telephone Operator*, June, 1921, pp. 2–3 +.

Reed, Harland. "Loyalty." *New England Telephone Topics*, September, 1913, p. 200.

Reinsch, Philomene. "The History of the Telephone Operators' Union." *Brookwood Review*, May, 1925, p. 3.

Schmitt, Katherine M. "Woman's Contribution to the Bell System Heritage." *Telephone Review*, December, 1923, pp. 366–67.

———. "I Was Your Old Hello Girl." *Saturday Evening Post*, July 12, 1930, p. 19 +.

Smith, Ethel. "Government Control and Industrial Rights." *Life and Labor*, April, 1919, pp. 85–88.

Smith, Laura. "Opportunities for Women in the Bell System." *Bell Telephone Quarterly*, January, 1932, pp. 34–43.

Taylor, G. M. "Selection and Development of a Supervisor." *New England Telephone Topics*, July, 1910, pp. 16–17.

Thomas, Norman. "Norman Thomas on Workers' Education." *New Republic*, May 9, 1923, p. 296.

Thorne, Dorothy. "Bayonne—Old Days and New." *Telephone Review*, March, 1917, pp. 75–78.

———. "Where the Genial Rest Time Goes." *Telephone Review,* July, 1917, p. 187+.

Turner, J. L. "Work of the Telephone Operator: The Art of Expression as Applied to Switchboard Operation." *New England Telephone Topics.* February, 1912, pp. 5–7.

Van Tassel, Frances. "800 Healthier and Happier Girls Get Health Course Certificates." *New England Telephone Topics,* July, 1928, p. 102.

Withington, Anne. "When the Telephone Girls Organized." *The Survey,* April 16, 1913, pp. 621–23.

———. "The Telephone Strike." *The Survey,* April 26, 1919, p. 146.

MAGAZINE ARTICLES (UNSIGNED)

"Annie Molloy." *New England Telephone Topics,* May, 1928, p. 37.

"Around the Circuit." *Journal of Electrical Workers and Operators,* September, 1916, pp. 102–3.

"Bazaar Briefs." *Union Telephone Operator,* June, 1921, p. 10+.

"Boston." *Life and Labor,* November, 1914, p. 344.

"The Busy Operator Is the Best Operator." *Southwestern Telephone News,* November, 1907, p. 5.

"The Call Circuit." *Union Telephone Operator,* July, 1921, p. 12.

"Chief Operator—Some Job!" *New England Telephone Topics,* August, 1916, pp. 97–99.

"Clothes Do Not Make the Girl." *Sacred Heart Review,* July 20, 1912, p. 79.

"Concerning the Boston Toll Office." *New England Telephone Topics,* April, 1915, p. 20.

"The Conspicuous Girl." *Sacred Heart Review,* July 19, 1913, p. 74.

"Convention Rhymes." *Union Telephone Operator,* January, 1922, p. 20.

"The Development of the Telephone in Los Angeles." *Pacific Telephone Magazine,* January, 1913, pp. 5–7.

"Editorial." *Cambridge Review,* April, 1906, p. 3.

"Editorial." *The Radiator,* December, 1906, p. 48.

"Emma Nutt, First of Our Thousands of Operators, Dies at 77." *New England Telephone Topics,* July, 1926, p. 120.

"The Employees' Benefit Fund." *New England Telephone Topics,* September, 1917, p. 146.

"Employees' Lunches for Health and Efficiency." *New England Telephone Topics,* March, 1913, pp. 319–22.

"England's Wild Women." *Sacred Heart Review,* April 12, 1913, p. 259.

"The First Florence Simms Scholarship." *Life and Labor Bulletin,* October, 1928, p. 3.

"Flying Squadron." *Southern Telephone News,* September, 1925, p. 8.

"Good Points and Bad of Telephone Operating as a Trade for Philadelphia Girls." *The Survey,* February 7, 1914, pp. 542–44.

"Indoor Athletics and Dance." *New England Telephone Topics*, February, 1914, p. 311.

"The International Congress." *Union Telephone Operator*, October, 1921, p. 13.

"Is the Younger Generation in Peril?" *Literary Digest*, May 14, 1921, pp. 9–12+.

"Jacksonville Telephone Girls Win Strike." *Life and Labor*, February, 1918, p. 40.

"The Journal and Its Mission." *Union Telephone Operator*, January, 1921, pp. 4–5.

"Ladies' League." *New England Telephone Topics*, January, 1916, p. 248.

"Life in Our Operators' Quarters." *New England Telephone Topics*, June, 1916, pp. 33–37.

"Lunches by the Thousands." *New England Telephone Topics*, December, 1914, pp. 244–47.

"Making Expert Operators." *New England Telephone Topics*, May, 1912, pp. 15–19.

"Meet Me in St. Louis." *Union Telephone Operator*, October, 1921, p. 10.

"New Chief Operators in Providence District." *New England Telephone Topics*, April, 1924, p. 506.

"New Chief Toll Instructress." *New England Telephone Topics*, July, 1924, p. 128.

"New England Tel & Tel Co. Bowling League." *New England Telephone Topics*, March, 1912, p. 29.

"Old Timers' Edition." *New England Telephone Topics*, March, 1915, pp. 333–66.

"Organization of the Traffic Department." *New England Telephone Topics*, May, 1909, pp. 5–8.

"Parents' Night." *New England Telephone Topics*, November, 1944, p. 11.

"Parents' Night at Newport." *New England Telephone Topics*, July, 1922, p. 119.

"Promotion in the Central Office." *New England Telephone Topics*, January, 1917, pp. 283–88.

"Rebuke to the Immodest." *Sacred Heart Review*, June 17, 1916, p. 3.

"The Religious Press on Youthful Morals." *Literary Digest*, May 21, 1921, pp. 27–28+.

"The Revival of the Bulletin Board." *Union Telephone Operator*, January, 1921, pp. 17–18.

"Rewards of Capitalism." *Union Telephone Operator*, February, 1922, p. 25.

"Saving Life and Property by Telephone." *Union Telephone Operator*, February, 1921, p. 20.

"Schenectady's Great Strike." *Journal of Electrical Workers and Operators*, January, 1914, pp. 30–32.

"Slaves of Dress." *Sacred Heart Review,* April 19, 1913, p. 281.
"Some Observations." *Union Telephone Operator,* December, 1921, p. 8.
"The Speech Weavers' School." *Pacific Telephone Magazine,* December, 1916, pp. 10–12.
"Standards of Operating." *New England Telephone Topics,* June, 1912, p. 44.
"The Story of a Union Bazaar." *Union Telephone Operator,* May, 1921, pp. 18–19+.
"Style and the Girl!" *Telephone Review,* November, 1918, p. 307.
"Supervisors' Instruction Course." *Telephone Review,* April, 1915, p. 136.
"Telephone Girls and Laundry Workers." *The Survey,* April 8, 1916, p. 57.
"Telephone Operators in Jacksonville, Florida Go on Strike." *Life and Labor,* January, 1918, p. 20.
"Telephone Operators' Strike." *Life and Labor,* August, 1913, p. 239.
"Telephone School in Houston." *Southwestern Telephone News,* November, 1907, p. 5.
"Telephone Settlement." *Journal of Electrical Workers and Operators,* June, 1919, pp. 556–57.
"Those Startling Styles." *Sacred Heart Review,* June 17, 1916, p. 4.
"Training Operators—Past and Present." *New England Telephone Topics,* December, 1908, p. 2.
"Untitled Poem." *Union Telephone Operator,* February, 1922, p. 28.
"Votes for Telephone Girls." *Life and Labor,* November, 1915, p. 173.
"Watch the Dance Programs." *Sacred Heart Review,* April 26, 1913, p. 292.
"Welfare Work on Behalf of Telephone Operators." *Pacific Telephone Review,* May, 1913, pp. 5–6.
"Why a Short Course?" *Life and Labor Bulletin,* April, 1923, p. 2.
"Why Telephone Operators Make Good Wives." *New England Telephone Topics,* February, 1916, pp. 265–66.
"Will You Hold the Line Please?" *Southwestern Telephone News,* August, 1926, pp. 7–9.

LETTERS IN MAGAZINES

Brady, May H. *Union Telephone Operator,* January, 1921, p. 8.
———. *Union Telephone Operator,* February, 1921, p. 8.
———. *Union Telephone Operator,* May, 1921, p. 8.
Castle, Janet. *Journal of Electrical Workers and Operators,* October, 1917, p. 144.
Chord, Miss [pseudonym]. *Union Telephone Operator,* January, 1922, pp. 8–9.
Cooney, Alice. *Union Telephone Operator,* March, 1921, pp. 7–8.

Crain, Kate. *Union Telephone Operator,* January, 1921, p. 10.

Donovan, Alice J. *Journal of Electrical Workers and Operators,* September, 1912, pp. 550–51.

———. *Journal of Electrical Workers and Operators,* December, 1912, p. 696.

———. *Journal of Electrical Workers and Operators,* June, 1913, pp. 983–84.

———. *Journal of Electrical Workers and Operators,* August, 1913, pp. 1094–95.

———. *Journal of Electrical Workers and Operators,* February, 1914, pp. 85–86.

Hickey, Margaret. *Union Telephone Operator,* February, 1921, p. 9.

Hill, Josephine. *Union Telephone Operator,* May, 1922, p. 6.

Hyman, Ethel. *Journal of Electrical Workers and Operators,* March, 1915, pp. 190–91.

Long Answer [pseudonym]. *Union Telephone Operator,* January, 1922, p. 9.

McKeon, Margaret. *Union Telephone Operator,* May, 1921, p. 9.

Para Chords [pseudonym]. *Union Telephone Operator,* January, 1922, pp. 9–10.

Plug, Miss [pseudonym]. *Union Telephone Operator,* December, 1921, p. 7.

Press Secretary, Local 124A. *Union Telephone Operator,* January, 1921, p. 9.

Weistroffer, Marguerite. *Journal of Electrical Workers and Operators,* December, 1916, pp. 334–36.

———. *Journal of Electrical Workers and Operators,* February, 1917, pp. 460–61.

DISSERTATIONS

Burke, William Maxwell. "History and Functions of Central Labor Unions." Ph.D. dissertation, Columbia University, 1899.

Endelman, Gary. "Solidarity Forever: Rose Schneiderman and the Women's Trade Union League." Ph.D. dissertation, University of Delaware, 1978.

Leon, Warren. "High School: A Study of Youth and Community in Quincy, Massachusetts." Ph.D. dissertation, Harvard University, 1979.

Matthews, Lillian. "Women in Trade Unions in San Francisco." Ph.D. dissertation, University of California at Berkeley, 1912. Also University of California Publication in Economics, Vol. 3, No. 1, June 19, 1913.

Ueda, Reed. "Avenues to Adulthood: Urban Growth and the Rise of Secondary Schools in Somerville, Massachusetts, 1800–1930." Ph.D. dissertation, Harvard University, 1980.

PAMPHLETS

Boston Trade Union College. "An Educational Institution for Workers." Boston: Boston Trade Union College, 1920.
————. "The Boston Trade Union College." Boston: Boston Trade Union College, 1922.
Cassidy, James. "The Saloon versus the Labor Union." Fall River, Mass.: n.p., November 26, 1911.

GOVERNMENT DOCUMENTS

Canadian Department of Labour. *Report of the Royal Commission on a Dispute Respecting Hours of Employment between the Bell Telephone Company of Canada, Ltd. and Operators at Toronto, Ontario.* Ottawa: Government Printing Bureau, 1907.
City of Somerville [Mass.]. *Annual Report for 1905.* Somerville, Mass.: Somerville Journal Print, 1906.
Commonwealth of Massachusetts. *Forty-fourth Annual Report on the Statistics of Labor—1913.* Boston: Wright and Potter Printing, 1913.
————. *Twenty-eighth Annual Report of the State Board of Arbitration, 1913.* Boston: n.p., 1914.
————. Bureau of Statistics of Labor. *Labor Bulletin of the Commonwealth of Massachusetts,* no. 44 (December, 1906).
Curry, Nelle B. *Investigation of the Wages and Conditions of Telephone Operating.* Report submitted to U.S. Commission on Industrial Relations, Washington, D.C., 1915.
Report of the President's Mediation Commission to the President of the United States. Washington, D.C.: Government Printing Office, 1918.
State of Arkansas. *Third Biennial Report of the Bureau of the Statistics of Labor of the State of Arkansas, 1917–1918.* N.p., [1918].
State of New York. Department of Labor. "The Telephone Industry." Special Bulletin 100. N.p., July, 1920.
Texas Penitentiary Investigating Committee. *Report and Findings of the Penitentiary Investigating Committee.* Austin, Tex.: Texas Penitentiary Investigating Committee, July 24, 1913.
U.S. Commission on Industrial Relations. *Final Report and Testimony Submitted to Congress by the Commission on Industrial Relations.* Vol. 10. Washington, D.C.: Government Printing Office, 1916.
U.S. Congress. Senate. *Investigation of Telephone Companies.* 61st Cong., 2d sess., 1910, S. Doc. 380.
U.S. Congress. Senate. *Report on Condition of Women and Child Wage-Earners in the United States.* Vol. 5, *Wage-Earning Women in Stores and Factories.* 61st Cong., 2d sess., 1910, S. Doc. 645.
U.S. Department of Labor. *Effects of Applied Research upon the Em-*

ployment Opportunities of American Women. Bulletin of the Women's Bureau, no. 50. Washington, D.C.: Government Printing Office, 1926.

U.S. Department of Labor, Bureau of Labor Statistics. *Characteristics of Company Unions, 1935.* Bulletin No. 634, June, 1937. Washington, D.C.: Government Printing Office, 1938.

CONVENTION PROCEEDINGS

American Federation of Labor. *Proceedings of the 1916 Convention.* Washington, D.C.: Law Reporter Printing Co., 1916.

Illinois State Federation of Labor. *Proceedings of the Thirty-eighth Annual Convention.* Chicago: Illinois State Federation of Labor, 1920.

———. *Proceedings of the Thirty-ninth Annual Convention.* Chicago: Illinois State Federation of Labor, 1921.

Massachusetts State Federation of Labor. *Proceedings of the Annual Conventions.* Worcester: Massachusetts State Federation of Labor, 1912–23.

Texas State Federation of Labor. *Proceedings of the Eighteenth Annual Convention.* Austin: Texas State Federation of Labor, 1915.

———. *Proceedings of the Twentieth Annual Convention.* Austin: Texas State Federation of Labor, 1917.

———. *Proceedings of the Twenty-first Annual Convention.* Austin: Texas State Federation of Labor, 1918.

United Textile Workers of America. "Proceedings of the Twenty-second Annual Convention of the United Textile Workers of America." Reprinted in *Textile Worker,* October, 1922.

Workers' Education Bureau. *Report of Proceedings, Second National Conference on Workers' Education in the United States.* New York: Workers' Education Bureau, 1922.

NEWSPAPERS

American Labor Union Journal (Butte, Mont.), 1903.
Anaconda (Mont.) *Standard,* 1907.
Arkansas Gazette (Little Rock, Ark.), 1917.
Atlanta *Constitution,* 1919.
Boston *Daily Advertiser,* 1913–14, 1919, 1923.
Boston *Evening Transcript,* 1912–13, 1919, 1923, 1928.
Boston *Globe,* 1912–13, 1915–16, 1918–20, 1923.
Boston *Herald,* 1913–14, 1918–20, 1922–23.
Boston Labor World, 1917–20.
Boston *Post,* 1913–15, 1917, 1919, 1922–23.
Brockton *Times,* 1923.
Brown *Daily Herald,* 1919.
Butte (Mont.) *Miner,* 1903, 1907–8.

Butte (Mont.) *Reveille,* 1907.
Carbondale (Ill.) *Free Press,* 1920.
Christian Science Monitor, 1912–13, 1919, 1923.
Cleveland *Plain-Dealer,* 1919.
Daily American (West Frankfort, Ill.), 1920.
Daily Kennebec Journal (Augusta, Maine), 1919, 1923.
Daily Oklahoman (Oklahoma City, Okla.), 1919.
Dallas *Morning News,* 1919.
Fall River *Globe,* 1919, 1923.
Florida Times-Union (Jacksonville, Fla.), 1917, 1919.
Fort Smith (Ark.) *Times-Record,* 1917.
Great Falls (Mont.) *Tribune,* 1907.
Harvard *Crimson,* 1919.
Helena (Mont.) *Independent,* 1907.
Idaho Daily Statesman (Boise, Idaho), 1908.
Labor News (Worcester, Mass.), 1910, 1911–13, 1915, 1918–19, 1921,
    1923–24.
Lawrence *Telegram,* 1919, 1923.
Lewiston (Maine) *Evening Journal,* 1919, 1923.
Los Angeles *Times,* 1920.
Lynn *Telegram-News,* 1919, 1923.
Manchester (N.H.) *Union,* 1919, 1923.
New Orleans *Times-Picayune,* 1919.
New York *Sun,* 1913.
New York Times, 1899, 1907, 1919–20, 1926, 1942.
The Pilot (Boston, Mass.), 1910.
Providence *Journal,* 1919, 1923.
Richmond *Times-Dispatch,* 1918.
St. Louis *Post-Dispatch,* 1913, 1919.
St. Paul *Pioneer-Press,* 1918–19.
San Francisco *Chronicle,* 1907.
San Francisco *Examiner,* 1907.
Salt Lake City *Tribune,* 1907–8.
Springfield *Republican,* 1919, 1923.
The State (Columbia, S.C.), 1919.
Virginian-Pilot and the Norfolk Landmark (Norfolk, Va.), 1919.
Washington *Post,* 1913.
Wichita *Eagle,* 1919.
Woman's Journal, 1910.
Worcester *Evening Gazette,* 1919, 1923.

HIGH SCHOOL STUDENT MAGAZINES

Cambridge Review (Cambridge, Mass. High School), 1906, 1917.
The Radiator (Somerville, Mass. High School), 1906, 1914, 1915, 1916.

INTERVIEWS

Coucher, Beatrice V. Telephone interview by Stephen H. Norwood, August 29, 1982.

Monro, Barta Hapgood. Telephone interview by Stephen H. Norwood, February 6, 1982.

Moriarty, Clare [pseudonym]. Interview by Stephen H. Norwood, Boston, Massachusetts, June 12, 1974; Telephone interview by Stephen H. Norwood, March 10, 1982.

Moriarty, Kathleen [pseudonym]. Interview by Stephen H. Norwood, Boston, Massachusetts, June 12, 1974.

Norwood, Rose Finkelstein. Interviews by Stephen H. Norwood, Boston, Massachusetts, January 28, June 12, and July 18, 1974 and May 2, 1975; Interview by Brigid O'Farrell, Boston, Massachusetts, [1977].

Schneider, Anna Weinstock. Interview by Stephen H. Norwood, Sudbury, Massachusetts, August 15, 1974.

Starr, Helen Norton. Interview by Stephen H. Norwood, New York, New York, October 9, 1982.

Swerbilov, Sally Parker. Interview by Stephen H. Norwood, New York, New York, February, 1978.

Wise, Henry. Interview by Stephen H. Norwood, Boston, Massachusetts, December 4, 1980.

Wise, Pearl Katz. Interview by Stephen H. Norwood, Boston, Massachusetts, September 27, 1980.

Wynne, Mary Quinn. Interview by Stephen H. Norwood, Springfield, Massachusetts, June 28, 1974.

Index

American Bell Telephone Company, 31
American Federation of Labor: and women workers, 73–74, 95, 134, 143–44, 223, 233; concern about Bell Company anti-unionism, 74; federal unions of telephone operators in, 83–84, 87; and Boston, 92, 98; and World War I, 156–58, 257; and workers' education, 224, 226–27; post-World War I decline, 255–56, 258; and 1923 New England operators' strike, 270, 281; 1933 campaign to reorganize New England operators, 306; mentioned, 83–84, 101, 260, 292, 302, 310
American Labor Union, 77–79
American Telephone and Telegraph Company (AT&T): established, 31; benefit plan, 51; labor policy, 74, 77; competition from independent telephone companies, 76; and 1913 Boston operators' near-strike, 111, 117, 119, 208; and company unionism, 255, 257–59, 306–8; and dial system, 263–64; and 1923 New England operators' strike, 280; mentioned, 47–48, 75, 78, 105–6, 131–32, 293
American Woman Suffrage Association, 91
Anti-Semitism: of New England Telephone Company, 42–43, 284

Baker, Loretta, 243–44, 253n, 273, 293
Balch, Emily, 140, 143–44, 154n
Bell, Alexander Graham, 30

Bell System. See American Telephone and Telegraph Company
Bethell, Union N., 117, 119, 167
Boston Central Labor Union: growth of, 92–93, 247; and 1913 Boston operators' near-strike, 108–10; and women, 137; and workers' education, 228–29, 247; and 1923 New England operators' strike, 281–82, 290; mentioned, 262–63, 268–70
Boston Chamber of Commerce, 108, 116, 119–20, 271
Boston Elevated Strike of 1912, 97, 109
Boston Equal Suffrage Association for Good Government, 94, 102
Boston Telephone Operators' Union (Local 1A): social programs of, 5, 145–46, 235–36; in 1923 New England operators' strike, 14–15, 146, 275–79, 282; in 1913 near-strike, 109–11, 114–16, 118–22; elections in, 137, 139, 265, 267; factionalism in, 138–40, 265–70, 272–73, 292; in 1919 New England operators' strike, 146, 180, 182–83, 185, 194; and workers' education, 228; use of military imagery, 274–75, 277, 282; mentioned, 8, 14, 98–99, 102, 104–8, 128–30, 136–37, 140–41, 143, 146–48, 150–51, 186
Boston Trade Union College, 226, 228–31
Boycott of Bell telephone: in Montana, 76, 78, 81; rejected by San Francisco Labor Council, 86; in Fort Smith, Ark., 160; in St. Louis, 203–4, 208; in Palestine, Tex., 207

Brandeis, Louis, 108
Brookwood Labor College, 226, 245–46
Bryn Mawr Summer School for Women Workers in Industry, 226, 228, 230–32, 247, 282
Bugniazet, Gustave: organizes operators, 107; and 1913 Boston operators' near-strike, 108, 110, 114, 117, 120; and 1919 New England operators' strike, 180, 275; at 1919 Telephone Operators' Department convention, 218
Burleson, Albert: background of, 163–64; hostility to trade unionism, 163–64, 199; uses convict labor, 164; criticized by Felix Frankfurter, 164, 169; and Norfolk telephone strike, 165; and Minneapolis-St. Paul telephone strike, 165–66; and Wichita telephone strike, 166; and government control of telephone system, 167; and women, 168; denounces Julia O'Connor, 168–69; and 1919 New England operators' strike, 170, 180–82, 184–85, 193–94, 197–98; and Order 3209, 198, 208; and Jacksonville operators' strike, 200; and Atlanta operators' strike, 200; and Columbia, S.C., telephone strike, 201; and Pacific telephone strike, 202; and Cleveland operators' strike, 205; mentioned, 162, 168, 258
Burns, Agnes, 225

Calhoun, Arthur, 245
Cassidy, James E., 188, 195–97
Catholic church, 15–18, 195–96, 276
Central States Council, 220–21
Chaffee, Zachariah, 229
Chicago Telephone Company, 43–44, 48, 138
Chief operator: work described, 32; mentioned, 37, 39, 43–44, 77–78, 103, 107, 127n, 166, 191, 270, 280
Christman, Elizabeth, 232
Clark, Sue Ainslee, 96, 154n
Cleveland Telephone Company, 204–6
Clothing and operators, 11–15, 41, 44,

48, 85, 110–12, 133, 165–66, 182–83, 236, 240, 277–78, 282
College Equal Suffrage League, 94
Collins, Peter, 110
Colpoys, John B., 114, 168, 289
Commercial Telegraphers' Union of America, 115, 200–201, 303
Common Cupboard, 244–45
Communications Workers of America, 308–9, 311
Company unionism, 204–6, 255, 257–61, 301, 305–9
Conboy, Sarah McLaughlin, 101–2
Connolly, James. *See* James Connolly clubs
Consumer culture, 11–12, 145, 311
Coucher, Beatrice V., 82, 89n, 221, 225
Crawford, Mary Caroline, 61, 106, 143, 154n
Curley, James Michael, 289–90

Dana, Henry Wadsworth Longfellow, 228–29, 232, 251n
Denison House, 94, 101–2
Dial system, 255, 262–65, 294, 307–9
Dolbear, Amos, 30
Donovan, Alice J., 110, 122, 138, 141, 145
Donovan, Mary, 18, 243–44, 253n
Douglas, Paul, 232
Driver, William, 170, 181

Evans, Elizabeth Glendower, 97, 108, 143

Family: and women workers, 2–3, 9; operators' desire for independence from, 5, 235, 241–42, 247, 311; Bell Company as, 12–13, 48–50; and Catholic church, 15–17; Irish-American, 18; and Bell Company hiring, 42; in mining towns, 76, 130, 221; operators' position in, 95, 100, 135–36; and unionism, 95, 141–42, 221, 239–41; in centers with high proportion of women working, 130; and Telephone Operators' Union leaders, 141–42, 301–2; mentioned, 11
Finkelstein, Rose: on operators' work-

ing conditions, 38–39, 140; on New England Telephone Company's anti-Semitism and racism, 42–43; on formation of Boston Telephone Operators' Union, 102; and WTUL, 141, 303; background of, 142; and 1919 New England operators' strike, 187; and workers' education, 226; later career of, 302–3

Fish, Frederick, 74, 77–78, 80, 116

Fitzgerald, John F., 108, 116

Fitzgerald, Susan Grimes Walker: helps organize Boston Telephone Operators' Union, 101; background of, 102; and women's suffrage, 102, 143, 145; mentioned, 154*n*, 269

Flapper, 1–20 *passim*, 111–12, 182, 234–38, 241, 248, 277–78, 282–83, 311

Foley, Margaret, 143

Frankfurter, Felix: as secretary, President's Mediation Commission, 159; criticizes Postmaster-General Burleson, 164, 169; and Boston Trade Union College, 229

Gatelee, John, 272

General strikes sparked by telephone operators' strikes: Helena, Mont., 7, 81; Fort Smith, Ark., 7, 161; Palestine, Tex., 7, 207

Gillespie, Mabel: helps organize Boston Telephone Operators' Union, 100, 103, 108; background of, 101, 145, 154*n*; and women's suffrage, 143; mentioned, 144

Gleason, Arthur, 225

Gompers, Samuel: complains of AT&T anti-unionism, 74; and WTUL, 95; and 1919 New England operators' strike, 181; and 1923 New England operators' strike, 270, 281; criticized by Mabel Leslie, 292–93; mentioned, 74, 224

Government control of telephone service, 157–58, 162–208 *passim*, 254

Gray, Elisha, 30

Hall, E. K., 117–18, 121, 293

Harding, Warren G., 256

Harrington, Mary E., 41, 43, 280

Henry, Alice, 232

Hickey, Rose, 200–201, 221, 259, 265

High school: and operators, 8–10, 16, 19, 21*n*, 22*n*, 38–40, 100; students as strikebreakers, 283

Hubbard, Gardiner, 30

Independent telephone companies, 70*n*, 76, 81, 160–61, 167, 170, 211*n*

International Brotherhood of Electrical Workers (IBEW): and women, 81, 83, 94, 128–29, 134–36, 141, 147–50, 152, 246–47, 309–10; on Pacific Coast, 83, 86, 158–60, 202, 259–60; organizes Boston operators, 101–3; organizes Boston telephone men, 102; in St. Louis, 130–32, 203; in South, 133, 200–201, 207; conflict between inside and outside workers, 147; classification of membership, 147–48; and 1919 New England operators' strike, 180–81, 191–92; and 1919 nationwide general strike, 180, 198–99; New England telephone men leave, 221, 255, 260–61; and Local 1A factional fight, 269–70; and 1923 New England operators' strike, 271, 275; mentioned, 79, 107–8, 110, 114, 117, 121–22, 134, 146, 151, 163, 165, 168, 208, 217–19, 242, 247–48, 259, 302, 304, 306

International Brotherhood of Telephone Workers (IBTW), 260–61, 267, 271–72

International Congress of Women at The Hague (1915), 14, 140

International Congress of Working Women: at Washington (1919), 14; at Geneva (1921), 234

International Ladies' Garment Workers' Union (ILGWU), 10, 224, 231, 235, 256, 310

Irish nationalism, 18, 219, 243–44

James Connolly clubs, 243–44

Johnson, E. A., 269, 281

Jones, Matt B., 266, 271, 284, 289–90

June, Mary E., 22*n*, 170, 221–22, 269

Kallen, Horace, 228
Kearney, John, 115, 184, 281
Keller, Jasper N., 105, 107, 109

Labor, U.S. Department of, 157, 159, 161, 169, 200, 205
Larkin, James, 244
Laski, Harold, 228–30
Leslie, Mabel: as Telephone Operators' Department organizer, 202–3; elected Department secretary, 219; background of, 219–20; as editor of *Union Telephone Operator*, 220; and workers' education, 229, 304; criticizes Samuel Gompers, 292–93; later career of, 303–4
Lewis, Sinclair, 199
Linehan, Peter F., 101–3, 105, 143
Lomasney, Martin, 7, 115
Lynch, Alice, 85

McAdoo, William Gibbs, 162–63
MacDonald, David, 78
McGrady, Edward, 281–82
McNulty, Frank, 129, 269
Mahoney, Mary, 116–17, 139–41, 265, 267
Male telephone workers: opportunities for advancement, 32–33; and AT&T athletic programs, 50; and AT&T disability program, 51; strike in Montana (1907–8), 81; refuse to support San Francisco operators (1907), 86; organized by operators, 105, 129; strike in Pennsylvania, New Jersey, and Delaware (1907), 107; and 1913 Boston operators' near-strike, 108; strike in St. Louis (1913), 131–32, (1919), 203–4; organize operators, 133–34; status compared with operators, 136; strike along Pacific Coast (1917), 158–59, (1919), 202–3, 259–60, (1920), 255, 260; strike in Norfolk, 165; strike in Minneapolis-St. Paul, 165–66; and 1919 New England telephone strike, 181, 185, 193–94; strike in Columbia, S. C., 201–2; strike in Cleveland, 205–6; strike in Palestine, Tex., 207; withdraw from

IBEW in New England, 255, 260–61; ridiculed by operators, 275, 282; mentioned, 48, 93–94, 111, 167, 208
Massachusetts Political Equality Union, 143
Massachusetts State Department of Public Utilities: survey of telephone service after 1923 operators' strike, 292
Massachusetts State Federation of Labor, 93, 101, 137, 247, 292
Massachusetts Woman Suffrage Association, 94, 142–43
Matron: duties of, 49–50; mentioned, 12, 85, 100, 280
Matthews, May: and WTUL, 121, 141; and women's suffrage, 143; as secretary of Telephone Operators' Department, 151, 219, 223; in 1919 New England operators' strike, 182–85, 194; in St. Louis operators' strike, 203–4; expelled from Local 1A, 267, 294; in 1923 New England operators' strike, 273, 277; mentioned, 105–6, 222, 269
Maurer, James, 226
Meagher, Mary: in 1913 Boston operators' near-strike, 116–17; elected to Boston Telephone Operators' Union's first adjustment board, 121; as organizer, 129; and Boston WTUL, 140; opposes Julia O'Connor, 219; promoted after 1923 New England operators' strike, 300*n*
Molloy, Annie E.: candidate for Boston city council, 19; in 1913 Boston operators' near-strike, 116–17, 120; elected to Boston Telephone Operators' Union's first adjustment board, 121; as organizer, 129; delegate to International Congress of Women at The Hague, 140; and Boston WTUL, 140, 145; compared with Julia O'Connor, 140, 266, 288–89; and women's suffrage, 143; and Local 1A factional fight, 265–70, 272–73; and 1923 New England operators' strike, 277, 280–82, 288–89; expelled from Massachusetts State

Federation of Labor convention, 292; later career of, 293
Monitor: work described, 36–37; mentioned, 39
Montana Federation of Labor, 79–81
Morison, Samuel Eliot, 229
Murphy, Michael, 17, 137, 229
Murray, Mary F., 116, 121
Muste, A. J., 245–46

National American Woman Suffrage Association, 102, 142, 304
National Bell Telephone Company, 30
National Civic Federation, 46, 74
National Federation of Telephone Workers, 307–8
National Recovery Administration: telephone code, 265, 305
National War Labor Board, 156–57, 256–57
New England Council of Telephone Operators' Unions, 221–22, 268–70, 281
New England Joint Council of Telephone Workers, 221
New England Telephone Company: hiring policy of, 41–43, 284; anti-Semitism and racism of, 42–43, 284; athletic programs of, 50–51; and benefit plan, 51; in 1913 Boston operators' near-strike, 98, 107–22 *passim*, 208; introduces "split trick," 99; labor policy of, 104, 208, 255, 262, 269, 271; fires Julia O'Connor, 140, 168; in 1919 New England operators' strike, 170, 180, 182–85, 189, 194; company unionism in, 260–62, 267, 271, 305–6, 309; in 1923 New England operators' strike, 280, 284, 289–91; mentioned, 8, 31–32, 36–38, 49–50, 64*n*, 105, 266, 292–93, 298*n*
New York Telephone Company, 13, 44, 49, 61, 65*n*, 71*n*
Noonan, James: and 1913 St. Louis telephone strike, 132; and formation of Telephone Operators' Department, 150; and 1919 New England operators' strike, 180; mentioned, 260, 269, 304

Norwood, Rose Finkelstein. *See* Finkelstein, Rose

O'Connell, William Cardinal, 17–18, 195
O'Connor, Julia S.: at 1919 Telephone Operators' Department convention, 1–2, 216–19, 242, 254–55; on formation of Boston Telephone Operators' Union, 98; in 1913 Boston operators' near-strike, 116; and Boston WTUL, 121, 139, 141, 302; background of, 139; elected president of Local 1A, 139; fired by New England Telephone Company, 139, 168; and workers' education, 139, 225, 228, 231; elected president of Telephone Operators' Department, 150–51, 219; and Ryan Commission, 167–70; leads 1919 New England operators' strike, 180–85, 189, 191, 193–94; conflict with James E. Cassidy, 195–98; salary of, 222–23; speaks at Dartmouth College, 232–33; visits England and Ireland, 233, 244; at 1921 Telephone Operators' Department convention, 233, 259; as Irish nationalist, 243–44; and Local 1A factional fight, 255, 265–70, 272–73, 278, 282; leads 1923 New England operators' strike, 255, 269–71, 274–78, 280–82, 287–91, 293–94; assails dial system, 262–63, 265; compared with Annie Molloy, 266, 288–89; revokes Local 1A's charter, 267–68; later career of, 293, 301, 306
O'Reilly, John Boyle, 24*n*
Operating Board, 167, 170

Pacific Telephone Company, 13, 84–86, 158–60, 202–3, 208, 259–60
Parker, Julia O'Connor. *See* O'Connor, Julia S.
Pesotta, Rose, 310
Peters, Andrew, 185
Police: and operators' strikes, 78–79, 161, 185–87, 192, 204, 277–79, 285–88; 1919 Boston police strike, 169, 186, 279; traditional

hostility toward labor, 186; mentioned, 75
Post Office Department, U.S., 157–58, 162–208 *passim*, 258
Pound, Roscoe, 229
Powers, Bridie, 185
Powers, Samuel, 110, 117
Poyntz, Juliet Stuart, 224
Private branch exchange operators (PBX), 46, 110–11, 267

Quinn, Mary: and 1919 New England operators' strike, 193–94; and 1923 New England operators' strike, 286–88; mentioned, 99, 107, 129
Quinn, Rose Hickey. *See* Hickey, Rose

Racism: of New England Telephone Company, 42–43; mentioned, 278
Railroad Administration, U.S., 162–63
Rand School for Social Science, 224
Riots: in 1919 New England operators' strike, 189–90, 192–93; in 1923 New England operators' strike, 278–79, 285–86, 288
Ripley, William Z., 229
Rocky Mountain District Council of Telephone Operators' Department, 82, 220–21
Rocky Mountain Telephone Company, 31, 75, 77–81, 132
Roxbury carpet weavers' strike of 1910, 97, 102
Ryan, John, 195
Ryan, William S., 167–68, 170
Ryan Commission, 167–68, 170, 289

Sacco-Vanzetti case, 243, 293, 303
St. John, Mary, 129
San Francisco Labor Council, 83–87
Sanders, Thomas, 30
Scientific management, 6, 33–38, 51–52
Settlement house movement, 83, 94–95, 101–2, 305
Sexual harassment and telephone operators, 45–47, 85–87, 106–7, 135–36
South End House, 94
Southern Bell Telephone Company, 31, 200–202, 208, 258, 264, 280

Southwestern Bell Telephone Company, 31, 131–32, 135–36, 160–62, 203–4, 206, 208, 280
Spalding, Philip L., 107–9, 117
Spraggon, Sarah, 130, 132, 204
Stites, Sarah, 232
Storrow, James Jackson, Sr., 116
Storrow, James Jackson, Jr., 109, 116
Strikebreakers: AT&T's massive shipment to Boston in 1913, 110–15, 117–22, 208; society women as, 183, 188–89, 283–84; in 1919 New England operators' strike, 183–84, 187–93; college students as, 188–93, 274, 279, 283–85; Molloy faction as, 273, 277, 281; in 1923 New England operators' strike, 277–78, 280–91; male telephone workers as, 282; mentioned, 78–79, 81, 86, 132–33, 161, 200, 202–3, 205–8, 308
Sullivan, Rose: assists operators of Midwest and West, 82, 221, 232; and Boston WTUL, 141, background of, 141–42; organizes Cleveland operators, 204–5; and workers' education, 225; assails dial system, 265; in 1923 New England operators' strike, 272, 278; later career of, 301–2
Sullivan, Teresa, 217, 221
Supervisor: position created, 31, 65*n*; work described, 31–32; mentioned, 33, 36, 38, 40, 48, 63, 89*n*, 127, 131, 138, 166, 183, 206, 221, 291–92

Taylor, Frederick Winslow, 33–34
Telephone operating: in late nineteenth century, 6, 26–30, 31–33; and scientific management, 6, 33–38, 51–52; equipment used in, 27, 29–31, 33–35, 37–38, 43, 66*n*; shift from males to females in, 27–28; training for, 29, 40, 43–44; work hierarchy in, 31–33; "A" and "B" work, 34, 66*n*; toll, 34–35, 100, 138; as "ladylike" occupation, 35, 42, 45, 62, 96, 136; uniform phraseology in, 35–37, 43, 63, 106, 131; double

supervision system in, 36–39, 63; and service testers, 37–38; recruitment for, 40–42; and married women, 41–42, 242; absence of blacks in, 42; night work in 45–47, 106–7; and traffic curve, 47; and "split trick," 47, 98–100, 103, 105–6, 119; investigations of, 52, 61, 71*n*; and nervous strain, 52, 61, 85, 110, 141; and demerit system, 131

Telephone Operators' Department, IBEW: 1919 convention, 1–2, 14, 216–19, 242, 254–55; and southern organizing, 2, 199–202, 206–7, 218; and workers' education, 4, 19, 225, 228, 232–33, 245–46; social programs of, 4–5, 234, 236–38; 1921 convention, 14, 220, 236–38; and Irish nationalism, 18, 219, 243–44; establishment of, 149–51; and regional councils, 220–22; absence of hierarchy in, 222–23; officers' salaries in, 222–23; and radicalism, 242–46; mentioned, 5, 10, 288, 292, 304

Telephone operators' strikes: New England (1919), 1, 169–70, 180–98, 222, 254, 266, 275, 310, (1923), 5, 255, 276–91, 293–94, 301, 304; Toronto (1907), 52, 61, 141, 233; Montana (1903), 77–79, (1907–8), 79–81, 87; San Francisco (1907), 84–87; threatened in Boston (1912), 105, (1913), 108–22, (1917), 141; St. Louis (1913), 131–32, (1919), 203–4; Port Arthur, Tex. (1916), 133–34; Winnipeg (1917), 134; Pacific Coast (1917), 158–60, (1919), 202–3, 259–60; Fort Smith, Ark. (1917), 160–62; Norfolk (1918), 165; Minneapolis-St. Paul (1918), 165–67; Wichita (1918), 165–67; Columbia, S. C. (1919), 199, 201–2; Atlanta (1919), 199–202; Jacksonville, Fla. (1917), 200, (1919), 199–200; Cleveland (1919), 204–6; Shawnee, Okla. (1919), 206; Palestine, Tex. (1919), 206–7; southern Illinois (1920), 221

Thayer, H. B., 106, 111, 258, 264

Toll operators: work described, 34–35, 100, 138; as faction in Local 1A, 138–40, 265–70, 272–73, 292

Toohig, Amanda, 300*n*

Tumulty, Joseph, 181

United Mine Workers' Union, 220–21, 256

Uprising of the 20,000, 3, 96–97, 169, 181, 309

Vail, Theodore, 74

Van Tassel, Frances, 267, 269, 273, 293, 300*n*

Velleman, Aaron, 281–82

Wages of operators: in 1880s–90s, 29; compared with Bell Company laborers, 33; in Boston (1909), 44–45, (1912–13), 98, 103, 115, 118, 120, 124*n*, (1915–17), 140–41, 197, (1918–19), 170, 180, 193–94, 196–97, 262, (1923), 255, 262, 269–71; in Bell System (1910), 70*n*; in Montana (1902–8), 79–80; in San Francisco (1907), 84–85, 89*n*; in Port Arthur, Tex. (1916), 133; in St. Louis (1919), 204; under NRA, 305–6; mentioned, 27, 48, 52, 130, 158, 165, 199–203, 206, 221, 308

Weinstock, Anna, 186, 289

White, Marjorie, 239, 252*n*

Wilson, William B., 157, 159, 169, 205

Wilson, Woodrow: labor policies of, 156–57, 159, 162, 257; and 1919 New England operators' strike, 181, 193; mentioned, 168–69

Wire Control Board, 167, 170, 199, 205

Withington, Anne, 101–2, 143, 145

Women's suffrage movement: and WTUL, 102, 142–45; and Telephone Operators' Union, 142–43, 147, 152; mentioned, 5, 17–18, 83, 102, 142–45, 147, 304–5

Women's Trade Union League, Boston: and formation of Boston Telephone Operators' Union, 95, 98, 100–103,

269; allies in, 96, 101–2, 108, 128, 139–40, 269; and Roxbury carpet weavers' strike, 97; and 1913 Boston operators' near-strike, 120–21; telephone operators and, 121, 136, 139–46, 151, 228; and women's suffrage, 142–43; relations with AFL, 143–44; social programs of, 144–46; mentioned, 96, 129, 146–47, 232–33, 247, 289, 302–3

Women's Trade Union League, Chicago, 95, 154n

Women's Trade Union League, National: establishment of, 4, 95; and workers' education, 4, 139, 220, 224–25, 230, 232, 246–47; as link between "social housekeeper" and flapper, 13–14; relations with AFL, 95; and women's suffrage, 142–43; emblem of, 238; mentioned, 17, 95–97, 106, 130, 146–47, 183, 302–3, 305, 310

Women's Trade Union League, New York, 95–96, 303–4

Women's Trade Union League, St. Louis, 95, 130, 204

Women's Trade Union League, Worcester, 129, 244

Workers' education, 4–5, 19, 139, 144–45, 147, 223–34, 301

Workers' Education Bureau, 227–28

Wynne, Mary Quinn. *See* Quinn, Mary

Youth culture: in early twentieth century, 7, 9–14, 39, 82, 111–12; striking operators' involvement in, 8, 182, 241, 277–78, 282–83; denounced by Catholic church, 15–16; and Telephone Operators' Union, 145, 234–38, 241, 311; mentioned, 100

Note on Author

STEPHEN H. NORWOOD received his Ph.D. from Columbia University. He has published several articles on women activists in the labor movement. He is currently assistant professor in the Department of History at the University of Oklahoma.

Books in the Series
The Working Class in American History

Worker City, Company Town:
Iron and Cotton-Worker Protest in Troy
and Cohoes, New York, 1855-84
Daniel J. Walkowitz

Life, Work, and Rebellion in the Coal Fields:
The Southern West Virginia Miners, 1880-1922
David Alan Corbin

Women and American Socialism, 1870-1920
Mari Jo Buhle

Lives of Their Own:
Blacks, Italians, and Poles in Pittsburgh, 1900-1960
John Bodnar, Roger Simon, and Michael P. Weber

Working-Class America:
Essays on Labor, Community, and American Society
Edited by Michael H. Frisch and Daniel J. Walkowitz

Eugene V. Debs: Citizen and Socialist
Nick Salvatore

American Labor and Immigration History, 1877-1920s:
Recent European Research
Edited by Dirk Hoerder

Workingmen's Democracy:
The Knights of Labor and American Politics
Leon Fink

The Electrical Workers:
A History of Labor at General Electric
and Westinghouse, 1923-60
Ronald W. Schatz

The Mechanics of Baltimore:
Workers and Politics in the Age of Revolution, 1763-1812
Charles G. Steffen

The Practice of Solidarity:
American Hat Finishers in the Nineteenth Century
David Bensman

The Labor History Reader
Edited by Daniel J. Leab

Solidarity and Fragmentation:
Working People and Class Consciousness in Detroit, 1875-1900
Richard Oestreicher

Counter Cultures:
Saleswomen, Managers, and Customers
in American Department Stores, 1890-1940
Susan Porter Benson

The New England Working Class and the New Labor History
Edited by Herbert G. Gutman and Donald H. Bell

Labor Leaders in America
Edited by Melvyn Dubofsky and Warren Van Tine

Barons of Labor:
The San Francisco Building Trades
and Union Power in the Progressive Era
Michael Kazin

Gender at Work:
The Dynamics of Job Segregation by Sex during World War II
Ruth Milkman

Once a Cigar Maker:
Men, Women, and Work Culture in American
Cigar Factories, 1900-1919
Patricia A. Cooper

A Generation of Boomers:
The Pattern of Railroad Labor Conflict
in Nineteenth-Century America
Shelton Stromquist

Work and Community in the Jungle:
Chicago's Packinghouse Workers, 1894-1922
James R. Barrett

Workers, Managers, and Welfare Capitalism: The Shoeworkers and
Tanners of Endicott Johnson, 1890-1950
Gerald Zahavi

Men, Women, and Work: Class, Gender, and Protest
in the New England Shoe Industry, 1780-1910
Mary Blewett

Workers on the Waterfront:
Seamen, Longshoremen, and Unionism in the 1930s
Bruce Nelson

German Workers in Chicago:
A Documentary History of Working-Class Culture
from 1850 to World War I
Edited by Hartmut Keil and John B. Jentz

On the Line:
Essays in the History of Auto Work
Edited by Nelson Lichtenstein and Stephen Meyer III

Upheaval in the Quiet Zone:
A History of Hospital Workers' Union, Local 1199
Leon Fink and Brian Greenberg

Labor's Flaming Youth:
Telephone Operators and Worker Militancy, 1878-1923
Stephen H. Norwood

Another Civil War: Labor, Capital, and the State
in the Anthracite Regions of Pennsylvania, 1840-1868
Grace Palladino

Books in the Series
Women in American History

Women Doctors in Gilded-Age Washington:
Race, Gender, and Professionalization
Gloria Moldow

Friends and Sisters: Letters between
Lucy Stone and Antoinette Brown
Blackwell, 1846-93
Edited by Carol Lasser and Marlene Deahl Merrill

Reform, Labor, and Feminism:
Margaret Dreier Robins and the Women's Trade Union League
Elizabeth Anne Payne

Private Matters: American Attitudes toward
Childbearing and Infant Nurture in the Urban North, 1800-1860
Sylvia D. Hoffert

Civil Wars:
Women and the Crisis of Southern Nationalism
George C. Rable

I Came a Stranger:
The Story of a Hull-House Girl
Hilda Satt Polacheck
Edited by Dena J. Polacheck Epstein

Labor's Flaming Youth:
Telephone Operators and Worker Militancy, 1878-1923
Stephen H. Norwood

Winter Friends:
Women Growing Old in the New Republic, 1785-1835
Terri L. Premo

Better Than Second Best:
Love and Work in the Life of Helen Magill
Glenn C. Altschuler

DATE DUE

WITHDRAWN
